Exploring
WASHINGTON'S
Wild Areas

Exploring
WASHINGTON'S
Wild Areas

A GUIDE FOR HIKERS, BACKPACKERS, CLIMBERS, X-C SKIERS & PADDLERS

Marge and Ted Mueller

Photos by Kirkendall/Spring

THE
MOUNTAINEERS

Published by The Mountaineers
1001 SW Klickitat Way
Seattle, Washington 98134

0 9 8 7 6
5 4 3 2

Published simultaneously in Canada by Douglas & McIntyre, Ltd., 1615 Venables Street, Vancouver, B.C. V5L 2H1

Published simultaneously in Great Britain by Cordee, 3a DeMontfort Street, Leicester, England, LE1 7HD

Manufactured in the United States of America

Edited by Miriam Bulmer
Maps by the authors
All photographs by Kirkendall/Spring except as noted
Cover design by Watson Graphics
Layout by Marge Mueller
Typesetting by The Mountaineers Books

Cover photograph: The Duckbush River in The Brothers Wilderness Area
Frontispiece: The view south from the summit of Norse Peak over the Norse Peak Wilderness; Mount Adams in the distance

Library of Congress Cataloging in Publication Data

Mueller, Marge.
    Exploring Washington's wild areas : a guide for hikers, backpackers, climbers, X-C skiers, and paddlers / by Marge and Ted Mueller : photos by Tom Kirdendall and Vicky Spring.
        p. cm.
    Includes index.
    ISBN 0-89886-351-1
    1. Outdoor drecreation—Washington (State)—Guidebooks. 2. Wilderness Areas—Washington (State)—Recreational use—Guidebooks. 3. Washington (State) Guidebooks. I. Mueller, Ted. II. Kirkendall, Tom. III. Spring, Vicky, 1953- . IV. Title.
796.5'09797—dc20   94-20224
                                                             CIP

CONTENTS

BELLING-HAM

542

Mount
Baker

Whatcom Peak

Challenger
Peak

10

10

10

11
11

12
12

12

SAN JUAN
ISLANDS

9

20

Dome Peak

14

Glacier Peak

15

16

22

PORT ANGELES

17

18

20

EVERETT

19
20

2

21

5
5

Mount Olympus

3

6

Stevens
Pass

25

SEATTLE

90

7

8

5

Snoqualmie Pass

1

101

4

ENUMCLAW

TACOMA

410

26

27

ABERDEEN

OLYMPIA

Mount
Rainier

29

28

31

7

30

PACIFIC

12

OCEAN

RANDLE

33

34

32

5

Mount
St. Helens

36

35

Mount
Adams

37

38

40

39

40

41

42

COLUMBIA RIVER

PUGET SOUND

Wilderness Area

50 Wilderness Area

National Park

44 Roadless Area

Roadless Area

National Recreation Area

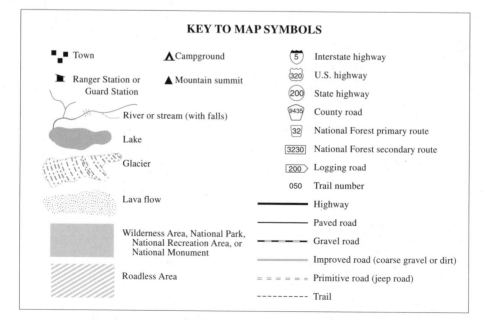

KEY TO MAP SYMBOLS

- Town
- Ranger Station or Guard Station
- River or stream (with falls)
- Lake
- Glacier
- Lava flow
- Wilderness Area, National Park, National Recreation Area, or National Monument
- Roadless Area

- Campground
- Mountain summit

- Interstate highway
- U.S. highway
- State highway
- County road
- National Forest primary route
- National Forest secondary route
- Logging road
- Trail number
- Highway
- Paved road
- Gravel road
- Improved road (coarse gravel or dirt)
- Primitive road (jeep road)
- Trail

INTRODUCTION

"An area where the earth and community of life are untrammeled by man, where man himself is a visitor who does not remain"—it was thus that the United States Congress defined a wilderness area when, in 1964, it passed the initial Wilderness Act. The Wilderness Act further defined a wilderness as undeveloped federal land that has retained its primeval character and that meets the following criteria:

• Appears to have been affected only by the forces of nature, not man;
• Has outstanding opportunities for solitude or primitive unconfined recreation;
• Is at least 5,000 acres in size, or of a size that makes its preservation and use in an unimpaired condition feasible;
• May contain ecological, geological, or other features of scientific, scenic, or historical value.

In the mid-1970s the Forest Service inventoried all national forest areas without roads or any substantial development, and assessed the impact of various potential uses of these areas. The results of this study were published in 1979 as the Roadless Areas Review and Evaluation (RARE II). In 1984, after examining this inventory, Congress passed the Washington State Wilderness Act, which designated several large parcels of this roadless land in the state as wildernesses. Those parcels not so designated were left without specific protection, their use to be established by normal Forest Service planning processes.

Each national forest developed its own management plan that further partitioned the RARE II roadless areas into various usage categories, ranging from Timber Harvest units and Motorized Recreation sections (read "roads") to Wildlife Habitat Areas, Scenic Preservation Corridors, Primitive Areas, and Semiprimitive Areas. The latter category was further divided between Nonmotorized and Motorized, depending on whether or not motorcycles were permitted on trails.

Today, Washington State is fortunate to have more than 4.1 million acres (6,400 square miles) of national forests and parks protected as "designated wilderness areas." The state ranks behind only Alaska and California in the total size of areas so designated.

This book covers not only designated wilderness areas that are legally protected from exploitation, but also selected Primitive and Semiprimitive Areas that are currently de facto wilderness. These lands have no formal protection other than the environmental impact statement review incorporated in the Forest Service planning process. The authors are unabashed advocates of extending formal wilderness designation to such areas before these precious and irreplaceable resources are lost to logging, mining, or other commercial development. It is also our conviction that motorcycles and ATVs are as inappropriate in Semiprimitive Areas as they are in a dedicated wilderness. Their raucous noise is incompatible with the sense of solitude treasured by wilderness visitors, and the damage they cause to trails and meadows is incompatible with the ethic of minimal impact use.

WILD AREA MANAGEMENT

Welcome to the Bureaucratic Maze

Both designated wildernesses and our broader category of wild areas fall under the administration of a complex collection of state and federal agencies. At a cabinet level, responsibility is shared between the Departments of the Interior and Agriculture. Interior's Fish and Wildlife Agency manages the islands off the Washington coast and in the San Juan Islands, both national wildlife refuges and designated wildernesses. The Bureau of Land Management, also part of Interior, administers the Juniper Dunes Wilderness. A third Interior agency, the National Park Service, manages Olympic, North Cascades, and Mount Rainier National Parks, as well as the Ross Lake and Lake Chelan National Recreation Areas. Although large portions of the parks and NRAs are also designated wildernesses, parts with roads and commercial and tourist facilities developed prior to the Washington Wilderness Act are excluded from this status.

The remainder of federal lands are the responsibility of Agriculture's US Forest Service. Portions of these forests have been formally protected as designated wilderness areas, a national recreation area, and a national monument. Even within the Forest Service, however, artificial administrative boundaries rarely coincide with the natural borders of the wild areas in this book. These areas are often split between two or more national forests, all of which have independent control over planning, forest area classification, and budgets within their own purview. National forests are further subdivided into ranger districts; this is where the shoe leather hits the trail. These units are responsible for construction and maintenance of trails, logging unit sales, and personal contact with wilderness visitors. Rangers are the people you want to reach for the most current information on road and trail conditions. But when a continuous trail, totally within any given wilderness or wild area, crosses a ranger district boundary, it suddenly acquires a different number, name, and maintenance status. This "your-turf, my-turf" game must be overcome to achieve coherent wilderness management.

Bordering federal lands are extensive state and private holdings. The latter are easy to identify: they are generally characterized by slope-balding clearcuts to within a millimeter of the national forest boundary and self-promoting signs about how this naked hillside is really a tree farm that will once again flourish, only to be slashed to the ground in another 75 years. State lands, most of which were ceded by the federal government at the time of statehood, are constitutionally committed to timber sales to maximize cash return to public school construction accounts. Other private inholdings in federal lands are mostly patented mining claims, vestiges of obscure and unrealistic mining laws created in 1872.

RULES AND REGULATIONS

Increased numbers of wilderness visitors, and the need to preserve the natural environment that they come to see, requires constraints on wilderness use—some general, some specific to individual areas. General rules are:

- Entrance into a wilderness area is by permit only. Permits may be obtained at the nearest ranger station, or in many cases at self-monitored trailhead stations.
- Maximum party size is 12, an aggregate of both pack animals and humans in the party.
- Maximum length of camping at any one site is limited, generally to 14 days.
- No mechanical means of transport are permitted in a designated wilderness: no ATVs, motorcycles, bicycles, or aircraft. In nondesignated wild areas this rule varies by trail. Specific restrictions are included with each trail description.
- No motorized equipment, such as generators or chain saws, is permitted in a designated wilderness.
- Caching or storing equipment is limited to 48 hours.
- Use of unprocessed hay or grain livestock feed is prohibited.
- Grazing, hitching, tethering, or hobbling livestock within 200 feet of the shore of any lake, stream, or pond is prohibited.
- Shortcutting switchbacks is prohibited.
- Collecting cultural artifacts or disturbing archaeological or pictograph sites is prohibited.
- Digging plants requires a permit, and picking flowers of threatened or endangered species is prohibited.

In addition, specific local restrictions may apply:
- Entry quotas have been established for certain high-use areas.
- Campfires may not be permitted; perhaps only camp stoves may be used.
- Cutting or trimming of trees, either live or dead, may be prohibited.
- Ecosystem restoration may preclude camping in certain areas, or preclude camping within a specified distance from lakes or streams.
- Pets (dogs, cats, or whatever) may not be permitted (and you should consider leaving pets at home in any case).
- Firearms may be prohibited, or if permitted may be subject to restrictions on where they may be discharged.

Always check in advance with local forest or Park Service rangers for current restrictions.

Aside from formal rules, there are other general guidelines for backcountry travel that all ethical visitors should follow in order to preserve the wilderness nature of the areas they visit. These include:

- Use existing campsites or unvegetated areas for camps rather than creating new sites and destroying more plants and grasses in the process.
- Minimize use of soaps, even biodegradable ones, wash cooking and eating utensils at least 100 feet from any stream or lake, and dump waste water on well-drained soil.
- Dig a cat hole, 4 to 6 inches deep, for human feces, and cover it with soil when finished. Locate the hole at least 100 feet from any water sources, and out of high-use camping areas.
- Pack out all refuse; don't burn or bury it. You packed it in full; it should be lighter going out.
- Store food in bags suspended from tree limbs at least 12 feet above the ground and 10 feet from the tree trunk to keep it away from animals.
- Follow the maxim "Take only pictures, leave only footprints."

TOPOGRAPHIC MAPS

The topographic maps listed in the information blocks are all USGS 7.5-minute-series maps, the most useful for wilderness navigation. These might not have the most current road and trail locations, so they may need to be supplemented by other maps, such as individual ranger district maps available from the Forest Service.

HIKING

Coding Conventions

Only selected trails, not a comprehensive list, are described in each section. Where space permits, additional trails are shown on maps accompanying the section.

Each trail description begins with the trail number and name, then the total trail mileage, followed by a difficulty rating.

---

e means easy. Easy trails offer a good near-level grade and well-maintained tread that should offer no problems to inexperienced hikers.

m means moderate. This rating covers a multitude of sins, but basically requires a fair degree of hiking and wilderness navigation ability. Moderate trails may include some miserable grades, rough treads, and a few obscure spots in the trail.

d means difficult. Difficult trails may have terrible tread, deadfalls and thick brush may be encountered, and extensive wilderness navigation experience is required. Some trails in this grouping are abandoned or no longer maintained, but should be followable by very experienced hikers with polished navigation skills.

The last letter(s) in the line, the letters in parentheses, define usage restrictions.

H means the trail is open only to hikers.
S means the trail is open to saddle and pack stock.
B means the trail is open to mountain bicycles.
M means the trail is open to motorized vehicles.

Beyond that, trail descriptions are deliberately brief; they are intended only to convey a sense of difficulty, both in length and elevation loss and gain, and some of the reasons to take the trail. For more extensive trail descriptions, refer to other guidebooks listed in the appendix of this book or contact local ranger stations for trail guides or recreational opportunity guides to trails within their district.

The condition of trails and the forest roads accessing them will vary over time. About 30 percent of the Forest Service budget comes from Congressional allocations, and in the past the remainder came primarily from timber sale proceeds. With growing restrictions on logging, this revenue source is greatly diminished, and funds for road and trail construction and maintenance are hard to come by. Trail conditions tend to degenerate, and remote, seldom-used, and difficult-to-maintain routes are often abandoned. More's the pity, for these trails are exactly the ones that can offer a degree of solitude not found on the more popular routes, as well as a way to disperse wilderness visitors and attract them away from more crowded areas. Unpopular though the idea is, maybe the time has come to charge hikers fees for trail usage. At any rate, before setting out for any trail described in this book, always check first with the local ranger district on its condition and access routes.

CLIMBING

This book is not meant to be a climbing guide, but the descriptions try to give a flavor of the climbing opportunities in a given region. Hundreds of peaks in the state offer every level of climbing challenge, but in general those mentioned in this book require technical climbing skills above mere scrambling, plus climbing equipment and experience in its use. As a short-hand means of giving a sense of a climb's difficulty, either of two commonly used classification schemes may be used.

The class system has five basic levels (C-1 to C-5), plus a decimal breakdown of C-5 into C-5.0 through C-5.11. In general, the higher the number, the more difficult the climb. C-1 and C-2 climbs are basically scrambles. A C-3 climb requires elementary climbing skills and involves moderate exposures, but a rope is generally unnecessary. A C-4 climb requires intermediate climbing skills, most often a rope is needed for safety, and sometimes pitons are required to se-cure belay points. C-5 climbs almost always require protection for safety on leads.

The grade system (G-I to G-VI) is more esoteric and subjective, and theoretically weighs factors such as length of climb, ascent time, route finding, weather problems, and so on. In general, a G-I technical segment can be completed in a few hours, a G-II takes half a day, and a G-III requires most of a day. A G-IV requires a long full day, and possibly a bivouac; usually its hard-est pitch is rated C-5.7 or above. A G-V is probably a one-and-a-half-day technical challenge with a hardest pitch above C-5.8. A G-VI climb is a multiday affair with extremely difficult climbing, most likely requiring aid.

For a more complete list of summits and detailed descriptions of specific routes, refer to one of the climbing guides listed in the appendix.

WINTER SPORTS

This category describes popular trips usually done on skis or snowshoes. They vary in length and difficulty from easy half-day tours up snowbound roads or trails to difficult cross-country routes that are only feasible when snow blankets rocks, brush, and other summertime obstacles. Some of the more difficult routes are exposed to avalanches when conditions are right. (Or per-haps wrong?) Again, further details on the features, experience level required, and hazards are found in guidebooks referenced in the appendix. Typically, taking tours over snowbound roads outside of a designated wilderness may mean encountering snowmobiles.

The Washington State Parks and Recreation Commission has a Sno-Park program, where parking areas are plowed at the start of more than 40 popular winter recreation tour sites. Sev-eral Sno-Parks have easy to intermediate groomed cross-country ski trails nearby, and some even have warming huts or sanitary facilities. A Sno-Park permit is required for use of these areas; as of 1994 the price is $20 per vehicle for the season. A guide to these areas and their associated trails is available from Washington State Parks at the address listed in the appendix.

WILDERNESS SAFETY

The very concept of a wilderness experience implies a good deal of self-reliance in an envi-ronment not designed to protect visitors from natural hazards. As the title of an old Seattle Mountain Rescue film states, *Mountains Don't Care.* Although there certainly are trails, or seg-ments of trails, that can be enjoyed by novice hikers, most of the recreational opportunities in this book demand backcountry experience, equipment, and map and compass navigation skills. The more remote and difficult routes may be physically punishing, with steep grades, boulder and tree root treads, and poorly marked or obscure sections. A great deal of determination, physical conditioning, experience, and wilderness navigation skills are required to safely sample

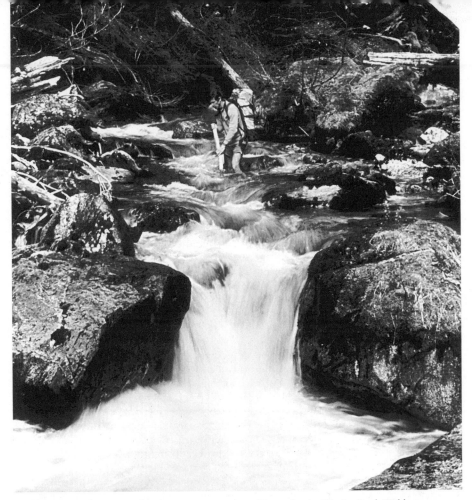

Wilderness travel may entail crossing streams such as this one in the Glacier Peak Wilderness. Exercise care whenever you are in the backcountry.

such trails. Outdoor clubs in several Washington cities offer courses in hiking, camping, and climbing, as well as group hikes and climbs led by experienced members of the organization. This is an excellent way to develop the skills needed before tackling a wild-area trip on your own.

Weather

We should start this brief survey of "what's out there that can get you" with the weather. Large portions of these wild areas are at elevations between 3,000 and 8,000 feet, and although summer temperatures are generally mild, sudden storms with wind, rain, or even snow are not unheard of. In open parkland or atop exposed ridge crests these conditions can quickly cause hypothermia in the unprepared, which if not treated rapidly will lead to death. On the eastern slopes of the Cascades the confluence of moist air from the west and the hot, dry air from the Columbia Plateau often builds midafternoon thunderheads, and the high country is not a fun place to experience a lightning storm. Snow often persists on ridges and north-facing slopes until mid- to late July, and safely traversing steep, open, sidehill slopes requires an ice ax and knowledge of how to use it.

Wildlife

Next in line are the critters out there in the woods. Although cougars, lynx, bobcats, coyotes, and, in some isolated instances, wolves, inhabit Washington's wild areas, consider yourself very lucky if you ever see one. You are therefore very unlikely to be harmed by one.

Almost all areas have a resident population of black bear, but they are more likely to run when sighted than to cause a problem. The exception is in areas where mindless campers have left food or garbage lying around, training bears where to find good pickings. Here otherwise timid bears will delight in ripping into packs and food bags that are not properly hung out of reach. They have little appetite for rare leg-of-hiker, and will depart to the tune of a banging kettle if they don't find a free lunch.

Wild areas in the northeast corner of the state are grizzly bear preserves; there are also reports of a few grizzlies in the North Cascades and one footprint was recently found in the South Cascades. However, the grizzly is an endangered species, which means that there are so few around that you'll likely hike a lifetime and never see one in these areas. Given the opportunity to avoid a hiker, old griz' will probably not cause a confrontation. Many hikers hang a bell on their packs to warn bears of their coming.

Smaller on the scale of annoying mammals are skunks, porcupines, squirrels, and mice, all of which delight in snaffling easy-to-reach food from campsites. The same precaution of hanging food bags out of reach should also thwart these creatures.

Next come reptiles, or, more specifically, rattlesnakes. They are found in many areas on the hotter eastern side of the state, such as lower portions of the Lake Chelan–Sawtooth, Wenaha–Tucannon, and Juniper Dunes Wildernesses. Given the opportunity, rattlers prefer to slither away and eat a mouse, and will strike out at a human only if surprised and without an avenue of retreat. Just watch out where you put your hands and feet. There are no poisonous snakes west of the Cascade crest.

In the insect world the most troublesome critters are ticks, which are found in profusion east of the Cascades, and in a few spots on the west side, in spring and early summer. Potentially harmful effects of tick bites include Rocky Mountain spotted fever and Lyme disease. Early summer also brings out clouds of mosquitoes and deer flies throughout the Cascades; their bites are annoying and sometimes painful, but have no long-lasting impact.

The smallest threat, microscopic in size, is *Giardia,* a paramecium that is transmitted into water supplies by the feces of mammals. This organism causes nausea and severe diarrhea that requires medical treatment to cure. Prevention, either by boiling water for at least ten minutes or by filtering it through pricey microfilters, is much easier than the cure.

Whole books have been written on recognizing and dealing with wilderness hazards, but no book can replace experience and prudent judgment for making trips safe and enjoyable. The recreational opportunities described in this book are in no way warranted to be hazard free; in fact, some are very difficult and even potentially dangerous for an inexperienced wilderness visitor. When you travel in the wild areas and over the routes described in this book, you are doing so at your own risk, and you must assume full responsibility for the safety and comfort of yourself and your party. Constant attention to potential problems from obscure treads, rockfalls, weather, avalanches, steep snow slopes, and the like, and a willingness to turn back in the face of conditions for which you are not prepared, are the keys to safe and enjoyable trips.

A NOTE ABOUT SAFETY

Safety is an important concern in all outdoor activities. No guidebook can alert you to every hazard or anticipate the limitations of every reader. Therefore, the descriptions of roads, trails, routes, and natural features in this book are not representations that a particular place or excursion will be safe for your party. When you follow any of the routes described in this book, you assume responsibility for your own safety. Under normal conditions, such excursions require the usual attention to traffic, road and trail conditions, weather, terrain, the capabilities of your party, and other factors. Keeping informed on current conditions and exercising common sense are the keys to a safe, enjoyable outing.

The Mountaineers

Opposite: *A stream near Lake of the Angels in Olympic National Park,
at the edge of the Skykomish Wilderness*

THE OLYMPIC PENINSULA

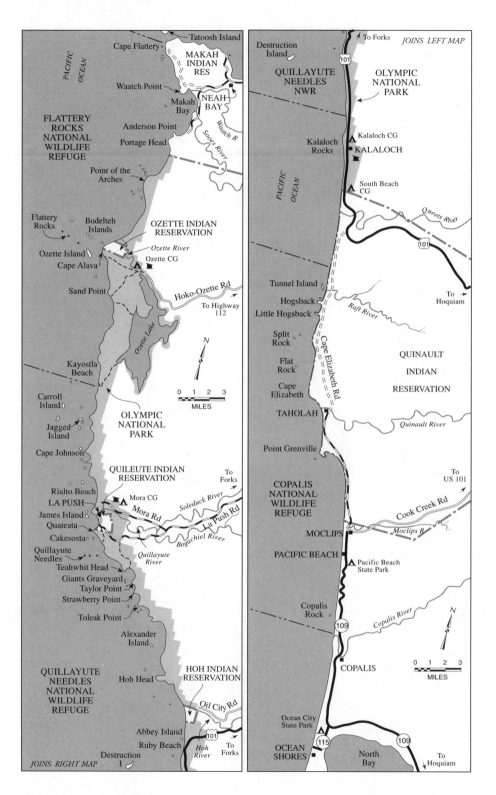

JOINS LEFT MAP

JOINS RIGHT MAP

1

WASHINGTON ISLANDS WILDERNESS

LOCATION: In Clallam, Jefferson, and Grays Harbor counties, along the Pacific Coast of the Olympic Peninsula, from Cape Flattery on the north to Copalis Rocks on the south

SIZE: About 486 acres of islands, rocks, and reefs, up to 3 miles offshore, stretching along 100 miles of coastline

STATUS: Designated Wilderness Area (1970), Designated National Wildlife Refuge (1940)

TERRAIN: 870 reefs, rocks, and islands ranging from less than 1 acre to 36 acres in size. Most have little to no shore below vertical rock cliffs washed by wild surf.

ELEVATION: 0 to 223 feet

MANAGEMENT: US Fish and Wildlife Service

TOPOGRAPHIC MAPS: Allens Bay, Bodelteh Islands, Cape Flattery, Destruction Island, Hoh Head, La Push, Makah Bay, Moclips, Ozette, Quillayute Prairie, Shale Slough, Taholah, Toleak Point, Tunnel Island

The three Washington Islands National Wildlife Refuges are a chain of offshore islands along the west side of the Olympic Peninsula that includes Flattery Rocks and the Quillayute Needles to the north, and Copalis Rock to the south. These islands are both home and breeding ground for a dozen species of marine birds, totaling more than 108,000 breeding pairs, as well as a stopover for thousands of migratory birds. Offshore waters teem with seals, sea lions, and whales.

Climate

The islands lie off the wet side of the Olympic Peninsula, exposed to weather patterns sweeping in from the Pacific. Annual rainfall ranges from 110 to 160 inches. Summers are cool and moist, with frequent stretches of persistent fog. Winter low-pressure systems bring storms with heavy rain, strong winds, and crashing seas. Temperatures are mild year-round, seldom dropping below 35 degrees or rising above 65 degrees.

Plants and Wildlife

The tops of the larger islands have a thin layer of soil that permits growth of shrubs such as salal and salmonberry; a few have stands of Sitka spruce. This vegetation supports a small population of Townsend's voles, shrew moles, Trowbridge's shrews, salamanders, and garter snakes, a food source for raptors.

The lower rocks and reefs are haul-out sites for harbor seals and northern and California sea lions. Other mammals common in the waters surrounding the islands include Pacific right whales, gray whales, piked whales, humpback whales, Pacific harbor porpoises, and fur seals. In 1970 sea otters were reintroduced after a nearly 100-year absence due to their near-extinction by fur hunters.

Among the birds known to nest on the islands are bald eagles, peregrine falcons, auklets, cormorants, petrels, oystercatchers, murres, gulls, and tufted puffins. These are joined annually by migrating flocks of passerines, scoters, shearwaters, and western grebes.

Sea lions haul out onto offshore rocks of the Washington Islands Wilderness.

Geology

The islands lie on the west side of the Olympic Peninsula, formed by the collision between the North American and Juan de Fuca plates some 50 million years ago. The western edge of this terrane consisted of sedimentary deposits overlaying the ocean floor. The repetition of submerging and uplifting transformed these sediments into metamorphic rock, and its differential erosion created the reefs and islands that comprise the wilderness today.

History

The sea and its resources were a vital part of the life of Northwest Indians, so these islands were undoubtedly frequented by them. Shell middens found on Tsakawahyah Island indicate native visitation there. The top of this island, as well as caves on Ozette Island, served as native burial sites.

In 1907 President Theodore Roosevelt designated Flattery Rocks, Quillayute Needles, and Copalis Rock as migratory bird sanctuaries. Further protection was afforded in 1940 when these areas, with the exception of Destruction Island, were made national wildlife refuges. All were designated as a wilderness area in 1970.

ACTIVITIES

All of the islands, by virtue of their wildlife sanctuary status, are closed to public entry and use. They can be viewed most closely from the coastal portion of Olympic National Park. Access points to this beach strip are at Ozette, Rialto Beach, Second and Third beaches near La Push, Ruby Beach, Kalaloch, Taholah, Moclips, and Pacific Beach.

2

OLYMPIC NATIONAL PARK—OCEAN BEACHES

LOCATION: In Jefferson and Clallam counties, along the Pacific Ocean shoreline of the Olympic Peninsula

SIZE: 42,900 acres

STATUS: National Park (1953), Designated Wilderness Area (1988)

TERRAIN: Sand, conglomerate, or rock beaches below steep rocky headlands. Hundreds of offshore rocks, reefs, and sea stacks. Headlands have wave-carved arches and caves, and are split by numerous creeks and rivers. Inland is low and densely forested, with a few lakes and several marshes.

ELEVATION: 0 to 650 feet

MANAGEMENT: National Park Service

TOPOGRAPHIC MAPS: Allens Bay, Destruction Island, Dickey Lake, Hoh Head, La Push, Makah Bay, Ozette, Queets, Quillayute Prairie, Toleak Point, Umbrella Creek

This portion of Olympic National Park consists of a 57-mile strip of Pacific Ocean shoreline. The southern third of the ocean beach lies only a few hundred feet from a coastal segment of US Highway 101, but the northern two-thirds are accessible only by hiking from one of four access points. Two sections, each more than 17 miles long, have no intermediate approaches.

Beaches range from long, wide expanses of sand to small coves framed by rocky headland cliffs, some impassable at sea level and others requiring low tide levels to round. Trails lead inland through dense, brushy forest to cross the most difficult of these heads. Offshore are more than 800 low rocks, submerging reefs, and spectacular sea stacks, all erosion-resistant vestiges of former heads and capes. Minus tides permit exploration of nearshore tide pools teeming with a fantastic variety of marine life.

The park-managed ocean strip is interrupted briefly in three spots by small Indian reservations: the Hoh Reservation on the south side of the Hoh River, the Quileute Reservation south of La Push, and the Ozette Reservation on the north side of Cape Alava. Indians have lived in these areas for centuries; archaeological digs at a village site at Cape Alava, covered by a sudden mud slide more than 500 years ago, have recovered priceless artifacts that chronicle the culture and life of these early Native Americans.

Over the last 200 years, rugged offshore reefs have claimed numerous ships and lives. Remnants of a wave-battered shipwreck lie on the rocks north of Shi Shi Beach; elsewhere along the coast, rusting anchors and chains recall the destruction of other ships. Chilean and Norwegian memorials, both located along the remote north wilderness beach, commemorate lives lost in nearby shipwrecks.

Near the north end of the beach strip, the park extends inland to enclose Ozette Lake, the third-largest natural lake in the state. The lake, with numerous bays and coves, is 8.5 miles long, and in most places nearly 2 miles wide. A small campground and a boat launch at the north end of the lake are its only means of access from civilization. Two trails lead from coves on the west side to the ocean beach; the rest of the lake's perimeter is rimmed with impenetrable brush and forest.

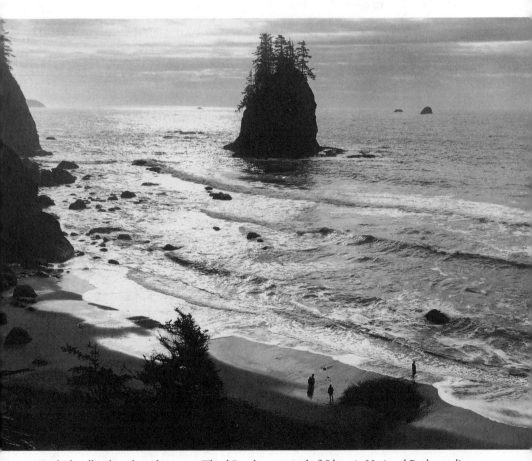

Rocky headlands such as this one at Third Beach are typical of Olympic National Park coastline.

Climate

The ocean beach strip is on the wet side of the Olympic Peninsula; precipitation here averages 120 inches per year, with three-fourths of this falling as heavy rains in fall and winter months. During this time a continuous series of low-pressure cells roll in from the Pacific Ocean, accompanied by high winds, torrential downpours, and heavy seas. Although precipitation during the summer averages only 3 inches per month, this season is still cool, moist, and frequently foggy. Temperatures are mild year-round, seldom dropping below 35 degrees or rising above 65 degrees.

Plants and Wildlife

The thick forest above the headland cliffs has a band of shore pine immediately above the beach. Inland this is replaced by hemlock, red cedar, Pacific madrone, and Sitka spruce. A dense growth of kinnikinnick, salal, and ocean spray is underlaid by mosses, ferns, deerfoot vanillaleaf, wood sorrel, and fireweed. Because of its low elevation and the heavy rains, the inland forest floor has numerous bogs, marshes, and mud holes, making cross-country travel difficult.

Residents of the forest, and visitors to the beaches, include black-tailed deer, black bear, raccoon, skunk, and, on rare occasions, elk and porcupine. The ocean strip and its offshore rocks are both home and breeding ground for glaucous gulls, great blue herons, double-crested cormorants, black oystercatchers, crows, and ravens. Bald eagles also nest in the area, and may be spotted perched on snags above the beach. Seals often haul out on the offshore rocks.

At low-tide levels, the nearshore wave-cut benches are laced with tide pools that harbor several types of seaweed, mussels, barnacles, limpets, periwinkles, snails, rock oysters, purple shore crabs, hermit crabs, starfish, nudibranchs, chitons, worms, anemones, and sea urchins.

Geology

The headwall of the beach south of Ozette Lake is made up of sandstones and conglomerates formed from continental and marine sediments deposited 10 million to 25 million years ago. The area from Kayostla Beach north to Shi Shi Beach is composed of glacial deposits laid down by Pleistocene ice sheets and more recent alluvium. In places the cliffs above the southern section of the ocean beach are intruded with breccia—fragments of broken sandstone compressed and cemented in subterranean trenches into solid rock. These outcrops are often permeated with crude oil compressed into spaces between the fragments.

The breaking surf focuses on projecting headlands, where it fractures blocks of rock by compressing air into small cracks, and undercuts the base of the sea cliffs, causing them to collapse. The resulting debris is eroded by the surf, carried off as sand and fine gravel, and deposited in the quieter water of coves. Over time the result of this erosion is the destruction of seaward headlands, the buildup of long stretches of sandy beach, and a smoothing of the coastline.

Offshore sea stacks are the less fractured, more erosion-resistant remnants of former headland cliffs. The rocks and reefs at or just below the surface are portions of harder rock that form a broad wave-cut bench near the shore.

History

Archaeological digs at Cape Alava indicate that Indians lived along the Northwest ocean beaches as long as 2,000 years ago. The first white explorers arrived in the area between 1774 and 1778. The natives were hostile to initial white contacts; a Russian expedition, shipwrecked near Rialto Beach in 1808, fought with both the Quileutes and Hoh before 22 of its members were either killed or captured.

In the early 1800s the territory was jointly claimed by the United States and Great Britain; a boundary settlement in 1846 ceded the area to the U.S. Treaties concluded in 1855 assigned then-recognized tribes to reservations near their traditional hunting and fishing grounds on the peninsula.

Around 1890 the first white settlers moved to the southern portion of the beach strip at Kalaloch to open a cannery. The first non-native settler arrived at La Push in 1860. As early as the 1870s, schooners brought staples there, and the village served as a supply point for the nearby western peninsula. To the north, homesteaders reached Ozette Lake in the 1890s, following rumors of a railroad or county road into the area. The road didn't arrive until 1935; meanwhile a tiny logging community grew at the site. The arrival of the road prompted the building of a small resort at the north end of the lake at Ozette.

Recognizing its natural resource value, President Grover Cleveland established the Olympic Forest Reserve in 1897. The unique geography and ecology of the area was further recognized in 1909, when President Theodore Roosevelt created the 651,000-acre Mount Olympus National Monument. National park status was conferred on the area in June 1938; the ocean beaches

Waves swirl around starfish clinging to a rock on the Olympic shore.

were added to the park in 1953. The latest addition, in 1977, was the beach strip between Point of the Arches and Shi Shi Beach.

At the onset of World War II, the vulnerability of miles of coastline caused the Coast Guard to appropriate resorts at Kalaloch and Ozette as part of the Coastal Lookout System. This system ultimately included isolated four-man outposts every 5 to 10 miles along the coast. A few old cabins near creeks and headlands are vestiges of this wartime effort.

ACTIVITIES

Hiking

Hikers along the remote ocean beaches must contend with several hazards not common to hikes in other wilderness areas. Sheer cliffs drop directly to the surf at some of the headlands, forcing travelers to cross them via short inland trails through the dense coastal forest. Other heads that can be rounded at low tides don't have such trails, and the steep sea cliffs and dense brush preclude crossing them. As a result, hikers must pay close attention to tide tables and schedule their travel to round such spots at low tide. Some creeks and rivers that can normally be waded become impassable with runoff from heavy rains or at extreme high tides. Severe storms combined with high tides can lash beaches with dangerous breaking surf that can toss huge driftwood logs around with ease. Detailed knowledge of tide levels and weather conditions is critical for a safe trip.

Point of the Arches. 3.5 miles/e (H). From the west end of Neah Bay find the road signed "OCEAN BEACHES" and follow it south. The road crosses the Waatch River, turns south along Makah Bay, then crosses the Sooes River. At 6.5 miles the passable road ends near some homes; the track that continues south across the reservation quickly degenerates to axle-deep mud. In 2 miles this path reaches the Olympic National Park boundary, above the north end of Shi Shi Beach. Slippery paths lead down to the beach at this point, and a short stroll north on the beach leads to small coves, tide pools, sea stacks, and the remains of a shipwrecked freighter.

The trail continues south along the bluff for another mile before wandering down to the beach near Petroleum Creek. The way follows the beach to Point of the Arches, an exquisite collection of tiny coves, tide pools, and a line of sea stacks stretching nearly a mile offshore. Many of these stacks have caves and arches cut through them by the surf, giving the point its name. A few nearshore stacks can be explored at minus tides, but the tide-exposed bench has sharp rocks and slippery footing. The headlands immediately south of the point are inaccessible by beach.

Cape Alava (Indian Village). 3.5 miles/e (H). Beginning at the campground on the north end of Ozette Lake, the route crosses the footbridge over the Ozette River and follows the north fork west through hemlock forest to the sandy beach on the south side of Cape Alava, the westernmost point of the coterminous U.S. Much of the trail is on puncheon logs that bridge bogs en route. The cape lies within the Ozette Indian Reservation, which stretches about a mile along the beach.

The sandy beach can be hiked north through the reservation to the mouth of the Ozette River, which can be waded at low tide. A narrow strip of sand leads north from the river for nearly 4 miles to the southern edge of Point of the Arches.

The beach south from Cape Alava to Sand Point is a narrow but easy 3-mile walk, except at very high tides. En route, at Wedding Rocks, are a series of Indian pictographs carved in the sandstone headland near the high tide level.

North Sand Point. *2 miles/e (H).* At the start of the Cape Alava Trail, take the south fork, which heads through brushy forest to reach Sand Point. A good portion of this path is also atop logs across bogs and marshes. A small rock spike marks the end of Sand Point, where a broad sandy beach sweeps south for 1.5 miles to cliffs north of Yellow Banks. A loop trip can be made by hiking north to Cape Alava.

Rialto Beach to Cape Alava (the North Wilderness Beach). *18.5 miles/m (H).* Because of the need to schedule rounding of several heads at low tide levels, this is generally a 3-day hike, typically done by hikers dropped off at one end and picked up at the other. The south end leaves Mora Campground at the Rialto Beach Picnic Area. Hike the broad sandy beach north for 0.5 mile, wade Ellen Creek, and in another mile reach Hole-in-the-Wall, a rock arch across the beach. A short distance north is the first headland that can be rounded only at low tide. Beyond, a sandy beach leads a mile north to the Chilean Memorial, commemorating the 1920 shipwreck of the schooner *W. J. Pirrie.* A small offshore island with rockbound tide pools can be reached at minus tides.

North of the Chilean Memorial, the cliffs of Cape Johnson require a low tide to round, as does a small head another 0.5 mile to the north. A sandy beach continues for 1.3 miles to a head with a short, low trail across the inland side. A mile-long sandy stretch, with views offshore of Sea Lion Rock and Jagged and Carroll islands, ends at a small, low-tide-only head, the last for several miles. In 2.4 miles the route reaches the Norwegian Memorial. The nearshore surf is peppered with low rocks from here to the next low-tide passage below a small head at the north end of Yellow Banks. The trip north to Sand Point and Cape Alava is described above.

Third Beach. *1.5 miles/e (H).* The trailhead is on the south side of the road, 2.3 miles east of La Push. A forest hike ends in a steep switchback descent of the headland to the center of Third Beach, a mile-long strip of sand sandwiched between Teahwhit Head and Taylor Point. At the south end of the beach a waterfall plunges from Taylor Point, and nearshore tide pools are accessible at low tide.

Third Beach to the Hoh River (the South Wilderness Beach). *17 miles/m (H).* This long wilderness beach segment requires inland treks to cross heads impassable at sea level, and crosses three creeks that may not be fordable during heavy runoffs. Taylor Head blocks passage at the south end of Third Beach (trail described above); a 1.5-mile wooded path leads inland across the head to a small cove on its east side. Here a scramble over or medium-tide-level passage around a protruding cliff reaches a sandy respite before Scotts Bluff. The bluff is passable at low tide or can be bypassed by a short inland trail.

In 0.5 mile the offshore stacks of the Giants Graveyard mark the former location of a present-day sea cliff passable only at medium or lower tides. Once this obstacle is rounded, a sandy crescent-shaped beach leads to Strawberry Point, where nearshore sea stacks and tide pools are accessible at minus tides. The broad beach continues south to Toleak Point, and more nearby offshore rocks and tide pools.

After another mile of broad sandy beach, cliffs force the route inland past a waterfall at Falls Creek and to a waded crossing of Goodman Creek before it once again returns to the beach. An easy hike of more than 2 miles leads to the ford of Mosquito Creek and a route choice. A minor head to the south can be skirted at minus tides, and the beach beyond can be followed for another mile before the cliffs of Hoh Head force the route inland. Alternatively, at Mosquito Creek, the Hoh Head trail climbs to the brushy rim of the sea cliff and follows it south, with glimpses of the beach below. Both routes join for an inland trek over Hoh Head to Jefferson Cove.

At the south end of the cove, a steep cliff is the final low-tide-only obstacle before reaching the Hoh River trailhead at Oil City, a grandiose name for a site with neither oil nor residents.

Southwest Beaches and US Highway 101 Accesses. Immediately south of the Hoh River, the park beach strip is interrupted by the Hoh Indian Reservation. US Highway 101 swings west into the park about a mile south of the reservation and follows the rim of headlands for 11.5 miles to the south park boundary near the Queets River. En route several short paths lead through the forest to the wide, sandy beach strip. There are only a few offshore stacks and rocks in this beach section; these occur near small eroded headlands, the only places where high tide levels may temporarily interrupt beach hikes. Beach 4 has tide pools accessible at low tide; a few sea stacks are offshore from Ruby Beach. Because of its accessibility, this strip is popular year-round, even in winter, when the surf hurls huge driftwood trees about and whips up a froth of spindrift along the water's edge.

Paths to the beach are located at Ruby Beach, on the north end of this strip; Beach 6, 0.9 mile to the south; a small stream, 0.9 mile south of Beach 6; Steamboat Creek, 0.4 mile farther south; Beach 4, in 2.4 more miles; Beach 3, 0.6 mile to the south; Kalaloch Beach, in another 2.5 miles; Beach 2, 1.3 miles south of Kalaloch; Beach 1, 0.9 mile to the south; and South Beach Campground, at the park's south boundary.

3

OLYMPIC NATIONAL PARK—INTERIOR

LOCATION: In Clallam, Jefferson, Mason, and Grays Harbor counties, in the heart of the Olympic Peninsula
SIZE: Park (interior): 878,973 acres; wilderness: 876,669 acres
STATUS: National Park (1938), Designated Wilderness Area (1988)
TERRAIN: A complex structure of rugged ridges, many supporting small glaciers or snowfields, divided by long, deep, glacier- and stream-carved drainages radiating from the high, remote interior of the region
ELEVATION: 80 to 7,965 feet
MANAGEMENT: National Park Service
TOPOGRAPHIC MAPS: Bob Creek, Bogachiel Peak, Bunch Lake, Chimney Peak, Colonel Bob, Elwha, Finley Creek, Hunger Mountain, Indian Pass, Kimta Peak, Kloochman Rock, Lake Crescent, Lake Sutherland, Lake Quinault East, Lake Quinault West, Maiden Peak, Matheny Ridge, McCartney Peak, Morse Creek, Mount Angeles, Mount Carrie, Mount Christie, Mount Deception, Mount Hoquiam, Mount Muller, Mount Olson, Mount Olympus, Mount Queets, Mount Skokomish, Mount Steel, Mount Tom, Mount Townsend, Mt. Washington, Owl Mountain, Port Angeles, Queets, Salmon River East, Salmon River West, Slide Peak, Spruce Mountain, Stequaleho Creek, The Brothers, Tyler Peak, Wellesley Peak, Winfield Creek, Wynoochee Lake

The inland portion of Olympic National Park is a huge wilderness, 50 miles wide east-to-west and 40 miles wide north-to-south. Here are a jumble of crumbling rocky summits between 6,500 and 7,700 feet high, flanked by sharp ridges, many topped by loose rock towers. The faces of the higher peaks host more than 60 small low-gradient glaciers. The heavy annual snow-fall leaves steep snowfields, many that never totally melt. The park has more than 350 lakes, most quite small and tucked into alpine cirques; however, one, Lake Crescent, is more than 5,000 acres in size. Approximately 586 miles of trails, several 20 to 30 miles in length, explore the interior of the park. Many trace the long, radiating river courses that drain from the high country.

Climate

The Olympic Range is a major barrier for storms from the Pacific Ocean; storm fronts drop tremendous amounts of precipitation on the range's western flanks, but the eastern slopes remain reasonably dry. The Hoh Rain Forest on the west receives an annual load of 133 inches of precipitation; the town of Sequim, on the northeast, sees only 16 inches. Most of this rain and snow falls between October and March, when few dry days are recorded. At lower elevations snow rarely remains on the ground for more than a few days, but a snowpack of 30 to 40 feet may accumulate on peaks and ridge tops. Year-round temperatures are relatively mild, ranging between the 20s to 40s in winter, and the mid-40s to 70s in summer. Weather is unpredictable, due to the proximity to ocean storm fronts; summer months frequently see persistent fog or low clouds below 3,000 feet that often disappear by early afternoon.

Plants and Wildlife

The wide altitude variation in the park spans multiple forest zones. At the lowest elevations forests are composed of Douglas-fir, western hemlock, Sitka spruce, and western red cedar, with bigleaf maple, red alder, and black cottonwood in drainage bottoms. The understory here contains salal, huckleberry, rhododendron, Oregon grape, devil's club, skunk cabbage, willows, salmonberry, and a variety of ferns and mosses. Farther up the slopes, trees change to Douglas-fir, western hemlock, silver fir, and western red cedar. Vine maple, alder, and devil's club are found along streams and in avalanche tracks. Near timberline, the trees are subalpine fir, mountain hemlock, and Alaska cedar, and ground cover is dominated by willows, slide alder, huckleberry, heather, and colorful displays of wildflowers such as beargrass, paintbrush, lupine, and avalanche lilies. The highest ridges, in the alpine zone, have a sparse cover of phlox, sedges, anemones, spirea, mosses, and lichens.

A wooden footbridge spans spectacular Soleduck Falls on the Soleduck River.

Common mammals include several species of shrews, coast mole, snowshoe hare, mountain beaver, squirrels, chipmunks, vole, raccoon, weasel, mink, river otter, skunk, coyote, black bear, cougar, bobcat, elk, and black-tailed deer. Over 200 species of birds have been recorded in the Olympics, and a few dozen more species are transient visitors. Those most commonly seen are wrens, crows, woodpeckers, sparrows, kingfishers, owls, hawks, grouse, jays, finches, ravens, kinglets, juncos, and golden eagles.

Geology

The rocks of the Olympic Peninsula were born in the waters off the western continental margin. Sediments and muds washed from the North American continent were layered and compressed offshore into sandstones and shales. Some 50 million years ago these deposits were intruded on their eastern edge by massive undersea lava flows that emerged as pillow basalts. These flows also penetrated the layers between the accumulated strata as sills. Collisions between the oceanic and continental plates caused shear fractures, and the strata layers overrode each other along the fault lines. Continued movement of the two plates toward each other tilted the strata sharply upward to a near-vertical plane. Further compression toward the northeast squeezed and distorted the strata into successive horseshoe-shaped bands wrapped around the north, east, and south sides of the Olympic Peninsula.

A general uplift raised the heart of the Olympics, and radial watercourses cut deeply through the base rock. Both continental and local glaciation during the last ice age, 12,000 years ago, further carved these drainages, leaving steep U-shaped valleys and glacial cirques in their wake. Since then erosion has worn, sharpened, and narrowed ridges, cleaving the loosely bonded rock into rotten peaks and towers along ridge crests, and deepening the gorges of major rivers and streams. Local alpine glaciers, and the rivers and streams they feed with abrasive, scoured waste, continue this shaping and carving today.

History

Native American tribes had several settlements on the shores of the Olympic Peninsula, some dating over 2,000 years ago. Artifacts found in high mountain meadows indicate natives visited the heart of the peninsula, now the Olympic National Park, between 4,000 and 8,000 years ago.

In 1774, crew members of the *Santiago*, under the command of Juan Perez, were the first Europeans to sight the Olympic Range. Mount Olympus was identified and named by Captain John Meares, a British explorer, in 1788; the name was applied to the entire range in the logs of the Vancouver Expedition in 1792.

The first homesteaders arrived on the lowland fringes of the Olympics in the 1850s. Although the U.S. Army built a trail from Fort Townsend to the Dungeness River in 1882, the interior of the range remained mysterious and unknown; some speculated that it contained a "Shangri-la" hidden valley. The first exploration into the range began in 1885, when Lieutenant Joseph O'Neil led an Army expedition through the northeast portion of the Olympics.

In 1889 the *Seattle Press* sponsored an expedition to cross the range and discover what lay hidden in its interior. A party of five headed into the Elwha Valley in December 1889. The group struggled upstream through deep snows in a tragicomic adventure. It took them until May 1890 to cross the range and reach the Quinault River, where they descended to the Pacific. The interior of the Olympics was no longer a mystery—and definitely not a Shangri-la!

O'Neil returned later in 1890 to lead a party into the range from the south. The expedition was intensive and thorough, mapping the Skokomish, Wynoochee, Quinault, Queets, Duckabush, and Dosewallips drainages. Although they claimed to have made the first ascent of Mount Olympus, evidence left by the party has never been found. When the Olympic Forest Reserve was created in 1897, a complete survey of the range was ordered. A USGS-contracted party led by Arthur Dodwell and Theodore Rixon completed this effort between 1898 and 1900, climbing many peaks in the range in the course of their activities. With the range and its peaks now plotted, a flurry of climbing activity took place in the early 1900s; by 1931 all major peaks had been climbed.

In 1909 President Theodore Roosevelt proclaimed 615,000 acres of the Olympic National Forest the Mount Olympus National Monument. The monument's size and boundaries shifted markedly in subsequent years due to political pressures and commercial greed for its natural resources. Olympic National Park, 648,000 acres, was created in 1938. Most of the interior was declared a designated wilderness in 1988.

ACTIVITIES

Hiking

DUNGENESS–GRAY WOLF RIVER TRAILS

Upper Gray Wolf Trail. 12.9 miles/m (H,S). The Lower Gray Wolf Trail enters the park from the Buckhorn Wilderness (2,260 ft), 0.9 mile from the Upper Gray Wolf Trail (2,100 ft). The latter follows the bank of the Gray Wolf River upstream through fir and cedar forest and across avalanche tracks. It climbs steeply, switchbacking into meadows (5,200 ft), to reach Gray Wolf Pass (6,180 ft). Here are wide views of Mounts Deception, Mystery, Constance, and Olympus, the Brothers, Lost Peak, and the Needles. The path continues south, zigzagging abruptly down to the Dosewallips Trail (3,600 ft).

Royal Basin Trail. 7 miles/m (H,S). From Trail #832 (2,680 ft) on the Dungeness River, just east of the park boundary, the way heads west up Royal Basin Creek through Douglas-fir and hemlock forest. The path crosses multiple openings swept by avalanches from Gray Wolf Ridge. At Royal Falls the creek and trail bend south and the grade flattens; the trail crosses lower Royal Basin and climbs to Royal Lake (5,118 ft). The upper basin is rimmed on the west by the rock towers of the Needles, capped at its head by Mounts Deception and Mystery, and flanked on the east by spires along the Olympic National Park–Buckhorn Wilderness boundary.

DOSEWALLIPS RIVER TRAILS

Lake Constance Trail. 2 miles/m (H). From the Dosewallips River Road (1,460 ft), this route shoots up along Constance Creek, clawing over roots, ledges, and small cliffs to reach Lake Constance (4,664 ft). North from this beautiful cliff-walled lake is 2-mile-long Avalanche Canyon, a snow-filled defile squeezed between cliffs and crags that rise abruptly 1,500 feet or more.

Dosewallips Trail. 15.4 miles/m (H,S). A long, easy-grade path from Dosewallips Campground (1,580 ft) follows the Dosewallips River northwest at the base of a deep, forested canyon. At Dose Forks, the West Fork Dosewallips Trail peels off, and shortly the Constance Pass Trail climbs to the north. The way follows the hook of the river west, then north, passing the south end of the Gray Wolf Trail. The forest opens at Dose Meadows, then the way contours around the head of the basin to Thousand Acre Meadow. Long, sweeping switchbacks climb to Hayden Pass (5,847 ft) to meet the trail of the same name. The pass is framed by Sentinel Peak and Mount Fromme, and has great views of Mount Anderson, Wellesley Peak, the Bailey Range, and Mount Olympus.

West Fork Dosewallips Trail. 9.1 miles/m (H,S). From Dose Forks (1,930 ft) the route climbs west to a bridge over the 100-foot-deep gorge of the West Fork, then follows the river upstream through fir and hemlock forest. At 2,750 feet the trail crosses the river into open country at Honeymoon Meadows (3,520 ft). Above, at Anderson Pass (4,465 ft), it joins the Enchanted Valley Trail. Here a steep switchback chain leads to the moraine of the Anderson Glacier (5,100 ft), the largest in the east Olympics. Tiny hardy wildflowers cling to niches in the rock; the glacier sweeps down from the two ragged summits of Mount Anderson.

Constance Pass Trail. 8.5 miles/m-d (H,S). Switchbacks through Douglas-fir climb the steep spur above the Dosewallips Trail (2,181 ft) to Sunnybrook Meadows, where a long traverse east leads to Constance Pass (5,850 ft) and views of the ragged cliffs of the Inner Constance Peaks. The way drops north to Home Lake (5,308 ft), then descends into the Buckhorn Wilderness to Trail #833 at Boulder Camp (4,920 ft).

DUCKABUSH RIVER TRAILS

Duckabush Trail. 22.2 miles/m-d (H,S). Trail #803 enters the park from the Brothers Wilderness (1,320 ft), then rolls along the broad bottom of the Duckabush drainage as it continues upstream to the North Fork Skokomish Trail (2,620 ft). The valley narrows, the way becomes steeper, and switchbacks climb to Marmot Lake (4,390 ft). The route snakes uphill through parkland to O'Neil Pass (4,980 ft), where it meets the O'Neil Pass Trail.

NORTH FORK SKOKOMISH RIVER TRAILS

North Fork Skokomish Trail. 15.6 miles/m (H,S). From Staircase Campground (840 ft), the route starts on an abandoned roadbed that heads up the North Fork of the Skokomish River. It passes the Flapjack Lakes Trail, then bends northeast as it thrusts upstream. The way leaves the timbered river bottom at Nine Stream (1,980 ft) to switchback up steep slopes and break into meadows at First Divide (4,688 ft). Here are views to Mount LaCrosse and White Mountain. Dropping down the north side of the pass, the way threads through meadows; Mount Steel frames the horizon to the west. Switchbacks descend steep wooded slopes north to the Duckabush Trail (2,710 ft).

Flapjack Lakes Trail. 5.6 miles/m (H,S). Beginning at the end of an abandoned-road section of the North Fork Skokomish River Trail (1,480 ft), the route heads up the forested slope east of the river, crosses Madeline Creek, then rounds a ridge into the Donahue Creek drainage. It weaves up to Flapjack Lakes (3,847 to 3,850 ft) at the base of the towers of Sawtooth Ridge. The path continues northeast through meadows, past tarns flanked by the spires of the Fin, Castle Spires, the Needle, and the walls of Mount Cruiser. Flower meadows at Gladys Divide (5,350 ft) sweep gracefully up to the top of Mount Gladys.

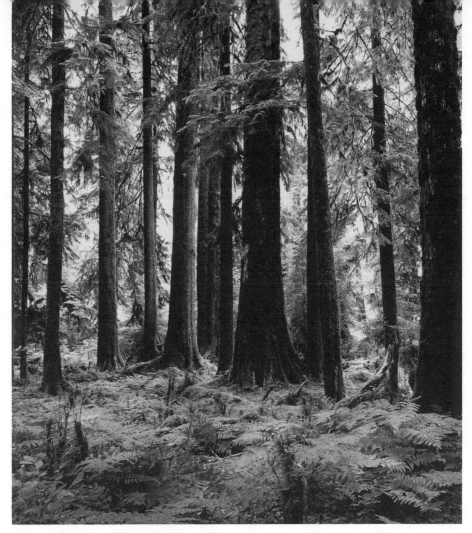

Ferns carpet the forest floor in the Hoh rainforest.

SOUTH FORK SKOKOMISH TRAILS

Upper South Fork Skokomish Trail. *7 miles/m (H,S).* Trail #873 enters the park (2,600 ft) 4.4 miles from its trailhead on FR 2361. To this point the grade is easy and well maintained, but at the park boundary it becomes rough and steep. After traversing a soggy basin (3,100 ft) the way switchbacks up to Sundown Pass (4,140 ft), then descends to the Graves Creek trail (3,760 ft) just south of Sundown Lake.

EAST FORK QUINAULT RIVER TRAILS

Enchanted Valley Trail. *18.9 miles/m (H,S).* From the end of the South Shore Quinault Road (620 ft) the route crosses Graves Creek, passes the Graves Creek Trail, then follows an abandoned roadbed up the ever-deepening Quinault River drainage. After crossing to the northwest side of the river, the road becomes a trail that traces the easy grade of the river upstream past numerous cascades from cliffs above. A suspension bridge over the river leads to the heart of Enchanted Valley and its two-story log chalet. Depending on the season, avalanches or myriad waterfall veils drop over the precipitous walls of Chimney Peak. Beyond Enchanted Valley, cliff walls constrict the route as it climbs past the O'Neil Pass Trail, then switchbacks steeply up to Anderson Pass (4,465 ft) to meet the West Fork Dosewallips Trail.

Graves Creek Trail. 8.6 miles/m (H,S). Near the start of the Enchanted Valley Trail (660 ft) this route climbs west through dense forest above Graves Creek to Success Creek. Here, creek and trail turn south and switchbacks climb the steep basin headwall. The way ascends east through meadows, passes the South Fork Skokomish Trail, and reaches Sundown Lake (3,811 ft).

O'Neil Pass Trail. 7.4 miles/m (H,S). From meadows west of Anderson Pass (3,250 ft) the route leaves the Enchanted Valley Trail and snakes southwest through forest and alpine meadows as it ascends past views of the cliffs of Chimney Peak above Enchanted Valley. It contours south through flower garden parks, rounds Overlook Peak, and climbs to O'Neil Pass (4,870 ft). The Quinault Valley stretches west to the Pacific, and close by is the massive summit of Mount Duckabush.

NORTH FORK QUINAULT RIVER TRAILS

Big Creek Trail. 7.1 miles/m (H,S). From rain forest bottomland on the North Shore Quinault Road, the route wanders west through fir and Alaska cedar to Big Creek. It heads abruptly uphill, breaks north along a steep-walled tributary drainage, then switchbacks up a wooded ridge to Three Lakes (3,180 to 3,230 ft) to meet the Skyline Trail.

North Fork Quinault Trail. 16.4 miles/m (H,S). Leaving the North Fork Ranger Station (500 ft), the way follows an abandoned road along the west bank of the North Fork Quinault River for 4 miles, then ascends into the narrowing valley. River and trail swing northwest, then hook sharply to the east. Steep walls near Geoduck Creek force the trail to the river. It crosses the river (hazardous at high water), climbs steeply through dense dark forest, and breaks into meadows as it meets the Skyline Trail. It reaches parkland at Low Divide (3,602 ft), where it joins the Low Divide Trail.

Skyline Trail. 20.5 miles/m (H,S). One of the most remote wilderness trails in the park leaves Big Creek Trail at Three Lakes (3,190 ft) to climb north past alpine tarns, meadows, and clumps of forest on the flank of Tshletshy Ridge. The way continues north above Three Prune Basin, then follows the divide between the Queets and Quinault basins north toward Kimta Peak. Ridgetop meadows afford views of Mount Olympus and the Bailey Range. After skirting the summit of Kimta Peak at 5,200 feet, the way bends sharply eastward, descends the north flank of Kimta Creek Basin, then switchbacks up to Promise Creek Pass (5,100 ft) and views of the heart of the Olympics—Mounts Zindorf, Christie, Seattle, Noyes, and Meany. Northwest the path gropes through snowfields broken by rocks and heather as it descends to Hee Haw Pass (4,550 ft), then climbs past a spur to Lake Beauty (4,681 ft), and Beauty Pass (5,070 ft). The way weaves around basin headwalls of Promise and Seattle creeks, switchbacks up to a traverse of the south rib of Mount Seattle, then snakes down to join the North Fork Quinault Trail (3,550 ft) west of Low Divide.

QUEETS RIVER TRAILS

Queets Trail. 15.4 miles/e-m (H,S). At Queets Campground (280 ft), ford the Queets River, follow the flat river bottom through huge moss- and fern-covered trees, pass the Kloochman Rock Trail, and continue upstream to enter a magnificent forest of Sitka spruce, Douglas-fir, and red cedar. The path fades at Pelton Creek (850 ft).

Kloochman Rock Trail. 3.4 miles/m (H,S). North from the Queets Trail at 2.3 miles (350 ft), the path passes a spur to the world's largest standing Douglas-fir, then begins a steep grind up the east bank of Coal Creek to Kloochman Rock (3,365 ft). A scramble to the summit reveals vast clearcuts stretching west from the park boundary, a sad vestige of once-virgin forest.

HOH RIVER TRAILS

Hoh Trail. 18 miles/e-m (H,S). This rain forest route leaves the Hoh Campground (600 ft) and meanders west through a flat bottomland forest of spruce, cedar, bigleaf maple, and Douglas-fir, draped in ferns and mosses. The path continues upstream on an easy grade to the Olympus Guard Station (948 ft) and the Hoh Lake Trail. In another 2 miles the canyon narrows and the way ascends to a bridge across the vertical walls of a 150-foot-deep gorge cut by the Hoh River. The route zigzags uphill past Martin Creek Falls to Elk Lake (3,011 ft). It climbs through Alaska cedar, mountain hemlock, and silver fir; crosses several avalanche tracks; then arrives at

Glacier Meadows (4,387 ft), high camp for climbs of Mount Olympus. The trail forks: the west branch leads to Indian Rock (4,700 ft), overlooking the snout of the Blue Glacier; the east branch continues up to a notch on the lateral moraine, then traces the glacier's edge to 5,000 feet.

Hoh Lake Trail. *6.5 miles/m (H,S).* About 0.5 mile beyond the Olympus Guard Station, the route leaves the Hoh Trail (990 ft) and immediately starts long switchbacks up the steep north wall of the drainage. It climbs through the heart of a 1978 burn where the forest is in the process of regeneration. From the crest the way contours into the Hoh Creek basin, climbs round its head, and snakes up to Hoh Lake (4,520 ft). The route ascends the east rim above the lake to meet the High Divide and Bogachiel trails (5,170 ft) on the south side of Bogachiel Peak

BOGACHIEL RIVER TRAILS

Bogachiel Trail. *32.7 miles/e-m (H,S).* From the end of FR 2932 (300 ft) the way continues up a former bottomland road bed for 2 miles to the park boundary, where it enters old-growth spruce and hemlock forest. At the mouth of the North Fork of the Bogachiel (770 ft) the canyon narrows; the route leaves the main river to follow its northwest fork. A steady ascent continues through thick forest to the river headwaters; it steepens as it climbs to a saddle (3,600 ft) in the basin headwall. East of Little Divide (4,130 ft), the route slides to the south side of the ridge, descends past Bogachiel Lake (3,540 ft), climbs over a saddle (4,120 ft), then weaves east down to Deer Lake (3,520 ft) and the Canyon Creek Trail. South from the lake the way passes a half-dozen tarns en route to the top of the divide (4,750 ft) between the Bogachiel and Soleduck rivers. A spur drops north down steep open slopes to the parkland of Seven Lakes Basin and its namesake collection of lakes. The narrow meadowed crest is followed east to a col just below the summit of Bogachiel Peak, where it ends at the junction with the High Divide and Hoh Lake trails (5,170 ft).

SOLEDUCK RIVER TRAILS

Soleduck Trail. *8.4 miles/m (H,S).* From the end of the Soleduck River Road (1,950 ft) the route heads up the north bank of the river on an easy grade through Douglas-fir forest. At Soleduck Falls it passes the Canyon Creek Trail, then wanders upstream to the Appleton Pass Trail. In less than a mile the way swings into the Bridge Creek drainage; switchbacks climb steeply to the meadows of Soleduck Park, where the path wraps around tiny Heart Lake (4,760 ft). It joins the High Divide Trail (5,050 ft) a short distance uphill at the crest.

Canyon Creek Trail. *3.1 miles/m (H,S).* At the start (1,950 ft) of the Soleduck Trail, an old wooden bridge crosses the river through the spray-filled air of Soleduck Falls. The way zigzags uphill, twisting along the convoluted, lushly vegetated slope above Canyon Creek to Deer Lake (3,520 ft). Here it meets the Bogachiel Trail.

High Divide Trail. *6.2 miles/m (H,S).* The Bogachiel and Hoh Lake trails join at a col (5,170 ft) just below the top of Bogachiel Peak. On the ridge to the east a spur leads to the summit (5,474 ft), an old lookout site with unbeatable views of the northwest corner of the Olympic Peninsula. The path follows the divide east; one side looks into the meadows of Seven Lakes Basin, the other over precipitous timbered slopes dropping to the Hoh River. As the way progresses eastward it meets the Soleduck Trail above Soleduck Park, then gradually descends to the rim above Cat Creek Basin. The path slides off the rising ridge, contours the steep, rocky south face of Cat Peak, then abruptly ends at the cliffs of the Catwalk (5,045 ft). Funding ran out before the trail could be extended through the Bailey Range, then plans were dropped to preserve the wilderness character of the range.

LAKE CRESCENT TRAILS

Aurora Ridge Trail. *15.5 miles/m (H,S).* After leaving the Soleduck River Road in clearcuts (1,400 ft), the way climbs east into virgin Douglas-fir forest as it heads up Aurora Ridge. At Sourdough Mountain (4,550 ft) the path breaks into meadows with views of Mounts Tom and Olympus. Here it descends to a saddle, then traverses east to just below the top of Aurora Peak (4,720 ft). Ridgetop forest and meadow alternate as the crest is traced east to the junction with the Aurora Divide Trail (4,750 ft), which it follows southeast to the Happy Ridge Trail.

ELWHA RIVER TRAILS

Happy Lake Ridge Trail. *10 miles/m (H,S).* The way leaves the Olympic Hot Springs Road (1,700 ft) and climbs northwest up forested slopes to the ridge top (4,550 ft). The narrow divide is followed west to a saddle (5,290 ft) with views north to the straits and south to Mounts Olympus, Anderson, and Carrie. A spur drops northwest to Happy Lake (4,870 ft); the main trail continues west along the crest to meet the Aurora Divide Trail. Ridgetop meadows are traversed southwest, then the way drops to the basin rim above Boulder Lake (4,332 ft), where it joins the Boulder Lake Trail.

Boulder Lake Trail. *2.8 miles/m (H,S).* About 0.5 mile above Boulder Creek Campground at Olympic Hot Springs (1,950 ft), the trail forks; left is the Appleton Pass Trail, straight ahead is the Boulder Lake Trail. The way climbs through Douglas-fir forest on the hillside north of Boulder Creek to the rim north of the lake, meets the Happy Lake Ridge Trail, then descends to Boulder Lake (4,332 ft).

Appleton Pass Trail. *7.8 miles/m (H,S).* From the junction (2,340 ft) above Boulder Creek Campground, the route bends south past a series of falls on the South Fork of the creek, then climbs via several switchbacks through forest and flower-splashed alpine meadows to Appleton Pass (5,000 ft). South of the pass more switchbacks drop steeply to the Soleduck Trail (3,100 ft).

Wolf Creek Trail. *8 miles/m (H,S).* From the end of the Elwha Road at Whiskey Bend (1,150 ft) the trail follows an abandoned road to the top of Hurricane Ridge. From deep forest in the lower portions, the way makes easy-grade switchbacks up to meadows near the end of the current Hurricane Ridge Road (5,050 ft).

Elwha Trail. *25.6 miles/m (H,S).* A long, hooked thrust into the heart of the Olympics leaves Whiskey Bend (1,150 ft) above Lake Mills, and ascends slowly east away from the river, through forest regenerating from a 1977 fire. The Long Ridge Trail heads off to explore country to the south. The Elwha Trail stays high above the Grand Canyon of the Elwha, wandering through dense old-growth forest, before descending to the river near Prescott Creek (1,300 ft). A level grade traces the riverbank south past Elkhorn Ranger Station, and the Dodger Point Trail, to Hayes River Ranger Station (1,700 ft), near the junction with the Hayden Pass Trail.

The broad bottomland and adjoining terraces are followed south, then east to the Low Divide Trail, as the river hooks back toward the Bailey Range. The canyon narrows and the way climbs to Elwha Basin (2,700 ft), where it deteriorates to a boot track up the drainage via the Elwha snow finger to Dodwell–Rixon Pass (4,780 ft).

Long Ridge Trail. *13.3 miles/m (H,S).* From the Elwha Trail (1,125 ft) the route descends to the Elwha River, crosses a suspension bridge, then begins a long sidehill ascent through Douglas-fir forest. The path swings back and forth across Long Ridge in a series of easy-grade switchbacks, then shifts this switchback pattern to the west side of the ridge. The trail finally stays atop or just below the crest as it enters meadows and subalpine forest with wide views east across the valley to the Bailey Range and beyond to Olympus. The path finishes its ascent through meadows to meet the Dodger Point Trail (5,290 ft). The trail was once to be extended across the Bailey Range, but these plans were abandoned.

Dodger Point Trail. *5.8 miles/m (H,S).* At Semple Plateau the route leaves the Elwha Trail (1,451 ft), fords the river, crosses terraces, then bends west above the Goldie River. Switchbacks surmount steep slopes as the way climbs a broad wooded ridge, then makes a long diagonal uphill to the northwest. Douglas-fir and hemlock forest change to subalpine growth with altitude, and flower meadows appear. The way reaches the crest (5,050 ft) northeast of Ludden Peak, where it meets the Long Ridge Trail and briefly shares tread with it en route to Dodger Point (5,760 ft). The old lookout cabin perched atop the point has unsurpassed views: Mount Olympus, the Bailey Range, the Elwha Valley, Mount Anderson, and, in the distance, Mount Rainier.

Hayden Pass Trail. *8.4 miles/m (H,S).* From the Elwha Trail at the Hayes River Ranger Station (1,710 ft) the way climbs to a small wooded terrace, then snakes through cliffs beside a plummeting creek. It begins a gradual diagonal ascent southeast, emerging into meadows at a rib west of Mount Fromme. Rounding the rib, the track contours around alpine meadows to

Hayden Pass (5,847 ft), tucked between Mount Fromme and Sentinel Peak. Here it meets the Dosewallips Trail.

Low Divide Trail. 3.1 miles/m (H,S). At the southernmost point of the hook of the Elwha River, the route leaves the Elwha Trail (2,190 ft), wanders through dense forest, then abruptly switchbacks up through headwall cliff bands to Lakes Mary and Margaret (3,590 and 3,630 ft). It continues uphill to Low Divide (3,602 ft), where it joins the North Fork Quinault Trail.

PORT ANGELES TRAILS

Heather Park Trail. 10 miles/m (H,S). The route heads southwest from Heart of the Hills (1,957 ft) and immediately begins climbing through second-growth forest on the north side of Mount Angeles. Increasingly steeper slopes force multiple switchbacks to reach the meadows of Heather Park (5,620 ft) in a lovely basin between the mountain's first and second summits. The way crosses the crest south of Second Summit, zigzags below the cliffs of Third Summit, then traverses to a notch in Klahhane Ridge (5,850 ft), where it meets the Lake Angeles Trail. Switchbacks drop south to a contour of the south face of Mount Angeles, then the way descends gradually over the meadow knolls and dips of Sunrise Ridge to the Hurricane Ridge Visitor Center (5,250 ft).

Lake Angeles Trail. 6.5 miles/m (H,S). From Heart of the Hills (1,790 ft) the way heads into forest alongside Ennis Creek, climbs 1,000 feet, crosses the creek, and heads up the steep ridge on its east flank. At the cliff-walled cirque embracing Lake Angeles (4,240 ft), switchbacks gain the narrow rim above the lake, and the way twists up open rocky slopes with increasing views of Port Angeles, the Strait of Juan de Fuca, and Victoria. A path crosses the top of Klahhane Ridge (6,046 ft), then traverses west on a cliff-blasted grade to join the Heather Ridge Trail (5,850 ft).

Grand Pass Trail. 8 miles/m (H,S). At the end of the Obstruction Point Road (6,120 ft) the trail fork to the south continues along the open tundra crest with expansive views into the heart of the Olympics. At a notch (6,400 ft) between two sharp knobs, the way swings east above a steep-walled basin, then drops in a switchback chain to a small meadow in a hillside bench. It descends to the Grand Creek valley and heads upstream to Moose Lake (5,056 ft). The way continues uphill through meadows past Gladys Lake (5,399 ft), then scales the rocky basin headwall to Grand Pass (6,420 ft). South of the pass it noses downhill, and nearly three dozen switchbacks later arrives at the Cameron Creek Trail.

Grand Ridge Trail. 7.6 miles/m (H,S). The east fork from the end of Obstruction Point Road (6,120 ft) stays above timberline for several miles, providing outstanding views of the eastern Olympics. The track follows the south rim of the ridge and gradually descends along the south flank of Maiden Peak. It wanders down the crest to the east, dropping into forest as it passes Green Mountain, then continues down the narrow wooded ridge to the road (5,233 ft) below Deer Park.

Climbing

Climbs of most of the major summits in Olympic National Park can be summarized as steep snowfields or modest-size glaciers, and C-2 to C-3 rotten rock. Since the climbs are, for the most part, multiday affairs, due to the remoteness of the region, most parties are content just to bag the summit of a significant peak and not worry about variations that exist on walls and faces of many peaks. There are hundreds of one- to two-lead rotten towers on ridgelines, but these are typically regarded as a nuisance en route to a summit rather than a climbing objective. For gendarme and face enthusiasts who enjoy loose rock, there are still many unclaimed firsts in the Olympics.

Probably the best rock climbing in the Olympics is found in the Sawtooth Range; since this range is on the border between the park and the Mount Skokomish Wilderness, the climbs are described in the latter section. Other major peaks (5,758 to 6,250 ft) in the southeast corner of the park are Mount Stone, Mount Steel, Mount Duckabush, and O'Neil Peak. All are C-3 except the west summit of Duckabush, rated C-4 via either an exposed ridge from the middle summit or the south ridge.

A challenging group of peaks is located on the east edge of the park surrounding Avalanche

Canyon just above Lake Constance. Here are Mount Constance (7,743 ft), a peak that dominates the skyline as seen from Seattle, with routes ranging from C-3 to C-5.7; Desperation Peak (7,150 ft) and Inner Constance (7,667 ft), mixed snow and rock routes between C-3 and C-4; the Thumb (6,600 ft), C-2 to C-4; and several towers on the ridge south of Inner Constance.

Immediately north of Constance is Warrior Peak (7,300 ft), a striking rock double summit. All routes are rated C-3. At the head of the West Fork Dosewallips is Mount Anderson (7,365 ft), the most prominent peak (with the largest glaciers) in the eastern Olympics. Exposed rotten rock routes, C-3, lead to both east and west summits.

Surrounding Deception Basin are Mount Mystery (7,639 ft), Little Mystery (6,941 ft), and Mount Deception (7,788 ft), the highest peak in the eastern Olympics. All are scaled via C-2 to C-4 routes. Rimming Royal Basin, west of the Buckhorn Wilderness, are another group of challenging, albeit rotten, rock climbs in the Needles (7,000 to 7,650 ft), with routes rated between C-3 and C-5.5. Among this group are Arrowhead, the Incisor, Sweat Spire, Gasp Pinnacle, and Devils Fang. On the east side of the basin, the Royal Shaft (6,000 ft) has a 120-foot C-5.3 route.

In the Hurricane Ridge area the most popular and easiest ascent is Mount Angeles (6,454 ft), which affords wide views north to Port Angeles, the Strait of Juan de Fuca, and Vancouver Island. Several routes from both north and south are at most C-3 in difficulty. Because of its proximity to the Obstruction Point Road, Steeple Rock (5,567 ft) sees intensive climbing activity, and a plethora of routes, ranging from C-3 to C-5.8, has been placed up its various faces, gullies, and crack systems.

The crown jewel of the Olympics, Mount Olympus (7,965 ft), was purportedly climbed by the O'Neil Expedition in 1890, but the first authenticated ascent occurred in 1907. The classic Blue Glacier–Snow Dome route is frequently used by climbing parties, although other routes climb the C-5.3 west ridge, and over lesser summits from the east. Mount Tom (7,048 ft), a subsidiary peak to the west, is most easily climbed from Olympus routes to avoid other lowland jungle approaches. A horseshoe of short rock pinnacles (6,246 to 7,365 ft) around the Hoh and Humes glaciers bears names from the pantheon of Greek gods and legends: Athena, Hermes, Aphrodite, Aries, and Icarus. All are relatively easy C-3 climbs, though exposed and rotten.

The Valhallas are an obscure group of rugged pinnacles encircling the Grei-Freki Glacier southwest of Mount Tom. Nordic gods rule here; among the pinnacles (5,400 to 6,038 ft) are Mimir, Thor, Woden, Baldur, Villi, and Freyja. All of these peaks are short, sometimes challenging C-2 to C-4 rock climbs.

Climbers negotiate crevasses on the Blue Glacier of Mount Olympus.

Striking through the heart of the inner Olympics is the Bailey Range. The highest summit in the range, Mount Carrie (6,995 ft), is little more than a narrow, exposed ridge walk to top. More challenging peaks in the range (6,283 to 6,950 ft) are Mount Fairchild, Mount Michael, Ruth Peak, and Mount Pulitzer, all involving exposed C-3 rotten rock.

In the vicinity of Low Divide are a number of easy walk-up summits and two that are more difficult: Mount Queets (6,476 ft), with four routes, and Mount Christie (6,177 ft), with mixed glacier and rock climbs. In the upper Quinault Valley are Chimney Peak (6,917 ft), with steep, exposed snow slopes; a nearby tower, the Chimney, a 100-foot C-5.3 lead; and Bicentennial Peak (6,722 ft).

Farther south, on either side of the Quinault Valley, are Mount Olson (5,289 ft), a C-3 scramble via the west ridge, and Muncaster Mountain (5,910 ft), snow and rock rated C-3 to 4. Along the park's south border, seldom climbed because of their remoteness, are the Five Ridge Peaks (5,077 ft), a series of short pinnacles on the ridge between Five and Six streams.

Winter Sports

The interior of the range is remote and fraught with avalanche hazards, so most winter recreational activities are found on the perimeter. The road to Hurricane Ridge is plowed in winter, and a small ski and tubing area operates at the visitor center atop the ridge. This is also a starting point for several cross-country tours. Excellent day trips with outstanding views are those to the top of Hurricane Hill, a 6-mile round trip; up the southwest ridge of Mount Angeles to the base of the summit block, 3 miles (the mountain is also climbed in winter); and following the Obstruction Point Road, to the north side of Eagle Point, 3.5 miles. The latter trip can be extended to Obstruction Point, 6 miles, generally as an overnight trek.

From the Elwha Road, cross-country tours follow unplowed roads and summer trails to Boulder Lake, 6 miles; Appleton Pass, 7 miles; and Happy Lake Ridge, extended to a loop via Boulder Lake. The latter trips are generally 2-day affairs.

On the west side of the park, a long 2- to 3-day tour for advanced skiers starts from the end of the Soleduck River Road and follows the Soleduck and Canyon Creek trails to the Bogachiel Trail atop the divide. After great open-bowl skiing in the Seven Lakes Basin, the trip climbs over the intervening ridge to Soleduck Park, and returns to the starting point via the Soleduck Trail.

At the southeast corner of the park a very popular tour heads out of Staircase and climbs to an overnight camp at Flapjack Lakes. From here there are excellent open meadow slopes to ski near Gladys Divide.

4

COLONEL BOB WILDERNESS

LOCATION: In Grays Harbor County at the southwest corner of Olympic National Park, immediately east of Lake Quinault
SIZE: 11,961 acres
STATUS: Designated Wilderness Area (1984)
TERRAIN: Heavily forested ridges rise steeply to alpine meadows and a few rocky peaks along ridge crests at the heart of the wilderness.
ELEVATION: 400 to 4,509 feet
MANAGEMENT: USFS, Olympic National Forest, Quinault Ranger District
TOPOGRAPHIC MAPS: Bunch Lake, Colonel Bob, Finley Creek, Lake Quinault East

On the south side of the Quinault River alluvial plain, foothills rise abruptly, gaining more than 4,000 feet of elevation in a horizontal distance of just over a mile. Two parallel ridges that run northeast to southwest join at the heart of the Colonel Bob Wilderness, then continue to the southwest as a single contorted crest. Several steep creek beds, bound by lateral ridges, drop from the upper reaches of this small wilderness to either the Quinault River or the Humptulips River, which border the north and south sides of the wilderness. Dense, lush rain forest cloaks the steep hillsides, making cross-country travel virtually impossible except in ridgetop alpine meadows.

A fire lookout once graced the small rock summit of Colonel Bob, the second-highest point of the wilderness. This location commands views spreading from northwest to south across miles of clearcuts, once virgin rain forest. Beyond, to the west, fog banks often define Pacific Ocean beaches. Cliff-bound Fletcher Canyon drops away steeply to the northeast, directing views to the jagged backbone of Olympic National Park.

As a result of the precipitous terrain, the few trails that penetrate the wilderness are strenuous. Access to streams is limited, and lakes, aside from a few minuscule tarns at the head of Fletcher Creek, are nonexistent; thus, camping is available at only a few primitive sites near sparse water supplies.

Climate

This rain-forest country is drenched by over 120 inches of precipitation annually. Clear weather occurs most frequently from mid-June to October, but rain can be expected every month of the year. Winter temperatures are mild, seldom dipping below freezing at lower elevations, while summer weather rarely exceeds 70 degrees. Snow blankets elevations above 3,000 feet during winter months. Because the wilderness lies so near the Pacific, winds off the ocean

A bridge crosses a moist gully near Ziegler Creek on the Colonel Bob Trail.

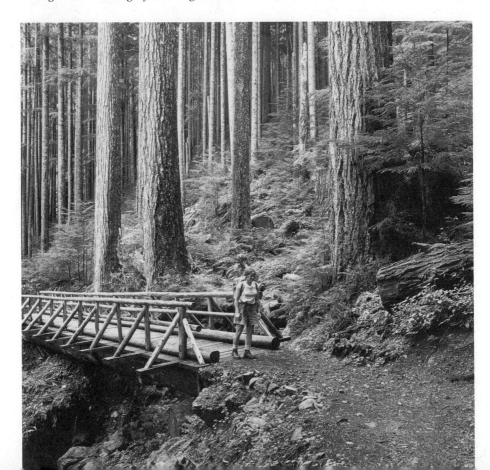

bring heavy precipitation and weather patterns change abruptly with little notice. Visitors should be prepared for drizzle or downpour, even if the day starts clear and sunny.

Plants and Wildlife

The ground cover in the lowest portions of the wilderness is a jumble of mosses, lichen, sword fern, and maidenhead fern, typical of rain forests. Creek beds are edged by dense borders of currant and salmonberry; vine maple and slide alder choke breaks in the adjoining forest. The low-level forest is a moss-encrusted profusion of western hemlock, Pacific silver fir, and western red cedar, with some Douglas-fir. Higher, western hemlock and silver fir predominate. Above 3,500 feet the forest thins to mountain hemlock and Alaska cedar, then gives way to grassy ridgetop meadows holding lush growths of huckleberry and salmonberry as well as beargrass and brilliant displays of daisies, avalanche lilies, lupine, and other alpine flowers. Steep, open talus slopes that drop from the highest ridge crests and rock outcrops are painted with hardy lichen. Short spiky rock summits cap these ridges.

The dense forest is home to black-tailed deer, elk, and black bear, and occasionally mountain goat and cougar may be seen. Look overhead or to tree snags for bald and golden eagles.

Geology

A crescent of uplifted, near-vertical strata of volcanic rock rims the north, east, and south sides of the Olympic Range. The Colonel Bob Wilderness lies at its southwest cusp, between two thrust faults. The steep narrow ridges were sculpted primarily by Pleistocene glaciers.

History

The first settlers arrived in the Lake Quinault region in the late 1800s. About 1915, Mart and Purl Mulkey roughed a trail up Ziegler Creek and built a trapper's cabin near the headwaters of its north fork. Although no trace of this trail can be found, in 1922 the Forest Service followed a similar route when it laid out the trail into the newly constructed fire lookout atop Colonel Bob. The Civilian Conservation Corps (CCC) replaced the Mulkey cabin with a trail shelter about the same time. The lookout collapsed under heavy snows and was removed in 1967.

ACTIVITIES

Hiking

Trail #851, Colonel Bob. 7.2 miles/d (H; S up to the junction with Trail #858). From the Quinault Lake South Shore Road (230 ft), the trail climbs steeply along the hillside northeast of Ziegler Creek to the Mulkey shelter at 4 miles. From here it switchbacks relentlessly to a 3,200-foot saddle on Quinault Ridge and traverses below cliffs to meet Trail #858. After crossing open, rocky slopes below Gibson Peak, it reaches Moonshine Flats at the head of Fletcher Creek. Switchbacks continue around the basin at the head of the creek and up the ridge to the final face of Colonel Bob, where steps carved in the rock lead to the summit (4,492 ft) and former lookout site.

Trail #858, Petes Creek. 1.8 miles/d (H,S). The trailhead is located northeast of Humptulips on FR 2204 (1195 ft). After a moderate 0.25 mile, the trail climbs a steep sidehill, crosses Petes Creek, and switchbacks up avalanche slopes below Gibson Peak to join Trail #851 (2850 ft).

Climbing

The eight or more rocky spikes that form the crown of the wilderness were once known collectively as McCallas Peak (3,865 to 4,492 ft). Four of these points are now named Wooded Peak, Mount O'Neil, Colonel Bob, and Gibson Peak. A trail leads to the top of Colonel Bob. The lookout formerly located there was not actually on the highest point in the wilderness; the true summit is on the ridge 1,200 feet to the east. All the other summits can be reached by cross-country routes no more strenuous than C-3. A spire on the ridge between Colonel Bob and Mount O'Neil, Mike's Spike (4,175 ft), requires one C-4 lead.

■————————— **5** —————————■

BUCKHORN WILDERNESS

LOCATION: In Jefferson and Clallam counties, in two sections on the east side of Olympic National Park. The northern section lies between Canyon Creek and the lower Dungeness River; the southern section is located between the lower Dungeness and Dosewallips rivers.

SIZE: 44,258 acres

STATUS: Designated Wilderness Area (1984)

TERRAIN: Creeks and rivers flowing from the eastern flank of the Olympic Range drain through glacier-carved canyons bounded by steep forested ridges. Alpine meadows at timberline give way to narrow, jagged, rocky ridges that end in rugged summits.

ELEVATION: 1,000 to 7,134 feet

MANAGEMENT: USFS, Olympic National Forest, Quilcene Ranger District

TOPOGRAPHIC MAPS: Mt. Deception, Mt. Jupiter, Mt. Townsend, Mount Zion, The Brothers, Tyler Peak

The northern portion of the Buckhorn Wilderness covers the transition zone between the peaks on the northeast corner of Olympic National Park and the forested lowlands south of Sequim. The Gray Wolf River splits the north end of this section; its tributaries cut through heavily forested lateral ridges. From the south side of the river these steep ridges rise to a 6,000-

foot-high rocky crest that arcs across the southern edge of this portion of the wilderness. High points along this ridge provide broad views north and northeast to the Strait of Juan de Fuca and Mount Baker, and west to the northern rim of Olympic peaks.

The southern section of the wilderness is larger and more rugged than the northern. From its headwaters, the Dungeness River threads along the west and north sides of the wilderness through a valley carved by Pleistocene glaciers. Steep forested hillsides on both sides of the river rise to rugged crests between 6,000 and 7,000 feet. Two large tributaries, Copper and Silver creeks, flow north to the Dungeness, cutting deep canyons into adjoining ridges. Their names reflect early prospectors' ambitious hopes for the region. A 216-acre plot of patented mining property, the Tubal Cain Mine, still exists on Copper Creek within the wilderness. The eastern face of the wilderness is gouged by glacier-cut valleys, down which flow Tunnel Creek and the Big Quilcene and Dosewallips rivers. The latter drainage forms the southern boundary of the wilderness.

More than 67 miles of trails penetrate the wilderness. Most reach the higher elevations along paths of least resistance—the valley floors. Other way-trails provide climbing, fishing, and exploring routes to more rugged sections of the wilderness. The region's dozen lakes are all quite small, and most are hidden in cirques high in the headwaters of creeks and rivers.

Climate

Because this portion of the Olympic Peninsula lies in the rain shadow of the Olympic Range, it is much drier than the western slopes. Annual precipitation, which usually accompanies winds from the south and southwest, ranges between 40 and 60 inches. Temperatures are mild at lower elevations, rarely going below freezing or above 80 degrees. Heavy snowfall occurs at elevations above 3,000 feet, generally between November and March.

Plants and Wildlife

Lower elevations host dense forests of western hemlock, Pacific silver fir, western red cedar, and Douglas-fir. Above 3,000 feet these trees give way to mountain hemlock, alpine fir, and western white pine, while the highest elevations see open stands of stunted alpine fir, white-bark pine, and dwarf juniper. In the northern portion of the wilderness a large area of virgin forest was destroyed in the early 1900s by a major forest fire, the Maynard Burn.

The understory below 3,000 feet consists of a rich tangle of mosses, ferns, salmonberry, huckleberry, Oregon grape, devil's club, and a profusion of native rhododendrons. Higher, the vegetation thins to mountain ash and mountain spirea accompanied by bunchberry, western columbine, pearly everlasting, and the cream-white wands of beargrass. Alpine meadows are covered with grasses, heathers, and bright seasonal flowers such as avalanche lily, phlox, and penstemon, while rock outcroppings shelter the white blossoms of saxifrage.

Large mammals include black-tailed deer, occasional black bear, cougar, and bobcat in forested areas, and a few mountain goats at higher elevations. In addition to a wealth of smaller birds, raptors such as northern spotted owls, bald eagles, and goshawks may be seen. Hikers in alpine meadows may be greeted by the shrill whistle of Olympic marmots.

Geology

The lower elevations at the north end of the Buckhorn Wilderness were part of the lateral moraine of the Vashon ice sheet that carved out Puget Sound and the Strait of Juan de Fuca some 14,000 years ago. The remainder of the wilderness consists mainly of older (40 million to 50 million years) upthrusted submarine volcanic flows that form a crescent around the north, west, and south rims of the Olympic Peninsula. This pillow basalt has limestone lenses containing bementite and hausmannite, a form of manganese ore that is unique to the peninsula. During the past 10,000 years, montane glaciers carved the deep, steep-sided valleys that frame most of the drainages and sculpted the spires, towers, and narrow, ragged ridgelines.

History

The Olympic National Forest, of which the Buckhorn Wilderness is now a part, was created in 1897 when President Grover Cleveland designated 1.5 million acres as the Olympic Forest Reserve. In 1902 visions of mineral wealth led prospectors to the Tubal Cain Mine, where the mining camp of Tull City (a cookhouse, two bunkhouses, and a blacksmith shop) sprang up. Manganese and copper ores were gouged from nearby hillsides, but fortune eluded the prospectors, and by 1920 active mining had ceased. Rotting fragments of cabins and campsites in the depths of the wilderness bear mute witness to later visits by prospectors, trappers, and hunters.

ACTIVITIES

Hiking

NORTH SECTION TRAILS

Trail #834, Gray Wolf. 9.1 miles/m (H,S). From its start on FR 2870 (970 ft), the trail meanders through a mix of virgin forest and clearcuts for 2 miles before reaching the Buckhorn Wilderness boundary. Canyon walls close in as the route continues up the steep sides of the Gray Wolf River gorge to Camp Tony (1,600 ft) to meet Trail #838. The trail leaves the river in a long diagonal ascent to Slide Camp (2,150 ft). From here it descends 2 miles through dense forest to the Olympic National Park boundary, then continues into the heart of the park.

Trail #838, Slab Camp. 3.1 miles/d (H,S). It's downhill all the way from the starting point (2,540 ft) on FR 2875 to the junction with Trail #834 at Camp Tony (1,600 ft). Trailhead views of Baldy quickly disappear as the path descends the forested hillside above Slab Creek in a series of gentle steps linked by short, steep segments.

DUNGENESS RIVER TRAILS

Trail #833, Dungeness. 7.8 miles/m (H,S). From the FR 2860 trailhead (2,520 ft), a near-level grade follows the Dungeness River upstream for 3.2 miles to Camp Handy (3,100 ft). Here a diagonal ascent features intermittent views of the precipitous west face of Mount Constance. At Boulder Shelter (4,950 ft) the Constance Pass Trail continues south into the park. From Boulder Shelter the Dungeness Trail switchbacks up alpine slopes to Marmot Pass (6,000 ft), where it retains the same number but becomes the Big Quilcene Trail.

Trail #840, Tubal Cain. 8.8 miles/m (H,S). From the north bank of Silver Creek (3,300 ft), this trail rounds an intervening ridge and begins a gentle ascent along Copper Creek, reaching the ruins of the Tubal Cain Mine in 3.6 miles (4,350 ft). Little is left of the mining operations; nearby mine shafts are unsafe for exploration. After crossing the creek, the trail heads upstream, climbing diagonally up open slopes with views to the imposing north faces of Iron and

Native pink rhododendrons decorate the Tubal Cain Mine trail in the Buckhorn Wilderness.

Buckhorn mountains. An unmarked spur 1.9 miles south of the Copper Creek crossing drops to tiny Buckhorn Lake. South from Buckhorn Pass (5,820 ft), an ascent along the west shoulder of Buckhorn Mountain, followed by a short drop to Marmot Pass (6,000 ft), leads to Trail #833.

Trail #847, Tull Canyon. 0.7 mile/e (H). A short spur leaves Trail #840 at the north end of the Tubal Cain property and swings up Tull Canyon to the site of the Tull City mining camp.

EAST-SIDE TRAILS

Trail #839, Mount Townsend. 6.2 miles/m (H,S). From FR 2760 (2,850 ft) rhododendrons crowd the trail as it climbs along Townsend Creek. At the head of the creek, switchbacks lead up a wall to a small lake and Camp Windy (5,300 ft). A stiff climb through alpine meadows gains the ridgetop. Rather than a definitive peak, Mount Townsend (6,280 ft) is a mile-long alpine meadow atop a narrow ridge. Wide, unobstructed views encompass Discovery Bay, the Strait of Juan de Fuca, the Cascades, Mount Constance, the Brothers, and a wall of Olympic National Park peaks. From the summit ridge, the trail descends north into forest to end near the midpoint of Trail #835; it can be hiked either east or west to access roads.

Trail #833, Big Quilcene. 5.3 miles/m (H,S). From FR 2750 at Tenmile Shelter (2,500 ft) the trail climbs through old-growth cedar, fir, and hemlock, and masses of rhododendrons as it follows the north side of the Big Quilcene River. In 2.5 miles the trail leaves the river on a steep traverse across scree and avalanche slopes below Buckhorn and Iron mountains. The way levels at Camp Mystery (5,400 ft), then continues to the head of the basin and switchbacks up a basalt cliff to Marmot Pass (6,000 ft).

Trail #841, Tunnel Creek. 7.3 miles/d (H,S; pack stock not recommended). From the north access at FR 2740 (2,600 ft) the track heads up the steep-walled, narrow valley of the South Fork of Tunnel Creek. The lower section is in old-growth hemlock and silver fir. In 2.7 miles the work begins; switchbacks lead up the valley wall to a small, wooded cirque that harbors tiny Harrison Lake (4,750 ft). A rocky path leaves the lake and climbs south to the Tunnel Creek–Dosewallips River divide (5,050 ft). En route, the vertical east walls of Mount Constance and Warrior Peak flash into view, seeming only an arm's-length away. The descent to the Dosewallips begins in gentle alpine meadows, then follows endless switchbacks through old- and second-growth forest to reach FR 2610 (500 ft).

Climbing

The northern section of the wilderness has no significant climbing challenges. Its highest points, Baldy (6,827 ft) and Tyler Peak (6,364 ft), are alpine scrambles.

In the southern portion of the wilderness there are numerous climbing opportunities in the small north–south subrange on the east side of the Dungeness River and on lateral ridges flowing east from that ridge. Most of the highest summits have routes no more difficult than C-3; their steeper faces are unappealing, loose, friable rock. The peripheral ridgelines are narrow, sheer, and serrated by 200- to 300-foot-high towers that offer several leads of C-4 to C-5 climbing.

At the northeast end of this subrange, Iron Mountain (6,826 ft) and Buckhorn Mountain (6,988 ft) are multi-summited rock arêtes with steep faces. Both can be climbed via talus gullies from the south. Iron Mountain and the northeast summit of Buckhorn are the most challenging.

South of Marmot Pass are a series of sharp ridges running northeast from the Mount Constance–Warrior Peak massif. The second narrow rib to the south, Ridge of Gargoyles (6,400 ft), has a number of precipitous rock towers that range from C-3 to C-5.3 in difficulty.

Alphabet Ridge (7,000 ft), which extends from the park into the wilderness northwest of Cloudy Peak, is a chain of C-3 to C-4 rock spires that can be reached from Charlia Lakes. A similar ridge northwest of Warrior Peak, Warrior Arm (6,900 ft), has a number of towers in the C-4 to C-5 range, as well as a few easier spires on the northeast end of the arm.

The basin at the head of the South Fork of Tunnel Creek has at least four challenging rock spires around its periphery: Destroyer, Enigma , April Peak, and the Nun. All offer steep, exposed slab climbing.

Winter Sports

Most of the upland country of the wilderness is sealed off in winter by steep, snow-laden, avalanche-prone slopes. The gentler terrain to the northeast, in the vicinity of Mount Townsend, offers opportunities for ski mountaineering or snowshoeing. Snow-covered forest roads permit ski access to the lower slopes; advanced ski-tourers can follow lightly timbered slopes along the approximate path of the summer trail to the long summit ridge of the mountain.

6

THE BROTHERS WILDERNESS

LOCATION: In Jefferson County, on the east side of Olympic National Park between the Dosewallips and Hamma Hamma rivers
SIZE: 16,682 acres
STATUS: Designated Wilderness Area (1984)
TERRAIN: A maze of steep forested ridges bordering the Duckabush River drainage that rise to two major rocky summits surrounded by a snarl of narrow rock-topped lateral ridges
ELEVATION: 600 to 6,866 feet
MANAGEMENT: USFS, Olympic National Forest, Hood Canal and Quilcene ranger districts
TOPOGRAPHIC MAPS: Mt. Jupiter, Mt. Washington, The Brothers

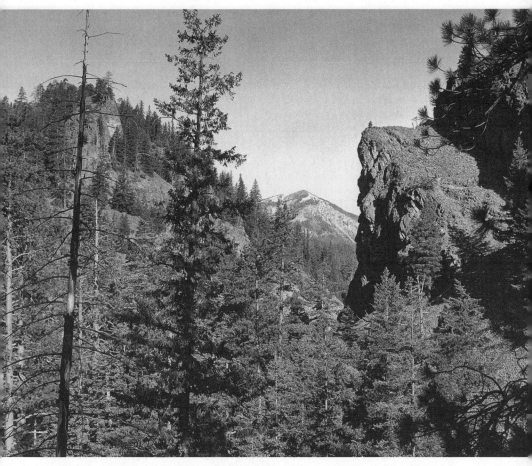

The Big Hump on the Duckabush River Trail in The Brothers Wilderness

The Duckabush River drains west from Olympic National Park through a deep, glacier-cut valley that slices through the center of the Brothers Wilderness. The backcountry centers around its two major summits: Mount Jupiter, north of the Duckabush, and the Brothers, south of the river.

Only three trails lead into the wilderness; one is an access route for climbs of the Brothers. The area's few lakes, with the exception of a sprinkling of small tarns north of the Brothers, are clustered around Mount Jupiter. None is accessible directly by trail; they are at best challenging cross-country scrambles from the Mount Jupiter Trail.

Climate

The wilderness lies on the dry side of the Olympics, in the rain shadow of the range. As a result, precipitation averages only 60 to 80 inches per year, and rain generally accompanies weather fronts moving in from the south or southwest. Temperatures are mild year-round, rarely getting above the 70s in the summer or below freezing in the winter at lower elevations. Snow is heavy in higher elevations during winter months, but most of it has cleared from the area by late July.

Plants and Wildlife

Heavy forests of western hemlock, western red cedar, and Douglas-fir cover lower elevations, with a thick understory of bracken fern, salal, and Oregon grape. Rhododendron, salmonberry, huckleberry, vine maple, alder, and devil's club crowd the forest floor. At mid-altitudes the timber is mostly Pacific silver fir and mountain hemlock; ground cover includes clumps of rhododendron, mountain ash, beargrass, and spirea, while trilliums, fawn lilies, and other delicate flowers provide springtime accents. Higher, phlox and buttercups snuggle into heathers and mosses amid subalpine fir. Finally, most vegetation gives way to ridgetop rock.

Black-tailed deer are the most common mammal in this wilderness, but the area also hosts elk, black bear, and mountain goat. Occasionally marmots, pine marten, cougars, and golden and bald eagles are seen as well as numerous other smaller birds and animals.

Geology

The Brothers Wilderness lies in the crescent of upthrusted submarine pillow basalt that rims the north, west, and south sides of the Olympic Peninsula. Pleistocene montane glaciers carved the major features of the area, including the immense canyon of the Duckabush drainage. Two of its major features, Little Hump and Big Hump, are steps cut from the underlying rock by the glacier that carved the valley. Big Hump appears to have dammed the melting glacier, forming a lake above it until the river finally breached the barrier.

History

Narrow-gauge railroads were used in the 1920s for logging the forest below Little Hump and the valley between Little Hump and Big Hump. Big Hump proved too formidable an obstacle for the trains, so the valley above was relatively untouched by ax and saw. A fire lookout once stood on the rocky summit pyramid of Mount Jupiter, and its sweeping views caused it to be used as an aircraft warning site during World War II. The lookout was removed in 1969.

ACTIVITIES

Hiking

Trail #809, Jupiter Ridge. 7.1 miles/d (H,S). The trail leaves FR 2610011 (2,000 ft), climbs steeply to the ridgetop (3,200 ft), and becomes a long slog along the ridge. It switchbacks up a rise and shifts to the south side of the crest, with the north wall of the Brothers in view. More switchbacks regain the rough basalt of the ridgetop, which is followed to the final zigzags up rock-hewn steps to the summit. The travail of the climb becomes worthwhile, as nothing obstructs the sweeping scenery. Nearby is the summit of the Brothers; to the south, distant Mounts Rainier, Adams, and St. Helens punctuate the horizon; the Cascades, Puget Sound, and the Seattle skyline lie to the east; Mount Baker and the Coastal Range of British Columbia are north; and to the west is the jagged eastern face of the Olympics.

Trail #803, Duckabush. 6.2 miles/m (H,S). From FR 2510060 (370 ft) the trail climbs leisurely up the wide river basin and over Little Hump to the flat track leading to the base of Big Hump. Switchbacks negotiate the 800-foot rise to the top (1,800 ft), where the bald rock of St. Peters Dome comes into view across the river. Canyon walls now close in, and the trail drops close to the river for the remaining ascent to the park boundary.

Trail #821, The Brothers. 4.5 miles/d (H). Take FR 25 to the Lena Lake trailhead (Trail #810, 780 ft). Hike the trail 3.5 miles to the lake and the start of the Brothers Trail (1,800 ft). The path follows the East Fork of Lena Creek through the "Valley of the Silent Men," where climbers purportedly pass silently in the early morning hours when headed to climb the Brothers. The maintained trail ends at a creek fork in 3 miles; beyond is a climbing route.

Climbing

The double-summited peak of the Brothers (6,866 ft), a distinct landmark on the horizon west of Seattle, is one of the most popular climbs in the Olympics. The traditional routes follow Trail #821 to the alpine meadows below the peak's south face. From here a variety of steep C-3 to C-4 chutes and gullies rise to the exposed ridge leading to the south summit. The north summit can be reached by a ridge traverse from the south summit or via climbs up the east ridge of the peak.

7

MOUNT SKOKOMISH WILDERNESS

LOCATION: In Mason County, at the southeast corner of Olympic National Park, immediately north of the upper end of Lake Cushman

SIZE: 13,105 acres

STATUS: Designated Wilderness (1984)

TERRAIN: The headwater basin of the Hamma Hamma River is bounded by two long ridges with several massive summits that radiate narrow, exposed rock arêtes crowned with sharp spires.

ELEVATION: 2,000 to 6,434 feet

MANAGEMENT: USFS, Olympic National Forest, Hood Canal Ranger District

TOPOGRAPHIC MAPS: Lightning Peak, Mt. Skokomish, Mt. Washington

The Mount Skokomish Wilderness is the southernmost of three wilderness areas created in 1984 to protect the remaining virgin forest on the east flank of Olympic National Park. The two parallel subranges of the wilderness, which run southwest to northeast, embrace the headwaters of the Hamma Hamma River. On the east, the chain of rock crests includes Mounts Ellinor, Washington, and Pershing. Narrow ridges that connect these summits are studded with smaller rock spires. Access to the range is limited to a few trails leading up to timberline, where climbing routes continue onward to the summits. For hikers, the ends of formal trails deliver unimpeded views east to Hood Canal, Puget Sound and the Cascades.

The only route into the headwater basin of the Hamma Hamma, the Mildred Lakes Trail, was created by the tread of boots, not shovels, axes, and pulaskis, and as a result it is steep and difficult. Any other access to this area requires cross-country brush beating. Sawtooth Ridge, bounding the west side of this basin, is a mecca for climbers; its chain of sharp peaks, towers, and needles offers some of the best rock climbing on the Olympic Peninsula. After being broken by a fork of the Hamma Hamma River, a continuation of this ridge to the north culminates in Mount Skokomish, the namesake of the wilderness.

The Mount Skokomish Wilderness holds seven lakes, ranging from 1 to 38 acres in size, as well as a sprinkling of smaller ponds. Although technically in Olympic National Park, Lake of the Angels' primary access leads through the wilderness. Another beatific name has been applied to a nearby col: St. Peter's Gate. Who knows, this may really be heaven on earth!

The view from the summit of Mount Ellinor into the Mount Skokomish Wilderness: Mount Pershing in the foreground, Mount Stone in the far distance

Climate

Because the wilderness lies in the rain shadow of the Olympic Range, precipitation is moderate, averaging 60 to 80 inches annually. Most of this accompanies weather systems from the south and southwest. Temperatures are mild, rarely exceeding 80 degrees in summer. Elevations above 3,000 feet receive snow between November and March, but by midsummer only the higher peaks retain snowfields.

Plants and Wildlife

Lower slopes of the Mount Skokomish Wilderness are heavily forested with old-growth western hemlock, western red cedar, and Douglas-fir. Ground cover is predominately ferns, salal, and kinnikinnick, with slide alder, willow, and vine maple choking the streambeds. At higher elevations the forest changes to hemlock, Alaska cedar, and silver fir, and then gives way to subalpine fir, western white pine, and dwarf juniper. Open hillsides sport thimbleberry and huckleberry, and in season small meadows high on the ridges burst into color with Indian paintbrush, buttercups, bluebells, anemones, and asters. Ridge crests are barren rock, adorned only by lichen and tiny flowers that can survive in this harsh terrain, such as tolmie saxifrage and spreading stonecrop.

The forests are home for elk, black-tailed deer, bear, cougar, and Olympic marmot. Isolated groups of mountain goats can be seen glued to crags along the rocky ridgelines. Ravens frequently announce the approach of hikers, while overhead bald and golden eagles circle.

Geology

The subrange that borders the east side of the wilderness, the Mounts Pershing–Washington–Ellinor massif, is uplifted pillow basalt, a portion of the crescent of such rock around the north, east, and south sides of the Olympic Peninsula. On the west side of the wilderness, the Sawtooth Range is composed of an erosion-exposed volcanic greenstone layer of the Soleduck Formation that makes up the core of the Olympic Mountains. Pleistocene glaciers gouged out the Hamma Hamma River drainage and shaped and sharpened the surrounding ridges and peaks.

ACTIVITIES

Hiking

HAMMA HAMMA RIVER TRAILS

Trail #813, Putvin. 3.7 miles/d (H). This gentle path leads from FR 25 (1,530 ft) up Boulder Creek, then along an abandoned logging road to the Mount Skokomish Wilderness boundary in 1.5 miles. The route steepens to a diagonal climb through second-growth forest along Whitehorse Creek. At 3,600 feet the way levels a bit, and subalpine forest opens to glimpses of the rugged north face of Mount Pershing. The respite is short, as switchbacks scale a pair of rock walls to reach the Olympic National Park boundary and a beautiful flowered meadow that surrounds a few small ponds. A short descent reaches Lake of the Angels (4,880 ft), tucked in a glacial cirque below the walls of Mounts Stone and Skokomish. A scramble to a saddle on the ridge between these peaks is rewarded with views west to Mounts Duckabush and Steel and distant Mount Olympus; to the east are Hood Canal, Puget Sound, the Cascades, and Mount Rainier.

Trail #822, Mildred Lakes. 4.5 miles/d (H). After a gentle start from FR 25 (1,800 ft), the trail quickly degenerates to a hard-to-trace boot-path that clambers over tree roots and around boulders, crosses a forested rib, and then descends to Huckleberry Creek. The route worsens as it crosses a ravine and heads straight uphill in a staircase of jumbled rock. At the ridgetop the grade eases, then descends past a series of pools to the first of the Mildred Lakes (3,754 ft). Above, Sawtooth Ridge comes into view, stretching from Mount Lincoln on the south to Mount Cruiser on the north. Paths continue through open forest and meadows, past more ponds, to the remaining two Mildred Lakes. The westernmost is one of the largest subalpine lakes in the Olympics. Campfires are prohibited at the lakes.

Climbing

The long, massive ridge between Jefferson Creek and the Hamma Hamma River has several interesting climbs, although approaches are quite brushy and the volcanic rock that pervades the area is often rotten. At the north end of the crest a steep, narrow ridge leads south to Tran Spire (4,943 ft), a 250-foot-high tower conquered in a couple of C-5.3 leads. Lesser spires along the ridge are also tempting. Jefferson (Thorson) Peak (5,720 ft) is a small cluster of rock summits 0.5 mile to the south; C-3 routes end in gullies up its north and east sides.

Another mile southwest is tri-headed Mount Pershing (5,600, 5,871, and 6,154 ft); a number of unnamed spires sprout from the ridges leading to Pershing's summits. The Jefferson Creek and Lake Ellinor basins separate Pershing from the next summit to the southwest, Mount Washington (6,255 ft). This popular peak has a dozen routes on either snow or solid rock. Mount Ellinor (5,944 ft) has a trail and scramble route up the south side, and a more challenging approach from the north via Lake Ellinor.

The north end of the wilderness is anchored by the massive triple summit of Mount Skokomish (6,434 ft), a relatively easy climb over rotten rock from Lake of the Angels.

The border between the west side of the Mount Skokomish Wilderness and Olympic National Park runs along the top of Sawtooth Ridge, renowned for its excellent rock climbing. This chain of pinnacles is composed of solid volcanic rock with few cracks for direct aid on vertical pitches. Most climbers approach the area from the west via the park's Flapjack Lakes Trail, rather than fight the heavy brush above Mildred Lakes. All of the pinnacles are near-vertical on their west faces, so most climbs attack less demanding east-side routes. The south end of the ridge is anchored by Mount Lincoln (5,868 ft), a relatively easy climb with steep, exposed rock. The lower North Peak of Mount Lincoln (5,690 ft) has a C-5.5 route up the south arête.

Along the ridge to the north are a series of gendarmes (5,600 to 5,700 ft), all with moderate single-lead routes. Two imposing towers, the Fin and the Horn (5,500 ft), have short exposed leads to the top on the south and east sides, and C-5.2 to C-5.5 routes up their near-vertical west faces. Castle Spires and the Needle (5,800 ft) have similar easy exposed routes on the southeast side and C-5 routes on the steeper north and west faces. The north end of the ridge, wholly within the Mount Skokomish Wilderness, is capped by Mount Cruiser (6,104 ft). The easiest route on the summit tower block is an exposed C-5, and other routes run up to 5.7. Several lower spires, all with short rock ascents, complete the north end of the ridgeline.

8

WONDER MOUNTAIN WILDERNESS

LOCATION: In Mason County, on the southeast side of Olympic National Park, northeast of the South Fork of the Skokomish River
SIZE: 2,349 acres
STATUS: Designated Wilderness Area (1984)
TERRAIN: Rugged, heavily forested slopes that rise to massive rock outcrops topped by steep pinnacles
ELEVATION: 1,741 to 4,758 feet
MANAGEMENT: USFS, Olympic National Forest, Hood Canal Ranger District
TOPOGRAPHIC MAPS: Mount Olson, Mount Tebo

Wonder Mountain Wilderness, a small triangle of land appended to the southeast side of Olympic National Park, is one of the smallest wilderness areas in the western United States. It lies in the headwaters of east-flowing McKay Creek and Five Stream. The high ridge that wraps around the south end of the wilderness is capped near its southernmost point by the precipitous rock summit of Wonder Mountain (4,848 ft). Four small unnamed lakes are hidden in cirques at the head of the two creeks that drain the wilderness. Two more lakes and a half-dozen tiny ponds lie to the north, across the national park border, at the head of forks of Five Stream. The ultimate in route finding, primitive camping, and solitude is virtually guaranteed by the remoteness and extreme difficulty of access to the wilderness. Campfires are prohibited at the lakes and above 3,500 feet.

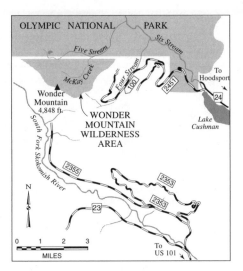

Climate

Annual precipitation ranges between 40 and 60 inches, as the wilderness is on the southern fringe of the Olympic Range rain shadow. A substantial portion of this occurs as snow. Temperatures are mild, rarely exceeding the 70s in summer.

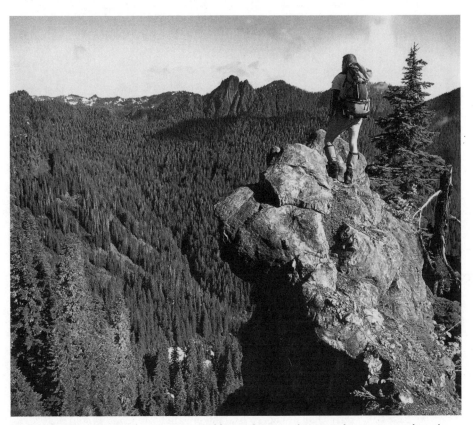

A climber surveys the Wonder Mountain Wilderness from a rocky point along its eastern boundary.

Plants and Wildlife

Lower elevations in the area are densely forested with western hemlock, Pacific silver fir, and Douglas-fir. Creek drainages are a tangle of slide alder, willow, and vine maple. Avalanche slopes off the north sides of the bordering ridge crests are covered in summer with thimbleberry, huckleberry, and vine maple. The wilderness is so seldom visited that there has been no attempt to identify its native wildlife.

Geology

The wilderness lies within the crescent of pre-Miocene uplifted volcanic rock that surrounds the north, east, and south sides of the heart of the Olympic Peninsula.

History

In the late 1890s several prospectors explored and staked claims in the area of the North Fork of the Skokomish River, east of the present wilderness. A few of these hardy souls were believed to have searched for copper and manganese ore in the Wonder Mountain area, but no active mining took place.

ACTIVITIES

Hiking

The Wonder Mountain Wilderness has no hiking trails either in it or accessing it. All approaches are cross-country via steep, difficult forested hillsides and ridges. The two forest roads that come closest to the wilderness lie on its southeast and southwest sides. Both roads are closed in fall and winter months to protect wildlife.

For the southeast approach, climb northwest from FR 2451100 (2,360 to 2,900 ft) up forested sidehills to small saddles that breach the 4,200- to 4,000-foot-high ridge crest. The north side of the ridge is very steep; beyond here cross-country routes depend on your destination.

The southwest approach from the end of FR 2355 (3,020 ft) follows the ridge east up steep wooded slopes to a flat (3,700 ft), then heads northeast toward the pinnacles on the end of the west ridge of Wonder Mountain. The ridge can be traversed west, then north, to lakes on the east side of the ridge. The ridges are all narrow, steep, and exposed.

Climbing

Climbing routes on Wonder Mountain (4,848 ft) all follow the southwest approach in the Hiking section above. The west ridge of the peak has several intermediate spires that must be either skirted or climbed before reaching the highest point on the east end of the summit ridge. The route is rated C-3.

------------------ **9** ------------------

SAN JUAN ISLANDS WILDERNESS

LOCATION: In San Juan, Whatcom, Skagit, and Island counties, in and around the periphery of the San Juan Island archipelago
SIZE: 355 acres
STATUS: Designated Wilderness Area (1976)
TERRAIN: 81 rocks, reefs, and islands ranging from 0.02 to 140 acres in size
ELEVATION: 0 to 174 feet
MANAGEMENT: US Fish and Wildlife Service
TOPOGRAPHIC MAPS: Anacortes North, Blakely Island, Deception Pass, Eastsound, Eliza Island, False Bay, Friday Harbor, Lopez Pass, Lummi Island, Mt. Constitution, Richardson, Roche Harbor, Shaw Island, Stuart Island, Sucia Island, Waldron Island

The San Juan Islands Wilderness includes a major part of the San Juan Islands National Wildlife Refuge. The refuge was established to protect nesting seabirds and marine mammals, and includes 9 acres of reefs, 29 acres of rocks, 157 acres of grassy islands, and 259 acres of forested islands. A total of 84 individual properties are included in the refuge, 81 of which are now protected by wilderness designation.

Climate

The San Juan Islands are located in the rain shadow of the Olympic Range and Vancouver Island; as a result they enjoy a comparatively dry climate, with an average annual rainfall of only 25 inches, mostly occurring during winter months. Temperatures are also mild, averaging 60 degrees in summer and 39 degrees in winter.

Plants and Wildlife

The reefs in the wilderness are awash at high tide, and low rocks have no soil, so both lack vegetation. Nearly half of the acreage in the wilderness consists of low islands, where a thin layer of soil supports a growth of fescue mixed with some wheatgrass and bluegrass. The tops of the larger islands have a tree cover of Douglas-fir and Pacific madrone, with some occurrences of Rocky Mountain juniper, lodgepole pine, and Oregon white oak.

Glaucous-winged gulls are the dominant species breeding in the wilderness. Other nesting species include Brandt's cormorants, pelagic cormorants, pigeon guillemots, tufted puffins, black brants, black oystercatchers, and rhinoceros auklets. In addition to these residents, some 200 migratory species of birds visit the islands annually. Bald eagles nest in the trees of forested

White Rock, in the San Juan Islands Wilderness, is a nesting site for several species of sea birds. (Photo: Marge and Ted Mueller)

1. Small Island
2. Rim and Rum islands
3. Fortress Island
4. Skull Island
5. Crab Island
6. Boulder Island
7. Davidson Rock
8. Castle Island
9. Three unnamed islands
10. Aleck Rocks
11. Swirl Island
12. Unnamed rock
13. Four unnamed islands
14. Three unnamed islands
15. Hall Island
16. Unnamed island
17. Secar Rock
18. Unnamed rock
19. Three unnamed islets
20. Thirteen unnamed islets
21. Mummy Rocks
22. Islets and rocks
23. Shark Reef
24. Harbor Rock
25. North Pacific Rock
26. Half Tide Rock
27. Seven unnamed islands
28. Low Island
29. Unnamed island
30. Barren Island
31. Battleship Island
32. Sentinel Island
33. Center Reef
34. Gull Reef
35. Ripple Island
36. Unnamed reef
37. Unnamed island
38. Gull Rock
39. Flattop Island
40. White Rocks
41. Mouatt Reef
42. Skipjack Island
43. Unnamed island
44. Clements Reef
45. Unnamed island
46. Parker Reef
47. The Sisters
48. Little Sister Island
49. Unnamed island
50. Tift Rocks
51. Unnamed rock
52. Turn Rock
53. Shag Rock
54. Flower Island
55. Willow Island
56. Lawson Rock
57. Pointer Island
58. Black Rock
59. Three unnamed rocks
60. Brown Rock
61. Unnamed rock
62. South Peapod Rocks
63. Peapod Rocks
64. North Peapod Rocks
65. Eliza Rock**
66. Viti Rocks**
67. Dot Island
68. Bird Rock
69. Unnamed island
70. Low Island
71. Nob Island
72. Unnamed island
73. Unnamed island
74. Unnamed rocks
75. Smith Island*/**
76. Minor Island*/**
77. Matia Island
78. Puffin Island
79. Turn Island*
80. Four Bird Rocks
81. Three Williamson Rocks
82. Colville Island
83. Buck Island
84. Bare Island

*Non-wilderness status
**Not within area of map

islands and are often seen perched in snags searching for prey, or feeding on fish along the shore-line. Harbor seals haul out on low rocks, and Dall's porpoises, harbor porpoises, pilot whales, minke whales, and pods of orca whales are common in surrounding waters.

Geology

The geology of the San Juan Islands is more complex than their physical size might indicate. The granites and gneisses of the Turtleback Complex occur along the north rim of Orcas Island and make up the bulk of Blakely Island. These are the oldest rocks in the islands, dating from pre-Devonian times, more than 400 million years ago. During the following 100 million years, most of this submerged base was overlaid with marine volcanic breccia and ash, and later with sedimentary deposits, which were metamorphosed into sandstones and shales.

Around 200 million years ago the entire region appears to have been lifted above sea level, after which portions subsided and were overlaid with more marine sediments. In the late Creta-ceous period, low-angle thrusting in a northwest direction deformed the region, raising a north-west-bearing mountain range, and metamorphosed the sedimentary deposits into sandstones and siltstones. The northern islands, Sucia, Stuart, Spieden, and Waldron, were bent into open folds along the direction of the thrusting.

Pleistocene glaciers provided the final tailoring of the region, gouging deep channels through the range parallel to the movement of the continental ice cap and smoothing and rounding its ridges. Later, the retreating ice left thick deposits of outwash sand and dropped large erratics throughout the landscape. Weathering and wave action have combined to erode the softer silt-stone and expose the harder layers of sandstone and conglomerate that form most of today's rocks and reefs.

History

The value of the smaller islands in the San Juan archipelago as bird refuges was first recog-nized in 1914, when the Smith Island Reservation was created. In 1937 Jones and Matia islands were added as independent migratory bird refuges. These three units were redesignated as na-tional wildlife refuges in 1940. A fourth refuge, the San Juan Islands National Wildlife Refuge, was created in 1960. It was composed of Williamson and Four Bird Rocks, and Colville, Turn, and Bare islands. Buck Island was added to this refuge in 1967.

In 1975 three of these four refuges were consolidated under the name of the San Juan Islands National Wildlife Refuge, and 58 additional rocks, reefs, and islands were added. Jones Island was excluded, pending a potential trade to the State Parks and Recreation Commission in re-turn for 74 state-owned rocks and islets in the San Juans. Sixteen more islands were added to the refuge in 1976, bringing it to 84 separate properties totaling 646 acres. In 1976, 355 acres of the San Juan National Wildlife Refuge were designated as the San Juan Islands Wilderness. Ex-cluded from wilderness status were Smith, Minor, Jones, and Turn islands, and the 5-acre state park property on Matia Island.

ACTIVITIES

Matia Island has four small coves that offer limited safe anchorage. Rolfe Cove, on the northwest end of the island, has a dock, float, and mooring buoys associated with an adjoining 5-acre state park. The rest of the island is part of the San Juan Islands Wilderness. A 0.5-mile trail leads from the campground past the remains of an old hermit's homestead to the island's south cove. From here a way-trail continues to the cove on the east end of the island, opposite Puffin Island. Public use of these trails is subject to revocation if the wildlife in the refuge is disturbed.

All other rocks, reefs, and islands of the wilderness are closed to any public use, including landing, day use, and camping. Kayakers and small boaters can skirt the shoreline of these wil-derness islands to observe birds and mammals, provided that wildlife is not bothered by their presence.

Opposite: *Mount Hardy as seen from Snowy Lake in the Liberty Bell Roadless Area*

THE NORTH CASCADES

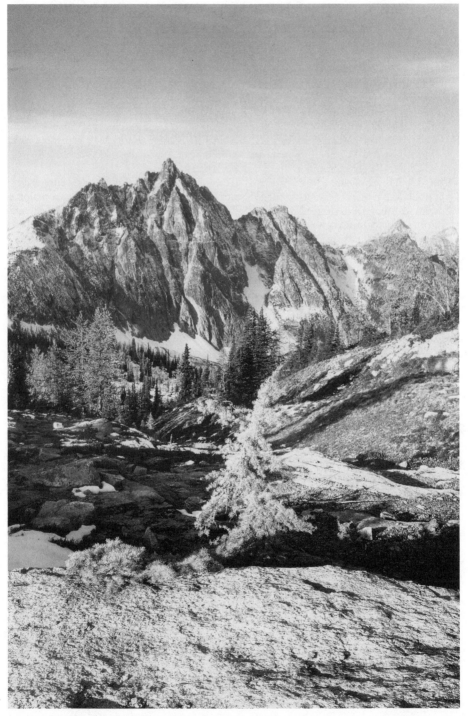

■———————————10———————————■

MOUNT BAKER WILDERNESS AND
MOUNT BAKER NATIONAL
RECREATION AREA

LOCATION: In Whatcom County, on the west side of North Cascades National Park, between Baker Lake and the Canadian border

SIZE: Designated wilderness: 117,900 acres; adjacent Primitive and Roadless areas: 45,000 acres; National Recreation Area: 8,600 acres

STATUS: Designated Wilderness Area and National Recreation Area (1984); Canyon Creek, Twin Lakes, and Loomis Mountain are Semiprimitive; Austin Pass is a Recreation Area; Twin Sisters Range is Primitive.

TERRAIN: The dominant feature of the wilderness is the ice-clad summit of Mount Baker. Surrounding terrain is extremely rugged, with steep slopes terminating in ridgetop alpine meadows. Above these, jagged rock ribs lead to the summits of glaciated peaks. Creeks and rivers cut deep canyons into the lower forested slopes.

ELEVATION: 1,800 to 10,778 feet

MANAGEMENT: USFS, Mount Baker–Snoqualmie National Forest, Mount Baker Ranger District

TOPOGRAPHIC MAPS: Bacon Peak, Baker Pass, Bearpaw Mountain, Cavanaugh Creek, Glacier, Groat Mountain, Mount Baker, Mount Sefrit, Mount Shuksan, Mt. Larrabee, Shuksan Arm, Twin Sisters Mountain, Welker Peak

Mount Baker, the fourth-highest summit in the state at 10,778 feet, is the northernmost of the chain of glaciated volcanoes that cap the Cascade Range in Washington. Although the mountain was first charted by explorers in 1790, dense forests, deep gorges cut by creeks and rivers flowing from its glaciers, and heavy snows lasting until midsummer thwarted exploration; it wasn't until 1868 that the first party reached its frozen summit. Fourteen glaciers cloak Mount Baker and its satellite summits. With the addition of smaller glaciers found on other high peaks in the area, the wilderness holds a total of more than 10,000 acres of permanent glacial ice.

The Mount Baker Wilderness, National Recreation Area, and adjacent roadless areas contain 59 trails totaling over 175 miles in length. Some are little more than climbing routes, others are brushy and poorly maintained, and a number are snowbound until mid-July. With the exception of the few routes that hug the bottom of densely forested drainages, the trails climb to alpine ridges with breathtaking vistas of glacier-shrouded Mount Baker, the photogenic summit pyramid of Mount Shuksan, and a host of other peaks along the backbone of the North Cascades and in Canada's Cheam and Coast ranges.

Most ridgetops have extensive, lightly forested heather meadows that burst into colorful displays of alpine flowers when the snow melts. A lush growth of huckleberries and blueberries ripens here in the fall.

Although lowland forests once covered the region, logging has nibbled its way to the fringes of the wilderness and is a constant threat to the remaining virgin forest in adjacent unprotected primitive and roadless areas.

Climate

Low-pressure systems from the Gulf of Alaska dominate the weather in the Mount Baker Wilderness. Heavy rain and snow are dumped on the region by successions of autumn and winter lows heavily laden with moisture gathered from the Pacific. Annual precipitation ranges from 80 inches in the lower areas on the western edge of the wilderness to 140 inches on the summit of Mount Baker and 150 inches at Baker Lake. Snow accumulates to an average depth of 18 feet in upper elevations. Even though most snow disappears below 3,500 feet by June, it persists above 5,000 feet until August. Glacial ice remains year-round above 6,000 feet; some permanent snowfields and pocket glaciers are found as low as 5,000 feet on north-facing slopes. When the Aleutian low retreats northward in summer, cool, dry air masses flow into the region.

Plants and Wildlife

Vegetation in the wilderness is typical of that found on west Cascade slopes. Where not logged, valley floors are covered by a forest of Douglas-fir, cedar, and true fir with a thick understory of ferns and salmonberry. Devil's club and skunk cabbage thrive along creek beds, and open slopes are matted with vine maple and red alder. On higher slopes trees shift to silver fir and mountain hemlock, with Alaska yellow cedar in more open spots; the understory consists of salal, Oregon grape, and huckleberries. Between 4,000 and 5,500 feet, clumps of mountain hemlock and alpine fir cluster in heather meadows covered by huckleberries, blueberries, and colorful wild flowers. Higher yet, trees shrink to dwarf evergreens, then disappear entirely as sedges and tiny hardy flowers mat rock ribs that climb to the permanent ice fields.

In 1937, 1,407 acres were set aside as the North Fork of the Nooksack Research Natural Area (RNA) to preserve a baseline forest of Douglas-fir and western hemlock. A 2,460-acre addition has been proposed to track regeneration of a 75-year-old burn through Douglas-fir and

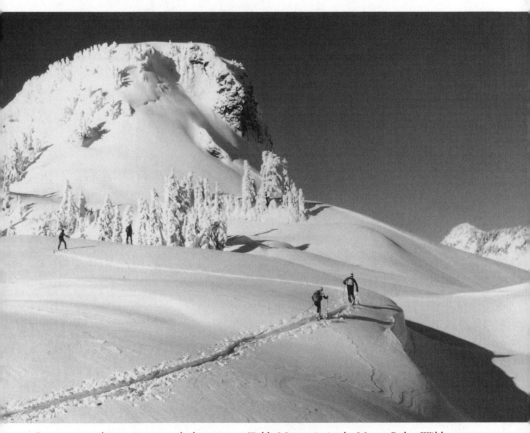

Cross-country skiers enjoy untracked snow near Table Mountain in the Mount Baker Wilderness Area.

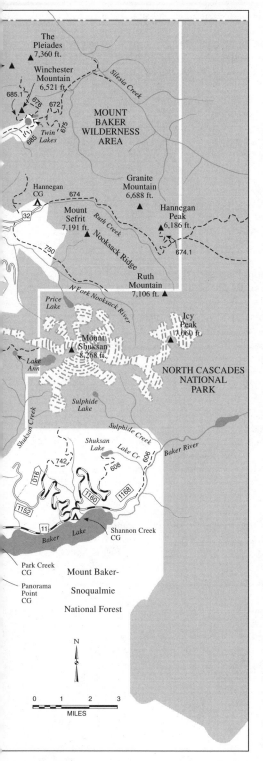

other subalpine ecological communities. A second RNA of 1,920 acres has been proposed at Chowder Ridge, where alpine plants, flowers, and dwarfed alpine fir (krummholz) are represented.

The forest is home to black-tailed deer, black bear, fishers, marten, blue grouse, and pileated woodpeckers. Mountain goats and hoary marmots are found at higher elevations. The basin on the south side of the wilderness between Dock Butte and Washington Monument has been designated as an elk refuge; it is one of the few places in the North Cascades where elk are found in any number.

Geology

The geology of the Mount Baker Wilderness is surprisingly complex for the size of the area. The North Cascades consist of a microcontinent that collided with, and became attached to, the North American continent about 50 million years ago. The dominate rock of this new addition is the Chilliwack Group, a thick sheet of dark sandstone, shales, and marine lava flows laid down between 200 million to 300 million years ago. The heart of this formation, from the Canadian border to Baker Lake, was overlaid 120 million to 150 million years ago by rock of the Nooksack Group, consisting of marine sediments, primarily of volcanic origin and rich in fossils. This formation was intensely folded and sheared along the Church Mountain Thrust at its north and east edge.

A long fault line runs along the eastern border of the Mount Baker Wilderness, from the Skagit River to the Chilliwack River in Canada. East of the fault, the rock is primarily of the Shuksan Suite, a huge thrust sheet of green schist and phillite metamorphosed from marine volcanic flows. The upward thrust of this sheet, interposed with fragments of older crystalline core rock, is exposed in the peaks at the northeast corner of the wilderness.

Mount Baker volcanics overlay the center of the Nooksack Group in an east–west direction. West of the present summit, the Black Buttes mark the location of an older eroded vent of the volcano. Mount Baker is relatively young; its flows were laid down over the past 10 million years, and there is less glacial erosion on the peak than on the other volcanoes farther south in the Washington Cascades. The mountain has been active in historic times, emitting steam and a little ash from the summit crater. The last significant activity of this nature occurred in 1975.

Glacial flows in Pleistocene times carved the underlying rock, creating most of the cirques and valleys that are presently recognizable. Even today, this erosion continues on a lesser scale where the massive glaciers of Mount Baker and smaller alpine glaciers on surrounding peaks carve and shape the surrounding rock.

The Sisters, at the southwest corner of the wilderness, is a massive intrusion of dunite, an ancient rock, probably of Precambrian origin, thought by some to be an exposed portion of the earth's mantle. The intrusion appears to have been emplaced 50 million to 60 million years ago. The surface of the rock is olivine, imbedded with grains of chromite, which weathers to a distinctive reddish-brown color. The tops of these peaks are rough textured, apparently having escaped significant glacial erosion.

History

Although there is evidence that Indians used a faint trail over Hannegan Pass to hunt mountain goats in the high Cascades, the first recorded explorations into the Mount Baker Wilderness occurred in connection with the boundary survey between 1857 and 1862. Tomyhoi Peak, Mount Larrabee, and either Goat Mountain or Winchester Mountain were possibly climbed by members of that survey party.

Prospectors poked into the South Fork of the Nooksack River in 1860 with scant success, but discoveries in the upper Skagit River and Ruby Creek in 1879 brought gold fever to the Nooksack as well. By 1885, the presence of gold in the South Fork was discounted, however, in 1896 promising prospects were found at the head of the North Fork of the Nooksack and its Swamp Creek and Ruth Creek tributaries. The Silver Tip Mine on Goat Mountain triggered a flurry of activity along Ruth Creek, and gold-laden veins of quartz were found at Twin Lakes and south of Skagway Pass. Word of riches quickly got out, and by 1902 nearly 500 miners inhabited five tent cities upriver from Nooksack Falls. Full-scale mining operations, complete with onsite stamping mills, began at the Lone Jack, above Twin Lakes, and the Great Excelsior, on Wells Creek. Mining was difficult; most sites were buried in snow for eight months a year, and transportation of materials, supplies, and ore relied on humans and pack strings.

Additional lode mining occurred at the Boundary Red Mine, on the north side of the Pleiades, the Gargett Mine on Mount Larrabee, at Yellow Aster Meadows, and east of Glacier. Placer mining flourished on the North Fork of the Nooksack and many of its tributaries. As the mines played out in the early 1900s, logging became the chief economic driver in the region, as it has remained to this day.

It wasn't until 1868 that a group led by Edmund Thomas Coleman made the first ascent of Mount Baker, via the glacier now named for him. Another 16 years passed before the second ascent, when a pair of climbers approached the mountain from the south via the Easton Glacier. Some contend that this party actually reached the top of Sherman Peak, the lower south summit of the mountain, rather than the true summit. Between 1911 and 1913, the Bellingham Chamber of Commerce introduced the annual Mount Baker Marathon. The race required contestants to get from Bellingham to the summit and back by auto, rail, bicycle, and foot, climbing to the summit via either the Coleman Glacier or Easton Glacier, and descending via the other. Poor weather, emotional stress, and the hazards of solo glacier travel caused cancellation of the marathon after its third year.

In the late 1920s, the CCC pushed a road to Baker Lake and built the Komo Kulshan Guard Station. A fire lookout was constructed atop Park Butte in 1936, and many of today's trails in were built to service the lookout and fire patrols in the area. The desire to exploit Mount Baker's scenic and recreational potential led to construction of a road to Heather Meadows, on the east side of the mountain, in 1924. By 1927, a resort there, complete with a lodge, hotel, and cabins, offered recreational activities that included skiing, hiking, and horseback riding. Most of the resort burned to the ground in 1931; the portions that were restored matured to today's Mount Baker Ski Area.

Federal management of the area was established in 1897 when President Cleveland created the Washington Forest Preserve, which included the region surrounding Mount Baker. From 1910 to 1917, Charles Finley Easton, the historian of the Mount Baker Club, was one of the chief lobbyists promoting Mount Baker as a national park. In 1926, the Mount Baker Recreation Area, encompassing the entire mountain, was established, however, the act still permitting logging, mining, and water development that did not impair recreational values. Renewed proposals for park status for Mount Baker were introduced in the late 1930s and early 1940s, but it wasn't until 1984 that the bulk of the mountain and its surrounding virgin forests were designated as wilderness.

ACTIVITIES

Hiking

HEATHER MEADOWS RECREATION AREA TRAILS

Trail #600, Lake Ann. 4.8 miles/m (H). From Austin Pass (4,700 ft), the trail drops to the north fork of Swift Creek and follows it through mixed heather, forest, and scree for 1.5 miles to a saddle overlooking Lake Ann (4,700 ft). The lake is perched in a small meadow at the edge of precipitous cliffs surrounding the head of Shuksan Creek. Across the basin, Fisher Chimneys and the lower 1,400-foot-high west wall of Mount Shuksan sweep up from the Lower Curtis Glacier.

Trail #681, Table Mountain. 2.6 miles/m-d (H). From the end of Highway 542 (4,700 ft), the northernmost trail climbs a steep basalt cliff to reach the near-flat top of Table Mountain (5,600 ft) and spectacular views of Mounts Baker and Shuksan. The path wanders along the south and west rims of the mountain, descends a steep snowfield (ice ax recommended), then weaves down cliffs on its west side to join Trail #682 (4,980 ft).

Trail #682, Chain Lakes. 5.5 miles/e (H). From the end of Highway 542 (4,700 ft), the southernmost path tiptoes along the south wall of Table Mountain to a saddle in a little over a mile. Here the trail drops north along the west side of Table Mountain, passes an unmarked junction with Trail #681, and arrives at tiny Mazama Lake, the first of the Galena Chain Lakes. Next in the chain is Iceberg Lake (4,793 ft); a short spur leads from here to Hayes and Arbuthnet lakes. The route climbs east to Herman Saddle (5,300 ft), then drops into the upper Bagley Creek Basin. A gradual descent past the flowered meadows surrounding Bagley Lakes reaches the lower Mount Baker Ski Area parking lot (4,200 ft).

Trail #682.1, Ptarmigan Ridge. 5 miles/m (H). At the saddle west of Table Mountain (5,200 ft), a branch of Trail #682 continues west toward Mount Baker, skirting one side, then the other, of Ptarmigan Ridge. The trail continues to Camp Kiser, a small bench (6,180 ft) amid clumps of mountain hemlock on the west side of Coleman Pinnacle.

UPPER NORTH FORK OF THE NOOKSACK RIVER AND RUTH CREEK TRAILS

Trail #750, Nooksack Cirque. 6.5 miles/m (H). From FR 32 (2,480 ft), a short barrier-free path leads to a bridge viewpoint of Ruth Creek plunging through a narrow 100-foot-deep gorge. The track wanders through logged-over land along the north side of the Nooksack River, then fades into the braided channels of the Nooksack as it enters the deepest and darkest portion of the drainage. Obscure paths continue upriver to 2,800 feet to seldom-seen views of the glaciers and rock walls at the head of the Nooksack Cirque.

Trail #674, Hannegan Pass. 5 miles/e (H; S from August 15 to November 1). From the end of FR 32 at Hannegan Campground (3,110 ft), a gentle climb up the forested hillside north of Ruth Creek reaches the heather meadows of Hannegan Pass (5,066 ft). The trail then enters the North Cascades National Park as the Chilliwack Trail. En route are glimpses south to Ruth Mountain, Mount Sefrit, and Nooksack Ridge.

Trail #674.1, Hannegan Peak. 1 mile/m (H). From Hannegan Pass (5,066 ft), lazy switchbacks head north up the ridge, through heather and wildflowers, to the summit of Hannegan Peak (6,186 ft). Look east to see the peaks of the Picket Range, including Redoubt, Whatcom, Challenger, and Triumph; south to admire the ragged north face of Mount Shuksan; and southwest at the ice crown of Mount Baker.

SWAMP CREEK TRAILS

Trail #699, Yellow Aster Butte. 3.5 miles/m (H). This route from FR 3065 (2,960 ft) climbs straight up the steep forested ridge south of Yellow Aster Butte. After a breath-catching pause at 4,000 feet, switchbacks continue the arduous ascent to a ridgetop meadow (4,700 ft). The way levels (5,500 ft) at a chain of beautiful tarns that dimple lush flower-tinted meadows. Old prospects and rusted mining gear testify to the origin of the trail. Late summer brings a feast of blueberries in the alpine meadows atop Yellow Aster Butte (5,600 ft). The lower section of this trail is unmaintainable, so plans are afoot to reroute it along the ridge west from Trail #686 at Gold Run Pass (5,410 ft).

Trail #686, Tomyhoi Lake. 4 miles/m (H). The way leaves FR 3065 (3,700 ft) at the base of an avalanche-swept face, climbs around a forested ridge, and continues up a minor drainage to Gold Run Pass (5,430 ft). Yellow Aster Butte looms high to the west, and Mounts Shuksan and Baker dominate the skyline to the south. After a steep descent from the pass, hazardous until it melts out, the trail follows a creek northward to Tomyhoi Lake (3,722 ft). A cliff sweeps up from the lake to a glacier falling from the summit of Tomyhoi Peak.

Trail #685, Twin Lakes. 1 mile/e (H). FR 3065 was built to haul ore from the Lone Jack Mine, not for recreational purposes. The final mile to Twin Lakes, a road occasionally graded by miners, is impassable most of the year; the county calls it a road, but the Forest Service considers it a trail. Beyond the start of Trail #686 (3,700 ft) the path passes near the site of the Union City mining camp, then switchbacks up the last mile to end between Twin Lakes (5,170 ft). The lakes are frozen until late summer. Rusting ruins and abandoned tunnels around the lakes mark faded dreams of easy riches.

Trail #685.1, Winchester Mountain. 2.1 miles/m (H). From Twin Lakes (5,170 ft), this route climbs north through alpine fir and small flower meadows, then traverses avalanche slopes. After rounding the ridge south of Winchester Mountain, the path switchbacks up through dwarf alpine fir to the summit and an historic fire lookout (6,510 ft) maintained by a local climbing club. A sweeping 360-degree view encompasses Tomyhoi Peak, Mount Larrabee, American Border Peak, the Pleiades, the glaciated spires of the Chilliwack Range, the sawtoothed Picket Range, Mount Shuksan, and the glistening mass of Mount Baker. An ice ax is mandatory in steep snow chutes until late summer.

Trail #676, High Pass. 3 miles/m (H). From 0.4 mile up Trail #685.1 (5,400 ft), a miner's route climbs north along the head of the Winchester Creek basin, then switchbacks up to Low Pass (5,650 ft). After ascending an open hillside to High Pass (5,900 ft), the trail climbs north up a ridge and a steep rock face to the shoulder of Mount Larrabee (6,730 ft). A spur northwest from High Pass leads to the abandoned Gargett Mine. The Forest Service plans to extend this trail from High Pass to Trail #686, just north of Gold Run Pass.

NORTH OF THE NORTH FORK OF THE NOOKSACK RIVER TRAILS

Trail #671, Church Mountain. 4.2 miles/m (H,M). Church Mountain is easily recognized from Highway 542 by its vertical green walls, which rise nearly a mile to a gable roof of rock and a slab-sided rock steeple. A fire lookout once stood atop the east peak, but weather collapsed the building; it was removed in 1966. From the trailhead on FR 3040 (2,313 ft) the route takes endless switchbacks up the forested hillside to reach heather meadows at the head of Deerhorn Creek basin. A long traverse and a steep ascent of a rock rib gains the summit ridge east of the lookout site. Here are imposing views a mile straight down to the Nooksack Valley, plus the panoramic sweep of the Sisters, Mount Baker, and Mount Shuksan, with the American Border peaks in the distance.

Trail #680, Nooksack River. 2 miles/m (H,S,M). Ambitious plans call for a "Bay to Baker" trail from Bellingham Bay to Heather Meadows on the east flank of Mount Baker. At the moment the only segment of this trail that exists is a brushy path that runs along the north bank of the river from Douglas Fir Campground, on Highway 542, east to Horseshoe Bend. Only 65 more miles of trail are needed to complete this dream.

Trail #670, Excelsior. 4 miles/m (H; S from August 14 to November 1). From the trailhead on Highway 542 (1,040 ft), incessant switchbacks climb a timbered mountain flank to Excelsior

Pass (5,375 ft). Here the route joins Trail #630 from the east, Trail #625 from the north, and a spur to a former lookout site atop Excelsior Peak.

Trail #698, Welcome Pass. 2.2 miles/d (H; S from August 15 to November 1). The east access to the High Divide leaves FR 3060 (2,450 ft) to zigzag up a steep forested ridge to Welcome Pass (5,400 ft). Here the trail becomes #630 as it continues west along the crest.

Trail #630, High Divide. 4.7 miles/m (H; S from August 14 to November 1). This trail winds through alpine meadows from Welcome Pass (5,400 ft) on the east to Excelsior Pass (5,375 ft) on the west. It rarely drops more than a few hundred feet below the ridgetop. Wildflowers adorn the route from late July to September, and the crevassed glaciers of Mount Baker are continuous visual companions.

CANYON CREEK TRAILS

Trail #689, Canyon Ridge. 9.1 miles/d (H,B,M; S from August 15 to November 1). From its west end at FR 3140 (4,470 ft) this trail wanders east along a 4,800- to 5,400-foot-high ridge crest, less than a mile south of the Canadian border. It was once part of the Whatcom Trail, which stretched from Bellingham to the Caribou gold fields of British Columbia. The path is gentle, sometimes in timber, sometimes in heather meadows. The west end is poorly maintained and difficult to follow, and is often obscured by snow until late summer. As the ridge swings south from the border, the trail begins a gentle descent through mountain ash forest to the junction with Trail #625 at its eastern end.

Trail #625, Damfino Lake–Excelsior Pass. 2.5 miles/m (H). Starting from FR 31 (4,277 ft), a gentle grade leads past Trail #689 to a meadow surrounding tiny Damfino Lake (4,470 ft). Beyond the lake the path wiggles up a steep hillside, then crosses a notch to more alpine meadows. A gentle traverse rises another mile to Excelsior Pass to meet Trails #670 and #630. Here is the familiar panorama of Mounts Baker and Shuksan, the Border Peaks, and the crests of the North Cascades.

SOUTH OF THE NORTH FORK OF THE NOOKSACK RIVER TRAILS

Trail #678, Skyline Divide. 5.5 miles/m (H; S from August 15 to November 1). From the trailhead at FR 37 (4,350 ft), switchbacks and a diagonal climb through a silver fir forest lead to the crest of Skyline Divide, between the Thompson and Deadhorse creeks. Atop the divide a short path leads north along the crest to a promontory (5,884 ft) with a clear view of the peaks lining the horizon and Church Mountain rising abruptly across the valley. Trees dissolve to alpine meadows as the path ascends the slowly rising ridge. With altitude the meadows fade to a mat of sedges; the trail continues south along the crest, then disappears into snowbanks at a cliff on the west end of Chowder Ridge (6,400 ft). The upper portion of the divide is snow-covered until August. Once above timberline, the horizon-spanning scenery includes the Canadian Coast Range, the Border Peaks, Mount Shuksan, and a wall of ice breaking from the summit of Mount Baker. Below are the deep canyons of north-flowing tributaries of the Nooksack.

Trail #677, Heliotrope Ridge. 2.7 miles/e (H). From the trailhead parking lot on FR 39 (2,880 ft), the route crosses Grouse Creek, zigzags uphill, then takes a climbing traverse through the forest to Kulshan Creek. An ascent east of the creek reaches the former site of Kulshan Cabin (4,700 ft), just below timberline. Here a path climbs a meadow-covered rib south to snowfields below Heliotrope Ridge (6,200 ft). These meadows are blanketed by wildflowers in late summer.

Trail #677.1, Hogsback Route. 1 mile/m (H). From the Kulshan Cabin site, the path east crosses Heliotrope Creek, then ascends a narrow rocky rib above the snout of the Coleman Glacier. The track continues uphill to climbers' campsites at the glacier's edge (6,000 ft).

MIDDLE FORK OF THE NOOKSACK RIVER TRAILS

Trail #697, Elbow Lake. 6.2 miles/m (H; S from August 15 to November 1). The route leaves FR 38, crosses a bridge over the Nooksack just below the trailhead (2,140 ft), and swings west to the mouth of Green Creek. It ascends the forested sidehill above the creek, then bends east up slopes above Hildebrand Creek. Canyon walls close in at tiny Hildebrand Lake. The way continues to Elbow Lake (3,380 ft) and nearby Lake Doreen; 200- to 400-foot-high walls embrace

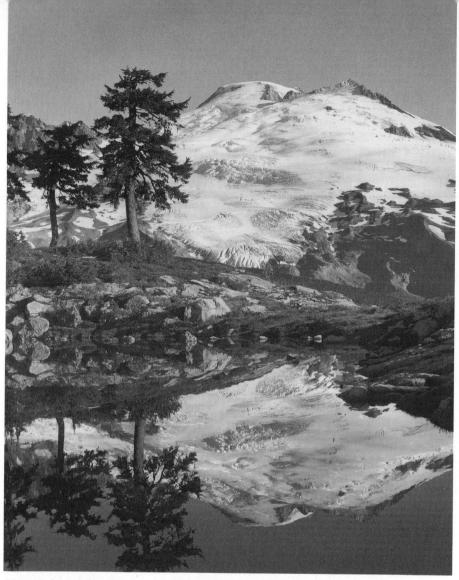

Mount Baker is reflected in a pool on the side of Park Butte.

both lakes. From Doreen the path threads through a breach in the wall, traverses south, and drops down a timber-covered ridge to a spur trail that meets Trail #603.3 (3,300 ft). The route crosses Doreen Creek twice before reaching FR 12 at Pioneer Camp.

Trail #696, Ridley Creek. 3 miles/m (H; S between August 15 and November 1). From the end of FR 38 (2,610 ft) the way climbs a timber-covered rib to a bridge over the Middle Fork of the Nooksack. After a traverse of forested slopes, switchbacks climb the steep north side of the Ridley Creek drainage. The route then traverses southeast along the upper edge of the flower meadows of Mazama Park to join Trail #603.3 (4,500 ft).

SOUTH FORK OF THE NOOKSACK RIVER TRAILS

Trail #604, Blue Lake. 0.7 mile/e (H,M). From the FR 1230 road end (3,930 ft), an easy path climbs to the alpine meadows surrounding the north and east sides of Blue Lake (3,984 ft). From its common start with Trail #604, Trail #604.1 climbs a forested rib north of Blue Lake, then breaks into an alpine meadow bench above the cliffs west of the lake. A narrow ridge leads south, where switchbacks climb to the summit of Dock Butte (5,239 ft). The fire lookout once here was removed in 1964, but the views of Mount Baker and south as far as Mount Rainier remain.

Trail #603, Park Butte. 3.5 miles/m (H; S between August 15 and November 1; open to snow-mobiles). From the trailhead at the end of FR 13 (3,364 ft) the route passes through Schriebers Meadow, then begins a gradual climb of the wooded hillside. The ridge is surmounted in a se-ries of switchbacks, and the forest is left behind at the lower end of Morovitz Meadows (4,600 ft). A diagonal ascent above the heather-covered basin south of Cathedral Crag leads to a saddle on South Fork Divide. A short hike up the ridge to the west reaches the fire lookout atop Park Butte (5,450 ft). The tower, constructed in 1936, is maintained by the Skagit Alpine Club. Views sweep up the Easton Glacier to the icy cap of Mount Baker; west is the ragged string of summits along the top of Sisters Mountain; north are the crags of Black Buttes.

Trail #603.1, Sulphur Moraine. 6.5 miles/m (H). This trail leaves Trail #603 (3,364 ft) just beyond its starting point, then makes a few lazy switchbacks up a forested ridge to the north between two forks of Sulphur Creek. At the head of the basin above the east fork, trees fade to heather meadows. The path climbs to 4,800 feet; a boot-track continues atop the snowfields and rocks of the moraine to Crag View, where the Squok Glacier focuses views upward to Sherman Peak, the south summit of Mount Baker. A recently constructed main trail traverses west above timberline along the 4,800-foot contour line to the headwaters of Rocky Creek on Metcalf Moraine. Here it drops to meet Trail #603 below Morovitz Meadows (4,600 ft).

Trail #603.2, Railroad Grade. 2 miles/m (H). From Trail #603 at the north end of Morovitz Meadows (4,670 ft), this way ascends the lateral moraine on the west side of the Easton Glacier. Above 5,000 feet a climbers' track continues along snow and jumbled rock to the edge of the glacier, 1,000 feet higher. This is the start of a climbing route to the summit.

Trail #603.3, Mazama Park. 6 miles/m (H; S between August 15 and November 1). At a saddle on the south side of Cathedral Crag (4,750 ft), the fork to the north is the upper end of Trail #603.3. It switchbacks downhill to a junction with Trail #696 (4,500 ft) near the south-east edge of the beautiful alpine meadow of Mazama Park. Trail #603.3 heads west over Bell Pass (3,964 ft) and ends on Trail #697 near Doreen Creek (3,300 ft).

BAKER LAKE TRAILS

Trail #608, Shuksan Lake. 2 miles/d (H). Starting from FR 1160 in a clearcut (2,980 ft), the trail enters old-growth forest and without respite zigzags up a seemingly vertical ridge to a saddle (4,720 ft) above two tarns. Dropping past these, the route swings west along a cliff rim above the south side of Shuksan Lake, then descends to a small meadow at the west end of the lake (3,694 ft).

Trail #606, Baker River. 1.6 miles/e (H). A short, near-level jaunt up the west bank of Baker River from FR 1168 (800 ft) ends at Sulphide Creek, just inside the national park boundary. Here are rewarding views up the wide glacier-carved basin, extending into the heart of the North Cascades to Easy Ridge and Whatcom Peak.

Climbing

The crown of the wilderness, Mount Baker (10,778 ft), was first climbed via the Coleman Glacier. This popular route on the northwest side ascends the glacier to the saddle between the summit and Black Buttes, then scales the steep ice of the Roman Wall to the flat summit pla-teau. South-side routes ascend the Boulder and Easton glaciers. The latter is the easiest on the mountain, but even it has seen fatalities in a midsummer avalanche on the upper Deming Gla-cier. From the northeast, climbs start at the end of Trail #682.1 at Camp Kiser, head up the Sholes Glacier to either the Rainbow Glacier or Mazama Glacier, then finish via the steep Park Glacier headwall. On the north, extremely challenging ice routes claw up the Coleman Glacier headwall, the upper Roosevelt Glacier, and the north ridge of the mountain. All glaciers become heavily crevassed and difficult to cross by early fall.

The ridge west from the summit leads to the Black Buttes, a maze of sawtooth basalt spikes above the west end of the Deming Glacier that are remnants of an earlier cone of Mount Baker. Vertical walls line both the east and west sides of a crescent-shaped arête. The four named sum-mits are Colfax (9,443 ft), Lincoln (9,096 ft), and Seward (8,005 ft) peaks, and Lee Promontory

(6,900 ft). Lincoln is the most difficult climb of the group, requiring exposed rock and glacier work. There are several other unnamed pinnacles along the crest between these peaks.

The Twin Sisters Range, southwest of Mount Baker, is named for the two distinctive pyramidal peaks, North Twin (6,570 ft) and South Twin (6,932 ft), which mark the north end of the range. The 6-mile-long crest to the southeast is topped by a number of towers ranging between 5,900 and 6,500 feet; small glaciers lie in pockets along the northeast side of the range. The rock throughout the range is rough-textured and solid, offering excellent short climbs in the C-4 to C-5 range. In keeping with the Sisters motif, many of the lesser peaks bear feminine names, e.g. Barbara, Nancy, Little Sister, and Cinderella.

The trails north from Swamp Creek access a group of peaks along the Canadian border. From Trail #699 at Yellow Aster Meadows, a boot-path heads up the ridge for an exposed C-3 scramble up Tomyhoi Peak (7,435 ft). From the south, the sharp summit pyramid of American Border Peak (7,994 ft) appears an imposing climb, although the long cross-country approach from the Gargett Mine is perhaps as difficult as the climb itself. A variety of rock features on the ridge southeast of the summit spices the C-3 to C-5 route. From the upper end of Trail #676 above the Gargett Mine, a scramble up talus, loose dirt, and rock reaches the top of Mount Larrabee (7,861 ft). The buttress east from the summit of Larrabee is capped by four ragged spires, the Pleiades (7,280 to 7,360 ft). Steep snow or ice gullies from either north or south reach a col between the east and west pairs of peaks, where C-3 scrambles over solid rock gain the summits.

Rugged Nooksack Ridge, between Ruth Creek and the North Fork of the Nooksack River, is anchored on the north end by Mount Sefrit (7,191 ft) and on the south by Ruth Mountain (7,115 ft). Ruth is a simple climb south from Hannegan Pass via the glacier on its north ridge, and the final summit pyramid of Sefrit has several C-4 to C-5 leads on solid rock. The crest between Sefrit and Ruth is laced with several lower pinnacles.

Winter Sports

Mount Baker Ski Area, a major commercial ski area at the east end of Highway 542, is surrounded by its namesake wilderness. The open alpine slopes of the enclosing wilderness are among the most popular cross-country ski touring areas in the state, with due caution paid to avalanche hazards. One of the Cascade's best cross-country trips heads south from the ski area, crosses the snowbound Bagley Lakes, and climbs to Herman Saddle. The return trip offers excellent runs down deep untracked snow. Another tour heads south from the ski lodge to Austin Pass and Artist Point for outstanding views of Mounts Shuksan and Baker in their cloaks of winter snow. The more daring can follow the general route of the summer trail along Ptarmigan Ridge to Camp Kiser, with due caution for the avalanche hazards on the south side of Table Mountain. Rewards include miles of untracked open basins.

While access roads are excluded from the wilderness, when snows seal them to vehicular traffic they become ideal ski tours. In the North Fork of the Nooksack drainage, such tours include FR 32 and 34 into the upper reaches of the Nooksack River and Ruth Creek, FR 3075 at the head of White Salmon Creek, FR 3071 up Anderson Creek above Silver Fir Campground, FR 33 up Wells Creek, and FR 3065 toward Twin Lakes. Farther west, FR 39 up Glacier Creek offers outstanding views of the northwest side of Mount Baker and access for skiing the open bowls below Heliotrope Ridge.

On the south side of Mount Baker, the difference between a recreation area and a wilderness area is readily apparent in the winter, when snowmobiles are permitted on roads and some of the trails of the recreation area. The snow-covered forest roads between Baker Lake and Schriebers Meadow are heavily used by adherents of this sport.

From Schriebers Meadow, the summer trail to Park Butte has excellent snow for advanced cross-country skiers well into late spring. Ski mountaineers often use the Railroad Creek route for glacier skiing on the lower Easton Glacier or even spring climbs from this side of the mountain. The snow-covered loop connecting FR 1144 up Morovitz Creek to FR 1130 up Park Creek has scenic side trips to Rainbow Falls and the opportunity for a welcome warming dip in Baker Hot Springs (nude bathing prohibited).

11

NOISY–DIOBSUD WILDERNESS

LOCATION: In Whatcom and Skagit counties, on the west side of North Cascades National Park between Highway 20 and Baker Lake

SIZE: Designated wilderness: 14,300 acres; adjacent Primitive and Roadless areas: 36,900 acres

STATUS: Designated Wilderness Area (1984), surrounded by Nonwilderness Primitive and Semiprimitive Nonmotorized areas

TERRAIN: Rugged, extremely steep, forested slopes split by numerous creek drainages. Ridges are topped by alpine meadows; those on the northeast border of the wilderness are capped by rocky summits.

ELEVATION: 900 to 6,234 feet

MANAGEMENT: USFS, Mount Baker–Snoqualmie National Forest, Mount Baker Ranger District. Also, a few sections outside the Designated Wilderness are managed by the State Department of Natural Resources (DNR) or are in private hands.

TOPOGRAPHIC MAPS: Bacon Peak, Damnation Peak, Lake Shannon, Marblemount, Sauk Mountain, Welker Peak

Ridges on the northeast and southwest sides of Noisy Creek (flowing to the north) and Diobsud Creek (flowing to the south) define the official boundaries of the Noisy–Diobsud Wilderness. The national forest land wrapping around three sides of the wilderness, about two and a half times the size of the designated wilderness itself, is currently managed by the Forest Service in a primitive or semiprimitive status, which gives it de facto, although not legal, protection similar to the wilderness. Eleven-mile-long Baker Lake lies along the northwest edge of this extended wilderness, at the foot of a steep hillside covered with old-growth forest. The southwest side of this region, including the lower portions of the Anderson, Welker, Thunder, and Jackman Creek drainages, has been heavily logged; fortunately, a 0.5- to 5-mile-wide buffer of old-growth forest still exists along the perimeter of the designated wilderness. Extremely steep rock walls rise from the Skagit River on the south and southeast sides of the extended wilderness.

Only 12 miles of maintained trails exist in the wilderness and adjacent roadless areas; another dozen or so miles of abandoned routes are so obscure and difficult that their use demands polished wilderness navigation skills. The wilderness itself holds only a dozen lakes, most above 4,000 feet; the roadless area outside the wilderness has more than double that number of lakes, most not reached by trails.

Hikers enjoy relatively easy trails to two abandoned fire lookout sites (Anderson Butte and Sauk Mountain). Both offer unparalleled views of hundreds of miles of forested ridges cut by lakes and deep river valleys. Above looms the jagged crest of the Cascades and the huge masses of the ice-clad volcanoes on the forefront of that range. Climbers are the most frequent visitors to the ragged rocky boundary between the wilderness and North Cascades National Park.

Climate

Alternating high- and low-pressure cells from the North Pacific dominate the weather pattern on the west side of the North Cascades. Summers are generally mild and dry, but a continuous series of low-pressure fronts from the south, southwest, and west bring rain and snow in the autumn and winter. Annual precipitation here is about 150 inches, much of it delivered as snow that reaches depths of 18 feet or more. The snow is generally gone below 3,500 feet by early June.

Plants and Wildlife

Vegetation in the Noisy–Diobsud Wilderness is typical of that found on the west side of the Cascades. Low-level forests are old-growth Douglas-fir, cedar, true fir, and western hemlock, with an understory of mosses, ferns, salal, Oregon grape, elderberry, and salmonberry, joined by vine maple and devil's club along creek beds. Buttercups, foam flower, and youth-on-age add color to the forest floor. With increasing altitude the timber shifts to mountain hemlock, and ultimately gives way to alpine meadows along ridgetops.

The dense forest canopy is habitat for black-tailed deer, elk, black bear, and northern spotted owls. Mountain goats are often seen in the Diobsud Buttes area, and peregrine falcons are occasionally spotted.

Geology

Most of the wilderness consists of Paleozoic sedimentary rocks, formed more than 250 million years ago as ocean sediments accumulated off a micro-continent impinging northeastward on the coastline of North American. At a thrust fault along the northeast side of the wilderness, pre-Jurassic metamorphosed rock overrode this plate, forming the crest of today's Diobsud

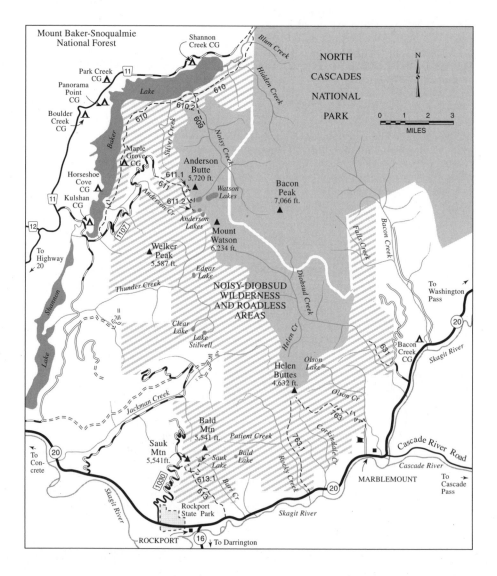

Buttes. A similar-aged metamorphic intrusion rises in the southeast end of the extended wilderness in the vicinity of Sauk Mountain.

History

Little is known of the early history of the Noisy–Diobsud Wilderness, although there are sketchy records of visitation by pioneer trappers. Most prospectors bypassed the area in their rush to more lucrative claims along the upper Skagit and Cascade rivers. Marblemount, the tiny community at the southeast corner of the wilderness, began the 1880s as the last point for miners to purchase supplies and slake their thirst for whiskey.

The first surveys of the region took place in the early 1900s, and records indicate exploration of the Baker River area in the 1920s. The present shoreline of Baker Lake was created in 1924 by the construction of Baker Dam, erected to supply power to the Bellingham area. Fire lookouts were built on Anderson Butte in 1920 and on Sauk Mountain in 1928. For a time, cattle were driven to alpine meadows for summer grazing; the path up to Helen Buttes is still known as the Cow Heaven Trail. In recent years logging, primarily on state and private land, has clearcut hundreds of acres along the southwest side of the extended wilderness.

ACTIVITIES

Hiking

Trail #610, East Bank. 13 miles/e (H,S). The trailhead (980 ft) is on the west side of the FR 1107. A gentle descent along a steep forested hillside crosses Anderson Creek, then drops to the east shore of Baker Lake, which it follows north to Maple Grove Campground (724 ft), accessible only by foot or boat. North from the campground a recently constructed trail follows the east bank of Baker Lake for 2 miles, then climbs over a forested knob at the elbow where the lake turns east. In another 1.5 miles an abandoned logging road that heads uphill has been transformed into a segment of Loop Trail #610.2. The mouth of Noisy Creek is the junction with the other end of this loop. The way continues northeast, maintaining altitude, to Hidden Creek, then descends to the east bank of the Baker River. Just beyond Blum Creek the way will cross a bridge over the Baker River and meet Trail #606.

Trail #611, Watson Lakes. 2.3 miles/e (H). From FR 1107002 (4,200 ft) a few switchbacks reach the ridgetop, and the path heads southeast along the gentle crest; in a little over a mile it climbs to the saddle above Watson Lakes. Switchbacks lead down to the upper lake (4,418 ft); the path follows its north shore, then descends to the lower lake (4,407 ft). The glassy surfaces of the two deep blue lakes mirror Anderson Butte and the snowfields leading to the summit of Mount Watson.

Trail #611.1, Anderson Butte. 1.5 miles/m (H). About 0.8 mile from the start of Trail #611, a fork leads east up switchbacks to the ridgetop, a former fire lookout site. Choice of the site is obvious, as views extend north over hundreds of acres of forest, crowned by the icy summits of Mounts Baker and Shuksan. The actual top of the butte (5,730 ft) is 0.25 mile to the east via an easy ridgetop scramble.

Trail #611.2, Anderson Lakes. 0.4 mile/m (H). At the point Trail #611 starts its climb to the Watson Lakes saddle, a spur continues downhill to the largest of the Anderson Lakes (4,475 ft). Two small ponds lie uphill in open basins south and west of this lake. The other three lakes of the group (5,000 to 5,300 ft) lie in a rocky basin above a band of cliffs to the east. These lakes usually remain frozen until mid-June.

Trail #613, Sauk Mountain. 2.1 miles/e (H). From Highway 20 at the west side of Rockport State Park, turn north onto FR 1030. A series of hairpin turns leads 7 miles uphill to the ridgetop, where a spur to the south ends at the present trailhead (4,500 ft). Be thankful—once the trail to this point was a tedious 5-mile grind from the highway up the steep ridge to the southeast. The remaining 2 miles of trail are not a snap, however; the path takes 29 switchbacks up a steep alpine meadow to reach the ridge leading north to the summit (5,541 ft). The original fire lookout was built here in 1928; its 1957 replacement was removed in 1985. To the north is a sweeping view of the entire Noisy–Diobsud Wilderness and beyond to the jagged

Valerian blossoms and hellebore decorate the hillside above Watson Lakes.

peaks of North Cascades National Park. Below, the blue ribbons of the Skagit and Sauk rivers thread through valley floors.

Trail 613.1, Bald Mountain. *1.4 miles/m (H).* At the point where Trail #613 gains the crest, follow a spur that heads south down the ridge, then contours northeast, crosses a finger ridge, and descends in a few lazy switchbacks to a cirque that holds Sauk Lake (4,104 ft). Plans call for extending the trail to the summit of Bald Mountain.

Trail #763, Cow Heaven. *6.4 miles/m (H).* The trail starts at the end of an unmarked road beyond the barn of the Marblemount Ranger Station (500 ft). Once herds of cattle were driven up this route for a summer feast on alpine meadows; now only hikers and hunters struggle up the steep, tedious path. An initial gentle grade through cool virgin forest soon leads to switchbacks up forested rock outcrops to a flat (2,200 ft). After a short respite, switchbacks continue up the steep sidehill to an indistinct ridge that breaks into alpine meadows (4,200 ft). The way becomes obscure; one fork traverses the slopes east of Corkindale Creek, and another continues up the crest to the top of Helen Buttes. The higher up the mountain, the better the views to the snowcapped peaks of North Cascades National Park and the upper gorge of the Skagit River.

Climbing

While Sauk Mountain (5,541 ft) has an easy trail to the summit, cliffs on three sides of the summit offer short, challenging rock climbs. In the winter, these faces are also used by ice climbers.

On the southeast side of the wilderness, dense vegetation covers a tangled succession of cliffs rising nearly 5,000 feet from Diobsud Creek to the near-vertical southeast rock face of Diobsud Buttes. A series of short, ragged summits lines the top of the buttes, and small glaciers hang from their northern edge. Most of these high points are scrambles, but a few have one or two leads of C-4 climbing.

The twin summits of Mount Watson (6,234 ft), nearly 1,000 feet higher than nearby Anderson Butte, offer even better views of the miles of forested valleys and ridges culminating in the glaciated summits of Mounts Baker and Shuksan and the sheer west face of Bacon Peak. Good C-3 to C-4 routes lead over rock or a rock-and-snow combination to the summit.

Winter Sports

The combination of snow and steep avalanche-prone terrain seals much of the Noisy–Diobsud Wilderness and adjoining roadless areas to winter recreation. The Sauk Mountain Road, from snowline to a cliff band at about 3,900 feet, offers a relatively safe intermediate midwinter tour, with good views of the Skagit and Sauk valleys from the upper portions of the road. Avalanche slopes make travel higher up the mountain inadvisable.

At the north end of the wilderness, the relatively gentle, lightly timbered ridge leading to Anderson Butte and Anderson Lakes (Trail #611) is an excellent advanced basic trip, with good downhill runs in the basin below the lakes. Snow levels will determine how much of FR 1107 must be skied to reach the ridge trail route.

12

NORTH CASCADES NATIONAL PARK COMPLEX (STEPHEN MATHER WILDERNESS)

LOCATION: In Whatcom, Skagit, and Chelan counties, between the Canadian border and Lake Chelan

SIZE: Total park: 505,000 acres; wilderness: 504,614 acres. Total Ross Lake National Recreational Area: 117,600 acres; wilderness: 74,000 acres. Total Lake Chelan National Recreational Area: 62,000 acres, wilderness: 56,000 acres

STATUS: National Park, Ross Lake NRA, Lake Chelan NRA, and Designated Wilderness Area (1988)

TERRAIN: Rugged, rocky, glaciated peaks rising locally as much as 7,000 feet above deep, forested, glacier-gouged and stream-cut valleys. Ross, Diablo, and Gorge lakes were created by Seattle City Light dams.

ELEVATION: 400 to 9,210 feet

MANAGEMENT: National Park Service

TOPOGRAPHIC MAPS: Bacon Peak, Big Devil Peak, Cascade Pass, Copper Mountain, Crater Mountain, Damnation Peak, Diablo Dam, Eldorado Peak, Forbidden Peak, Gilbert, Goode Mtn., Hozomeen Mtn., Jack Mtn., Marblemount, McAlester Mtn., McGregor Mtn., Mount Blum, Mount Sefrit, Mount Shuksan, Mount Triumph, Mt. Arriva, Mt. Challenger, Mt. Logan, Mt. Lyall, Mt. Prophet, Mt. Redoubt, Mt. Spickard, Pinnacle Mountain, Pumpkin Mtn., Ross Dam, Shuksan Arm, Skagit Peak, Sonny Boy Lakes, Stehekin, Sun Mountain

The Challenger Glacier and Mount Challenger in North Cascades National Park

The "National Park Complex" consists of three components: the park itself, and the Lake Chelan and Ross Lake National Recreation Areas. The latter area divides the park into two separate pieces, one to its north, and one to its south. Each of these segments is a vast wilderness in its own right, with outstanding peaks, spire-laden ridges, and an extensive collection of alpine glaciers.

The North Cascades National Park encompasses some of the wildest, most rugged, and untracked terrain in the Cascade Range. Although there are nominally 390 miles of maintained trails in the park, this figure is somewhat misleading, as most individual trails are quite long, and vast stretches of the park are accessible only by cross-country travel, much of which requires mountaineering skills. Multiday mini-expeditions are required to reach many of these remote areas. The most popular day-use area is Cascade Pass, due to its relative ease of access as well as its spectacular alpine scenery. Unfortunately, hordes of visitors are severely stressing this fragile environment, despite valiant efforts by the Park Service to preserve it.

The Ross Lake National Recreation Area consists of a narrow corridor along the North Cascades Scenic Highway, which bisects North Cascades National Park, and a similar corridor along the east side of the park enclosing Ross Lake. The highway and the exploitation of the Skagit River drainage for hydroelectric power are the reasons for excluding the NRA from the national park. Recreation in the area is heavily boat-oriented; there are 19 different campsites along the shores of Ross and Diablo lakes, many accessible only by boat. The outstanding alpine scenery of the adjacent park and Pasayten Wilderness, with their many glaciers and jagged peaks, can be admired from a number of spots along the area's lakes and trails.

The broad, deep, glacier-carved valley of the Stehekin River, in the Lake Chelan NRA, is one of the most remote such valleys in the state. It can be reached only by steamer from Chelan, 51 miles to the south, by private boat, floatplane, private aircraft, or by hiking or riding horseback over connecting trails to the east and west. The valley floor is framed by steep cliffs rising more than 7,000 feet to rugged peaks. Streams cascade down these slopes, often ending in beautiful waterfalls near the valley floor. One of these, 312-foot Rainbow Falls, can be seen from a campground and picnic area 2 miles northwest of Stehekin. During summer months, the park runs a shuttle van service (fee charged) up the Stehekin Valley Road, with stops at trailheads and campgrounds en route.

Climate

The climate varies dramatically by location: the west side of the park complex receives much heavier precipitation than the east slopes. West of the north–south backbone ridges, the annual precipitation is near 110 inches, most falling between November and May in the form of snow; annual snowfall exceeds 500 inches. Although the Ross Lake RNA is technically on the wetter western side of the Cascade crest, it is in the rain shadow of the Skagit and Picket ranges, and therefore receives significantly less precipitation than one would expect for a west-side region. The mean annual precipitation at Ross Lake ranges between 66 to 75 inches.

West-side temperatures tend to be mild; mean January temperatures on the lower slopes range between 15 and 25 degrees, with temperatures dropping below that at higher altitudes. Average summer highs are in the mid-70s in the valleys, and in the 60s to low 70s at upper elevations.

Because Lake Chelan is on the drier east side of the Cascades, annual precipitation there averages only 33 inches. Most of this falls between October and April as snow, 109 inches of it, that accumulates to depths of 5 to 7 feet. The higher trails are generally clear by July. Rain in the east is a rarity between May and September. Temperatures here reach the high 80s to 90s in summer, and lows in winter average between zero and 20 degrees.

Plants and Wildlife

Forest communities within the park vary both by location, east or west of the backbone ranges, and altitude. Forests in west-side valleys consist of western hemlock, Douglas-fir, western red cedar, and red alder, and in damper spots willows, vine maple, big-leaf maple, birch, dogwood, black cottonwood, and chokecherry. In the understory are salal, Oregon grape, huckleberry, Oregon boxwood, twinflower, and bracken fern, and in drier spots kinnikinnick, dogbane, and spirea.

With increasing altitude the forest mix is dominated more by Pacific silver fir; some Alaska cedar joins the community, as do Sitka alder and mountain hemlock. In the highest zone on the west, mountain hemlock and subalpine fir prevail; there are local occurrences of alpine larch, whitebark pine, juniper, and several species of willow. Alpine meadows above treeline have a ground cover of grasses and heathers, and summer wildflowers such as glacier lily, cinquefoil, phlox, lupine, saxifrage, and penstemon.

At the highest levels east of the crest, mountain hemlock and subalpine fir make up large portions of the forest; Sitka alder, whitebark pine, juniper, and willow are still present, but a new addition to the forest is Englemann spruce. With decreasing elevation, Douglas-fir, western hemlock, Alaska cedar, western larch, and western white pine reappear.

Lower-level forests east of the divide shift to Pacific silver fir, grand fir, Douglas-fir, western hemlock, western red cedar, ponderosa pine, lodgepole pine, whitebark pine, willows, Sitka alder, vine maple, and dogwood. The Big Beaver Valley in the Ross Lake NRA holds one of the

CANADA
UNITED STATES

Silver Lake

Mount Spickard
8,979 ft.

Mox Peaks
8,504 ft.

Silver Creek

Perry Creek

Hozomeen Mountain
▲ 8,066 ft.

Hozomeen CG

Willow Creek Tr

Hozomeen Lake

Ridley Lake

Willow Lake

Lightning Creek

Freezeout Creek

Freezout Creek Tr

ROSS LAKE NATIONAL RECREATION AREA

Desolation Peak
6,102 ft.
▲

Skagit Peak
6,663 ft. ▲

Little Beaver Tr

Little Beaver Creek

Arctic Creek

Mist Creek

Ross Lake

Desolation Lookout Tr

Lightning Creek Tr

749

Three Fools Creek

No Name Creek

No Name Lake

Skymo Creek

Skymo Lake

Mount Prophet
7,640 ft.

PASAYTEN WILDERNESS AREA

Luna Creek

Luna Peak
8,285 ft. ▲

McMillan Creek

Elephant Butte ▲
7,379 ft.

Big Beaver Creek

Big Beaver Tr

Dry Creek

Dry Creek Tr

752

Devils Creek

East Bank Tr

May Creek

NORTH CASCADES NATIONAL PARK

McMillan Spire
8,000 ft.

Azure Lake

Mount Degenhart
8,000 ft.

Range

Sourdough Lake

Sourdough Mountain
6,107 ft. ▲

Pierce Mountain
4,777 ft.
▲

Jack Mountain
9,066 ft.
▲

Crater Mountain
8,128 ft.
▲

Stetattle Cr Tr

Stetattle Creek

Sourdough Mtn Tr

Pierce Mtn Wy

Diablo Lake Tr

Ruby Arm

Jack Mtn Tr

Crater Creek

Mount Ross
6,053 ft. ▲

Davis Peak
7,051 ft. ▲

Diablo

Gorge Cr

Gorge Lake

Diablo Lake

Thunder Arm

Ruby Creek

20

To Winthrop

Goodell Creek Tr

Skagit River

Pyramid Lake

Pyramid Peak
7,182 ft.

Ruby Mountain
7,408 ft.
▲

Panther Creek Tr

Silwell Creek

Goodell CG

Ladder Creek

Paul Bunyan's Stump
7,480 ft. ▲

Colonial Cr Colonial Creek CG

Colonial Peak
7,771 ft. ▲

Neve Creek

Thunder Creek Tr

Panther Creek

NCNP

Newhalem

Newhalem Creek CG

Newhalem Creek Tr

The Needle
8,152 ft.

Snowfield Peak
8,347 ft. ▲

NCNP

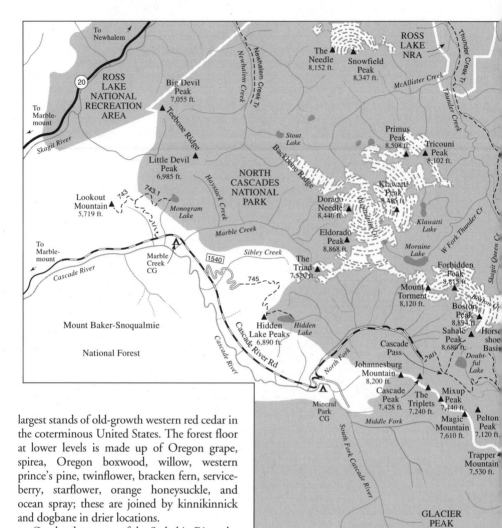

largest stands of old-growth western red cedar in the coterminous United States. The forest floor at lower levels is made up of Oregon grape, spirea, Oregon boxwood, willow, western prince's pine, twinflower, bracken fern, serviceberry, starflower, orange honeysuckle, and ocean spray; these are joined by kinnikinnick and dogbane in drier locations.

On the slopes east of the Stehekin River the woodlands shift to Pacific silver fir, whitebark fir, and western larch; higher still the forest becomes subalpine fir, Englemann spruce, and subalpine fir. At upper elevations the forest tapers to subalpine larch, and underfoot, heather and rock.

Among the larger mammals found in the park's interior are elk, mule deer, white-tailed deer, moose, mountain goat, black bear, mountain lion, lynx, and red fox. Smaller inhabitants include porcupine, mink, raccoon, striped skunk, wolverine, ermine, river otter, beaver, marten, snowshoe hare, and long-tailed weasel. The smallest creatures found here are moles, pika, hoary marmot, chipmunks, squirrels, voles, deermouse, and bog lemming.

The most often seen of the 150 bird species in the area are blue and ruffed grouse, American flicker, red-breasted nuthatch, black-capped chickadee, Steller's jays, and ptarmigan. Species on state or federal threatened and endangered lists that have been sighted in the park are fishers, gray wolf, grizzly bear, peregrine falcon, bald eagle, northern goshawk, pileated woodpecker, northern spotted owl, sandhill crane, American white pelican, Swainson's hawk, trumpeter swan, ferruginous hawk, and common loon.

Geology

The southeast–northwest orientation of the major geological structures in the North Cascades tends to confirm tectonic theories that the region was once a micro-continent located in the mid-Pacific that collided with the North American continent some 50 million to 90 million years ago. This terrane is thought to have made initial contact in southern California, then slid northwest before becoming firmly docked to North America between the Pacific Northwest and Alaska. The collision triggered the uplift of the Cascade crest, and folding and fracturing, oriented in the direction of the movement of the plates, created the sheer north faces characteristic of peaks in this region.

The backbone of the area is composed of older metamorphic gneisses formed between 500 million and 700 million years ago, the crystalline core of the micro-continent. A long thrust fault runs north–south along the west side of Mount Shuksan. On its west side are slates and

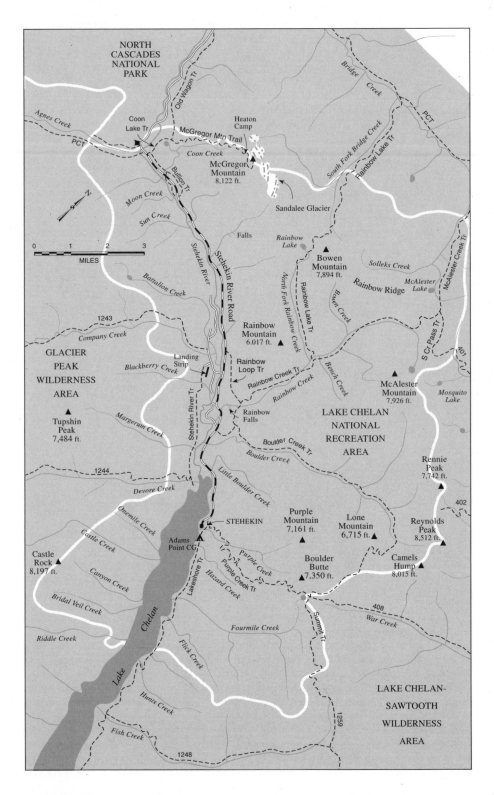

schists ranging between 300 million and 600 million years in age. The rock on the east side of the complex consists of metamorphosed schists, gneisses, and a good deal of migmatite, more than 180 million years old, formed off the east coast of the North Cascades micro-continent long before it joined the west coast of North America.

This base was intruded about 100 million years ago by granodiorite and quartz diorite in the area northeast of Bridge Creek and along the line of ridges between the upper Stehekin River and the town of Newhalem. The Picket Range and the Mount Redoubt area are made up of relatively young granite and granodiorite intrusions that occurred 10 million to 40 million years ago, after the docking of North Cascades terrane.

A major north–south fault line runs along the east bank of Ross Lake. The region between this fault and the Hozomeen fault line to the east that marks the west boundary of the Methow graben, is composed of uplifted greenstone, a metamorphosed basalt. Jack Mountain, on the southwest edge of the Ross Lake RNA, is believed to have been thrust to the east along a horizontal fault line as it overrode younger sedimentary rocks.

An ice age that began 2 million to 3 million years ago created thick glaciers that carved deep valleys in the underlying rock. About 15,000 years ago the Puget lobe of the Cordilleran ice sheet reached east up the Skagit Valley to the vicinity of Newhalem. Another lobe of that glacial ice rode down the Skagit headwaters from Canada, flowing over divides untouched in previous periods of glaciation. However, the portion of the Skagit Valley between Newhalem and Ross Lake was not in the route of the glacial flow; the deep V-shaped river course here was cut solely by erosion.

As the glaciers that formed the Stehekin Valley and Lake Chelan retreated, a lobe of the continental ice sheet advanced across the Columbia River Plateau to deposit a moraine that blocked the lower end of the valley now filled by Lake Chelan, causing the level of the lake to rise by hundreds of feet. The 51.5-mile-long, 1,548-foot-deep lake has seen many adjustments in its water level over the ages, some caused by earthquakes, others by man. Today it is the largest lake in the coterminous U.S. that is so deeply carved through the mountains that frame it. Damming the Chelan River at its outlet in 1928 stabilized the lake at its current level.

Most of the present surface features of the park are a result of glacial erosion by both continental ice sheets and alpine glaciers. The major drainages have steep walls and the wide U-shaped floors characteristic of glacier-formed valleys. The lower ends of many creeks and rivers have carved narrow, steep-walled gorges through alluvial deposits near their mouths. Alpine glaciers, the ancestors of those remaining today, are responsible for cutting the dozens of cliff-walled cirques and chiseling the sharp ragged peaks that line the major ridges throughout the region.

History

There is some evidence of prehistoric use of the North Cascades by natives who quarried chert for tools and weapons, fished for salmon, and visited the high country to hunt mountain goat. Artifacts found near Hozomeen Mountain indicate a long period of Indian habitation, and two tribes lived in or regularly visited the area: the Lower Thompson tribe above the Skagit Gorge, and the Skagits below it. Fading lines of petroglyphs on lakeside cliffs opposite Stehekin retain an indecipherable record of early inhabitants in the Lake Chelan area. The few passes through the rugged mountains were critical trade routes between tribes in the Puget Sound and those in the Columbia River Basin. One of the most popular routes, still followed by today's trails, crossed the Cascade crest at Twisp Pass, descended along Bridge Creek to the Stehekin River, then headed upstream over Cascade Pass and dropped to the Skagit River via the Cascade River.

The earliest non-natives in this part of the Cascades were trappers and fur traders who first entered the area in the late 1700s via Cascade Pass, using the old Indian trade route. A Swiss topographer surveyed the boundary between Great Britain (Canada) and the United States between 1857 and 1859, and mapped some of the upper Skagit drainage.

The first whites to explore the head of Lake Chelan were surveyors who, in the 1870s, were seeking possible rail routes over the Cascades. In 1882 an Army group under Lieutenant H. H.

Pierce claimed to have discovered the head of the lake and the river flowing into it; the officer graciously named the river for himself, but it is now called the Stehekin.

In 1877 prospectors headed up the Skagit but found only traces of placer below the mouth of its gorge. They later struggled upstream to the vicinity of Ruby Creek, where they found increasingly better placers, enough to trigger a minor gold rush. Prospectors poured into the area at the end of the 1870s, but access was a constant inhibitor to mining production, since the Skagit Gorge could only be traversed via precarious cliff-wall ledges and, at Devils Elbow, a shaky suspension bridge and a system of ladders. The Fraser River and Caribou gold strikes soon lured most prospectors north, although limited mining was carried on in the area until the 1950s.

Between 1885 and 1889, highly promising galena ledges were discovered in Boston Basin, near Cascade Pass. These were traced into the Doubtful Lake and Horseshoe basins. All three basins were rapidly plastered with claims over the next three to four years. The ore, rich in silver and lead, with traces of gold, piled up near tunnel mouths for lack of a means to get it to market.

In 1889 the first steamer on Lake Chelan was launched, and settlers moved to the head of the lake during 1889 and 1890. By 1891, a trail ran 6.5 miles up the south side of the river, then crossed it and followed its north side into the upper valley. The initial road up the valley was platted in 1891, and the current route was built in 1897. In ensuing years prospectors worked downstream from Cascade Pass to Bridge Creek, Flat Creek, Agnes Creek, Coon Lake, Company Creek, Rainbow Creek, and Boulder Creek. The influx of 700 to 800 miners in 1892 eventually dissipated as the value of the ore played out. Limited mining activity continued in Horseshoe Basin until 1948. A rich silver strike was discovered at the head of Thunder Creek in 1892, but again transportation difficulties thwarted exploitation of the find, and operations there folded by 1913. Today the economic mainstays of the tiny community of Stehekin are recreation and tourism.

Opening access to the upper Skagit and creating a link between the Skagit and Methow val-

Remnants of the old Black Warrior Mine above Horseshoe Basin

leys concerned both regions as early as 1893. Whatcom County partisans lobbied for a route over Hannegan and Whatcom passes, while Skagit County citizens preferred one up the Skagit River and over Cascade Pass. When the former route was ruled not feasible, proponents of the latter split into the Cascade Pass crowd and another faction that wished to extend the crude road that had been cut from Winthrop to the Harts Pass mines.

Cascade Pass was selected, money was appropriated in 1895, and construction in 1896 pushed a rough road on the west to within three miles of the pass, where the road end remains today. A dirt road was cut up the east side of the pass from Stehekin to Bridge Creek in 1899, and was later extended to the Black Warrior Mine in Horseshoe Basin. Despite heavy lobbying to complete the road across the pass, nothing was achieved by 1929, when the stock market crash eliminated funding. The scenic and wilderness value of the area was recognized before momentum for construction could be regenerated, and in 1934 it became part of the newly created North Cascades Primitive Area.

The die was cast in 1940 when Forest Service managers, probably out of a desire to retrieve logs cut during the Ross Dam construction, convinced the Highway Department to back a route over Rainy and Washington passes. Road construction from Newhalem to Thunder Creek was started in 1958, and from the Methow toward Washington Pass in 1962. The long-awaited North Cascades Scenic Highway opened in 1972.

Skagit Power was the first to attempt damming the Skagit in 1909; the effort failed due to problems getting construction materials into the gorge. In 1918 Seattle City Light began construction of a diversion dam at Gorge Creek to supply power to the city and to other dam projects upriver. The railroad was extended up the Skagit to Newhalem in 1921 to support construction, and the first dam was finished in 1924. The design and construction of a second dam at Diablo began immediately. After delays caused by the financial market crash in 1929, the 389-foot Diablo Dam was finished in 1936. A year later the need for additional power triggered design work on the Ross Dam. This 540-foot-high structure was completed in 1949. The last dam built replaced the original diversion dam at Newhalem with the present 300-foot-high Gorge Dam in 1960. Although City Light applied for permits for three additional dams in the drainage, rising environmental consciousness in the 1980s stymied any further hydroelectric projects.

Vestiges of the region's history still remain within the park, and have been designated or proposed as National Historic Register sites. These include old log cabins and backcountry shelters, the Black Warrior Mine, monuments marking the international boundary, and the three remaining lookouts of the six originally constructed in the region.

ACTIVITIES

Hiking

NOOKSACK RIVER TRAILS

Although some references list the trail from Hannegan Campground to Whatcom Pass as the Hannegan–Whatcom Trail, we will follow the more traditional segmentation into the Hannegan Trail, between the campground and Hannegan Pass; the Chilliwack Trail, from the pass to the Canadian border; and the Brush Creek Trail, between the Chilliwack Trail and Whatcom Pass.

Copper Mountain Trail. 15 miles/m (H). At a junction (4,240 ft) northeast of Hannegan Pass, this path heads up the steep forested face on the north side of the drainage. After a few switchbacks it crosses the upper forks of Hells Gorge, where it breaks into alpine meadows and traces the ridgetop (5,500 ft) east. The open crest offers endless views of Ruth Mountain, Mount Shuksan, and the vast expanse of the wilderness heart of the park. At 3 miles a spur drops to tiny Egg Lake (5,180 ft); the main route continues along the scenic ridgetop to the lookout atop Copper Mountain (6,260 ft). Here a sweeping panorama embraces the Border Peaks, Slesse, Nodoubt, Redoubt, Bear, Mox Peaks, and the whole jagged crest of the north Pickets. Switchbacks descend northeast from the open crest past the tight cliff-bound cirque containing Copper Lake (5,263 ft). The way enters broken subalpine forest, then continues down through long switchbacks in old-growth forest to rejoin the Chilliwack Trail north of Indian Creek (2,320 ft).

Chilliwack Trail. 17 miles/m (H,S). This is an old miner's route to the Caribou gold fields in Canada. From Hannegan Pass (5,046 ft) a few switchbacks through subalpine forest lead to meadows at the head of the Chilliwack River, where the Copper Mountain Trail takes off. The rapid, wooded descent to Copper Creek Camp (3,100 ft) is followed by a gentler grade that works its way down near the river. In another mile a cable car provides safe passage across the Chilliwack for hikers. The route bends around a ridge nose and past a junction with the Brush Creek Trail, then continues down the widening valley bottom, most of the way in brush and dense timber. Beyond Indian Creek it meets the north end of the Copper Mountain Trail. The Chilliwack is followed downstream to the Canadian border (2,050 ft), and on to Chilliwack Lake.

Brush Creek Trail. 5.1 miles/m (H,S). Near the mouth of Brush Creek (2,640 ft) this route leaves the Chilliwack Trail and traces the north side of the creek upstream, always deep in woods and along brushy stream bottom. A gradual climb gives way to a steady uphill grind to Whatcom Pass (5,206 ft) and the Little Beaver Trail. Spectacular views from the pass are but a hint of what is available from short boot-paths south to the shoulder of Whatcom Peak or north to the meadowed arm above Tapto Lakes (5,670 to 5,750 ft). To the south lie the massive summit of Whatcom Peak and the immense white swath of the Challenger Glacier sweeping up to rugged, rocky summit pinnacles.

WEST-SIDE ROSS LAKE TRAILS

Big Beaver Trail. 15 miles/m (H,S). Reach Ross Dam either by boat uplake from Diablo or via the Happy Falls Trail from Highway 20. Cross the dam (1,617 ft) and pick up the trail on its north side as it contours the sidehill 200 feet above the lake. After passing Ross Lake Resort, a gentle grade ascends across open sidehills with views of the lake, Ruby Arm, and Jack Mountain. The path swings north; contours northwest through Douglas-fir, hemlock, silver fir, and cedar; then drops in a few lazy switchbacks to a footbridge across Big Beaver Creek (1,618 ft). This point can also be reached by water taxi from the resort to Big Beaver Camp.

The way follows the north side of the creek up the broad glacier-carved valley, passing lush green creek-bottom marshes, ponds, small lakes, and huge western red cedar. At 6.2 miles (1,900 ft) the trail enters the park and climbs rapidly along plunging Big Beaver Creek. Upstream the grade eases as it ascends to Beaver Pass (3,620 ft). The way is mostly in heavy forest with occasional avalanche-track vistas west to the vast glacial cirques and towers of the Pickets. After crossing the pass, switchbacks wind down into the Little Beaver Valley to meet the Little Beaver Trail (2,440 ft).

Little Beaver Trail. 16.9 miles/m (H,S). The trailhead, on the trackless west shore of Ross Lake, must be reached via a boat to Little Beaver Campground (1,650 ft). The path climbs switchbacks above the narrow channel at the mouth of Little Beaver Creek, then heads west above the creek. At 2.5 miles it enters the park and wanders up the bottom of a wide glacier-cut valley between high, forested walls to meet the Big Beaver Trail (2,440 ft). A gradual ascent continues up an ever-narrowing valley, with cliffs encroaching on either side. At 2,950 feet kiss the easy grade good-bye and fight through 56 switchbacks hacked up wooded cliffs to Whatcom Pass (5,206 ft). Here are outstanding views of the northern Pickets and the immense white expanse of the Challenger Glacier.

SKAGIT RIVER TRAILS

Thornton Lakes Trail. 4.8 miles/m (H). From the end of the Thornton Creek Road (2,500 ft), 11 miles east of Marblemount, the tread swings into the Thornton Creek drainage on an abandoned logging road, passing through clearcuts. After crossing the creek and reversing direction, the old road gives way to a true trail, which turns uphill with a vengeance. The route switchbacks up through old-growth forest, then pauses briefly in a small flat at the park boundary before switchbacks resume to gain the ridge crest (5,050 ft). A ridgetop scramble north to Trappers Peak (5,966 ft) is rewarded by an outstanding view of the ragged Picket Range. The path drops a short distance west to lower Thornton Lake (4,486 ft), nestled below the cliff wall of Trappers Peak. Scramble routes work up to Middle (4,700 ft) and Upper (5,040 ft) Thornton Lakes. These two lakes are not free of ice until mid- to late summer.

Newhalem Creek Trail. 6.6 miles/e (H,S). An old logging road leaves the campground (520 ft) on the south side of Highway 20 at Newhalem, and heads south up Newhalem Creek. In 2.8 miles it enters the park and passes through a series of large clearcuts to a trail-end campsite (2,300 ft). The slashes in the forest offer views of jagged Teebone Ridge.

Sourdough Mountain Trail. 5.5 miles/m (H,S). The route starts at the northwest side of Diablo (900 ft), and shoots straight up the wooded hillside, resorting to switchbacks only when the slope gets *really* steep. The nose of the ridge is gained at 3,800 feet, where the route enters the park and continues a long gradual ascent north to Sourdough Creek. It climbs east and, with a few more switchbacks, reaches the rocky meadow atop Sourdough Mountain. The lookout, originally built in 1916 and rebuilt in 1933, sits atop the high point (5,985 ft) at the east end of the mountain. The panorama includes nearby Colonial, Snowfield, Pyramid, and Pinnacle peaks, and in the distance Boston and Buckner, the Picket Range, Canada's Chilliwack Range, Skagit Peak, and Jack and Crater mountains. Below are Diablo and Ross lakes.

Pyramid Lake Trail. 2.25 miles/e (H). The track leaves the south side of Highway 20 (1,100 ft) east of the spur road to Diablo, and climbs a forested rib on the east side of Pyramid Creek. A gradual ascent through old-growth Douglas-fir and hemlock and up a last few switchbacks ends at the pocket meadow holding tiny Pyramid Lake (2,630 ft). The clearing gives a glimpse of the impressive 1,000-foot-high summit block of Pyramid Peak.

Diablo Lake Trail. 3.8 miles/m (H). About 1.5 miles east of the spur to Diablo, turn north on the road down to Diablo Dam, cross the top of the dam, and in little over a mile reach a onetime resort, the future home of the North Cascades Environmental Center (1,227 ft). A path leaves east and wanders upstream along the banks of Deer Creek to the base of cliffs above Buster Brown Flat. It picks its way up and across a narrow bench between cliff bands and contours a rocky bluff (1,820 ft) with great views down to Diablo Lake and Thunder Arm and up to the Colonial Glacier and its surrounding peaks. The route rounds a steep ridge nose, traverses lightly forested cliffs, then descends to the suspension bridge (1,220 ft) across the Skagit below Ross Dam. From the east side of the river, the powerhouse road is followed uphill to the Happy Falls Trail, which leads back to Highway 20.

Thunder Creek Trail. 18.9 miles/m (H,S). From the south end of Colonial Creek Campground (1,220 ft) a path heads along the bank of Thunder Arm to a bridge across Thunder Creek. The way continues through dense old-growth Douglas-fir, hemlock, and cedar into the heart of the Thunder Creek valley. A few meadows resulting from old forest fires offer dramatic views up to the Neve Glacier and Snowfield and Colonial peaks. At 6 miles (1,940 ft) the trail enters the park south of McAllister Creek. It crosses Fisher Creek and follows it steeply uphill to avoid a large valley-bottom swamp in the Thunder Creek basin. At 3,130 feet the Fisher Creek Trail breaks away, and this route descends steep slopes to the valley floor (1,950 ft) near the south end of the swamp.

Creek and trail climb a narrowing drainage to Skagit Queen Creek (3,040 ft), then the route switchbacks up a steep shelf to an alpine valley as it traces the creek bed upstream through narrowing canyon walls. The way weaves up the basin headwall above the source of Thunder Creek to the rock cleft of Park Creek Pass (6,080 ft), where it meets the Park Creek Trail from the Stehekin.

Fisher Creek Trail. 10.5 miles/m (H). After leaving the Thunder Creek Trail (3,130 ft), this route follows the densely forested bottom of Fisher Creek east below Ragged Ridge to a basin meadow (5,200 ft) north of Mount Arriva. The trail turns abruptly up the steep north slopes and grinds in switchbacks to Easy Pass (6,500 ft).

Easy Pass Trail. 2 miles/m (H). Easy? Not really. The name is relative, comparing this pass to other passes across Ragged Ridge that are real bears. From the pass (6,500 ft) the way wiggles down talus slopes along Easy Pass Creek, then enters open alpine forest as it continues its rapid, rough descent northeast to Highway 20 (3,680 ft), 6.2 miles west of Rainy Pass.

EAST-SIDE ROSS LAKE TRAILS

East Bank Trail. 20 miles/m (H). From the Panther Creek Bridge (1,800 ft) on Highway 20, the trail drops north to cross Ruby Creek, then heads west above the shore of Ruby Arm. In 3 miles the route passes the Jack Mountain Trail, then swings north through Hidden Hand Pass (2,540 ft). It wanders slowly downhill to the north to close with the east bank of Ross Lake near Roland Point. The trail remains near the shore of this inland fjord for the remainder of its 20-mile length. The Dry Creek Pass Trail heads east into the Pasayten Wilderness about a mile north of Devils Creek, and the Lightning Creek Trail heads inland on the north side of its namesake. The East Bank Trail ends at the lakeshore 2 miles farther, at the start of the Desolation Lookout Trail (1,750 ft).

Jack Mountain Trail. 3 miles/m (H). From the 3-mile point of the East Bank Trail (1,930 ft) this route heads in the only direction it seems to know—up! Fifty-four switchbacks later the way breaks into beautiful meadows for a more gradual lateral ascent east to its end at a ridgetop saddle (6,000 ft). Gentle open slopes lead north to a pair of knobs with breathtaking views of Jack and Crater mountains, the Picket Range, and Pyramid, Pinnacle, Colonial, and Snowfield peaks.

Desolation Peak Lookout Trail. 4.5 miles/m (H). At the north end of the East Bank Trail (1,720 ft) the route heads sharply upward, switchbacking all the way, through young forest regenerated after a 1926 burn. Occasional open spots give glimpses down to Ross Lake. The way breaks out into meadows at 4,500 feet, but unrelenting switchbacks continue up to the ridge crest and north along the crest to a bald knob (5,895 ft). Fields of flowers escort the track to the lookout atop Desolation Peak (6,102 ft). North, the sheer 2,000-foot walls of Hozomeen Mountain loom close at hand. South, the icy expanse of the Nohokomeen Glacier sweeps up to the massive summit of Jack Peak. In the distance are the Pasayten highlands, Eldorado, Snowfield, Colonial, the Picket Range, and Mount Baker, and below is the blue ribbon of Ross Lake.

Lightning Creek Trail. 10 miles/m (H,S). This link between the East Side Trail and the Canadian border leaves that trail at Lightning Creek (1,700 ft). It switchbacks out of the narrow creek bottom to the sidehill above the creek, follows the drainage east and north, then descends gradually to meet the creek at Deer Lick Cabin (1,920 ft). Just beyond, Trail #749 heads east into the Pasayten Wilderness. The route continues north, along the east bank of Lightning Creek to the dense, foreboding cedar grove of Nightmare Camp. A gradual ascent traces Lightning Creek as it swings west to its source, Willow Lake (2,853 ft).

Willow Creek (Jackass Pass) Trail. 5 miles/e (H,S). The last link between the East Bank Trail and Canada heads west from Willow Lake (2,853 ft), descending a shallow, forested valley. It

Columbia tiger lily

passes a short spur to Hozomeen Lake (2,923 ft), then wanders down to the Hozomeen Campground, on Ross Lake just south of the Canadian border. This trailhead can be reached via the road south into the Skagit Valley Recreation Area from Trans-Canada Highway 1, near Hope, B.C.

STEHEKIN RIVER TRAILS

Pacific Crest National Scenic Trail. 13.2 miles/m (H,S). This trail, commonly known as the PCT, continues its journey north from the Stehekin River Road at Bridge Creek (2,170 ft), 16 miles upstream from Stehekin. It follows the broad, forested rim above the 200-foot-deep Bridge Creek gorge, with occasional glimpses northwest to Ragged and Memaloose ridges, then drops to meet the Walker Park Trail (2,580 ft) at the mouth of the North Fork. The route continues upstream above the steep north bank of Bridge Creek, then enters a widening valley floor as it drops to the creek bank. Avalanche swaths provide breaks in the forest cover as the way heads east past the Rainbow Lake Trail to the Twisp Pass Trail. The path continues along the west bank of the creek to Highway 20 at Rainy Pass (4,900 ft).

Walker Park (North Fork of Bridge Creek) Trail. 9.5 miles/m-d (H,S). This old miner's route leaves the PCT at its 2.7-mile point, and heads north along the North Fork of Bridge Creek in a deep, densely wooded, U-shaped valley. Avalanche tracks offer brief brushy peeks to the high cliffs that frame the drainage. The original trail led north past prospects in Grizzly and Fisher creeks to Fisher Pass. The present trail fords Grizzly Creek (3,150 ft) and continues along the North Fork, breaking into valley-bottom meadows with breathtaking views of waterfalls cascading from the hanging glaciers at the base of the faces of Goode and Storm King mountains. The way fades into meadows (4,200 ft) in the great cirque on the south side of Mount Logan.

Twisp Pass (Fireweed) Trail. 5 miles/m (H,S). From the PCT at the mouth of McAlester Creek (3,640 ft), this old Indian path climbs gradually but relentlessly along the East Fork of McAlester Creek to Dagger Lake (5,508 ft). The way then climbs to the head of the drainage and Twisp Pass (6,064 ft), where it becomes Trail #432 as it leaves the park.

Stiletto Peak Trail. 3.5 miles/d (H). From Trail #2172, 0.6 mile north of the Twisp Pass Trail, switchbacks climb a steep wooded slope with no respite for 2,100 vertical feet. The way then contours ridgetop meadows, crosses a small notch to a tiny creek-head cirque, then climbs once more through parkland to the site of a fire lookout (7,223 ft) removed in 1953. The 360-degree views remain; these include Goode Mountain's face and broad glacier, Mount Benzarino, Frisco Mountain, Early Winter Spires, and Silver Star.

Park Creek Trail. 8 miles/m (H,S). Starting on the Stehekin River Road (2,310 ft) 18.5 miles from Stehekin, the route switchbacks up above the Park Creek gorge, bends into the drainage, skirts 800-foot-high cliffs at the southeast end of Park Creek Ridge, and enters the broadening valley bottom to the northwest. The way breaks into meadows as the valley opens to a wide cirque surrounded by waterfall-laced walls rising 4,000 feet to Booker and Buckner mountains, the Buckner Glacier, Storm King, and Goode Mountain. The track leaves the valley floor in a chain of switchbacks up a steep face to a pocket valley, where flowered meadows, heathers, and snowfields lead to the narrow rockbound notch of Park Creek Pass (6,080 ft).

CASCADE RIVER TRAILS

Cascade Pass Trail. 6.5 miles/m (H). This historic trail, a route across 5,423-foot-high Cascade Pass that was used by Indians and early explorers, has been so loved to death in recent years that the Park Service has turned it into a near city-park path to protect the fragile ecology. On the west the trail leaves the end of the Cascade River Road (3,650 ft). Easy-grade switchbacks crawl through forest to break into parkland, fingertips away from Cascade Peak, the Triplets, and the rumble of ice peeling off the north face of Johannesburg. The route descends east of the pass to Pelton Basin campsites, the Horseshoe Basin Trail, and a constantly changing horizon of jagged peaks on either side. At its east terminus the path joins the Stehekin River Road at Cottonwood Camp (2,750 ft).

Horseshoe Basin Trail. 1.5 miles/m (H). In pre-wilderness days this road was used to transport ore and mining supplies between Stehekin and the Black Warrior Mine. Today the path leaves the Cascade Pass Trail between Doubtful and Basin creeks (3,640 ft), then bends north into the latter's basin. A few switchbacks at the end of the gradual climb end at the mine (5,000 ft), wrapped in lower cirque cliffs draped by dozens of ribbon waterfalls. The mine ruins are interesting to explore (with care). Don't remove artifacts! The more hardy may choose to search for old miner's tracks through the cliffs east of the mine to gain the wider upper cirque, which blazes with a rainbow of wildflower colors soon after the snows melt. Mining claims once filled this basin up to the base of aptly named Ripsaw Ridge, as prospectors chased galena ledges exposed by glaciers.

Trail #745, Hidden Lake. 4.5 miles/e-m (H). From the clearcut end of FR 1540 (4,000 ft), the path climbs first through forest, then breaks into meadows and wildflowers as it switchbacks up to the head of the East Fork of Sibley Creek. A long diagonal ascent followed by a lazy pair of

Horseshoe Basin and Ripsaw Ridge

zigzags reaches a saddle (6,590 ft) above Hidden Lake. The main trail continues a short distance to the lookout cabin atop Hidden Lake Peaks (6,890 ft), maintained by volunteers. A rough way-trail drops from the saddle down talus slopes to the tight cirque holding Hidden Lake (5,733 ft).

Trail #743, Lookout Mountain. 4.7 miles/m (H). East of Lookout Creek the track leaves the Cascade River Road (1,250 ft) for a knee-numbing switchback assault on the wooded ridge to the north. The grade tapers to just steep 2,200 feet higher as it continues its climb to the junction with Trail #743.1 (4,150 ft). More twisty trail gains a meadowed side slope with views into the Cascade River drainage. After zigzags conquer a steep cliff, the way winds around the east and south sides of a knob to a volunteer-maintained fire lookout (5,699 ft) with grand views of the Skagit River valley and the peaks of Cascade Pass.

Trail #743.1, Monogram Lake. 2.2 miles/m (H). Leaving Trail #743 (4,150 ft), this spur climbs steep timbered slopes and breaks into meadows as it swings around an open nose (5,400 ft), then descends to the shore of Monogram Lake (4,873 ft). North slopes sweep up to the Monogram Glacier and the peaks at the south end of Teebone Ridge.

LOWER STEHEKIN TRAILS

In summer a twice-a-day Park Service or concessionaire shuttle van will carry you up the Stehekin Valley Road for a fee. Private businesses also have taxi services available.

Lakeshore Trail. 4 miles/e (H,S). From the Golden West Visitor Center in Stehekin, the path heads south along the northeast shore of the lake. The grade is easy, with a few ups and downs that never rise more than 500 feet above the shore. The trail runs through stands of ponderosa pine and Douglas-fir with an understory decorated by a botanical dictionary of flowers, running from balsamroot to yellow bells. There are two campgrounds along the route, one a short distance from the trailhead and one near the RNA boundary beyond Flick Creek. At the RNA boundary, the route enters the Lake Chelan–Sawtooth Wilderness as Trail #1247, then continues another 13.2 miles to Prince Creek.

Purple Creek Trail. 8 miles/m (H,S). Also starting at Stehekin's Golden West Visitor Center, this route strikes uphill through Douglas-fir, ponderosa pine, and whitebark pine, twisting through 27 tight switchbacks before crossing Purple Creek. Another 30 switchbacks in mountain hemlock and subalpine fir, then in larch-rimmed meadows, reach tiny Lake Juanita (6,665 ft). A 0.5-mile spur leads west to the top of Boulder Butte (7,350 ft), the site of a fire lookout in the 1930s and '40s. Views span Lake Chelan, the Stehekin Valley, and a horizon of jagged peaks. Just above the lake, the Summit Trail heads southeast, and a few hundred feet farther is War Creek Pass (6,770 ft). Here Trail #408 heads east into the Lake Chelan–Sawtooth Wilderness, and the Boulder Creek Trail drops to the valley below.

Summit Trail. 2.4 miles/m (H,S). From Lake Juanita (6,665 ft) this path heads through larch and side-slope meadows below a southeast-trending ridge. After a gentle drop into open stands of ponderosa and whitebark pine the way ascends rocky meadows to a saddle (7,230 ft) and the NRA boundary. It continues as Trail #1259.

Rainbow Loop Trail. 3.2 miles/e (H,S). The south trailhead (1,170 ft) is 2.7 miles up-valley from Stehekin Landing. It climbs to a forested bench, and after passing the start of the Boulder Creek Trail, reaches an open bluff (2,200 ft) with views down to the valley and Lake Chelan. The path contours the bench, then crosses Rainbow Creek to the lower end of the Rainbow Creek Trail. A gradual descent rejoins the Stehekin Valley Road (1,230 ft) 5 miles from Stehekin Landing.

Boulder Creek Trail. 11.5 miles/m (H,S). Starting 0.8 mile from the south end of the Rainbow Loop Trail (2,100 ft), this route begins a steady grind up Boulder Creek, first through Douglas-fir, ponderosa, and whitebark pine, then through meadows. A traverse closes to the creek at 3,700 feet; the way traces the bank as the creek swings south into the head of the drainage. Here switchbacks gain the shoulder (6,530 ft) of Lone Mountain, where the forest opens to views of flowered meadows flowing from the summits of Reynolds and Rennie peaks. The wooded rib is followed southeast to a ridgeline hump (7,484 ft), the NRA border. The boundary is followed south across a few undulations to War Creek Pass (6,770 ft), to meet the Purple Creek Trail and Trail #408.

Rainbow Creek Trail. *10 miles/m (H,S).* This route leaves the Rainbow Loop Trail 1.5 miles from its south trailhead. Switchbacks climb above the west side of Rainbow Creek, then a traverse merges with the rising creek. Crossing to the east bank, the ascent continues through meadows to Bench Creek, the beginning of the Rainbow Lake Trail. A climb through dense old-growth forest recrosses the creek, and switchbacks gain McAlester Pass (6,017 ft). At the pass, meadows spotted with a few pines afford views of the steep north side of McAlester Mountain and the summits of the crest running north to Twisp Pass. The McAlester Creek Trail continues northwest, and the South Creek Pass Trail strikes southeast for 1.4 miles to South Pass (6,300 ft), where it continues into the Lake Chelan–Sawtooth Wilderness as Trail #401.

Rainbow Lake Trail. *6.1 miles/m (H,S).* From the Rainbow Creek Trail at Bench Creek (3,750 ft) this path switchbacks down to cross Rainbow Creek, then back up the opposite side as it heads west along the north fork of the creek. The track continues a gradual ascent through meadow breaks in the spruce forest to the head of the drainage. A brief climb of a rocky basin headwall reaches Rainbow Lake (5,630 ft), which sits in a forested bowl with meadows at either end. From Rainbow Lake the route climbs to the west shoulder (6,230 ft) of Bowan Mountain, then switchbacks down steep rocky meadows to the South Fork of Bridge Creek. The trail follows the creek downstream to the PCT at Bridge Creek (3,250 ft).

McAlester Creek Trail. *5.5 miles/m (H,S).* From McAlester Pass (6,017 ft) gentle switchbacks drop to McAlester Lake (5,507 ft), where lake-edge meadows poke out of open forest cover. From the lake the track drops down steep, wooded side slopes to follow the bank of McAlester Creek to the Twisp Pass (Fireweed) Trail (3,820 ft).

Stehekin River Trail. *4 miles/e (H,S).* This valley-bottom path follows the original wagon trail used before the present road was built. From the road spur along the southwest side of the Stehekin landing strip (1,200 ft), the near-level path weaves through open woods along the southwest side of the river, passing tiny flowered clearings and beaver ponds to reach Weaver Point Campground (1,100 ft), the original starting point of the Stehekin Valley wagon road. Just above the campground, Trail #1244 heads up Devore Creek into the Glacier Peak Wilderness.

Coon Lake Trail. *1.2 miles/m (H,S).* Heading north from the High Bridge Guard Station (1,600 ft), a couple of lazy switchbacks gain the bench (2,210 ft) holding shallow Coon Lake, an excellent spot for watching waterfowl. A pretty waterfall cascades from a narrow cleft in the cliffs on the northeast side of the lake. The McGregor Mountain Trail leave the north end of the lake.

A climber traverses a steep slope in the North Cascades; Ripsaw Ridge and Mount Buckner in the distance

McGregor Mountain Trail. *6.8 miles/d*

(H,S). Steep is an understatement! This route leaves the north end of Coon Lake (1,980 ft) and heads up the precipitous slope along the west side of Coon Creek. One hundred forty-four tedious switchbacks later, it reaches a small larch-rimmed basin holding Heaton Camp (7,000 ft). Beyond the camp, a tough scramble follows paint splotches marking a path over talus and ledges to the summit (8,122 ft). Breathtaking scenery abounds: the valley floor is a vertical mile and a half below; to the south are Bonanza, Agnes, Dome, Spire, and a host of other jagged summits; at the head of the Stehekin Valley are the Cascade Pass peaks; farther north are the Park Creek Pass summits; and due north is Mount Benzarino, with Ragged Ridge in the distance.

Climbing

North Cascades National Park combines glaciers, technical rock, and local altitude differentials exceeding 5,000 feet for some of the best alpine climbing in the coterminous U.S. Limited trails and rugged cross-country terrain mean that, with the exception of Mount Shuksan and some of the Cascade Pass peaks, most climbs are multi-day efforts, with much of this time spent getting to and from climbing bases near objective peaks.

In the southeast corner of the park, a line of glaciated rock summits (7,760 to 8970 ft) stretches northwest from Frisco Mountain. Some are nontechnical ascents; others are rock climbs of varying difficulty. The more difficult climbs, C-4 to C-5.5, are the narrow rounded thumb of Fisher Peak, the 1,000-foot north face of Meulefire Peak, and the wide, unstable 1,400-foot north face of Arches Peak. At the northwest end of this group is Ragged Ridge, a chain of ridgetop spikes between 7,230 feet and 8,795 feet. The highest of these, Mesahchie Peak, is the only real challenge, between C-3 and C-5.

In the triangle between Fisher, Park, and Thunder creeks are three huge glaciated massifs: Mount Logan (9,087 ft), Storm King (8,520 ft), and Goode Mountain (9,200 ft). Logan has challenging ice and rock routes, some in the high C-5 range. Storm King has four summits of nearly the same altitude, with rock routes rated C-4. Goode, with a dramatic glacier on the northeast face, has a half-dozen different approaches between C-3 and C-5.5.

Major summits along the crest north and east of Cascade Pass include Booker (8,280 ft), with a C-5.8 face; Buckner (9,080 ft), scramble and C-3 to C-4 ridge routes; Ripsaw Ridge (8,000 ft), dozens of closely spaced spires rated C-3 to C-5; Boston Peak (8,894 ft), C-3 to C-4; and Sahale Peak (8,680 ft), a relatively easy ascent.

The Boston Basin peaks offer several striking challenges for rock climbers. Sharkfin Tower (8,120 ft) and Sharks Tooth are narrow ridge-crest blades with all routes rated above C-5. Forbidden Peak (8,815 ft) is a stark tower rising above the huge Boston Glacier, with several exposed ridge and face routes between C-4 and C-5.10. Nearby Mount Torment (8,120 ft) has rock ledges and towers mostly in the C-3 to C-4 range.

Framed between McAllister, Thunder, and Marble creeks are a host of rugged glacier-bound crags capped by the distinctive ice slope leading to the top of Eldorado Peak (8,868 ft). This glacier route is easier than several others rated as high as C-5.7. Southwest of Eldorado is the Triad (7,520 ft), with an exposed, steep C-5.6 wall. To the north are a host of spectacular needles (8,102 to 8,508 ft) between Eldorado and Klawatti Peak (8,485 ft). There are weeks of climbing challenges here, on solid C-3 to C-5.5 granite. Backbone Ridge (7,160 to 7,675 ft), to the northwest, has a string of short one- to four-pitch climbs up spires whimsically named the Coccyx, Sacrum, and Lumbar and Thoracic points.

Along the western rim of this segment of the park is Teebone Ridge, rising sharply above surrounding valleys. The ridge, between 6,840 and 7,055 feet, includes Little Devil Peak, Baksit, and Big Devil peaks; Fallen Angel; and a group of short gendarmes known as the Six Hellions. Although approaches are tedious, the rock summits are mostly short, enjoyable C-3 climbs.

Clustered south of Highway 20 in the vicinity of Diablo and Gorge lakes are a group of pinnacles (7,182 to 8,347 ft) framing two good-sized glaciers. Here are Pyramid, Pinnacle, Colonial, and Snowfield peaks; Paul Bunyan's Stump; the Needle; and the Horseman. All rise more than a vertical mile above nearby valleys. Climbs are mixed ice and rock, with some routes up 40- to 45-degree ice and narrow, knife-edge arêtes rated C-4 to C-5.6.

Northwest from Diablo is the renowned Picket Range, a jumble of sharp rock summits rising above hanging glaciers that peel off 1,000-foot-high walls into deep valleys below. The southern component of this range, between 6,800 and 8,000 feet, contains McMillan Spire, twin summits that rise more than 2,000 feet from the glacier at their base. Inspiration Peak has a long, slabby, exposed C-5.9 face. The Pyramid, Mount Degenhart, and the Chopping Block all have classic, mixed ice and rock alpine routes. Mount Terror has C-3 to C-5.5 routes up various ridges and faces.

The northwest continuation of the Pickett Range presents more jagged peaks. Mount Fury (8,292 ft) has no route easier than C-4, and several more difficult. Phantom Peak (8,045 ft) and Crooked Thumb (8,124 ft) are spectacular rock needles with sheer east faces. The capstone of the north Pickets is Mount Challenger (8,236 ft), with an imposing 2-square-mile glacier on its northeast flank. Steep crevassed ice leads to rock summit blocks rated in the C-5 range. Anchoring the north end of the range is Whatcom Peak (7,754 ft), a massive ice and rock summit.

Another small subrange is framed by Goodell Creek, the East Fork of Bacon Creek, and Bald Eagle and Lonesome creeks. The two significant peaks in this group are Mount Triumph (7,270 ft) and Mount Despair (7,292 ft). Triumph is a rock thumb with near-vertical to overhanging faces on three sides. Dual-summited Despair has a slabby 4,500-foot east face and a hanging glacier.

The group of summits along the park's west boundary south of Baker River are seldom climbed, due to long tedious cross-country approaches. Among these is Bacon Peak (7,066 ft), a massive, heavily glaciated summit with a broad, exposed 2,000-foot west face. Hagan Mountain (6,800 ft) is a string of short rock pyramids flanking an alpine glacier. The summits are interesting one- to two-lead pitches between C-3 and C-5.5. Mount Blum (7,680 ft) is a bulky peak with both nontechnical and exposed C-3 to C-5.9 ridge climbs.

The classic alpine beauty, featured on more postcards, calendars, and book covers than any other peak in the North Cascades, is Mount Shuksan (9,127 ft). Shuksan's distinctive pyramidal peak is draped with a jumble of hanging glaciers and flanked with knife-edge arêtes that offer some of the best mixed alpine climbing in the park. A dozen or more routes have been put up Shuksan itself; these run from a romp up the Sulphide Glacier and the traditional Fisher Chimneys combination of rock and ice to the broken 55-degree ice cascade of the Price Glacier and the C-5.7 Northwest Rib. East of the summit, enclosing the huge Nooksack Cirque, are the impressive Nooksack Tower and Jagged Ridge. The Nooksack Tower combines near-vertical ice couloirs and a headwall face with 7 of 16 pitches classed over C-5.7.

In the remote north-central portion of the park is another subrange with rugged glaciated summits, long ridgelines of gendarmes, and striking near-vertical north faces. Bear Mountain (7,942 ft) has a wide 2,500-foot-high north wall, the upper third of which overhangs. Routes on this face run to 17 leads rated between C-5.3 and C-5.9. Mox Peaks (also known as Twin Spires; 8,407 and 8,504 ft), at the north end of Ridge of Gendarmes, are a pair of exposed rock fangs with no easy routes. The signature summit of this group is Mount Redoubt (8,956 ft); although it has a 1,700-foot rock wall to the northeast, easier routes reach the top from other sides and ridges. The third major summit in the area is Mount Spickard (8,879 ft), one of the few peaks in the area that has a steep glacier route to within 200 feet of the top.

The narrow confines of the Ross Lake RNA enclose few peaks of climbing interest. Hozomeen Mountain, marking the northeast border, is an impressive exception. This massive multi-summited peak rises abruptly more than 5,000 feet above the valley floor on the east side of Ross Lake. The sharply pointed summit pyramids have precipitous 2,000-foot rock faces and numerous individual crags on flanking ridges. The North Peak (8,066 ft) is the highest point on the massif; it has been climbed by several long C-4 to C-5 routes. The South Peak (8,003 ft) is the most difficult, with upper pitches ranked C-5.4 to C-5.6. The lesser Southwest Peak (7,471 ft) has a relatively easy route from the southwest and two from the south and west rated C-4 to C-5.

There are no truly difficult climbs in the Lake Chelan NRA, but a number of the summits have impressive faces. At the southwest corner of the RNA is Castle Rock (8,137 ft), named for the imposing west flank that rises 7,000 feet above the lake. Cross-country routes from Devore

Canoeing on Diablo Lake

Creek gain the south ridge for an easy approach.

McGregor Mountain (8,122 ft), is a huge east–west trending massif that rises in a continuous succession of cliffs above the north side of the Stehekin Valley. The McGregor Mountain Trail (see Hiking, above) climbs the west corner of the peak, where a scramble continues to the top. Several other lower satellite summits are scattered along the arête to the east.

The crest along the boundary between the RNA and the Lake Chelan–Sawtooth Wilderness has the highest peak in the area, and probably its best climbing. Reynolds Peak (8,512 ft) has an awesome 2,500-foot north face and two distinct summit pyramids. Approaches from War Creek Pass or Trail #402 lead to C-3 to C-4 leads on the final summit block. The crest continues north, then west to Rennie Peak, Mount Gibbs, and McAlester Mountain. All follow the vertical north-face theme of the other peaks, but are easy scrambles from the southeast.

Winter Sports

Although most of the backcountry in the park is sealed by heavy snows and avalanches during winter, Mount Shuksan's Sulphide Glacier is an excellent late-spring trek once roads in the Baker Lake area melt out and make the approach viable. The lower portion of the trip roughly follows Trail #742 up the steep timbered slopes of Shannon Creek to the lower edge of the Sulphide Glacier, then continues up the broad, easy-grade slope to the summit pyramid. Weather, crevasses, and lower-altitude avalanche slopes all add spice to the trip.

Water Sports

The Skagit River between Newhalem and Copper Creek is popular for rafting and kayaking. In addition to high mountain scenery, wildlife such as deer, raccoon, fox, coyote, beaver, and otter may be spotted along the river. Fall brings spawning salmon runs, and bald eagles winter along the river. The put-in point is Goodell Campground, and take-out spots are at Bacon Creek and Copper Creek. The water level fluctuates daily, depending on the power demands on the dams, but the river is always runnable by paddlers with Class 3 experience.

The lower Stehekin offers diverse paddling opportunities. For the first 0.5 mile below the High Bridge Guard Station the river runs through a narrow channel with very challenging white-water rapids. Below that point, the river is rated Class 2 or lower, with major hazards being downed trees and logs, and the propensity of the river to shift its channel periodically. Put-ins are found at Bullion Camp and Harlequin Campground, and the take-out is at Weaver Point Campground at the mouth of the river.

13

LIBERTY BELL

LOCATION: In Okanogan, Skagit, and Chelan counties, between the Pasayten and Lake Chelan–Sawtooth wildernesses
SIZE: 141,760 acres
STATUS: Semiprimitive Nonmotorized, with the exception of the North Cascades Scenic Highway, which crosses the lower portion of the area
TERRAIN: Steep rugged mountains frequently capped by serrated knife-edge ridges. Streams and rivers drop abruptly from lakes in rock-rimmed cirques or headwall basins to broad, U-shaped, glacier-cut valleys. Some small pocket glaciers, mostly below sheer north faces of peaks
ELEVATION: 1,904 to 8,444 feet
MANAGEMENT: USFS, Okanogan National Forest, Winthrop Ranger District
TOPOGRAPHIC MAPS: Azurite Peak, Crater Mountain, Gilbert, Mazama, McAlester Mtn., McLeod Mountain, Mt. Arriva, Robinson Mtn., Slate Peak, Silver Star Mtn., Washington Pass

It is said that the Liberty Bell Roadless Area is Washington's equivalent of Yosemite Valley. Although not directly comparable, the two regions have many similar features. The Liberty Bell area is nearly bisected by the long, deep, U-shaped valley of the upper Methow River, a beautiful and classic example of the cutting and shaping action of glacial ice. The dominant features of the southern half of the area are massive peaks and ridges formed by granitic intrusions through the metamorphic base rock. These peaks exhibit sheer, solid granite faces, several more than 1,000 feet high, a challenge to the best of climbers. Other ridges are crowned with a series of fins, spires, and towers of comparable difficulty, though with lesser vertical extent.

The area cannot truly be called roadless, as it is spanned by Highway 20, the North Cascades Scenic Highway. However, as its name implies, it was constructed and is maintained for minimal intrusion into the scenic beauty of the region. Aside from this road, the remainder of Liberty Bell deserves protection similar to that afforded the areas along its boundaries: the Pasayten Wilderness, North Cascades National Park, and the Lake Chelan–Sawtooth Wilderness. Its exclusion from wilderness status was possibly prompted by about 150 mining claims that still exist in the area.

An abundance of trails leads into the region; many originated as narrow-gauge wagon roads built to serve the area's mines and prospects. While several of these routes ply brushy creek bottoms and are poorly maintained, others, including a segment of the Pacific Crest National Scenic Trail, cross high passes and traverse alpine slopes that offer breathtaking scenic views. Lakes are sparse—there are just 28 in the entire area, and only 10 are significant enough to bear a name. However, most are scenic gems, set in tight cirques surrounded by imposing cliffs with tiny shoreside meadows bordered by subalpine fir and larch. They are especially beautiful in the fall, when their turquoise surfaces reflect the golden larch and crimson bushes.

Climate

Because the Liberty Bell area straddles the Cascade crest, weather varies markedly over its 20-mile east–west span. On the west side, average annual precipitation is about 100 inches; on the east, about 60 inches. Most of this precipitation occurs between November and April, with as much as 45 feet of snow falling on higher west-side elevations over the winter period. Average winter minimums are 16 degrees on the west side of the range, and 9 degrees on the east side. Maximum summer temperatures average in the low 70s on both sides of the crest.

Plants and Wildlife

The forest in the lower portion of the region west of the crest is dominated by Douglas-fir and lodgepole pine, with an understory of Oregon grape, spirea, willow, bracken fern, Oregon boxwood, ocean spray, twinflower, serviceberry, honeysuckle, starflower, and prince's pine. At higher elevations, Englemann spruce, mountain hemlock, western red cedar, Pacific silver fir, and subalpine fir join the forest mix. East of the crest, the mid-elevation forest is a mix of ponderosa pine, lodgepole pine, and western larch, while at higher elevations grand fir, white fir, white pine, mountain hemlock, and subalpine fir replace the ponderosa. The understory here includes huckleberry, prickly currant, Oregon boxwood, baldhip rose, and beargrass.

Among the forest animals are mule deer, cougar, black bear, and, at high elevations, mountain goat. Rarer species, in need of special preservation efforts, are spotted owl, lynx, wolverine, water vole, western gray squirrel, and three-toed woodpecker.

Geology

Approximately 50 million years ago the North Cascades micro-continent collided with the west coast of North America; the metamorphic rocks off the east coast of that terrane were twisted and uplifted to form this segment of the Cascade Range. South from Rainy and Washington passes, the base had already been intruded by the granitic Black Peak batholith prior to the meeting of the two plates. About 40 million years ago, the Golden Horn batholith pushed up into the heart of the Liberty Bell area. The intrusive contact zones between this batholith and the base metamorphic suite are highly mineralized, thus the extensive mining in this region.

Mountain goats at Cutthroat Pass in the Liberty Bell Roadless Area

The Gardiner Mountain fault, which marks the west side of the Methow graben, runs north-west to southeast through the area, roughly in the vicinity of the South Fork of Slate Creek. The fault line is not discernible; it is masked by the Golden Horn batholith. The sedimentary base of the sunken Methow graben has been overlaid by a thick layer of glacial debris.

About 15 million years ago the continental ice sheet covered all but a few of the high points of the Liberty Bell area, and its advance can be recognized in the deep U-shaped valleys that were carved by the glacier, and in the scrape marks etched into exposed granite outcrops. The steep knife-edge crests, with their many towers and spires, are a result of flaking caused by the expansion of water that accumulated in fine cracks in rock structures and then froze.

History

The early history of the Liberty Bell area is dominated by its mineral riches. Prospectors probed the area in the late 1880s, entering it from both the Skagit and Methow valleys. In 1892, Alex Barron discovered a rich strike near Harts Pass. The mining camp of Barron blossomed quickly to a population of 1,000, and reached 2,500 at the peak of its activity. More than $300,000 in gold was extracted from this one claim.

Transportation of supplies in, and ore out, was a major obstacle to capitalizing on the area's riches. In 1893, Charles Ballard was hired to put a road into Harts Pass. When completed, the road was so narrow it required specially built narrow-gauge wagons to negotiate it. One precarious section at Deadhorse Point consisted of planks laid over steel pins that had been driven into the face of a sheer cliff. A panicky runaway pack string gave the location its name. Despite this hazardous route, huge compressors with 9-foot-diameter flywheels, multi-ton rock crushers, and tons of ore were moved in and out via the primitive Harts Pass road.

In 1915, Ballard opened the Azurite Mine, one of the richest in the area. It produced nearly $1 million in gold and silver between 1929 and 1939. Lode mines were located around Barron, Tatie Peak, Hells Basin, Boulder Creek, Mill Creek, Majestic Mountain, and Granite Creek. Placer mines along the creeks of the region took out more than $225,000 in gold. In total, more than 3,000 claims were staked in the area between 1894 and 1937. Today 140 unpatented claims and 10 patented claims still remain.

At peak production, some of the mines were operated year-round, but avalanches took a heavy toll in buildings and lives, and dog teams were the only source of supplies during winter months. Access was an ongoing nemesis, and the Harts Pass road wasn't improved to its present condition (still not for the faint-hearted) until the 1930s. Methow Valley miners and merchants lobbied fruitlessly for a road across the Cascades to the Skagit Valley, but it wasn't until 1962 that the route over Washington Pass was selected. The road was finally completed in 1972, but this highway is still closed by heavy snow from late November to mid-May.

In the early 1900s sheepherders arrived on the scene and drove flocks from their winter pastures in the Columbia Basin to high alpine meadows in the Pasayten for summer grazing. As many as 300,000 sheep per year were taken to the high meadows via a "driveway" that went over Driveway Butte, then up Rattlesnake Creek. Grazing permits have since been drastically reduced; at present only one herd is permitted into the area in alternate years.

The primitive scenic beauty of the North Cascades was recognized in 1934, when the Whatcom Primitive Area was expanded to the 801,000-acre North Cascades Primitive Area. In 1968 most of this primitive area became North Cascades National Park. Unfortunately, Liberty Bell was excluded from both the park and the wilderness classification. Its striking topography certainly merits such protection.

ACTIVITIES

Hiking

RUBY CREEK TO RAINY PASS TRAILS

Trail #754, Chancellor. 15.5 miles/e (H,S). From Granite Creek Guard Station on Highway 20 (1,930 ft) this path enters the dense old-growth forest along Canyon Creek. It follows the creek upstream, crossing several tributaries, passing moldering fragments of cabins and piles of rusting mining equipment. Just after the route crosses Mill Creek, Trail #755 heads off to the east. Trail #754 widens as it follows an old narrow-gauge wagon road for the remaining distance to Chancellor Campground (2,844 ft), at the end of FR 5400700 northwest of Harts Pass. Chancellor was once the site of a booming mining camp. The trail continues into the Pasayten Wilderness.

Trail #755, Mill Creek. 10 miles/m (H; S, but not recommended). Branching off from the 5.9-mile point on Trail #754 (2,820 ft), this scenic, rarely used trail began as a route to the Azurite Mine. Its narrow track follows the steep, forested sidehill along Mill Creek. At 3.5 miles the path passes the west end of Trail #754 from Cady Pass, the main route to the mine, and at 4.7 miles the mine itself is reached (4,500 ft). Open spots at tailings give glimpses up to the rugged west face of Mount Ballard. The route continues south along Mill Creek through a 1987 burn, then switchbacks up to Azurite Pass (6,700 ft). Here are great views of Azurite Peak and the impressive north face of Golden Horn. The track descends a steep forested slope along Jet Creek to join the PCT (4,390 ft).

Trail #756, Meebe Pass–East Creek. 8 miles/m (H,S). From Highway 20 (2,580 ft), switchbacks up a forested nose lead to a rock outcrop with good views down Granite Creek, and beyond to Crater Mountain. A long, timbered traverse crosses East Creek, then gradually climbs above its north bank to the Gold Hill Mine (4,700 ft). The route drops back to East Creek and follows it south, becoming more obscure as it crosses and recrosses the creek. A mile from the head of the basin the trail zigzags up steep wooded slopes to Mebee Pass (6,500 ft), once a lookout site. From the pass the way descends gradually to the West Fork of the Methow, where it joins the PCT, 0.3 mile south of Jet Creek (4,370 ft).

RAINY PASS TRAILS

Trail #740, Lake Ann–Maple Pass Loop. 1.9 miles to Lake Ann/e (H); 6.5 miles for Maple Pass Loop/m (H). A wide, gentle track leaves south from Rainy Pass (4,900 ft), switchbacks a few times up through dense forest, traverses an open avalanche track, then splits. The spur to the west soon arrives at the cliff-walled cirque containing Lake Ann (5,475 ft); a tiny island pokes through its turquoise surface. The northwest fork climbs above the north side of the lake, then makes a few steep switchbacks to Heather Pass (6,200 ft) and views west across Lewis and Wing lakes to the imposing summit of Black Peak. The track continues along the top of the cliffs above Lake Ann to Maple Pass (6,300 ft). Imposing scenery includes nearby Corteo Peak

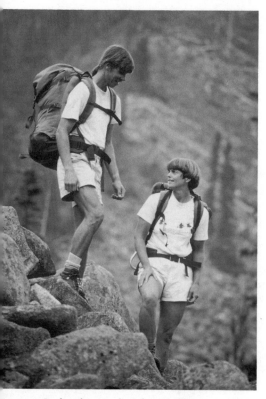

Backpacking in the Liberty Bell area

and, in the distance, Dome Peak, Spire Point, and Glacier Peak. The route continues along the narrow, open crest above the Lake Ann cirque, then tiptoes down rock steps along the divide between Lake Ann and Rainy Lake. It descends this steep forested rib to meet Trail #310 and follow it back to Rainy Pass.

RAINY PASS TO WASHINGTON PASS TRAILS

Trail #2172, Bridge Creek. 3.1 miles/m (H,S). A short path from Highway 20 (4,510 ft) joins the PCT, whose tread is shared for 1.4 miles to a Y intersection. This route heads southeast, crosses State Creek, and passes junctions with the old Crest Trail route and Trail #426. After a boulder-hop crossing of Copper Creek, the way continues another 0.6 mile to the national park boundary. In 1.4 miles farther the route ends on the Twisp Pass Trail (3,870 ft).

Trail #426, Copper Pass. 4.8 miles/d (H,S). This brushy, seldom-used path leaves Trail #2172 just north of Copper Creek (4,250 ft) and heads east up that creek's drainage. A few switchbacks take the route out of the creek bottom to wooded slopes above its north bank, where it continues a gentle, but obscure, ascent to bouldery meadows at the head of the drainage. Here it climbs to Copper Pass (6,700 ft), then descends into the Lake Chelan–Sawtooth Wilderness as Trail #426.

Trail #314, Blue Lake. 2.2 miles/e (H). From a pullout on Highway 20 (5,200 ft) this National Recreation Trail enters the forest and parallels the road for a short distance. It then heads up ever-steepening slopes, surmounting them by switchbacks, to reach the north shore of Blue Lake (6,254 ft). The surface reflects a 1,000-foot rock wall above it. East of the lake the towers of Liberty Bell and Early Winter Spires jut into the sky, and ragged Cutthroat Peak decorates the northwest horizon.

WASHINGTON PASS TO MAZAMA TRAILS

Trail #483, Cutthroat Lake. 5.5 miles/e (H,B,S). A gentle path leaves Lone Fir Campground (4,500 ft) and follows the bank of Cutthroat Creek southwest for 1.7 miles to a junction. The spur south leads to Cutthroat Lake (4,935 ft), set in a wide basin surrounded by rugge d peaks. The west fork switchbacks up through huge old-growth forest, then enjoys a respite at a bench meadow framed with immense larch. The climb resumes, swings around the head of a small rocky basin, and arrives at Cutthroat Pass (6,820 ft), where it joins the PCT. At the pass, a panorama of peaks—Silver Star, Liberty Bell, Cutthroat, Dome, Azurite, Ballard, Golden Horn, Tower, and the Needles—encircles the horizon.

Trail #481, Driveway Butte. 4 miles/m (H). This segment of an old sheep drive leaves Klipchuck Campground (2,900 ft) and heads north alongside Indian Creek. The climb through forest to the head of the creek is steep, but from there the grade eases. It becomes brushy and obscure as it continues northwest, then turns northeast up open slopes to the top of Driveway Butte (6,982 ft). This old lookout site has expansive views down the Methow Valley and across Early Winters Creek to the crags and spires of Silver Star Mountain.

Trail #476, Cedar Creek. 9.2 miles/m (H,B,S). From the gravel pit at the end of FR 5310200 (3,030 ft), the route, a National Recreation Trail, starts gently up the Cedar Creek drainage, passing through old-growth fir, spruce, and cedar. At 2 miles (3,500 ft) the creek drops 50 to 60 feet over a beautiful falls. The path continues upstream along the bank, reaching meadows with views of Gardiner and Silver Star mountains and the long row of towers that cap the ridge at the head of the valley. The track leaves the meadow for forest as it continues uphill and crosses the west and main forks of the creek. It heads steeply uphill toward seemingly impenetrable Abernathy Ridge. Switchbacks gain the narrow defile of Abernathy Pass (6,420 ft), where the trail drops into North Creek and joins Trail #413 (5,450 ft). Knobs above either side of the pass offer views of Silver Star and the spires along Kangaroo and Snagtooth ridges.

HARTS PASS TRAILS

Trail #480, West Fork of the Methow. 8 miles/e (H,B,S). The route leaves Rattlesnake Campground (2,710 ft) and wanders along the bottom of the deep West Fork of the Methow drainage, most of the way in lodgepole pine, except for a few brushy meadows cut by avalanche chutes. At 7 miles the track heads uphill along Brush Creek to join the PCT (4,280 ft).

Left to right: *Early Winter Spires (pair of tall peaks on the left), Lexington Tower (mid-level peak with small knob on top), Concord Tower, and Liberty Bell*

Trail #475, Cady Pass. 8.5 miles/m (H,B,S). The trail was once a narrow-gauge road over which supplies were hauled to, and ore from, the Azurite Mine. It heads south from FR 5400500 (3,850 ft) into the South Fork of Slate Creek drainage. In 1.5 miles the route crosses the creek, then heads northwest in a long lateral climb through beautiful old-growth forest to meadows at 5,200 feet. Switchbacks up an open rib reach Cady Pass (5,980 ft) and a grand scenic display that includes Mount Ballard, Majestic Mountain, Jack Mountain, and Snowfield Peak. A scamper northwest along the ridge for 0.9 mile to an old lookout site at Cady Point has even better views. West of the pass the track swings back and forth as it gradually descends open hillside, then forest, to meet Trail #755 (4,240 ft) a mile north of the Azurite Mine.

Pacific Crest National Scenic Trail. 30.7 miles/m (H,S).

PCT: Rainy Pass to Methow Pass. 10.5 miles. From the north side of Rainy Pass, the trail enters dense fir forest as it gradually climbs into the Porcupine Creek drainage. After crossing the creek, switchbacks take the track high on the slopes above the west bank, where a gradual ascent swings around the head of the basin. A chain of easy-grade switchbacks climbs to Cutthroat Pass (6,830 ft), to meet Trail #483. Here grand views open to Silver Star, Liberty Bell, Cutthroat, and Kangaroo and Sawtooth ridges. The route continues north from the pass, staying high as it swings across the rocky east side of the crest. It then switchbacks down a narrow rib to Granite Pass (6,300 ft), with views north to the Needles and Tower Mountain. Northwest of the pass, the path contours the steep headwall below Tower Mountain to meadows in a small alpine bowl. A boot-path heads a short distance uphill to Snowy Lakes. The PCT climbs west out of the basin, then traverses to Methow Pass (6,590 ft).

PCT: Methow Pass to Glacier Pass. 12 miles. After leaving Methow Pass the path switchbacks down the forested lower flank of Golden Horn to the headwaters of the West Fork of the Methow, then follows the dense river bottom north past Trails #755 and #757. As the river bends east, the trail climbs higher above its bank and swings into the Brush Creek drainage, where it meets Trail #480, then ascends along the narrow creek bottom. Near the head of the basin it zigzags uphill to Glacier Pass (5,580 ft), a low saddle between Brush Creek and the South Fork of Slate Creek. There are a few glimpses here of Azurite Peak and Mount Ballard.

PCT: Glacier Pass to Harts Pass. 8.2 miles. From Glacier Pass, switchbacks climb the steep west end of Handcock Ridge, where more meadows overlook Azurite and Ballard. The crest is followed north to the wide meadow of Grasshopper Pass (6,750 ft), where the path crosses into the South Fork of Trout Creek drainage. A contour north near timberline leads to a col (6,890 ft) on the shoulder of Tatie Peak and more views of Mount Ballard. The track traverses around the head of the wide basin southeast of Tatie Peak, passes a col (6,950 ft) at the head of Ninetynine Basin, then swings around a buttress ridge to yet another saddle (6,660 ft) above the North Fork of Trout Creek. A descent north passes the Brown Bear Mine and reaches FR 5400500 (6,420 ft) 0.5 mile south of Meadows Campground. The road is hiked north to Harts Pass (6,194 ft).

Climbing

The Liberty Bell area has some of the most challenging rock climbing in the Washington Cascades. There are both Dolomite-like spires and Yosemite-like faces within easy hiking distance from Highway 20. Rising dramatically above the south side of Washington Pass is Liberty Bell Mountain (7,720 ft), a dome-shaped peak with near-vertical granite walls jutting more than 1,100 feet above the valley floor. Eleven routes have been put up the peak, all ranging between C-5 and C-5.9. The massif south from Liberty Bell is fractured into five more distinct granite towers: Minuteman, Concord, and Lexington towers, and North and South Early Winter spires. All range around 7,500 feet, and all offer vertical wall climbs in the C-5 to C-5.10 range.

Paralleling the Liberty Bell massif to the east is Kangaroo Ridge, a wild 3-mile-long collection of fins, spires, and crags with vertical north and east sides; each has at least 200 to 500 feet of C-5 to C-5.10 climbing.

Northeast of Kangaroo Ridge is another mile-long group of towers atop Snagtooth Ridge, all with 100- to 300-foot final pitches ranging between C-4 and C-5.7.

North of Snagtooth Ridge is the massive bastion of Silver Star Mountain (8,876 ft), with a star-shaped glacier on its northeast flank and two distinct sets of towers on its northwest ridge. The easiest ascent is a C-3 glacier and rock route, but other climbs reach the summit from the south, southwest buttress, southeast face, and west face; the latter is a complex C-5.8 challenge.

The first group of towers (8,350 to 8,441 ft) north of Silver Star are the Wine Spires: Chablis, Pernod, Chianti, and Burgundy; the latter is the most difficult, C-5.6 to C-5.9. The next group of crags, with moderate faces on the west and sheer ones on the east, are collectively referred to as Vasaliki Ridge. The individual towers are Vasaliki Tower (7,920 ft) and the Acropolis (8,040 ft), C-4 to C-5.5 in difficulty. Farther north are Charon, Ares, Juno-Jupiter, Aphrodite, and Bacchus towers, all with relatively easy C-3 routes.

On the north side of Highway 20, between Washington and Rainy passes, is another massive ridge, anchored on the south by Whistler Mountain (7,990 ft), a small, pointed peak with C-4 to C-5.7 routes. The most prominent summit here is Cutthroat Peak (8,050 ft), whose summit block has no trivial routes; all are rated between C-4 and C-5.10. Near Cutthroat Pass is Molar Tooth (7,547 ft), a fang requiring six leads, one C-5.6.

At the east end of the granitic Golden Horn batholith are the Needles (8,140 ft), an isolated group of spires, each with a few leads of rock climbing. The highest has 200 feet of solid rock, with one C-5.5 lead. Tower Mountain (8,444 ft) has an impressive 1,400-foot north face, but can be topped by C-3 to C-4 routes from the south and west. Golden Horn (8,366 ft) is a distinctive-looking rock horn with a sheer 1,700-foot north face, an easy C-3 climb from the south.

A long ridge north of the Golden Horn–Tower massif is capped by Azurite Peak (8,400 ft) and Mount Ballard (8,301 ft). Both have impressive-looking faces, but neither is a technical challenge.

South of Meebe Pass are the Methow Pinnacles, a group of three pyramidal summits atop a long 1,400-foot-high wall. The highest of these (7,564 ft) has some delicate slab climbing rated C-5; the others are less difficult.

Winter Sports

Although the Methow Valley is renowned for its ski touring, most of this activity is associated with valley-bottom lodges and ski trails, and very little winter activity penetrates the backcountry of the Liberty Bell Roadless Area. The treeless scars that lace the steep slopes in the heart of the area testify to winter avalanche hazards that justify its avoidance. A few cross-country tours are safe either in early fall when the snow is light, or in late spring when the snowpack is mostly stabilized. These offer an opportunity to enjoy the scenic beauty of the area enhanced by a blanket of snow.

After the first fall snows, but before Highway 20 is closed for the winter, a ski tour to Lake Ann and above it to Heather and Maple passes offers a winterized sample of the stunning scenery found along this summer trail. Once snows close Highway 20, the road is a popular snowmobiling route, except in conditions of high avalanche danger.

A popular midwinter tour continues up the barricaded highway above Early Winters to the Cedar Creek Trail #476, then heads up that trail to Cedar Falls. The trail is narrow, however, so the downhill run can be dicey.

After Highway 20 reopens in late May, and with stable snow conditions, the PCT can be skied north from Rainy Pass into Porcupine Creek and up to Cutthroat Pass. Avalanche slopes in upper Porcupine Creek must be watched carefully, however. Cutthroat Pass can also be reached by skiing Cutthroat Lake Trail #483, a beautiful trip that is safe from any avalanche hazard until it reaches the final small bowl just below the pass.

When the Harts Pass road first opens, a great, relatively safe, tour heads south past Meadow Campground, then up the ridge above the Brown Bear Mine. After skiers feast on the views from a 7,200-foot knob at the head of the ridge, a downhill run through the forested basin to the east leads back to the campground.

Opposite: *Mount Stuart dominates the Alpine Lakes Wilderness Area.*

THE CENTRAL CASCADES

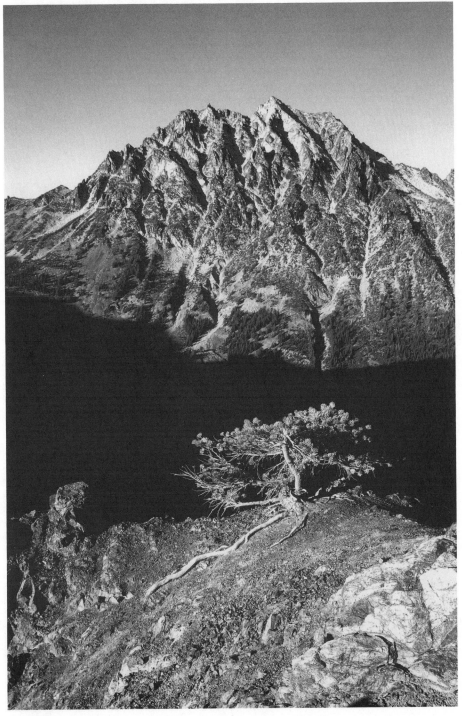

14

MOUNT HIGGINS

LOCATION: In Skagit County, on the north side of Highway 530, 4 to 12 miles west of Darrington
SIZE: 10,700 acres
STATUS: Semiprimitive Nonmotorized
TERRAIN: Extremely steep timbered ridges culminating in sharp rocky summits
ELEVATION: 500 to 5,274 feet
MANAGEMENT: USFS, Mount Baker–Snoqualmie National Forest, Darrington Ranger District
TOPOGRAPHIC MAPS: Fortson, Mt. Higgins

West of Darrington, the valley floor drained by the North Fork of the Stillaguamish River is rimmed on the north and south by steep, forested hillsides that sweep nearly a mile to the sky. To the south lies the Boulder River Wilderness, and to the north is a small, rugged, roadless area surrounded by an onslaught of logging roads and clearcuts. Only its precipitous terrain and the presence of old-growth spotted owl habitat have saved the area from a similar fate. A high, Y-shaped ridge, bounded by near-vertical walls, runs east and west through the center of this roadless enclave. Four small lakes are tucked into shelves below the ridgetop.

The area contains a single trail that leads to the westernmost summit of the ridge, the site of a former fire lookout. The other two major summits of the Mount Higgins massif can be gained only by cross-country climbing routes. The highest point in the area, Round Mountain (5,274 ft), was once scheduled for a lookout; a trail was put in to the top, but the structure was never built. Portions of the abandoned trail may still be found.

The summits offer spectacular views down to the valley floor and across to the nearby ragged summits of Whitehorse and Three Fingers on its south side. The backbone of the Cascades, capped by ice-clad Glacier Peak, frames the eastern horizon. To the west, the Olympic Range rises above the waters of Puget Sound.

Climate

Annual precipitation in the area ranges between 80 and 100 inches, mostly falling as snow during fall and winter. The steep walls of the backbone ridge are laced with avalanche tracks from the heavy snowfall. Higher slopes become accessible by July, when most of the snow has melted. Temperatures are relatively mild year-round, with an average high in the mid-80s and an average low in the 20s.

Plants and Wildlife

Although the lower slopes have some Douglas-fir, true fir, and western red cedar, the bulk of the dense forest consists of western hemlock at lower elevations, and mountain hemlock higher up. A few small alpine meadows are found near the heads of creek drainages. Clearcuts and ava-

The valley of the North Fork of the Stillaguamish River from Mount Higgins; Whitehorse Mountain on the right

lanche slopes along the access routes have a dense brush cover of vine maple, slide alder, and dwarf willow.

The forest is home to black-tailed deer, black bear, blue grouse, marten, and pileated woodpeckers. Old-growth forest remaining along the northwest edge of the area hosts spotted owls.

Geology

The Mount Higgins massif is composed of metamorphosed sandstone and shale sharply folded into steep southwest-dipping strata.

ACTIVITIES

Hiking

Trail #640, Mount Higgins. 4.5 miles/m (H,B,M). Although the trailhead is on the east side of the #SL-0-5500 road at 1,460 feet, a boot-path departs from the end of a switchback in another 1.5 miles (2,500 ft), shortcutting the lower first mile of the formal trail, and meeting it near the national forest boundary. Both trailheads are on DNR land. The route climbs up the west side of the Dicks Creek drainage, eases at 3,400 feet, and passes a spur that drops west to Myrtle Lake (3,515 ft). After wending through a meadow at the head of Dicks Creek, the trail resumes its ascent through forest broken by boulder fields. The path ends at the top of the westernmost of the three summits of the massif (4,849 ft), the site of a former fire lookout built in 1926. The building collapsed from heavy snow in 1965.

Climbing

Skadulgwas Peak (4,785 ft) is the middle of three peaks along the Mount Higgins massif. The 1,000-foot north face of the summit block is nearly vertical, and its south face is a steep rock slab, however, there is a scramble route via the southwest ridge.

Mount Higgins (5,176 ft) is the easternmost, and highest, of the three summit peaks. Its east ridge is reached via a cross-country route that leaves FR 1850 near Deer Creek Pass, or from the end of FR 1890, north of Swede Heaven. The ridge can be followed west to a 200-foot, C-3 rock pitch just below the summit.

■ —————15————— ■

BOULDER RIVER WILDERNESS

LOCATION: Located in Snohomish County, between the North and South Forks of the Stillaguamish River, 15 miles east of Granite Falls

SIZE: 49,000 acres

STATUS: Designated Wilderness Area (1984)

TERRAIN: Brushy wooded slopes rise steeply from 1,000 feet to ridgetops in the range of 4,000 to 5,000 feet. The north–south backbone ridge has several rock peaks and pinnacles.

ELEVATION: 1,000 to 6,850 feet

MANAGEMENT: USFS, Mount Baker–Snoqualmie National Forest, Darrington Ranger District

TOPOGRAPHIC MAPS: Helena Ridge, Mallardy Ridge, Meadow Mountain, Mount Higgins, Silverton, Whitehorse Mountain

The Boulder River Wilderness is located at the heart of a small subrange framed on the north and south by forks of the Stillaguamish River, and on the east by the Sauk River. A narrow, north–south axis ridge, serrated with sharp rock summits, runs through its center. Numerous steep, heavily wooded lateral ridges run east and west from this backbone. Cross-country travel below timberline is extremely difficult due to the steep terrain and thick brush, slide alder, and devil's club. However, exquisite alpine meadows are found on some ridgetops at timberline.

Several small glaciers fill cirques on Whitehorse Mountain and Three Fingers, and a number of small permanent snowfields are found in other pockets throughout the area. The wilderness has 22 charted lakes and ponds.

Climate

Average annual precipitation for the area ranges between 80 and 100 inches per year. Southwesterly storm patterns during winter months bring heavy rain and snow, especially on the south and west sides of the area. Snowfall can be expected by early November, with snow persisting down to 2,000 feet until late May. Most snow is gone below 4,000 feet by early July. Temperatures are relatively mild year-round.

Plants and Wildlife

Dominant trees at lower altitudes are western hemlock, Douglas-fir, and western red cedar. One of the few lowland old-growth forest areas in this part of the state can be found in the lower reaches of the Boulder River, where ancient stands of Douglas-fir, true fir, western red cedar, and western hemlock can be found. The 640-acre Long Creek Research Natural Area, located in the southwest corner of the wilderness area, was established in 1947 to preserve a baseline forest of western hemlock and climax red alder, some nearly 2 feet in diameter and 100 feet tall. Creek drainages hold a dense understory of slide alder, dwarf willow, vine maple, ferns, and devil's club.

The forest at mid-altitudes consists mainly of mountain hemlock, Pacific silver fir, Alaska cedar, and subalpine fir. Alpine parks can be found between 4,000 and 5,000 feet. Typical of these are the top of Meadow Mountain and Goat Flat on the west side of the axis ridge, where the forest dwindles to patches of subalpine fir and mountain hemlock, and meadows support heather, huckleberry, blueberry, dwarf lupine, phlox, salmonberry, anemone, fleabane, valeria, paintbrush, penstemon, bistort, and avalanche lilies.

Lowland wildlife includes black-tailed deer, elk, and black bear; mountain goats inhabit cliffy areas above timberline.

Geology

This portion of the North Cascades lying west of the Straight Creek fault was created about 50 million to 90 million years ago when a micro-continent carried by tectonic plates became attached to the western edge of the North American plate. Over time the edges of this terrane had been overlaid with sedimentary layers and basalt flows that were later metamorphosed into Darrington phyllite. The binding of the terrane to the continent was accompanied by uplift, folding, and faulting of the ancient rock base.

Volcanic activity that occurred between 10 million and 40 million years ago was followed by another major uplift of this area, and intrusions of granodiorite along the east side of its high north–south axis ridge. Between 2 million and 12,000 years ago the alpine glaciers that formed on the higher peaks flowed down to merge with thick ice sheets covering the lowlands, in the process carving out most of the presently recognizable geographic features.

Peaks of the backbone ridge consist mainly of older metamorphosed shale and sandstone exposed by erosion of younger volcanic rocks. Granite walls on the east side of Salish Peak and along Squire Creek are examples of the Squire Creek granodiorite intrusion. Mineralization in the form of veins, disseminated sulfides, and gold-containing placers occurred along the contact zones between the intrusion and the older metamorphic rock.

History

As late as 1890 the entire Boulder River Wilderness area was uncharted, and the headwater sources of the Stillaguamish River were unknown. In 1889, the discovery of lead, silver, and gold ore just east of here in the Monte Cristo basin brought miners and speculators into the area. Surveys of routes by which heavy machinery could be brought in and ore could be taken out led to the construction, in 1891, of a wagon road from the north following the Sauk River. In 1892, another road was built along the South Fork of the Stillaguamish. By the fall of 1893 the rails of the Everett and Monte Cristo Line were added to the latter route.

The Monte Cristo finds led to other prospecting in the region, and the mining camp at Silverton served as a base for prospectors staking claims in the vicinity of Long Mountain, on the southern rim of the present wilderness area. Prospecting out of Darrington, on the northeast side of the area, led to several active claims on Whitehorse Mountain, Jumbo Mountain, and in Buckeye Basin, which all lie within the present wilderness area.

Rough mining trails laced the area; prospectors showed total disdain for precipitous ridges if there was a vein of gold or silver to be found. Their only concern on the equivalent of a C-5 climbing route was whether they could make it with a cast-iron cookstove lashed to their packs. During the 1920s and '30s, the Forest Service expanded the rough miner's trail network with

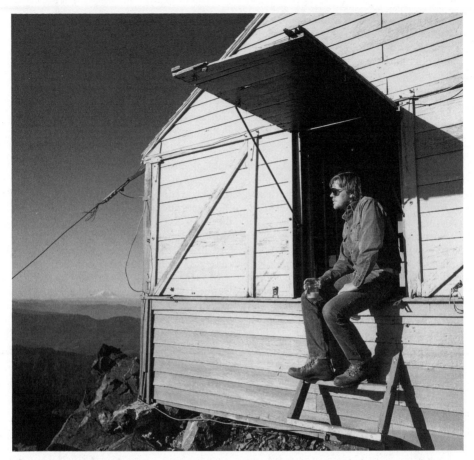

The old fire lookout, held in place by steel cables, still sits on the summit of Three Fingers; Mount Rainier in the distance

routes to reach and supply the fire lookout perched atop Three Fingers and patrol cabins spotted about the area. When logging supplanted mining as the area's major industry, most of this older trail system was either obliterated or abandoned.

ACTIVITIES

Hiking

Trail #734, Boulder River. 4.3 miles/e (H). The trailhead is located at the end of FR 2010. Old-growth forest and waterfalls from side streams are prime attractions as the trail meanders up and down above the north side of the canyon carved by the Boulder River. Due to its low elevation, this trail is hikeable year-round, but it offers no views of wilderness peaks.

Trail #654, Squire Creek. 4 miles/m (H). The trail runs between the end of FR 2040, on the north, and Squire Creek Pass. The route climbs along Squire Creek, offering spectacular views of the precipitous east side of the peaks on the backbone ridge of the wilderness.

Trail #641, Three Fingers. 6.2 miles/m (H). The path starts from FR 41 at Tupso Pass. A short spur 2 miles east of the pass leads to Saddle Lake; the main trail continues to Goat Flat, 4.5 miles from the trailhead. Goat Flat is a pleasant alpine meadow thick with early-season flowers and late-season berries. A crude path continues climbing westward to reach Camp Saddle and Tin Can Gap, two cols that lead to the Queest-Alb Glacier at the west base of Three Fingers. From here a climber's track over glacier and rock reaches the South Peak summit block, where ladders lean up the final sheer face to a lookout cabin atop a minuscule rock platform blasted from the top of the mountain.

Trail #653, Niederprum Trail. 2 miles/d (H). This trail from FR 2030 is a classic miner's track that doesn't dilly-dally in switchbacks—it climbs from 1,000 feet to 4,000 feet up the north side of Whitehorse Ridge by the shortest (and steepest) route possible. It ends in a brush-covered meadow where miner Mat Niederprum once worked his claims. A track that continues over Lone Tree Pass is the most popular route for climbing Whitehorse Mountain.

Climbing

With the exception of Jumbo Mountain, climbing activity is concentrated on the peaks along the major north–south axis ridge. Most of these have near-vertical faces ranging from 600 to 2,000 feet on one or more sides, but many have other relatively easy routes. Several of these peaks are climbed in the winter, when snow covers the brush and makes cross-country travel easier.

Whitehorse Mountain (6,563 ft) rises dramatically above the town of Darrington, offering a combination of glacier or rock climbing routes, most of the latter below C-5. The most popular route leaves the end of Trail #653. South from Whitehorse are Buckeye Peak (5,896 ft), Mount Bullon (5,974 ft), and Salish Peak (5,690 ft), as well as intermediate short towers along intervening ridges. Although approach routes involve brush-beating up valley floors and steep sidehills, routes of C-4 or lower can be found on all of these peaks. The southeast face of Salish Peak is 600 feet of excellent granite with routes varying from C-5.6 to C-5.8.

The visual showpiece of the area is Three Fingers, its highest summit. The South Peak (6,850 ft), which tops the Boulder River Wilderness, has a restored lookout cabin perched on its top. It is reached via Trail #641 and a climber's path across steep snow and rock to a vertical face, where a ladder spans the final 40 feet to the lookout. The Middle Peak (6,600 ft) is an easy rock climb from the col between it and the North Peak. The North Peak (6,720 ft) has several interesting routes combining glacial ice and C-4 to C-5 rock climbs.

South of Three Fingers are Big Bear Mountain (5,641 ft) and Liberty Mountain (5,688 ft). Both require brush-beating approaches but have easy rock routes to the final summits. Liberty also has a more challenging C-5.6 route on its north ridge. At the southeast lobe of the axis ridge is Long Mountain (5,111 ft), where a series of individual rock summits are linked by a mile-long exposed ridge.

Jumbo Mountain (5,801 ft) lies between the Squire Creek and Clear Creek drainages, east of the main line of peaks. Once above timberline, its three summits are easy rock scrambles.

■—————16—————■

HELENA RIDGE TO BARLOW PASS

LOCATION: In Snohomish County, between the Sauk River and the South Fork of the Stillaguamish River
SIZE: 29,640 acres
STATUS: Semiprimitive Nonmotorized
TERRAIN: Steep forested ridges capped by rocky peaks
ELEVATION: 1,040 to 6,610 feet
MANAGEMENT: USFS, Mount Baker–Snoqualmie National Forest, Darrington Ranger District
TOPOGRAPHIC MAPS: Bedal, Helena Ridge, Silverton, White Chuck

A small tarn on the Perry Creek Trail reflects alpine scrub.

At the southeast end of this roadless area, thick forests climb near-vertical slopes to knife-edge ridgelines surmounted by sharp peaks. Lush alpine meadows line the ridgetops to the north and west, and two dozen lakes fill alpine cirques above most of the drainages. Trails lead to only a half-dozen of these lakes—the remainder require cross-country brush-beating to reach. One trail at the southeast end of the area reaches a high meadow; a second leads to a rocky summit with outstanding views south to the nearby range of peaks that run from Big Four to the Monte Cristo group.

Climate

Precipitation, 80 to 100 inches annually, starts in the form of rain in early October, changing to snow at higher elevations before the month is out. By the end of November the snow level is generally down to 2,000 feet, where it remains until May. By July snow has disappeared below 3,500 feet, and most of the higher elevations are clear by early August. Temperatures are relatively mild, seldom below zero in winter or above 80 in summer.

Plants and Wildlife

By virtue of the extremes in altitude in the area encompassed within the Helena Ridge to Barlow Pass area, the complete range of western Washington forest zones is represented. Lower old-growth forests are western hemlock, Douglas-fir, and western red cedar; creek drainages are clogged with slide alder, vine maple, ferns, dwarf willow, and devil's club. The mid-altitude forest is mostly mountain hemlock, mixed with Pacific silver fir, subalpine fir, and Alaska cedar.

Ridgetops, lakes, and drainage headwaters have meadows of heathers, huckleberry, blueberry, salmonberry, and a variety of colorful wildflowers. Rocky peaks have a sparse cover of heather and sedge, interspersed with a few hardy flowers.

The Perry Creek drainage has been proposed as a 2,066-acre RNA. It contains various rare species of ferns, along with untouched stands of Alaska cedar, mountain hemlock, subalpine fir, and a heather and huckleberry community.

Forest inhabitants include black-tailed deer, black bear, spotted owl, marten, and pileated woodpeckers. Isolated groups of mountain goats are found in the higher elevations.

Geology

The area is mostly 60-million-year-old sedimentary deposits, overlaid at the southeast corner near Barlow Pass with more recent volcanic flows interbedded with sedimentary rock. Mount Forgotten is composed of loose volcanic breccia, and the area northwest from it is predominately pre-Jurassic metamorphic rock. Helena Ridge and the ridge to its west are a mix of sandstone and conglomerates, intruded on the western edge by Squire Creek granodiorite.

History

Although the mineral wealth of Monte Cristo, south of Barlow Pass, was discovered in 1889, all initial approaches to that area were from the south, from the vicinity of Index. The upper South Fork of the Stillaguamish River was unexplored until 1891, when surveys of the drainage were followed rapidly by a government trail and, by 1893, a railroad. Prospecting and mining in the mountains between Silverton and Monte Cristo was heavy between 1894 and 1897, but by 1900 the mines had begun to play out.

Logging followed mining as the next economic boom for the region, and major timber sales in ensuing years have pushed logging roads into the periphery of the Helena Ridge to Barlow Pass area, along Clear Creek, Coal Creek, Beaver Creek, and several of the tributaries flowing north into the Sauk River. Only the heart of this (for the time being) de facto wilderness remains roadless and covered by old-growth forest.

ACTIVITIES

Hiking

COAL CREEK TRAILS

Trail #712, Independence Lake. 0.7 mile/e (H). The trail starts at a clearcut at the end of FR 4060 (3,580 ft), then traverses a steep sidehill through old-growth forest to reach Independence Lake (3,720 ft). Meadows at either end of the lake flank a rock wall that rises above its east shoreline.

Trail #712.1, North Lake. 2.5 miles/m (H). This path starts at the northeast end of Independence Lake, where switchbacks twist up the steep hillside to a pair of saddles on the ridgeline (5,000 ft). The first of these offers views of Mount Baker and the peaks of the Boulder River Wilderness, the second overlooks Glacier Peak. More switchbacks lead east from the saddle down to the cirque filled by North Lake (4,158 ft).

Trail #711, Perry Creek. 3.6 miles/e-m (H). The trailhead is located at Perry Creek on FR 4063 (2,100 ft). The track follows the sidehill above Perry Creek, alternating between forest and open talus slopes. Falls are visible in streams cascading off the south side of Stillaguamish Peak; at 1.9 miles the trail crosses just above a waterfall on Perry Creek itself (3,300 ft). The ascent continues to a hillside covered by old-growth forest. Ridgetop meadows (5,000 ft) offer exhilarating views of the Cascade peaks from Mount Baker to Mount Rainier; to the south Big Four looms just a touch away. The climbers' scramble route to the summit of Mount Forgotten (6,005 ft) follows the narrowing ridge to the north.

Trail #710, Dickerman Mountain. 4.3 miles/m (H). From the Mountain Loop Highway (1,940 ft), never-ending switchbacks work up the sheer south flank of Mount Dickerman through a dense forest, regrown from a major fire in the early 1900s. At 4,400 feet the climb moderates at meadows containing a tiny lake. The pause is brief, however, and the way continues up the steep west ridge to the summit (5,723 ft). The vertical north face of the peak overlooks Perry Creek and the rock spires surrounding its headwaters: Stillaguamish, Twin, and Chokwich peaks, and Mount Forgotten. To the east are Sloan and Glacier peaks, and to the south the chain of Monte Cristo–area summits serrate the skyline.

EAST-SIDE TRAILS

   Trail #656, Peek-a-boo Lake. *2.5 miles/m (H).* From FR 2086 (3,160 ft), the trail enters old-growth forest as it climbs the broad drainage at the head of Dutch Creek. At 3,800 feet, switchbacks up a forested face gain a ridgetop meadow (4,300 ft) with views northeast to White Chuck and beyond to Dome Peak and Mount Shuksan. The path then descends to beautiful Peek-a-boo Lake (3,902 ft), tucked in a forested hillside pocket.

Climbing

There are two areas of climbing interest on the west and southeast sides of the area. On the far west side are Voodoo Peak (5,193 ft), a short C-4 ascent; Helena Peak (5,401 ft), a walkup with a C-3 face; and the more challenging Devils Peak (5,170 ft), C-4. Several short rock towers along the ridge to the south offer one- to two-lead challenges. Nearby Devils Thumb (5,172 ft), an exposed outcrop of dunite, has a C-4 approach from Devils Lake. Independence Peak (5,445 ft), a small rock outcrop, is accessible by C-3 scrambles from Trail #721.1.

The higher southeast portion of the area includes several peaks above 5,500 feet. Northern-most are Stillaguamish Peak, a scramble, and Mount Forgotten, an exposed C-3 ridge scramble; both are reached from Trail #711.

The triple summits of Twin Peaks (5,836 ft) are normally approached from the Perry Creek basin, where notches lead to the sheer exposed C-4 slabs protecting the summits. A spire-studded ridge leads northeast to Chokwich Peak (5,662 ft), a flat-topped summit with several short towers on ridges to the north, west, and south.

Winter Sports

The Mountain Loop Highway is not plowed beyond the vicinity of Silverton during the winter, but ski tours from here can follow summertime logging roads for excellent winter scenery and reasonable downhill runs. One of the more popular tours follows snow-covered FR 4060, from its start 2.5 miles beyond Silverton, up the Coal Creek basin to Coal Lake. More experienced skiers can continue on to either Pass Lake or Independence Lake. The wide Coal Creek drainage frames wondrous winterscapes of Big Four Mountain, Hall and Sperry peaks, and Mount Pilchuck.

■├─────────────────**17**─────────────────┤■

MALLARDY RIDGE TO SILVERTIP PEAK

LOCATION: In Snohomish County, along the south side of the Mountain Loop Highway between Silverton and Monte Cristo
SIZE: 20,280 acres
STATUS: Semiprimitive Nonmotorized
TERRAIN: Rugged, extremely steep, forested hillsides rising to a chain of jagged rock summits
ELEVATION: 1,500 to 6,610 feet
MANAGEMENT: USFS, Mount Baker–Snoqualmie National Forest, Darrington Ranger District; the Washington State Department of Natural Resources; and isolated patented mining claims
TOPOGRAPHIC MAPS: Bedal, Mallardy Ridge, Monte Cristo, Silverton

The 15-mile-long crest on the south side of the South Fork of the Stillaguamish River, between Mallardy Ridge and Silvertip Peak, bristles with some of the most beautiful alpine summits on the western flank of the Cascades. Although the area has remained roadless, mainly due to its rugged topography, it has still seen heavy use by humans.

Discovery of gold, silver, and copper lodes here in the 1890s led hordes of prospectors into the rugged peaks, which were soon plastered with mining claims. The few trails that exist today were put in by miners, intent at getting from place A to place B via the shortest distance possible. As a result, these trails are strenuous and challenging, more often used as climbing routes rather than for casual hiking. Several other paths are abandoned and overgrown; those inter-

Opposite: *Sheep Gap Mountain rises above Gothic Basin.*

ested in bushwhacking their way into the area's history can locate their traces using old maps.

A dozen distinct peaks, all topping 6,000 feet, and many more smaller spires and towers line the crest of the region. Hikers are lured here by the scenic beauty; climbers are challenged by the solid rock pyramids with vertical faces framed by knife-edge ridges.

Climate

Summer weather is generally dry and mild, with temperatures rarely exceeding the 80s. Rains start in October and turn to snow at higher elevations by month's end. Precipitation—80 to 100 inches annually—continues to fall as snow throughout winter, when snow levels drop to around 2,000 feet. Temperatures remain mild through winter, seldom dropping below zero. Snow is gone below 3,500 feet by July, but upper elevations are not snow-free until August.

Plants and Wildlife

The lower portions of the backbone ridge are heavily forested, primarily with western hemlock, some Douglas-fir, and western red cedar. Avalanche tracks that lace the steep ridges are covered with slide alder and vine maple, joined by dwarf willow and devil's club along creek beds. A few alpine meadows, with seasonal wildflower displays, are found atop the ridges at the western end of the area. The ragged rock summits support little vegetation other than patches of heathers and sedges. Unique local climatic conditions at the Big Four Ice Caves foster the growth of subalpine wildflowers, rarely seen at this low elevation.

Geology

The geology of the area reflects dramatic deformations of the base metamorphic rock. The phyllite and slate of Big Four dates to pre-Jurassic times. The peaks southwest of Big Four are mostly younger metamorphosed sandstones, shales, and conglomerates formed from Cretaceous and Paleocene continental deposits about 70 million years ago. The folded strata here dip steeply to the east and northeast. Vesper Peak and the area south of Big Four are made up of a Tertiary intrusion of quartz diorite. Sheer rock faces, narrow ridgelines, and high cirques were carved by local alpine glaciers 15,000 to 20,000 years ago.

History

Prospectors and miners poured into the area between 1891 and the 1920s, beating out hardscrabble trails to impossible spots in their search for mineral riches. The Everett and Monte Cristo Railway was completed in 1893 to support mining operations. Portions of the railroad grade are still recognizable today along the bank of the South Fork of the Stillaguamish River.

In 1897 a 2-mile-long aerial tram was run from Silverton (1,500 ft) south over 4,200-foot Marble Pass to reach the "45" copper mine at the head of Williamson Creek. Unfortunately, the very week the tram was completed, heavy snows and floods wiped out the railbed, and mining operations were suspended. The railway was not restored until the spring of 1900, and the "45" tram was returned to operation in July of 1901. The operation was never profitable, and the mortgage on the mine was foreclosed in 1903.

Despite the decline in mining activity at Monte Cristo itself, in 1911 the Del Campo Metals Company opened prospects on Weden Creek, and by 1913 it had announced that they were ready to produce. However, by 1918 these two mines in Gothic Basin were also abandoned.

As mining played out, the scenic value of the area was recognized, and in 1921 Everett investors built an elaborate resort with a lodge, cabins, golf course, tennis courts, and a man-made lake at the base of Big Four Mountain. The 1929 depression cut deeply into the inn's clientele, and a devastating blow was dealt in 1933 when the railroad discontinued operation. Automobiles with wheels modified to run on the railroad track continued to serve the inn until 1937, when the CCC converted the old railbed to the present Mountain Loop Highway. The inn burned to the ground in 1949. A picnic area now stands near its foundation.

ACTIVITIES

Hiking

Trail #723, Ice Caves. 1 mile/e (H). A near-flat path leaves the Big Four Picnic Area parking lot (1,715 ft) on a boardwalk over beaver-pond marshes, enters the woods, then crosses a footbridge over the South Fork of the Stillaguamish. After a short forest hike, the trail breaks out to close-up views of the mile-high face of Big Four Mountain and the avalanche-born snowfield that harbors the ice caves. The caves form when meltwater from the face of the mountain creates pockets under the ice, which are then enlarged by warm drafts of summer air. The caves are subject to sudden collapse, so are dangerous to enter or climb upon. Avalanches that create the snowfield obviously also make close approaches dangerous in winter.

Trail #707, Sunrise Mine. 3 miles/m (H). The trail starts from FR 4065 in a clearcut (2,380 ft), then enters forest as it heads to a log crossing of the South Fork of the Stillaguamish River. It continues up a branch of the river, breaking out to a steepening avalanche slope. The final mile, marked by cairns, heads straight uphill to Headlee Pass (4,600 ft). The rock in the final chute below the pass is very steep and loose. The pass, a knife-edge slot in a spire-dotted ridge between Sperry and Morning Star peaks, is the start point of climbing routes for these peaks.

Trail #724, Weden Creek. 1.8 miles/d (H). From Barlow Pass (2,361 ft) hike the old Monte Cristo Road 1.7 miles to the trailhead on the southwest side of the road. The Sauk is sometimes difficult to cross here; an alternative path on the opposite bank, cut by volunteers, runs from the Twin Bridge Campground, 1 mile from Barlow Pass, to the normal trail at Weden Creek.

The trail was originally put in to reach the two Del Campo mine sites at the head of the creek. A steep diagonal up a forested hillside crosses several gullies en route that require ice axes for safety when filled with snow. From the lower mine site (3,700 ft), switchbacks gain the top of a cliff above Weden Lake, the site of the upper mine. Here the way enters the Foggy Lake basin, framed on both sides by 1,000-foot faces rising to the craggy summits of Del Campo and Gothic peaks and Castle Rocks. The snow-covered basin melts to meadows in late summer, but the lake often remains frozen year-round.

Climbing

The ridge between Mallardy Ridge and Silvertip Peak is a climber's mecca, with challenges for all skill levels. Big Four (6,135 ft) is a massive mountain with an imposing near-vertical north face. Two bands of cliffs, one between 2,000 and 4,000 feet and a second between 4,800 feet and the summit, are its major challenges. Several routes have been put up the mountain; most range from C-3 to C-4, with one variant rated C-5.8.

North of Headlee Pass are two sharp rock towers, Vesper (6,214 ft) and Sperry (6,125 ft) peaks. Vesper's north face is a near-vertical 900-foot slab, with routes ranging from C-5.6 to C-5.9. The summit pyramid of Sperry has three sheer faces separated by steep narrow arêtes. Routes are C-2 to C-5.8.

On the south side of Headlee Pass is Morning Star Peak (6,020 ft). The final summit pyramid has no routes below C-3 to C-4. There are several minor spikes on the spur ridges from both Sperry and Morning Star. One of these, Vega Tower (5,480 ft), is a striking spire offering both C-3 and C-5.8 climbs.

North of Foggy Lake is Del Campo Peak (6,610 ft), a solid rock summit pyramid, difficult from all sides. On the rim above the lake is Gothic Peak (6,213 ft), solid sandstone with precipitous east and west faces. Along the ridge north from Gothic are Castle Rocks (5,800 ft), a series of difficult crags.

South of the Foggy Lake basin is the multi-summited massif of Sheep Gap Mountain (5,683 to 5,819 ft). The lower north peak is an easy scramble, but near-vertical walls of the bell-shaped main peak are rated C-3, as is Rams Horn (5,400 ft), a tower south of the main peak.

▪———————18———————▪

RAGGED RIDGE

LOCATION: In Snohomish County, between Spada Lake and the North Fork of the Skykomish River

SIZE: 35,300 acres

STATUS: USFS, Semiprimitive Nonmotorized; unprotected DNR and private land

TERRAIN: Rocky crags line the narrow tops of steep forested ridges, indented by deep creek drainages

ELEVATION: 720 to 5,550 feet

MANAGEMENT: USFS, Mount Baker–Snoqualmie National Forest, Skykomish Ranger District; the Washington State Department of Natural Resources; and private patented mining claims

TOPOGRAPHIC MAPS: Baring, Gold Bar, Index, Monte Cristo, Mount Stickney, Wallace Lake

Ragged Ridge is one of the most remote and impenetrable areas still remaining on the western flank of the Cascades. Miners once staked nearly a hundred claims here, mainly along the edges of the Silver Creek drainage, but all mining ceased long ago. The edges of the area have been chewed by logging, especially in the state DNR properties. Three short trails penetrate the periphery of the area; the seldom-visited interior is untouched by man-made accesses, and (thankfully) has yet to see a chain saw.

The convoluted crests for which Ragged Ridge is named have steep, densely forested walls cut by creek drainages. Narrow ridgetops are liberally sprinkled with rock horns and spike-like gendarmes. Two large lakes, Greider and Boulder, lie on the northwest, and a third, Isabel, is on the southwest. A sprinkling of smaller lakes is found west of Mount Stickney and along the southern border of the region.

Climate

Average rainfall in the area ranges from 60 to 80 inches per year, mostly accompanying storm fronts approaching from the southwest. A large portion of the precipitation falls during winter months as snow. Summers tend to be dry and mild. Snow levels lower to 2,000 feet during winter; by early July the snow retreats to 4,000 feet, and most is gone by the end of that month. Temperature highs average in the 80s in summer and lows are in the 20s in midwinter.

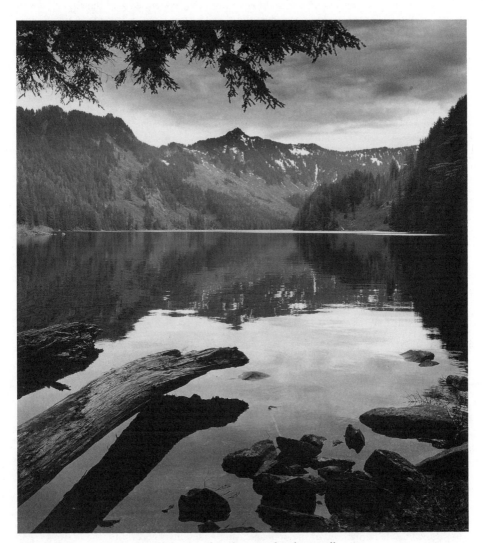

Lake Isabel is one of three large lakes found in the Ragged Ridge Roadless Area.

Plants and Wildlife

Beyond the clearcuts and their second-growth spawn that surround Ragged Ridge, the heart of the area is virgin forest. The dominant species is western hemlock, but mountain hemlock, silver fir, and red cedar also share the hillsides. Avalanches bare strips down the precipitous hillsides, which then grow dense with vine maple, dwarf willow, and slide alder. Red mountain heather, western cassiope, blueleaf huckleberry, luetkea, and elephant's-head pedicularis are found in subalpine meadows near creeks and lakes.

Forests are inhabited by elk, black-tailed deer, and black bear. Both deer and elk descend to lower elevations adjoining the North Fork of the Skykomish for winter range, and bald eagles use the river as a winter feeding ground. Spotted owls are found in the vicinity of Snowslide Lake on the South Fork of Salmon Creek.

Geology

At the northern edge of the area, near Red Mountain, strata of metamorphosed sedimentary and volcanic rock are cut by a dike of serpentine. The western edge of the region consists mostly of older Mesozoic sedimentary deposits. The heart of Ragged Ridge is an intrusion of 35-million-year-old granitic rock, a part of the Index batholith. Local alpine glaciation during the Pleistocene epoch is responsible for carving out the steep-walled valleys and for shaping the ragged ridge crests.

History

In the mid-1800s the dense virgin forests of the Pacific Northwest presented a serious obstacle to new settlers in the region; thus, rivers were relied on for transportation and commerce. The first trading centers along the Skykomish River were located at Snohomish City and Gunn's Place (present-day Index). In 1859 a syndicate was organized to push roads into the area, and Ed Cady was hired to explore the upper Skykomish to look for a possible route across the Cascades to the Columbia River basin. Cady and his partner discovered that local Indians traded with tribes east of the Cascades using a route that went up the North Fork of the Skykomish River, through a pass (now named Cady Pass), and down the Wenatchee River. In 1860 Cady began blazing a path along this route that is still used by forest roads and trails. The trails themselves are not in the Ragged Ridge area proper; look for them in the Henry M. Jackson Wilderness. The present-day North Fork Snoqualmie River Road follows the route of one along the north side of the Ragged Ridge area.

The new trail brought prospectors into the region, and a small way station called Scott's Camp was built at the confluence of Silver Creek and the Skykomish. This later became the mining camp of Galena, a site still marked on today's maps, although it has long since disappeared. By 1874 prospectors had filed claims on Silver Creek, upstream from Scott's Camp, and by 1880 another mining camp, Mineral City, was thriving at the junction of the north and south forks of Silver Creek.

ACTIVITIES

Hiking

Greider Lakes Trail. 2.5 miles/d (H). From the trailhead picnic area on FR 61 (1,580 ft), a path leads into the forest, then starts endless switchbacks up a jarring root-and-boulder tread. In just under 2 miles, a scramble traverse of a steep cliff leads to Little Greider Lake (2,910 ft). A path around the northwest shore continues 0.5 mile to Big Greider Lake (2,932 ft). Both lakes are rimmed by a 1,000-foot-high band of cliffs. Just before the second lake, a spur switchbacks 0.7 mile up the steep brushy hillside to the base of a rock wall and great views up Williamson Creek to Big Four, Vesper, and Little Chief peaks.

Boulder Lake Trail. 4 miles/d (H). The trail leaves the south side of FR 61 (1,650 ft) on an abandoned logging road that deteriorates to a rough traverse of a large rock slide above the east bank of Boulder Creek. In 0.5 mile the path enters forest and zigzags up, then traverses as it climbs the hillside to the head of the drainage. After a final marshy contour, the northwest end of Boulder Lake (3,706 ft) is reached. Cliffs 600 feet high border the cirque that holds the lake.

Climbing

Although individual summits in the Ragged Ridge area are not high in comparison to other Cascade peaks, many rise nearly 4,000 vertical feet above the adjoining drainages, presenting a climbing challenge belied by their altitude. Since most of the area is intrusive granite, the rock offers solid, stable climbing. Ridges throughout the area are topped with a multitude of short gendarmes worthy of a lead or two of serious rock climbing.

Mount Stickney (5,367 ft) is the highest peak on the west edge of the Ragged Ridge area. Cross-country approaches from the northwest reach narrow ridge-crest scrambles from its east or west ribs. The convoluted crest dividing the North Fork of the Sultan River and the Salmon Creek and Elk Creek drainages has several attractive rock horns and pyramids ranging from C-3 to C-5.5 in difficulty; all approaches require considerable bushwhacking. The ridge encircling Greider Lakes is capped by Greider (4,829 ft) and Static (5,100 ft) peaks. The latter has excellent climbing routes up solid granite, with short leads to C-5.8.

The highest point in the Ragged Ridge area is Red Mountain (5,550 ft). The summit block is protected on all sides by near-vertical faces, breached only by steep brush-choked gullies; a C-4 route climbs from the Sultan River basin.

The northeast end of the area is anchored by Crested Buttes (5,318 ft), a ragged subridge south of Sheep Gap. A series of crags atop the ridge can be approached from either the east via Silver Creek or from the west via the Sultan River. Thick brushy approaches lead to C-3 to C-4 rock spires.

19

EAGLE ROCK

LOCATION: In Snohomish and King counties, between the Beckler River and the North and South Forks of the Skykomish

SIZE: 35,035 acres

STATUS: Semiprimitive Nonmotorized

TERRAIN: Three major ridges trending northwest to southeast rise abruptly 3,000 to 4,000 feet above intervening drainages. Ridge crests are capped by rock gendarmes and rugged craggy peaks with near-vertical faces.

ELEVATION: 660 to 6,240 feet

MANAGEMENT: USFS, Mount Baker–Snoqualmie National Forest, Skykomish Ranger District; Washington State Department of Natural Resources; private patented mining claims

TOPOGRAPHIC MAPS: Baring, Blanca Lake, Evergreen Mountain, Grotto, Index, Monte Cristo

East from Gold Bar on US Highway 2, the stupendous, 3,000-foot vertical north face of Mount Baring suddenly looms dead ahead. On the opposite side of the valley the massive, jagged thumbs of Gunn and Merchant peaks protrude above forested hillsides. These peaks mark the southwest corner of the Eagle Rock Roadless Area. This de facto wilderness fills a triangular wedge framed by the North and South Forks of the Skykomish River and the Beckler River. Although logging has gnawed at the south and east sides of this area, and mining has made deep intrusions into its western edge, the heart of the region remains virgin forest at elevations below 4,000 feet, with precipitous ridges and peaks rising steeply above.

Mount Baring, Grotto Mountain, and Klinger Ridge form the southern rim of the Eagle Rock area; behind them lie the Barclay Creek drainage to the west and the Eagle Creek drainage to the east. A second line of peaks rises along the north sides of these creeks, on the west rising to Jumpoff Ridge. At the east end of this ridge is the highest point in the area, Gunn Peak; a jumble of rock towers continues east to Merchant Peak. The crest then tapers southeast past Townsend Mountain, Flapjack Point, and Eagle Rock before dropping to the Beckler River.

North of this extended ridge, the Trout Creek valley nearly cuts the area in two. A series of smaller creeks subdivide the northern portion of Eagle Rock into several interlocking ridges that culminate in the sharply spiked arêtes of Spire and Bear mountains and the forested summits of massive Iron and Conglomerate mountains.

Once past the peripheral logging and mining roads, access to the interior of Eagle Rock follows faint boot-paths; only two short trails are maintained. Nonetheless, many of the dozen and a half alpine lakes that dot the heart of the area are reached by determined fishermen. Climbers also visit Eagle Rock, drawn by the beauty and challenge of its jagged peaks.

Climate

Precipitation averages between 60 and 80 inches annually. Although there is intermittent rainfall year-round, most precipitation falls as snow between September and May. Snow accumulates to depths of 20 feet or more at higher elevations. Temperatures are relatively mild, with highs averaging in the 80s in summer, and lows averaging in the 20s in winter.

Plants and Wildlife

Lower elevations are covered with a dense forest of western hemlock, with some Douglas-fir and red cedar. The forest understory is very brushy, as are creek beds, clearcuts, and avalanche tracks. Cover here is primarily vine maple, dwarf willow, and slide alder. Subalpine meadows, most commonly found along and at the head of creek drainages, contain red mountain heather, huckleberry, western cassiope, and luetkea. The steep rock at higher elevations is lightly forested, primarily with mountain hemlock. Cliffs, basins, and talus slopes have light coats of heathers and sedges that are color-dabbed with small hardy wildflowers.

The forested portions of the Eagle Rock area hold black bear, black-tailed deer, bobcat, cougar, and a few elk. Mountain goats are also found in the high mountain areas. Creeks and lakes support beaver, marten, mink, otter, muskrat, and ermine. Bald and golden eagles, osprey, and spotted owls roost in tall old-growth trees, and blue grouse, ruffed grouse, and several species of songbirds are found in the brush below.

Geology

The core of the Eagle Rock area is a portion of the Grotto batholith, a 25-million-year-old granodiorite intrusion, flanked on the east by metamorphosed pre-Miocene volcanics and Permian sedimentaries, and on the west by Paleozoic sedimentary rock. Quartz veins containing a variety of sulphides are found along the borders of the intrusion. Trout Creek, the major drainage north of the Gunn Peak massif, has been a significant producer of copper ores. Prospectors working along the Mount Baring ridge have discovered quartz veins containing tourmaline, blue shorl, albite, and epidote.

The deep, U-shaped valleys between the area's major ridges show clear evidence of their origins in the scraping and carving of local Pleistocene alpine glaciers. These same glaciers sculpted the narrow, sometimes knife-edge arêtes between the rock summits and gendarmes.

History

Although the earliest visitors to the region were trappers, they were soon followed by prospectors working their way north from Index along the North Fork of the Skykomish. In 1897, rich copper ores were found in lower Trout Creek, and other claims were staked higher up the creek on the north side of Gunn Peak. The lower of these, the Sunset Mine, operated continuously from the time of its discovery until 1932, with the peak of its production occurring between 1918 and 1920.

ACTIVITIES

Hiking

Only two short trails in the area are maintained by the Forest Service. Several more paths have been informally beaten into popular recreation spots. Many of the mining and logging roads that edged the Eagle Rock area in the past are no longer maintained. Although gated or impassable to vehicles, the old roads serve as unofficial, though usable, trails.

Trail #1070, Heybrook. 1 mile/m (H). This is the earliest trail to be free of snow in the Skykomish Ranger District; snow is usually so light that it can be hiked year-round. From the north side of US Highway 2 (900 ft), the trail climbs in a few lazy switchbacks through second-growth forest to the Heybrook lookout (1,700 ft). (The tower is unsafe—stay off!) Here are awe-inspiring views of the sheer north and east walls of Mounts Index and Persis, and the broad

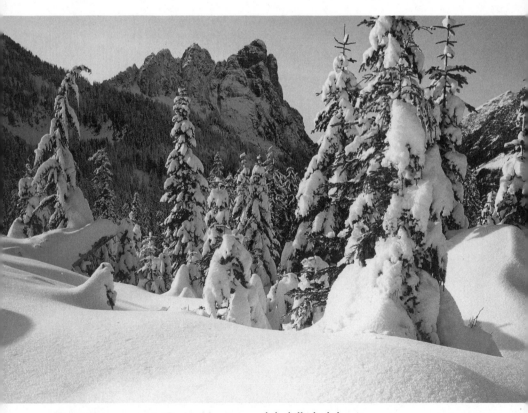

Heavy winter snow coats Baring Mountain and the hillsides below it.

Skykomish River valley. FR 6260 services the radio facilities on the summit, so the site can also be reached by hiking this road. Gated near its start, this route is 4 miles long.

Trail #1055, Barclay Lake. 2.2 miles/e-d (H). The trail leaves the north side of FR 6024 (2,200 ft) and slogs through mudholes along the riverbank as it wanders up to the inlet of Barclay Lake (2,422 ft). A footpath from the lake inlet heads northeast up the hillside and across talus slopes to a low saddle and Stone Lake (3,875 ft). From here it continues northwest through Paradise Meadows to Eagle Lake (3,888 ft), which lies just below the east face of Merchant Peak.

Climbing

The imposing 3,100-foot-high vertical north face of Mount Baring (6,125 ft) has long been regarded as one of the most difficult climbs in the western Cascades. Some of the northwest's top climbers struggled with this C-5.8 to C-5.10 challenge before it was finally conquered in 1960. Since then it has been climbed several times, including once in the winter. Its equally challenging north prow, Dolomite Tower, is a C-5.9 climb, first done in 1986.

Baring and the striking thumbs of Gunn and Merchant peaks are bookends on either side of Barclay Creek. Gunn (6,240 ft) is approached from Barclay Creek, where gullies and slabs lead to a notch on its southeast ridge. A basin traverse leads to the C-3 ascent of the final summit block. The northwest face of this block can be climbed in three C-4 to C-5 rock leads. Merchant Peak (6,113 ft) is topped by relatively easy C-3 ridge routes from the saddle between its east and west summits.

On the Bear Creek–Howard Creek divide, Spire Mountain (6,213 ft) is a sharp, narrow rib topped by three distinct summits and several other rock gendarmes. C-3 to C-4 routes up chimneys on the east face access the tops of the spires. Bear Mountain (5,519 ft) is a triple-towered, rough, rock peak at the northeast corner of the Eagle Rock area. Ascents start from FR 6574 at the north end of the Beckler River Road. Ribs connecting the individual summits are sharp knife-edges; traverses on them are rated C-3 to C-5.

—20—

HENRY M. JACKSON WILDERNESS

LOCATION: In King, Snohomish, and Chelan counties, straddling the Cascade crest between Stevens Pass and the North Fork of the Sauk River

SIZE: 103,591 acres, plus about 35,100 acres of adjacent roadless areas

STATUS: Designated Wilderness Area (1984), adjoined by Semiprimitive Nonmotorized areas

TERRAIN: Steep slopes and finger ridges separated by glacier-cut valleys. Ridgetop alpine meadows to the south and east; glaciated, sharp, serrated ridges with distinctive peaks to the northwest

ELEVATION: 1,800 to 7,835 feet

MANAGEMENT: USFS, Mount Baker–Snoqualmie National Forest, Darrington and Skykomish ranger districts; Wenatchee National Forest, Lake Wenatchee Ranger District; some private patented mining claims

TOPOGRAPHIC MAPS: Bedal, Bench Mark Mountain, Blanca Lake, Captain Point, Evergreen Mountain, Labyrinth Mountain, Monte Cristo, Poe Mountain, Scenic, Skykomish, Sloan Peak, Stevens Pass

The Henry M. Jackson Wilderness honors Washington's longtime senator, who was a major force in creating large portions of the state's present wilderness areas. The area straddles more than 30 miles of the Cascade crest from Stevens Pass to Kodak Peak, traversed by a portion of

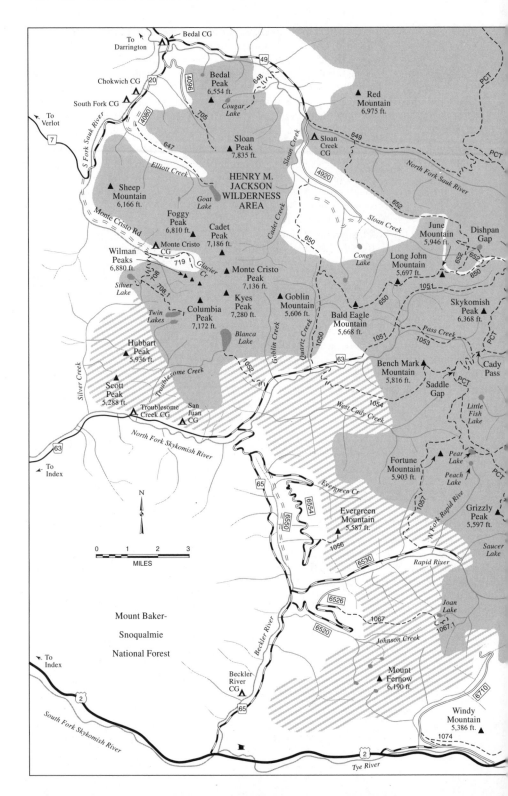

the Pacific Crest National Scenic Trail. Ridges separated by deep glacier-carved valleys radiate east and west from the crest; many are routes for other trails leading from the perimeter of the wilderness to the PCT.

The northwest corner of the wilderness encompasses several glaciated basins rimmed by narrow ragged ridges capped by spires, towers, and toothlike summits ranging between 6,000 and 7,800 feet. Their imposing 4,000- to 5,500-foot local relief makes them a mecca for mountain climbers, hikers, and photographers who relish Alps-like scenery. Since this area saw major mining activity in the late 1800s, history buffs can have a field day exploring the ruins of mines and mining camps, envisioning what the area must have looked like in its heyday.

More than 60 alpine and subalpine lakes are spattered about the area, ranging from pond size to the substantial 179 acres of Blanca Lake. Although several roadless areas on the periphery of the designated wilderness were not included under its protection, they are included here in the hope they may be joined to the wilderness before they succumb to timber harvest or development. These include the Troublesome, lower West Cady, and Evergreen creek drainages; Johnson Ridge; the Mount Fernow and Beckler Peak area; Windy Mountain; and the Fish, Fall, and Lake creek drainages.

Climate

Annual precipitation ranges from 60 to 80 inches, mostly falling in the form of snow at medium and high elevations. Periods of heavy precipitation start in November, often causing runoffs in rivers and streams late in the year. Snow accumulates as deep as 20 feet on higher terrain, and often remains there until late July. Elevations below 3,500 feet are generally snow-free by early June, when snowmelt again causes peak flows of rivers and streams.

Temperatures are relatively mild year-round. Summer highs average in the 80s, and winter lows average in the 20s, with a few extended below-zero periods.

Plants and Wildlife

On the west side of the Cascade crest, most valleys and ridges up to about 4,500 feet are covered with western hemlock, Alaska cedar, Douglas-fir, true fir, Pacific silver fir, and spruce. Drainages contain a tangled web of slide alder, vine maple, dwarf willow, ferns, and devil's club, and avalanche slopes have a thick cover of slide alder and vine maple. At higher elevations the timber changes to subalpine fir and mountain hemlock. Basin heads and ridgetops frequently have open parklands carpeted with heathers and mosses and fringed by blueberry and huckleberry bushes. When snows melt these meadows are ablaze with colorful wildflowers, avalanche lilies, dwarf lupine, penstemon, phlox, bistort, valerian, and Indian paintbrush.

Black-tailed deer are the most common species in the area, but the forest also harbors black bear, cougar, marten, lynx, spotted owls, and blue grouse. At rocky upper elevations, mountain goats and hoary marmots may also be seen.

Geology

The geology of the Henry M. Jackson Wilderness is complicated by the Straight Creek fault, which cuts through it from north to south. According to plate tectonic theories, this fault line marks a slippage between sections of the northwest-moving North Cascades micro-continent.

The base rock east of the fault is older continental crust, mostly metamorphosed sedimentary deposits that accumulated on the eastern coastal plain of the North Cascades terrane over 180 million years ago. The base rock west of the fault is thick volcanic ocean crust overlaid with metamorphosed mudstones and sandstones, all heavily folded 25 million to 35 million years ago. Most of the peaks of the Monte Cristo group represent eroded remnants of this base.

The area east of the Straight Creek fault and north of Stevens Pass was intruded by a large mass of granitic rock between 60 million and 100 million years ago. Later granitic intrusions, about 25 million years old, occurred east of the fault in the vicinity of Sloan and Foggy peaks, and to the west in the vicinity of Hubbart Peak.

The sharp, jagged, spire-laden arêtes and incisor summit blocks in the north end of the wilderness all result from the carving of local alpine glaciers that reached their maximum about 15,000 years ago. These same glaciers are responsible for shaping the steep-sided drainages that pervade the region.

History

Trappers and prospectors made the first non-Indian explorations in the area. To facilitate their travel, Ed Cady blazed a trail across the Cascades in 1860, following a route used by coastal Indians to trade with tribes east of the mountains. Cady's trail across the pass now named for him never materialized into the wagon road and railroad envisioned by his Everett business patrons. Today it remains accessible only to boots and hooves.

Prospectors worked north from the Skykomish River up Silver Creek, lacing the area with claims and dreaming of rich gold, silver, and copper strikes. In 1889, Joseph Pearsall, prospecting north of Hubbart Peak, reached a saddle now known as Wilmans Pass, where he saw the peaks surrounding Glacier Basin. Spotting rust streaks on the basin walls and the red-gold glint of galena, he worked his way into the basin to collect ore samples. Assays showed both gold and silver; Pearsall got a grubstake and headed back to the basin to stake claims. By fall a dozen claims marked rich-looking prospects in Glacier Basin and Seventysix Gulch. In 1890 more claims were filed, and the campsite in the valley was named Monte Cristo, after the wealthy count of that name in the novel by Alexander Dumas.

The year 1893 saw the town of Monte Cristo platted, the construction of a concentrator, and the arrival of the first train via a new route up the Stillaguamish River. Aerial tramways were built from the mines to the concentrator in 1894. In 1896 a wagon road reached mines at Goat Lake in the drainage north from Glacier Basin. Tunnels were bored 250 feet beneath the floor of Glacier Basin, and a hole was started through lower Wilmans Peak between Glacier Basin and Seventysix Gulch.

More than 22,500 tons of ore concentrate had been shipped out of Monte Cristo by 1897, but for the next two years floods and washouts closed the railroad line to the town, shutting down mining. The railroad was restored in 1900, and mining resumed at a steady pace the following year. Although more than $7 million in gold was taken from Monte Cristo, the mines were never profitable, and 1904 mine closures and bankruptcies foretold the end. The mines closed in 1907; in 1915 heavy snows crushed most of the town's buildings, leaving it a ghost town save for visits by tourists to the remaining hotel. The last mines shut down in 1920; the final vestige of mining, the remaining tramway cable, fell in 1973.

The southern perimeter of the wilderness was opened by the construction of the Great Northern Railroad line across Stevens Pass in 1893. The original path over the summit required

A hiker surveys a sea of peaks in the Henry M. Jackson Wilderness Area. Sloan Peak is in the center distance.

a series of switchbacks on either side; spurs at the ends of the switchbacks held trains while switches were thrown to permit them to reverse direction for the next section of track. This laborious method of crossing the pass was eliminated in 1900, when a 2.6-mile-long tunnel was completed through the mountain just north of the pass. Despite construction of massive snowsheds above the section of track west of the tunnel, a 1910 avalanche killed 96 people aboard two trains that had been trapped by prior slides. The track was relocated to a new 7.79-mile-long tunnel south of the pass in 1929.

ACTIVITIES

Hiking

NORTH FORK OF THE SAUK RIVER TRAILS

Trail #648, Sloan Peak. 4.5 miles/d (H). From FR 49 (1,900 ft) the trail follows an old road across beaver ponds to the North Fork of the Sauk River; it must be forded in the vicinity. The miner origin of the route becomes apparent as it climbs relentlessly up a forested rib, then delicately tiptoes across Cougar Creek between two waterfalls. A respite in the ascent, followed by two more crossings of Cougar Creek and a chain of short switchbacks, surmounts the final 1,000 feet. Here the path breaks out to meadows (4,800 ft) with awesome views of nearby Sloan Peak and more distant ones of Red Mountain and Glacier Peak. Travel beyond here requires mountaineering skills.

Trail #650, Bald Eagle (Curry Gap). 10 miles/m (H,S). A footbridge crossing Sloan Creek (2,400 ft) leads to a 2.5-mile hike up abandoned FR 4920 to the trailhead (2,950 ft). The trail enters the forest and ascends to Curry Gap (3,950 ft), where meadows open to views of glaciers falling from the east side of the Monte Cristo peaks. The trail continues southeast, switchbacks to the ridgetop (5,000 ft), then follows the crest to the north side of Bald Eagle Mountain.

The route follows a ridge northeast to Long John Mountain, then continues east atop the crest to June Mountain. A side-trip scramble to the top the mountain (5,946 ft) opens expansive views of Sloan, Glacier, and the Monte Cristo peaks. The trail meets Trail #652 from the north at a small saddle east of June, then swings across the ridge to traverse south-slope meadows. It gains the ridgetop, then hooks south to join the PCT at Dishpan Gap (5,600 ft).

SOUTH FORK OF THE SAUK RIVER TRAILS

Trail #647, Elliott Creek. 5.2 miles/e (H). From the gate near the start of FR 4080 (1,850 ft), walk the road through forest and clearcuts for 3.5 miles to its end, the beginning of the foot trail to Goat Lake. The trail follows an 1896 wagon route to mining claims in the basin. In 0.5 mile a side path leaves the trail and crosses Elliott Creek to the site of a former hotel and mining camp. Switchbacks surmount a steep hillside below the lake outlet; glimpses here of McIntosh Falls. The trail rounds the east side of Goat Lake (3,161 ft) and is overwhelmed by brush near its south end. Views here rise up the basin to cliffs below the glaciers hanging from the sides of Cadet and Foggy peaks.

Trail #708, Poodle Dog Pass. 2.4 miles/m (H). From the Monte Cristo townsite (2,756 ft) this steep, eroded track climbs past several mine shafts to a wooded breather at 3,400 feet. The rest is brief, and the path stumbles over roots and boulders as it switchbacks up to Poodle Dog Pass (4,350 ft). From the pass a short spur continues west to the cirque surrounding Silver Lake (4,260 ft).

Trail #708.1, Twin Lakes. 2.7 miles/m (H). From Poodle Dog Pass (4,350 ft) a rugged path climbs east to Wilmans Pass (4,850 ft), the original route used by the prospector who discovered the Monte Cristo basin. Here the way follows a steep, narrow rib with views down the wall of Seventysix Gulch to the pinnacles of Wilmans Peaks, and up to the summit of Columbia Peak. Beyond a col between the Twin Peaks summits (5,350 ft), the trail scrambles along a shelf above a 600-foot-high cliff, then descends to the east bank of the northern, and larger, of the Twin Lakes (4,710 ft).

Trail #719, Glacier Basin. 2.1 miles/m-d (H). From the south side of the bridge over Glacier Creek near Monte Cristo (2,850 ft), the trail follows a gentle railroad grade for nearly a mile, to a no-nonsense climb that heads straight up badly eroded dirt and rock where trailside tree roots provide vital hand holds. As it rounds Mystery Hill, the path breaks into meadows at the heart of Glacier Basin (4,700 ft). On all sides vertical glacier-pocked walls sweep up to rugged peaks: Wilmans, Monte Cristo, Cadet, and the Cadets. Ruins and rusting debris are all that remain of the mine shafts, ore bins, and aerial tramways that once filled this beautiful place.

NORTH FORK OF THE SKYKOMISH RIVER TRAILS

Trail #1052, Blanca Lake. 3.5 miles/d (H). There is no hesitation in the uphill grind from FR 63 (1,900 ft) through 37 switchbacks to reach a tiny meadow enclosing the perfectly circular shoreline of Virgin Lake (4,220 ft). From here a 0.5-mile path swings down a forested sidehill to the south shore of Blanca Lake (3,972 ft). Rock cliffs rise above the east shore of the lake, whose water is stained a pale turquoise green by glacial till. At the north end of the lake is a broad talus fan, plowed by the Columbia Glacier before it retreated farther up the basin. Rimming the glacier are walls and pocket glaciers below the summits of Kyes, Monte Cristo, and Columbia peaks.

Trail #1054, West Cady Ridge. 8 miles/m (H,S). After numerous switchbacks climb through old-growth forest from FR 63 and the Skykomish River (2,470 ft), the route breaks into meadows atop West Cady Ridge (4,800 ft). The heather parkland follows a ridgetop arc to Bench Mark Mountain. A short spur to the top of the mountain (5,816 ft) offers vistas to the Monte Cristo peaks, Sloan, Baker, Glacier, and Rainier. The route continues a short distance east, dropping to meet the PCT just north of Saddle Gap (4,700 ft).

Trail #1051, North Fork of the Skykomish River. (8 miles/m H,S). At the end of FR 63 (3,000 ft) this path heads up the valley floor of the North Fork of the Skykomish River. It continues up the narrowing drainage to the river headwaters and an open alpine park (4,500 ft). Switchbacks attack the steepening hillside, and the route gains the ridgetop at Dishpan Gap (5,600 ft) to merge with Trail #650 and the PCT.

BECKLER RIVER TRAILS

Trail #1067, Johnson Ridge. *4.3 miles/m (H; M,B to the wilderness boundary).* This trail originally started at the Beckler River, but logging roads and clearcuts annihilated its lower portion. It now begins near the upper end of abandoned FR 6526 (3,800 ft) in an area burned by a 1967 forest fire. The sometimes obscure path follows the crest east; as it passes over Sunrise Mountain (5,056 ft) trees give way to views of Mount Fernow and Glacier Peak. The ridgetop trail descends to a saddle, then climbs again to Scorpion Mountain (5,540 ft). A spur drops from the mountaintop to tiny Joan Lake (5,040 ft), cupped in a bench on Scorpion's east slope.

Trail #1057, Meadow Creek. *8 miles/m (H,S).* The route leaves the Rapid River and FR 6530 just east of Meadow Creek (2,000 ft) and switchbacks up the slope above the creek through the remains of a 1967 forest fire. A gradual ascent reaches the head of the creek, then heads uphill to reach alpine meadows surrounding Fortune Ponds (4,700 ft). A short scramble to the top of Fortune Mountain (5,903 ft) opens views of the backbone of the Cascades. South from the ponds the way follows the tread of the old PCT to meet its new route above Pear Lake (4,809 ft).

US 2 TRAILS

Trail #1074, Iron Goat. *7.3 miles/e (H).* Once the railroad route across Stevens Pass, the portion of track between the old Cascade tunnel and Scenic was abandoned when the trains were rerouted to a new tunnel on the south side of the pass. Seven miles of this railbed have since been converted to a trail. There are two segments, both starting at a switchback on the east side of Martin Creek (2,600 ft). The lower piece of trail traces the old track from the switchback down to Twin Tunnels, 1.2 miles. The upper part of the route ends at Wellington townsite, once a railroad camp west of the Stevens Pass tunnel. The trail will eventually be extended to the old tunnel entrance.

SMITHBROOK ROAD TRAILS

Trail #1590, Smithbrook. *1.5 miles/e (H,S).* The shortest east-side approach to the PCT leaves FR 6700 (4,200 ft) in clearcuts, then climbs uphill west to Union Gap (4,700 ft) and its junction with the PCT.

LITTLE WENATCHEE RIVER TRAILS

Trail #1506, Top Lake. *5 miles/m (H,S).* From the end of FR 6701500 (3,700 ft) the trail traverses a forested hillside below Shoofly Mountain until it reaches cliffs rising above the north fork of Lake Creek. Switchbacks gain the ridge above the cliffs, where the route follows the crest northwest to Fall Mountain, skirts its south side, then descends to Top Lake (4,580 ft). The trail continues west through the meadows to join the PCT north of Wenatchee Pass.

Trail #1501, Cady Pass. *5 miles/m (H,S).* Three trails leave the Little Wenatchee Ford Campground (2,960 ft); this is the shortest of the three to reach the PCT. For most of its length the route follows the valley bottom beside Cady Creek, in places quite muddy. When the main drainage of the creek swings north, the trail climbs west and joins the PCT at Cady Pass (4,500 ft).

Trail #1532, Cady Ridge. *6 miles/d (H).* This fork leaves Trail #1501 (3,000 ft) 0.2 mile beyond the Little Wenatchee Ford Campground and begins a grueling 1-mile climb north to the top of Cady Ridge (5,000 ft). Once the crest is gained, the path follows it northwest through open forest and ridgetop meadows to join the PCT south of Wards Pass (5,700 ft).

Trail #1525, Little Wenatchee River. *7.5 miles/m (H,S).* From the Little Wenatchee Ford Campground (2,960 ft), the trail heads north up the brushy valley floor of the Little Wenatchee River. In 5 miles the route leaves the Little Wenatchee and climbs an eroded path up a steep hillside to Meander Meadow (4,900 ft). Here heathers, sprinkled with colorful wildflowers, line the path as it continues the gentle ascent to the PCT at Sauk Pass (5,500 ft).

Pacific Crest National Scenic Trail. *32 miles/m (H,S).*

PCT: Stevens Pass to Union Gap. 7 miles. The trail crosses US Highway 2 just east of Stevens Pass (4,030 ft) and initially follows an old railroad grade across slopes with low brush cover and open views of the Nason Creek drainage and Nason Ridge. It traverses west into the headwaters of Nason Creek, where it ascends through marshes and meadows to a rock knob (5,010 ft) above the west shore of Lake Valhalla. The route drops into a meadow at the northwest end of the lake (4,900 ft), then climbs, staying well below the east side of the crest until it reaches Union Gap (4,700 ft), and meets Trail #1590.

PCT: Union Gap to Wenatchee Pass. 10.5 miles. From Union Gap the track drops down the west side of the crest to meadow-wrapped Lake Janus (4,146 ft). After climbing west from the lake, it regains the crest (5,200 ft) with the path weaving from one side to the other. Passing high above Glasses Lake, a few switchbacks gain the top of Grizzly Peak (5,597 ft), with views down to Heather Lake and northeast to Glacier Peak. Beyond a balding knob north of Grizzly Peak the route follows the forested crest as it descends to Wenatchee Pass (4,210 ft).

Pride Glacier and peaks of the Monte Cristo region. Left to right: *Kyes Peak, Columbia Peak (in distance), Wilmans Peaks (either side of U-notch), the Cadets (far right)*

PCT: Wenatchee Pass to Cady Pass. 6.2 miles. A short climb from Wenatchee Pass reaches meadows west of Top Lake, and Trail #1506. A slow ascent gains a saddle above the east end of Pear Lake (4,790 ft). The trail was rerouted in 1987 to continue along the ridge and bypass Pear Lake, Frozen Finger Pass, and Fortune Ponds. Trail #1057 from Meadow Creek now incorporates the old route from Fortune Ponds past Pear Lake to the PCT. The route swings west of the ridge for a long traverse to Saddle Gap (5,050 ft) and, just north of it, Trail #1054. A series of switchbacks descends to Pass Creek, to meet Trail #1053. The route then reaches Cady Pass (4,300 ft) where it is joined by Trail #1051.

PCT: Cady Pass to Wenatchee Ridge. 8.3 miles. After dodging east of the crest at Cady Pass, the track regains the top at 5,400 feet, then maintains that altitude across talus slopes and alpine meadows on the south side of Skykomish Peak. Tiny cliff-rimmed Lake Sally Ann (5,479 ft) is passed, and Trail #1532 merges from the east. The path continues through flower-laced heathers and crosses Wards Pass (5,700 ft) to reach Dishpan Gap (5,600 ft); here it is joined by Trails #1051 and #650. More alpine meadows are crossed to Sauk Pass (5,500 ft), where Trail #1525 ascends from Meander Meadow. A short traverse below the east side of Kodak Peak (named for a camera lost there by a USGS topographic survey party) leads to Wenatchee Ridge, the south boundary of the Glacier Peak Wilderness.

Climbing

The northernmost peak in the Henry M. Jackson Wilderness is tri-summited Bedal Peak (6,554 ft). Routes vary from a scramble up timbered slopes on the north to several C-5.7 leads up solid rock on the southeast face. South of Bedal is the signature mountain in this part of the Cascades, Sloan Peak (7,835 ft). It is the highest point in the wilderness, and its distinctive "Matterhorn" summit is easily identified from any viewpoint within a hundred miles. Climbs combine alpine meadow treks, glacier travel, and steep solid rock. The easiest route, a C-3, follows a shelf traversing the south side to the upper southwest face. The southwest face and the north ridge are a tougher C-4 to C-5. The vertical east, southeast, and west faces require several leads from C-5.7 to C-5.8.

The horseshoe ring of peaks around Monte Cristo and Glacier Basin have climbs enough to fill a season. At the northwest corner is Addison Ridge, a long jagged massif divided into three distinct summits and a multitude of ridgetop crags (6,640 to 6,799 ft). The highest are Gemini North, Gemini South, and Pirate Peak. Farther east along this arête are Eyre Tower and the rock pyramid of Foggy Peak (6,810 ft), whose various routes range from C-4 to C-5.

On the north side of Glacier Basin are Cadet Peak (7,186 ft) and the Cadets (6,800 ft), a row of easy-scramble crags. Capping the head of the basin is Monte Cristo Peak (7,136 ft). Combination snow and rock routes up its ridges and faces are in the C-3 to C-4 range, although one rates C-5.5. The south side of the basin is framed by multi-towered Wilmans Peak and several companion spires. West Wilmans (6,840 ft) and East Wilmans (6,880 ft) peaks have two small glaciers hanging from their east flanks, and vertical rock faces on both north and south sides. Most ascents are ranked C-3 to C-4. Farther west along the ridge are East Wilmans Spire, C-5.4, South Wilmans Spire, C-3, and North Wilmans Spire, C-4 to C-5.2. Lower down on the ridge is an impressive stone monolith, the Count of Monte Cristo, with several routes ranging from C-5.4 to C-5.10.

A companion basin south of Glacier Basin surrounds the broad Columbia Glacier. On its east side is Kyes Peak (7,280 ft), with pocket glaciers wrapped around a jagged crest. Monte Cristo Peak is also at head of this basin. On the west rim, a series of C-5 towers leads to the summit of Columbia Peak (7,172 ft). An easy C-3 route up the west spur gains its summit, although C-4 to C-5 routes exist on other ridges and faces.

More remote and less known summits lie on the outer flanks of the Monte Cristo group. These include Goblin Mountain (5,606 ft), east of Kyes Peak, and a long rugged ridge south of Poodle Dog Pass capped by Hubbart Peak (5,936 ft) and Scott Peak (5,288 ft). Both of the latter peaks have impressive vertical east faces.

The terrain south and east in the Henry M. Jackson Wilderness, while rugged and remote, has few appealing climbs. A possible exception is Mount Fernow (6,190 ft) a subalpine mass south of Johnson Creek and west of Kelly Creek. A few crags of C-3 difficulty stand atop its steep, forested ridges. Lichtenberg Mountain (5,844 ft), rising above Lake Valhalla, north of Stevens Pass, has a west face and northwest ridge of solid rock with C-5.7 routes.

Winter Sports

Most of the Henry M. Jackson Wilderness is locked in deep snow all winter, and its high-angled, remote slopes present too great an avalanche hazard for winter travel. The exceptions are areas immediately north of Stevens Pass, which are accessible to cross-country skiing and snowshoeing from the ski area. Skyline Ridge, on the north side of the pass, is a strenuous 1,000-foot climb from the highway past the radio relay shed to the snow-covered flat of Skyline Lake. A continuation of the tour uphill to the ridgetop offers views of Mount Stuart and Glacier Peak. Downhill runs are good via the ascent route or in the powder snow in the timbered basin northwest of the ridge (with due caution for lower avalanche slopes above Nason Creek). Under stable snow conditions the open slopes on the east side of the summit ridge offer excellent advanced skiing; ridgetop cornices often make them difficult or dangerous to reach.

The open bowl of Smithbrook Basin can be reached from snow-covered Smithbrook Road, 4.7 miles east of the pass. Halfway up the basin, avalanche slopes on both sides bear a cautious watch, as do those farther into the basin on the north side of Lichtenberg Mountain. Expert skiers can pick up the general route of the PCT near the head of the basin and follow it south across a saddle to steep slopes leading to Lake Valhalla. The tour should only be taken under very stable snow conditions.

—21—

NASON RIDGE

LOCATION: In Chelan County, between US Highway 2 and the Little Wenatchee River
SIZE: 19,567 acres
STATUS: Roadless Special Interest Area for scenery and recreation
TERRAIN: A long, steep, east–west ridge with a broad, rounded top capped by spurs leading to
    rock summits. Lower slopes are covered with open mixed-conifer forest, but the ridgetop is
    barren rock and talus.
ELEVATION: 2,200 to 7,063 feet
MANAGEMENT: USFS, Wenatchee National Forest, Lake Wenatchee Ranger District; plus a
    few private sections owned by Longview Fiber
TOPOGRAPHIC MAPS: Labyrinth Mountain, Lake Wenatchee, Mount Howard, Plain

Throughout its 16-mile east–west length, Nason Ridge rises abruptly for 4,000 feet above adjoining drainages. Its top is broader and less jagged than other Cascade massifs of similar altitude, but the barren crest above 6,000 feet is marked with steep cliffs falling away to broad talus slopes. Small lakes and tarns hide in basins and cirques below. Several peaks mark the top of the ridge, but none presents any climbing challenge. Although the total acreage enclosing the ridge is relatively small, the wide vistas of the Cascade crest from the open upper slopes make the ridge area feel larger than it actually is.

Many sidehills, especially those above Nason Creek and US Highway 2, are regularly swept clean of trees by avalanches. The low-lying replacement growth of vine maple, mountain ash, and slide alder turns these slopes into palettes splashed with brilliant golds and scarlets in late fall.

Climate

Nason Ridge receives 55 to 65 inches of precipitation annually, more than half in the form of snow between the months of October and April. Snow accumulates to an average of 6 to 7

Mountain goats are commonly seen on Nason Ridge.

feet during winter months, but most of the area is snow-free by mid-July. Summer temperatures are warm, with highs averaging in the upper 80s, and winter is chilly with lows averaging in the teens.

Plants and Wildlife

Lower elevations are covered by grand fir and Douglas-fir. The mid-elevation forest is western hemlock, western red cedar, and Pacific fir, with an understory of vine maple, salal, salmonberry, Oregon grape, sticky currant, elderberry, and devil's club. The upper-elevation forest is mostly subalpine fir, lodgepole pine, whitebark pine, and Englemann spruce. Alpine meadows have a profusion of wildflowers. Steep avalanche-swept sidehills are covered with willow, mountain maple, mountain ash, Sitka alder, huckleberries, forbs, and grasses. The highest elevations are barren, save for sedges and heathers.

Nason Ridge is known for its concentration of mountain goats, which are often seen around Alpine Lookout early or late in the day. For study purposes, the herd in the lookout vicinity is protected from hunting.

Geology

The central portion of Nason Ridge, from Rock Mountain to Round Mountain, is primarily folded metamorphic biotite schist and gneiss of the continental crust that makes up the Cascade core. It is probably 100 million to 200 million years old. The far west end of the ridge is a portion of the Mount Stuart batholith, a younger granitic intrusion that occurred 50 million to 60 million years ago. The Leavenworth fault, marking the west edge of the Chiwaukum graben, runs north–south along the east side of the ridge. The graben is thought to have subsided as the area was overlaid with sedimentary deposits. Cobbles and boulders mark the fault boundary. Although adjoining drainages were gouged by alpine glaciers, the upper portion of the ridge appears to have escaped glaciation; its rock outcrops are rugged and angular, not smoothed by glacial polishing.

History

The earliest use of the Nason Ridge area was for grazing sheep. In the early 1900s herds were driven up to ridgetop meadows for summer forage. Fire lookouts were constructed between 1933 and 1936 atop Rock Mountain and Alpine Lookout. The former was abandoned in 1973; the latter, replaced in 1975, is one of the few forest lookouts actively manned for fire detection.

ACTIVITIES

Hiking

LAKE WENATCHEE TRAILS

Trail #1583, Nason Ridge. 16.7 miles/m (H,S,B; M from its east end to the Alpine Lookout spur trail). From the Kahler Glen trailhead (1,980 ft) south of Lake Wenatchee State Park, the track follows and crosses old logging roads as it heads up the east end of Nason Ridge for 3 miles to 5,270 feet, where it meets Trail #1529. It traverses the south slope of Round Mountain, then follows the crest west. In 2.5 miles, a spur leads uphill to a ridge high-point and Alpine Lookout (6,235 ft). Motorized vehicles are prohibited beyond the start of this spur. Views north are down to Lake Wenatchee, the White River drainage, Dirtyface Mountain, and the peaks of Chiwawa Ridge. To the south, US Highway 2 follows Nason Creek far below, and across the valley are the Chiwaukum Mountains and the north end of the Alpine Lakes Wilderness.

From Alpine Lookout, the path continues west on the south slope of the ridge, first through meadows, then in open alpine forest. In 3.2 miles it switchbacks down to Merritt Lake (5,003 ft). From the lake it descends to a basin where the upper end of Trail #1588 is met (4,840 ft). A traverse west along south slopes reaches the meadows of Royal Basin (4,900 ft); horse travel is not recommended west of here. Switchbacks up talus gain a forested bench that continues west to Crescent Lake (5,450 ft). A climb from the lake basin rounds a narrow rib, then traverses rock and talus slopes to the open bowl above Rock Lake (5,870 ft). Skirting cliffs above the lake, the path rounds a bare rib to join Trail #1587 (6,110 ft).

US 2 TRAILS

Trail #1529, Round Mountain. 1.6 miles/ m (H,M,B). This is the shortest of the trails that reach the east end of Nason Ridge and its spectacular viewpoints at Round Mountain and Alpine Lookout. From FR 6910 (3,960 ft), the route uses a dozen easy-grade switch-backs up the hillside to gain the ridgetop just east of Round Mountain. Here it joins Trail #1583 (5,270 ft) as the latter continues west along Nason Ridge.

Trail #1588, Merritt Lake. 3 miles/m (H,S,B). From the end of FR 657 (3,040 ft), 23 switchbacks through old-growth forest gain a basin above the west side of Mahar Creek, where Trail #1583 is met (4,840 ft). That trail can be followed 0.5 mile uphill to Merritt Lake (5,003 ft), a tarn with a small meadow near its outlet and rock cliffs framing the opposite shore.

Trail #1587, Rock Mountain. 4 miles/m (H,S,B). From the end of a power-line service road east of Berne on US Highway 2 (3,010 ft), this grueling trail heads up the avalanche-stripped hillside where, 62 switchbacks later and 2,000 feet higher, it gains the top of a rib projecting southeast from Nason Ridge. There is little respite, however, as the path continues up steep heather-covered slopes. At the south rim of the basin enclosing Rock Lake, the west end of Trail #1583 is met (6,110 ft). The Rock Mountain Trail climbs a rock rib to the crest of Nason Ridge and Trail #1531 (6,600 ft). The way goes straight up the narrow crest to the Rock Mountain summit (6,850 ft), a former lookout site atop cliffs that drop 1,000 feet east to Rock Lake. A ridge leads 1.5 miles to the north, to the top of Mount Howard, the highest point on Nason Ridge. Beyond, Sloan and Glacier peaks loom above a host of lesser summits. To the south, the tip of Rainier rises above the summit of Mount Daniel.

Trail #1531, Snowy Creek. 4 miles/m (H,S,B). Where FR 6705 crosses Snowy Creek, find the trailhead on the south side of the road (3,580 ft). The track climbs gently south through cool streamside forest, then takes switchbacks east up to a large flat meadow. The pleasant hike is over, and 32 switchbacks, first in open timber, then up rock and heather, gain the top of Nason Ridge (6,600 ft). Here Trail #1587 is joined as it begins its final thrust to the Rock Mountain summit.

Winter Sports

Nason Ridge is too steep and avalanche-prone for much winter recreation, however, the summer route up the logging roads of Butcher Creek and Trail #1529 to the top of Round Mountain offers a safe, though strenuous, 5-mile winter trip to the top of the mountain. Here are shimmering views of snowclad peaks and lakes, and an excellent downhill run through open timber.

■┌────────────────**22**────────────────┐■

GLACIER PEAK WILDERNESS

LOCATION: In Skagit, Snohomish, and Chelan counties, astride the Cascade crest between Cascade Pass and the Wenatchee River

SIZE: 576,900 acres, with adjacent roadless areas of 48,800 acres

STATUS: Designated Wilderness Area (1964, 1984); adjacent areas are Semiprimitive Roadless

TERRAIN: Deep glacier-cut valleys with steep sidehills, heavily forested up to 5,000 to 6,000 feet. Above, meadows and parklands along lower ridge crests give way to heavily glaciated, ragged rock summits ranging between 7,000 and 9,000 feet. Centerpiece of the wilderness is the ice-draped volcanic cone of Glacier Peak.

ELEVATION: 1,600 to 10,541 feet

MANAGEMENT: USFS, Mount Baker–Snoqualmie National Forest, Mount Baker and Darrington ranger districts; and Wenatchee National Forest, Chelan, Entiat, and Lake Wenatchee ranger districts. Also some private patented mining claims

TOPOGRAPHIC MAPS: Agnes Mountain, Bench Mark Mtn., Cascade Pass, Clark Mountain, Dome Peak, Downey Mtn., Gamma Peak, Glacier Peak East, Glacier Peak West, Goode Mtn., Holden, Huckleberry Mtn., Illabot Peaks, Lime Mountain, Lucerne, McGregor Mtn., Mount David, Mt. Lyall, Pinnacle Mountain, Prairie Mtn., Pugh Mountain, Pyramid Mountain, Saska Peak, Schaefer Lake, Sloan Peak, Snowking Mtn., Sonny Boy Lakes, Stehekin, Suiattle Pass, Trinity, White Chuck Mtn.

A glorious hodgepodge of peaks and glaciers along the Cascade crest surrounds Glacier Peak, the most remote of the range's high volcanoes. Creeks drop from snow- and ice fields to rush through deep glacier-scoured drainages. Walls swoop up from the brush-choked valley bottoms past avalanche scars on forested slopes to vertical rock faces and knife-edge summits. Wilderness ridges are pocked with cirques and basins holding 210 lakes, many so remote that only half of them have been named.

One hundred cataloged trails spread through the region, offering 450 miles of hiking. These range from easy well-maintained paths to rugged old sheep drives, poorly marked and seldom cared for. Once above timberline, experienced cross-country hikers have many more miles of alpine country at their disposal. Such treks include the classic Ptarmigan Traverse, a 15-mile-long climber's route, mostly on rock and glaciers, from Cascade Pass south to Dome Peak. The exit south from Dome requires another 10 to 20 miles of cross-country and trail travel to reach the nearest road.

Glacier Peak, 10,541 feet, is the highest summit in its namesake wilderness. The remainder of the significant peaks in the region range between 7,000 and 9,500 feet; most have either alpine glacier skirts or hanging glaciers plastered to their sides. The wilderness has more active glaciers than any other region in the Lower 48 states. The relatively low elevation of the wilderness peaks belies their climbing challenge and scenic beauty; most rise about 5,000 vertical feet above adjacent valley floors, and many sheer faces are more than 2,000 feet high.

Climate

Because the Glacier Peak Wilderness spans the Cascades, its climate varies by location—east or west of the crest. The high range blocks storm systems that sweep in from the Pacific; as the damp, warm ocean air bumps into the mountains, it rises, cools, and deposits its moisture content on the western slopes. Once across the crest precipitation levels drop significantly as the cool, dry air continues east across the state. On the west side of the wilderness the average annual precipitation is 110 inches, much falling as snow between October and April, accumulating up to 45 feet deep. On the east side of the Cascades the annual precipitation averages only 35 inches, and snow depths range from 10 to 12 feet. Temperatures follow much the same pattern. West of the crest the ocean air patterns keep summer highs down to the balmy 80s, and

Glacier Peak and Image Lake

winter lows in the teens to lower 20s. East of the crest summers are warmer, with highs in the 90s, and winter lows range slightly above zero.

Plants and Wildlife

Valley bottoms are covered by a dense forest of hemlock, spruce, cedar, fir, cottonwood, alder, and willow, with an understory of woody plants such as huckleberry. Side-wall forests consist of true fir, spruce, and hemlock, and some larch in upland meadows. Eastern slopes also have substantial pine, mostly lodgepole. Steep slopes are regularly cut by avalanche tracks where alder and low alpine plants are the primary survivors. Clusters of subalpine fir and mountain hemlock frame alpine meadows carpeted with sedges, heathers, and a variety of wildflowers.

Wildlife includes both mule and black-tailed deer, a few elk, black bear, marten, fisher, and lynx. Among smaller animals are Douglas squirrels, chipmunks, and golden-mantled ground squirrels. Higher rocks and cliffs are home to mountain goats, pika, hoary marmots, and ptarmigan. Rarely seen, though possibly present, are grizzly bear, gray wolf, and wolverine.

Birds of the area include grouse, goshawks, red-tailed hawks, gray jays, red-shafted flickers, Clark's nutcrackers, great horned owls, and the more rare spotted owls and peregrine falcons.

Geology

The core rocks in the area are schists and gneisses, metamorphosed from sediments and lava flows beneath the ocean on the coast of the North Cascades micro-continent, before it reached North America. The core rock was lifted above the sea, and granitic plutons such as the one forming the Dumbell Mountain peaks intruded through the newly raised crust in places, as long as 220 million years ago. As this micro-continent drove northeast and impinged on the west coast of North America about 50 million years ago, these metamorphic rocks were squeezed and

folded to form the base structure of the northwest-trending Cascade Range. When the rocks cooled and hardened, the residual northward motion of the newly accreted North Cascades caused shear stresses resulting in several parallel fault lines, generally running in a northwest–southeast direction.

Erosion wore away the surface of the new mountain range, carrying the sediments down to valley floors to form sandstones and conglomerates. Uplifting of the region continued, accompanied by lava flows from volcanoes along the Cascade crest, until about 25 million years ago, when most volcanic action ceased. Fissures caused by faulting were intruded with still more granite from deep within the earth's crust: The largest of these intrusions, in the heart of the wilderness, is the Cloudy Pass batholith, which formed about 22 million years ago.

The cone of Glacier Peak began to build atop the western edge of the Cloudy Pass batholith about 700,000 years ago in a series of passive dacite flows. Lime Ridge, to the east, first blocked the westward flow of lava, so most spread to the east into the Suiattle River valley. As the volcano cone grew higher, flows surmounted Lime Ridge and poured into the White Chuck River drainage as well. Most volcanic flows that built the primary cone of the peak ceased after 12,000 to 15,000 years, however, two more recent eruptions formed smaller subcones on the flanks of Glacier Peak. Extruded dacite formed Disappointment Peak on a rib to the south. A second cone on the east flank of the mountain, beneath the Chocolate Glacier, collapsed and oozed down in the form of mud flows and debris fans to push the Suiattle River into the bedrock to the east. In a (hopefully) final burst of activity about 12,000 years ago, the mountain exploded violently in nine or more closely spaced eruptions, sending pumice mud slides into the White Chuck and Suiattle valleys, and distributing a carpet of ash and pumice up to 12 feet thick over the mountains downwind to the east. This ash has been traced as far east as Saskatchewan.

About a million years ago the final sculpting of the region was begun by glaciers, which waxed and waned until the last advance of the continental ice sheets about 12,000 years ago. The glaciers cut the deep U-shaped valleys characteristic of the region, carved the sharp peaks and ridges, and scooped out the bowls now filled by mountain lakes. Since then the glaciers have been in retreat, but their past work can be observed in the long moraines extending well beyond today's glacial snouts, and in the high rock ribs from the summit of Glacier Peak that mark the original surface level of the volcanic cone prior to glacial grinding.

History

The earliest users of the Glacier Peak Wilderness were nearby Indian tribes, who foraged its forests and meadows for plants and game. Indian trails used for trade between the coastal tribes and those of central Washington crossed Cloudy, White, and Indian passes. The first Euro-Americans in the area were traders and trappers; their travel through the area followed existing Indian trails. In the 1870s railroads sent survey crews into the region in search of Cascade crossings suitable for rail lines.

The Northwest gold rush of the 1880s and '90s brought in prospectors, with the first claims filed in the Chiwawa River valley, Phelps Creek drainage, and along Railroad Creek. Prospectors found not only gold, but ores of copper, silver, lead, zinc, and molybdenum. By 1896, red stains had led to prospects at Red Mountain and other spots on Phelps Ridge; the Royal Development Company bought out claims and built a large mill at Trinity. Mines extracted low-grade copper ore in the 1930s, but production ceased to be profitable, and the operation closed.

A railroad survey in 1887 reported copper ore outcrops along Railroad Creek, and J. H. Holden staked claims there in 1896. Although Holden could never raise capital for a full-scale operation, Howe Sound Company later bought the property, and by 1938 began production. In 1939 a 2,000-ton mill was built at Holden, and the population of the mining community grew to 450. Over the next 19 years, the Holden mine produced more copper than any other in the state; 106,000 tons of concentrate were shipped to the Tacoma smelter, and 600,000 ounces of gold were recovered. The total value of the minerals extracted exceeded $66 million. A precipitous drop in copper prices in 1957 made Holden's low-grade ore no longer profitable. Mining ceased, and the property was eventually sold to the Lutheran church for a retreat village.

Settlers first arrived in the Wenatchee Valley in the 1870s, and by the 1900s sheepherders had blazed trails into the Glacier Peak Wilderness and were regularly moving herds from valley bottoms to alpine meadows for summer pasture. Many of the more rugged (and, unfortunately, poorly maintained or abandoned) trails in the high country are old sheep drives. Fire-prevention strategies in the 1920s prompted the Forest Service to build more trails to support fire lookouts on peaks throughout the region and to provide access for fire patrols and fire suppression crews. Lookouts were located atop Green, Huckleberry, Red, Johnson, Domke, and Poe mountains, Sulphur Point, Miners Ridge, Flower Dome, Glacier Creek Ridge, and Mount David.

The Glacier Peak Wilderness Area was created in 1963; it encompassed portions of what is now the south end of North Cascades National Park, but did not extend as far south or west as the current wilderness boundaries. In 1984 the boundaries were expanded, adding 112,600 acres to the wilderness.

Mining took place at Big Copper Mine near Holden from the 1930s through the 1950s. The mine is now closed.

ACTIVITIES

Hiking

SUIATTLE RIVER TRAILS

Trail #780, Huckleberry Mountain. 7 miles/m (H,S). From FR 26 (990 ft) long switchbacks sweep up a hillside to the ridgetop (5,180 ft). The trail follows the crest northwest, where subalpine meadows give views of Glacier Peak and the north face of White Chuck Mountain. A ridgetop ramble to a bald knob (5,856 ft) opens views of the snow-draped span of Mount Chaval, Snowking Mountain, Mutchler Peak, Mount Buckindy, and beyond the ragged backbone of the Cascade crest. At the end of the ridge, 0.6 mile north, is the site of an abandoned lookout (6,267 ft).

Trail #768, Downey Creek. 6.8 miles/m (H,S). From Downey Creek Campground on FR 26 (1,450 ft), the track slogs steadily up through forest, streams, and mud holes above the east side of Downey Creek, occasionally dropping near the creek itself. In 6 miles, at Bachelor Creek (2,440 ft), the trail passes the start of Trail #796, then follows Downey as it bends east from Goat Creek and fritters away about a mile upstream.

Trail #796, Bachelor Creek. 5.5 miles/d (H). An abandoned trail Trail #768 at Downey Creek (2,440 ft), stumbling over roots and rocks as it climbs above the north bank of Bachelor

Creek. It crosses to the south side of the creek (3,800 ft), traverses a meadow below Pilot Peak, then climbs to the steep headwall of the basin. Picking a route through high angle slopes, the track reaches the ridge south of Spire Lake. Here the razor-sharp pinnacles on ridges radiating from Spire Point, the massive Dome Glacier, and the rocky summit of Dome Peak come into view. A descent south from a narrow saddle leads to Cub Lake (5,338 ft). Cross-country climbing routes head east to Dome Glacier.

Trail #784, Suiattle River. *10.8 miles/e (H,S).* The major west-side gateway to the Glacier Peak Wilderness leaves the end of FR 26 (1,592 ft), then wends east up the deep Suiattle drainage to its junction with the PCT (2,800 ft). At 9.4 miles, Trail #785 swings northeast up Miners Ridge.

Trail #785, Miners Ridge. *9.9 miles/e (H,S).* At 9.4 miles on Trail #784 (2,760 ft), switchbacks head north up the forested hillside. Above the west end of Trail #795, switchbacks continue up to flowered meadows atop Miners Ridge. A spur heads west 0.1 mile to a lookout site; the cabin here is used in summer as a wilderness ranger station. The main trail continues east through ridgetop parkland to Image Lake (6,056 ft), one of the most photogenic spots in the wilderness. The lake, set amid flower garden meadows, reflects the icy summit of Glacier Peak. A path circles the grassy basin east of the lake, and other spurs lead away from the lake to separate camp areas for backpackers and horses. Scrambles east along the heather crest to Plummer Mountain (7,870 ft) open vistas of the Dome Peak area. From Image Lake the trail traverses east, then switchbacks down to meet Trail #795 at the Glacier Peak Mine property (5,630 ft).

Trail #795, Miners Cabin. *2.1 miles/e (H).* This track avoids the final ascent to the top of Miners Ridge; instead, it traverses the south side of the ridge at the 5,400-foot level as it heads toward Suiattle Pass. It is rejoined by Trail #785 at some miners' shacks (5,630 ft), then ends as it meets the PCT (5,470 ft) 0.7 mile west of Suiattle Pass.

WHITE CHUCK RIVER TRAILS

Trail #657, Meadow Mountain. *17.6 miles/m (H,S).* After a 5-mile hike up gated FR 2710, the trail leaves the north side of the road (3,570 ft), makes a gentle traverse, then switchbacks up to open meadows (4,900 ft) on the south slopes of the crest. At a saddle in 0.5 mile is a spur that descends to Meadow Lake (4,763 ft). The path continues east through forest and meadows that become wildflower gardens in early summer, berry patches in fall. At a sharp saddle (5,800 ft) south of the Meadow Mountain summit, switchbacks drop to a traverse above Owl Creek. The route continues east around creek-head basins to a tiny bench (5,400 ft) below the cliffs of Fire Mountain. It zigzags down to Fire Creek (3,720 ft), crosses it, heads west along a bluff, then switchbacks down a nose to join Trail #643 (2,570 ft).

Trail #643, White Chuck. *6.9 miles/e (H,S).* At Owl Creek Campground at the end of FR 23 (2,240 ft), this path heads east into the old-growth forest of the White Chuck valley. The junction with Trail #657 is passed at 1.4 miles, as the route continues into the steep-walled river drainage. At 4.2 miles, Trail #643A leads to Kennedy Hot Springs and the east end of Trail #646. Trail #643 switchbacks up a nose to the east to join the PCT at Sitkum Creek (3,900 ft).

NORTH FORK OF THE SAUK RIVER TRAILS

Trail #646, Lost Creek Ridge. *11.1 miles/m (H,S).* The route shows no mercy as it switchbacks from FR 49 (1,849 ft) up the slopes to Bingley Gap (4,390 ft), then zigzags up the ridge to a saddle (5,520 ft) where a spur to Round Lake (5,070 ft) drops off. Here are unobstructed views of Bedal and Sloan peaks. The track becomes vague as it traverses the parkland on the south slopes below the crest; it becomes recognizable again near Hardtack Lake (5,430 ft). The path crosses to open north-facing slopes, climbs briefly, then descends to the cirque containing Camp Lake (5,681 ft). A climb up the rib north of the lake leads to a meadow bench, then switchbacks down to the north shore of Lake Byrne (5,544 ft). The trail swings back and forth through the forest as it drops with knee-jarring vengeance to Kennedy Hot Springs (3,300 ft).

Trail #649, North Fork of the Sauk. *8.4 miles/m (H,S).* From Sloan Creek Campground on FR 49 (2,072 ft), a gentle track heads east along the North Fork of the Sauk River. Huge cedars decorate the river bottom as the way passes the beginning of Trail #652 at 2 miles. At Mackinaw

Shelter (2,970 ft) the gentle grade is history as switchbacks press up forest and avalanche slopes to timberline (5,260 ft). A long traverse through a subalpine park meets the PCT, 0.5 mile west of White Pass (6,000 ft).

Trail #652, Pilot Ridge. 11 miles/d (H,S). This route leaves Trail #649 at the 2-mile point (2,400 ft). After a foot-log crossing of the Sauk, the path zigzags up the steep wooded slope to gain the top of Johnson Ridge (5,175 ft). The way follows the crest southeast for 7 miles as it undulates between 5,000 and 5,700 feet, alternating between forest and meadows with unsurpassed views of Glacier Peak, the Monte Cristo–area summits, and Mount Rainier. The path rounds the head of the Sloan Creek basin, passes a spur to Johnson Mountain, then twists around a rib and drops to Little Blue Lake (5,194 ft). After contouring a basin above another fork of Sloan Creek, the trail climbs to join Trail #650 east of June Mountain (5,700 ft).

WHITE RIVER TRAILS

Trail #1521, Mount David. 7 miles/m (H). From the end of FR 64 (2,300 ft), follow Trail #1522 downstream along the west bank of the White River for 1 mile to the start of Trail #1521. The route leads southwest up a steep forested slope, where switchbacks gain the ridge crest (5,200 ft). After a brief respite, the climb resumes, and with ups and downs reaches timberline. It continues, weaving through ridge-crest cliffs, to the summit pinnacle, where a lookout once stood. Concrete steps set in holes blasted from the rock cliff lead to the top (7,420 ft). Wide views here stretch to Sloan Peak, Clark Mountain, Mount Daniel, Mount Rainier, Lake Wenatchee, and, way below, the White River and Indian Creek.

Trail #1502, Indian Creek. 11 miles/m (H,S). Cross the bridge at the end of FR 6400 (2,300 ft) to the west side of the White River, and wander the valley floor upstream for 2 miles. After crossing Indian Creek the route switchbacks above the lower creek gorge, then returns to the level creek bottom upstream. After a gradual grind upstream the grade steepens near the upper end of the Indian Creek drainage, and the forest thins and breaks into intermittent meadows. A few final zigzags reach Indian Pass (4,990 ft) and the PCT.

Trail #1507, White River. 15 miles/m (H). At the end of FR 6400 (2,300 ft), the route on the east side of the White River wends through old-growth forest as it follows the river upstream. At mile 4, Trail #1562 branches east at Boulder Creek; the White River Trail then makes two rather tenuous crossings of the river and heads uphill southwest to Lower White Pass and the PCT (5,600 ft).

Trail #1562, Boulder Creek. 9.5 miles/d (H). At Boulder Creek (2,530 ft) this route leaves Trail #1507 and switchbacks east up forest slopes. The way crosses the creek in an upper basin and continues a moderate ascent along its east bank. It threads through cliffs of the basin headwall to reach the meadows of Boulder Pass (6,200 ft) for a peek into the upper Napeequa Valley. The downhill grade northeast from the pass is moderated by a long chain of switchbacks. Crossing the Napeequa River (4,290 ft) is a final challenge; it can be nearly impossible during high-water periods. On the opposite side of the river the way meets Trail #1518 from Little Giant Pass, and Trail #1562A up the Napeequa Valley.

Trail #1562A, Napeequa River. 5 miles/d (H). From the junction of Trails #1562 and #1518, this path heads up the wide green swath of the Napeequa River valley. An imposing rim of glaciers and peaks rise above. A number of cross-country routes probe the enclosing walls.

CHIWAWA RIVER TRAILS

Trail #1518, Little Giant. 8.5 miles/d (H). A mile north of Nineteenmile Campground on FR 62, the trail drops east from the road (2,606 ft) to the Chiwawa River, where a barricade indicates the obvious—the bridge is out. Cross the river on a nearby logjam, or in low water wade, and follow old roads through an abandoned campground to the trailhead. The original sheep drive that went straight uphill has been enhanced by switchbacks, but the tread is very eroded. A pine forest is traversed to the south fork of Little Giant Creek, where the steep ascent resumes, first in forest, then brush, and then atop a rocky rib to finally reach Little Giant Pass (6,408 ft). A rough tread leads down to the valley floor to meet Trails #1562 and #1562A.

Trail #1511, Phelps Creek. 9.5 miles/m (H,S). From the gate on FR 6211 (3,500 ft) the track heads up an old mining road, past the start of Trail #1508, to the road end near Chipmunk Creek. The path continues along the creek bottom, alternating between meadow and forest to reach Spider Meadows (4,700 ft), framed by 2,000-foot-high cliffs topped by Dumbell Mountain. At 5,300 feet the trail splits; one path continues a short distance to the headwaters of Phelps Creek, the other heads west toward a seemingly impenetrable wall. A miner's path picks its way up the cliff to a gully that contains the Spider Glacier. A scramble up the rib east of the glacier leads to Spider Gap (7,100 ft), with good views of Mount Maude and Seven Fingered Jack en route. On the north side of the gap, a snow and rock descent along the side of the Lyman Glacier reaches the end of Trail #1256B from Lyman Lake.

Trail #1508, Carne Mountain. 3.5 miles/m (H,S). Moderate-grade switchbacks climb through forest from Trail #1511 (3,500 ft) to the open slopes of a small basin (4,800 ft) on the southwest side of Carne Mountain. The larch-rimmed meadows of the basin are stippled with wildflower colors in early summer. At the head of the basin (6,420 ft) the way meets Trail #1509, joining from the northeast. A short amble south to a small saddle gives views of the vertical north face of Old Gib, and a ridge scramble north reaches the top of Carne Mountain (7,085 ft).

Trail #1550, Chiwawa River. 4.9 miles/e (H,S). An old mining road to the Red Mountain prospects near the head of the Chiwawa River starts on private mine property at the end of FR 62 at Trinity (2,772 ft). At 1.5 miles pass the beginning of Trail #1513 and climb away from the river along the west flank of Phelps Ridge. The river is rejoined as it swings north. In another mile the trail forks (4,760 ft). Trail #1550A continues up the basin to a meadow at the forks of the Chiwawa River; views sweep up to Fortress and Chiwawa mountains. Trail #1550 switchbacks through avalanche-scored timber to prospects on the west slope of Red Mountain (6,440 ft).

Trail #1513, Buck Creek. 8 miles/m (H,S). From the 1.5-mile point of Trail #1550 (3,200 ft) the route crosses the Chiwawa River, then follows Buck Creek northwest. After rising over a pair of glacier-cut benches, the way breaks into a meadow with views to hanging glaciers on the face of Buck Mountain. A long switchback takes the path out of the creek bottom to a traverse of slopes high above the creek. The trail rejoins the creek at its source in a basin at 5,600 feet. Continue west to Buck Creek Pass (5,810 ft) and tremendous views of Glacier Peak. Trails #1513, #789, and #792 meet at the pass.

Trail #789, Buck Creek Pass. 5 miles/m (H,S). The route northwest from Buck Creek Pass (5,180 ft) wends through meadows as it descends to Small Creek, then ascends again to cross Middle Ridge (6,245 ft). An easy wooded grade leads to the PCT (4,640 ft) near Miners Creek.

ENTIAT RIVER TRAILS

Trail #1400, Entiat River. 10.5 miles/e (H,S). From Cottonwood Campground, at the end of FR 51 (3,144 ft), a wide track heads northwest through river-bottom timber along the Entiat River. Leaving this route to the west are Trail #1404, at 3.5 miles; Trail #1430, at 5 miles; and Trail #1405, at 8.3 miles. Headed east at 6.5 miles is Trail #1230A. As the Entiat River hooks west, the dense forest occasionally breaks into meadows. The valley widens, and the trail finally ends (5,482 ft) in a cliff-bound meadow below glaciers hanging from the summit blocks of Mount Fernow, Seven Fingered Jack, and Mount Maude.

Trail #1404, Cow Creek Meadows. 3.2 miles/e (H). From Trail #1400 (3,749 ft) the path passes the north end of Myrtle Lake, climbs northwest through a notch, then contours a forested rib to reach Cow Creek, where a short spur leads to Cow Creek Meadows (5,180 ft). The trail continues uphill in a chain of switchbacks through rocky meadows and larch on the east side of Fifth of July Mountain to intersect Trail #1408 from the Entiat Mountains (6,637 ft).

Trail #1430, Larch Lakes. 5.4 miles/m (H,S). After leaving Trail #1400 (3,784 ft) and crossing the Entiat River, the path climbs through timber beside Larch Lakes Creek. Trees give way to the brushy slopes of an old burn, and tedious switchbacks weave uphill to the small bench holding lower Larch Lake (5,670 ft). A short ascent leads to the meadow encircling the upper lake (5,750 ft), and the north end of Trail #1408. The route now crosses a saddle (6,450 ft) on the northwest rim of the basin and begins a long traverse to Pomas Pass (6,420 ft), where it meets Trail #1453.

Trail #1230A, Snow Brushy Creek. 5 miles/m (H,S). From Trail #1400 (3,981 ft), this aptly named route climbs through timber and brushy creek bottom, passes the north end of Trail #1434 at 1.7 miles, then reaches avalanche-cut meadows with views of the north faces of Gopher Mountain and Saska Peak. At 3.7 miles Trail #1433 joins in from the south. The path climbs ever-steepening larch-covered slopes at the head of the basin to reach the narrow gash of Milham Pass (6,663 ft), then continues north to Emerald Park as Trail #1230.

Trail #1405, Ice Creek. 4.1 miles/e (H,S). After leaving Trail #1400 (4,363 ft) and crossing the Entiat River on a log, the route swings west into the Ice Creek drainage, where it meets the north end of Trail #1453. The path continues up Ice Creek valley, in forest at first, then in alternating trees and meadows. At the head of the creek the trail ends in a pretty basin (5,210 ft) surrounded by the rock walls of the Entiat Mountains.

From these meadows a rugged 2-mile boot-tread heads east to the base of cliffs, then scrambles up alongside a fork of Ice Creek to a rock and pumice bench that holds lower Ice Lake (6,822 ft). Follow the bench southwest to the creek cascading from the upper lake. The route scrambles up along the creek to Upper Ice Lake (7,188 ft), tucked below the 1,600-foot-high face of Mount Maude.

Trail #1453, Pomas Creek. 3.1 miles/m (H,S). As Trail #1405 enters the Ice Creek drainage, this path drops off south (4,398 ft), then climbs a hogback on the west side of Pomas Creek. A traverse beneath cliffs and a few switchbacks lead to Pomas Pass (6,420 ft), where the route meets Trail #1430.

LUCERNE TRAILS

Trail #1230, Emerald Park. 7 miles/m (H,S). At the 2.2-mile point on Trail #1280 (2,182 ft), between Lucerne and Domke Lake, this route strikes southwest along the flat west of the lake. A long traverse of a forested hillside leads to Emerald Park Creek; here the trail steepens as it climbs above the northwest side of the drainage. The way levels as it enters the meadows of Emerald Park (5,200 ft). Farther up the drainage the meadows expand, with views opening to jagged Bearcat Ridge to the south. The path climbs to steep-walled Milham Pass (6,663 ft) and views east to Lake Chelan and the Sawtooth Range. From the pass, Trail #1230A continues west to the Entiat River.

Trail #1256, Railroad Creek. 10.5 miles/m (H,S). An easy grade route leaves the end of FR 8301 at Holden (3,310 ft) and heads west up the Railroad Creek drainage. The track through the dark green jungle continues upstream, to a hillside ascent past waterfalls at the outlet to Hart Lake (3,982 ft). Switchbacks up a side-slope bypass cliffs below Crown Point and offer views of the cascades. The route ascends past another waterfall to its source, Lyman Lake (5,598 ft), a picture-postcard spot below the Lyman Glacier and Chiwawa Mountain. To the west, subalpine forest gives way to meadows as the route climbs to Cloudy Pass (6,438 ft). From Cloudy Pass the route switchbacks down into the basin at the head of Agnes Creek to meet the PCT.

Trail #1256B, Lyman Lake. 3 miles/m (H). A relatively new trail from the north end (5,580 ft) of Lyman Lake heads along a rib east of the lake, then crosses an old moraine into a meadow that holds four upper lakes at the snout of the Lyman Glacier. From the lower edge of the glacier, gullies, rock, or snow (depending on the season) lead up to Spider Gap (7,060 ft) and the north end of Trail #1511.

STEHEKIN RIVER TRAILS

Trail #1244, Devore Creek. 16 miles/m (H,S). From Weaver Point Campground (1,150 ft) the route switchbacks up the hillside to bypass a short gorge near the mouth of Devore Creek. It then follows the creek bottom south through steep, narrow walls, occasionally passing through avalanche-cut meadows. At the head of the creek in Fourth of July Basin, switchbacks climb the headwall to Ten Mile Pass (6,442 ft), then more drop south through larch and pine into the Ten Mile Creek drainage. At 5,200 feet a side-slope traverse to the northwest joins the upper reaches of the creek. The route continues upstream to meadows below basin-rimming cliffs.

Zigzags up a rocky gully on the east side of the cliff reach Hilgard Pass (6,638 ft), the south end of Trail #1243.

Trail #1243, Company Creek. 11 miles/m (H,S). The route leaves the Stehekin Valley (1,250 ft) and climbs a rib above cliffs on the north side of Company Creek. It traverses high above the creek at the base of cliffs; a flat grade continues south until Company Creek rises to meet it. The trail proceeds up the creek bottom, and at 5 miles makes a difficult crossing to the east side of the stream. At the confluence of Company and Hilgard creeks the route swings up the Hilgard drainage, following it south to basin-end cliffs. Switchbacks work up the headwall to Hilgard Pass (6,638 ft), where the south end of Trail #1244 is met. The pass can be dangerous until snow melts.

Trail #1272, West Fork of Agnes Creek. 3 miles/e (H,S). Near the confluence of the south and west forks of Agnes Creek, 5 miles south of the Stehekin, this trail branches west from the PCT (2,400 ft). After crossing both creek forks, the path follows the bank of the West Fork as it heads into the heart of a spectacularly scenic basin. Meadows en route and at the trail's end (2,600 ft) look up to feathery falls cascading down polished granite cliffs from a rim of glaciers. The peaks rising above the ice include some of the most remote and difficult climbs in the wilderness: Agnes Mountain, Blue and Dome peaks, and Spire Point.

Trail #1271, Flat Creek. 3.5 miles/e (H,S). From the Stehekin Valley Road (2,285 ft), 14.5 miles from Stehekin, this route heads southwest up the Flat Creek drainage. An easy grade through forest and meadows ends in a bowl (2,800 ft) below the impressive cliffs of Rimrock Ridge. The glacier-wrapped summit of Le Conte Mountain rises to the west above the end of the valley.

Pacific Crest National Scenic Trail. 60.3 miles/m (H,S). The PCT enters the Glacier Peak Wilderness from the Henry M. Jackson Wilderness at Indian Pass. It follows the Cascade backbone north, and next contacts civilization at the High Bridge Guard Station on the Stehekin River, at the mouth of Agnes Creek.

PCT: Indian Pass to Sitcum Creek. 12.4 miles. The ridge at Indian Pass (4,980 ft) can be reached from the south via the PCT from the Henry M. Jackson Wilderness or from the east on Trail #1502 from Indian Creek. The route climbs gently through meadows to Lower White Pass (5,590 ft), where it meets the upper end of Trail #1507. The ascent continues on open northeast slopes to White Pass (5,904 ft), with Glacier Peak in view the entire way. At White Pass the trail crosses the ridge, traverses below White Mountain, and meets the east end of Trail #649. The way climbs gradually to Red Pass (6,550 ft), a narrow defile south of Portal Peak, where the Monte Cristo group of peaks lines the western horizon. The way swings east after crossing the pass; meadows give way to cliffs and talus slopes on the south side of White Chuck Cinder Cone, a remnant of a small volcano. The trail drops to Glacier Creek Meadows in a broad basin at the head of the White Chuck River, then descends through subalpine forest. After crossing the White Chuck, a long river bottom descent reaches Sitcum Creek (3,900 ft) and Trail #643 from the west.

PCT: Sitcum Creek to Vista Ridge. 18.6 miles. The route heads north, traverses the valley wall to Kennedy Creek, crosses the creek, and climbs the opposite wall to Kennedy Ridge (4,250 ft). The parkland crest is followed up to timberline, close to the snouts of the Scimitar and Kennedy glaciers. A long ascent weaves northwest, crossing meltwater creeks, to reach Fire Creek Pass (6,350 ft), the most technically troubling pass on the PCT. Switchbacks east of the pass drop first to cliff-bound Mica Lake (5,443 ft), then to Milk Creek (3,800 ft). Thirty-six switchbacks up the opposite side of the drainage regain lost altitude and reach the meadows of Milk Creek Ridge (5,600 ft). A gentle grade through the basin at the head of the East Fork of Milk Creek leads to Vista Ridge (5,900 ft) and a sweeping view up the Vista Glacier to the summit of Glacier Peak. Here are the first glimpses northwest to the glaciers in the Dome Peak area.

PCT: Vista Ridge to Suiattle Pass. 12.3 miles. After a chain of switchbacks drops through cliffs to Vista Creek, the route follows the wooded creek bottom downstream to Skyline Bridge over the Suiattle River (2,780 ft), where it crosses Trail #784. The route zigzags up the nose of Middle Ridge, traverses east above Miners Creek, crosses it, and climbs to Suiattle Pass (5,984

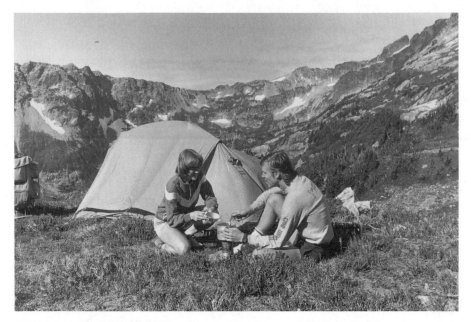

Campsite on a shoulder of Red Mountain

ft), passing Trails #789 and #785 en route. The pass overlooks the deep Agnes Creek drainage and the jagged knife-edge ridge on its east border.

PCT: Suiattle Pass to the Stehekin River. 17 miles. The route drops into the headwaters of the South Fork of Agnes Creek, where it meets Trail #1256 (5,600 ft). As the path swings around a basin southeast of Bannock Mountain, glimpses open east to Bonanza Peak (9,511 ft), the highest nonvolcanic summit in the Cascades. The way descends to rejoin Agnes Creek at Glacier Creek (3,600 ft); the long trek down the valley floor passes Trail #1272 (2,400 ft), leading up the West Fork of Agnes Creek. Meadows in this section of the trail offer views upstream to the rock finger summit of Agnes Mountain, and downstream to the south face of McGregor Mountain. Civilization of sorts is reached at the High Bridge Guard Station on the Stehekin (1,600 ft).

Climbing

Climbing guides catalog routes up 140 peaks and spires in the wilderness, far too many to list individually here. Many of these have impressive faces exceeding 1,000 feet in height, but also have easy ridge scrambles to their summits. Following is a summary of the most impressive or technically challenging climbs.

In the northwest corner of the wilderness, the highest and most glaciated peak is four-summited Snowking Mountain (7,433 ft). Routes exist from all sides, but none are technically difficult. Southwest of Snowking is Mount Chaval (7,127 ft), with three craggy summits. Easiest routes are from the west; more challenging are the northwest flank, C-3 to C-4, and the north ridge, 1,500 feet of solid granite with moves up to C-5.7. The third peak of interest in this area is Mount Buckindy (7,320 ft), the highest of a group of fractured, loose breccia spires that rise above the Kindy Glacier. Routes from the north and east combine snow and rock pitches. A half-dozen lesser spires in the group have short vertical faces of low C-5 difficulty.

The remoteness of Glacier Peak (10,541 ft), the highest summit in the wilderness, adds to the difficulty of its ascent. Routes have been put up all of its major glaciers: the Sitkum, Scimitar, Kennedy, Ptarmigan, Vista, Ermine, Dusty, North Guardian, Chocolate, Cool, and Gerdine. The upper reaches of most of these are very steep and heavily crevassed. The only rock route to the summit follows the southern rib via Disappointment Peak, then up the cleaver beyond to the summit. Southeast of Glacier is Tenpeak Mountain (8,281 ft), a long summit block above the Honeycomb Glacier with several rock routes in the C-5 range.

Popular, easily accessible peaks (7,240 to 8,200 ft) lie along the boundary between the wilderness and North Cascades National Park at Cascade Pass. Most impressive of these is Johannesburg Mountain, with its wide, vertical, 2,200-foot-high north face; several routes rate up to C-5.8. Next along this ridge is Cascade Peak, with C-3 to C-5.8 ascents on all sides. East of Cascade are the Triplets, three rock spikes with several hundred feet of C-3 to C-5.3 leads. The ridge turns southeast to Mixup Peak, a long knife-edge crest rising from a steep downsloping rock apron. Routes vary from C-4 to C-5.

The classic 15-mile-long, cross-country Ptarmigan Traverse south from Cascade Pass reaches some of the best climbs in the wilderness. The traverse crosses Cache Col south of the pass to its first summit, Magic Mountain (7,610 ft). Its summit tower has an impressive vertical west face, however, most climbs involve only C-3 to C-4 chimney or ridge routes. A traverse south leads to a col between Mount Formidable (8,325 ft) and Spider Mountain (8,280 ft). Formidable is a massive peak above the Middle Cascade Glacier with a summit chopped into several towers. Steep routes on both snow and rock have a few exposed leads. Spider is renowned for its loose rock, which endangers otherwise simple C-4 ascents.

A long traverse south leads to Le Conte Mountain (7,762 ft), an elongated summit. The highest point is an easy ridge climb, but the 100- to 200-foot spires at the south end of the summit block are more challenging. The Le Conte Glacier is traversed south past Sentinel Peak (8,261 ft) and its companion, Old Guard (8,240 ft); both are easy snow and rock scrambles. After contouring the upper South Cascade Glacier the route crosses a saddle and drops to White Rock Lakes (6,194 ft). Sharp knife-blade spires along an arête southwest of the lakes culminate in Spire Point (8,264 ft), at the apex of the Dana and Spire glaciers. This crag has several difficult rock routes ranging from C-4 to C-5.7.

East of Spire, on a rib between the Dome Glacier to the west and the massive Chickamin Glacier to the east, is the highest summit in the area, Dome Peak (8,920 ft). Travel over crevassed glaciers leads to the final assault on the narrow summit flake. There are also several interesting towers on ridges radiating from Dome, and two more peaks rise above the Chickamin Glacier. East of Dome is Sinister Peak (8,440 ft), a bulky rock summit with a steep snowfield on its shoulder. Ice and rock routes are rated C-4. Northeast of Sinister is Blue Mountain (8,198 ft), sometimes known as Gunsight Peak for the pair of rabbit-ear flakes that form its top. It is a striking peak with a solid vertical 700-foot granite face. There are no easy routes, and those on the face range as high as C-5.10.

Agnes Mountain (8,115 ft) is a rugged, isolated peak 1.5 miles east of Blue. Its distinctive Matterhorn shape protrudes high above surrounding crags. The slabs and blocks of the summit pyramid hold several C-5 to C-5.6 routes. The South Fork of Agnes Creek is framed by two impressive ridges. To the west is Bannock Mountain (7,760 ft), with a massive northwest face rising 1,700 feet above a glacier base. On the east side of the creek is a long jagged ridge with Needle Peak (7,880 ft) at its north end. The pointed summit is an exposed C-3 climb. The ridge continues south past Dark Peak (8,504 ft) to culminate in the huge mass of Bonanza Peak (9,511 ft), the highest nonvolcanic summit in the Cascades. The top of the mountain is a complex multi-horned rib that long thwarted climbing attempts. Glacier approaches lead to several rock pitches of C-5 and above on any summit routes.

At the northeast end of the wilderness three impressive peaks rise above the west side of Devore Creek. The northernmost, Tupshin Peak (8,320 ft), has a broad 1,300-foot north face and a series of pinnacles along its summit ridge. Ticklish, exposed C-4 to C-5.4 rock work is required to reach the top. Southwest of Tupshin is White Goat Mountain (7,800 ft), a narrow granite blade with sheer 1,000-foot sides. Even the normally easier arête approaches are rated C-5.3 to C-5.5. The southernmost of this trio is Devore Peak (8,360 ft), with a vertical 900-foot north face. Ridge routes have a few brief C-4 leads.

Fortress Mountain (8,674 ft) is the highest summit in the Chiwawa Mountains, but a relatively easy scramble from the southwest flank or east ridge. The Entiat Mountains terminate in three peaks of climbing interest. Mount Maude (9,082 ft) is a bulky summit rising above the Entiat Glacier. A difficult icefall route ascends from the glacier; all other routes, none higher than C-5, are on rock. North of Maude is Seven Fingered Jack (9,077 ft); as its name implies, its crest comprises seven pointed crags. All may be climbed via moderately difficult gullies. Mount Fernow (9,249 ft), the third peak, is the highest point in the Entiat Mountains. Its three main ridges are all easy climbs.

Winter Sports

Few visitors venture into the interior of the Glacier Peak Wilderness in winter, as the proliferation of avalanche tracks on side-slopes makes such expeditions inadvisable; nonetheless, winter ascents have been made on some of its peaks. Several classic ski/snowshoe tours on the west side of the wilderness can be recommended. One of these is Green Mountain, best done early or late in the season to reduce avalanche danger. The route follows Trail #782 from the Suiattle River. There is some avalanche danger in the steep meadows near timberline, before reaching the ridgetop. The reward is a panorama of peaks, including Sloan, Glacier, Dome, Shuksan, Baker, and nearby Buckindy.

A safer tour, with equally spectacular views of Glacier Peak, is Meadow Mountain via Trail #657. It is a 5-mile road slog to reach the trailhead, and the lower portion of the trail is a narrow path through dense timber with only light snow cover. Once into timberline meadows, the deep snow on the broad ridge crest offers endless skiing opportunities.

An expert-level trek follows Trail #643 up the White Chuck River to Kennedy Hot Springs. The feasibility of this trip depends on snow depths; too much and it is impossible to drive the 11 miles up FR 23 to the trailhead, too little and the low-altitude trail will have only sparse snow cover. In the "just right" case, the reward for the long valley-bottom trip is a dip in the warm springs before heading back.

23

ENTIAT MOUNTAINS

LOCATION: In Chelan County, on the southeast border of the Glacier Peak Wilderness Area, between the Chiwawa and Entiat rivers
SIZE: 89,755 acres
STATUS: Approximately 65 percent is designated as Roadless, but most trails are open to motorcycle use.
TERRAIN: A high-altitude plateau, with steep side-slopes leading to interconnecting alpine ridgetops that rise to rugged summits at the northeast end of the range
ELEVATION: 2,500 to 7,610 feet
MANAGEMENT: USFS, Wenatchee National Forest, Lake Wenatchee and Entiat ranger districts
TOPOGRAPHIC MAPS: Brief, Chikamin Creek, Plain, Pyramid Mountain, Saska Peak, Schaefer Lake, Silver Falls, Sugarloaf Peak, Trinity, Tyee Mountain

The Entiat Mountains are a southern extension of the Glacier Peak Wilderness Area, and their exclusion from it is somewhat illogical. Perhaps it was because their geography was less rugged, more a transition from the ice-clad peaks of the wilderness to the alpine and mid-range forest of central Washington. Or perhaps it was because of their extensive trail use by motorcycles—more's the pity.

The mountain range rises abruptly from the base level of about 2,500 feet in the two wide glacial-cut valleys that frame either side. The center of the range varies between 5,000 and 7,000 feet. The Mad River has carved a deep longitudinal drainage through the heart of the area. Its tributaries, as well as those of the Chiwawa and Entiat rivers on either side, further dissect the range into an interconnecting series of ridges and valleys.

The forests are typical of the Cascades' east slopes, giving way to broad meadows along and near the heads of creeks, and alpine meadows on ridgetops. The entire range has only a half-dozen lakes larger than pond-size, and most of these are shallow and heavily silted. In a few centuries they will probably be swallowed by encroaching meadows.

Some 185 miles of trail lace the Entiat Mountains Roadless Area; however, the roadless designation does not preclude motorized use. About 145 trail miles are open to motorcycles, and a half-dozen trails have been widened and graded (nearly paved) specifically for motorized use. Some of the remaining miles default to foot travel only by virtue of being abandoned and unmaintained. The snarl of engines certainly does not contribute to a wilderness experience, and the ash and pumice soil of the mountains is easily eroded by boots, let alone speeding, spinning wheels. It may be too late to protect this wonderful area with a wilderness designation, but we should at least lobby for no further degradation.

Climate

The west side of the Entiat Mountains receives more precipitation (45 to 90 inches annually) than the east side (35 to 50 inches annually). On both sides, from 60 to 70 percent falls between November and April in the form of snow. Valley snow depths reach an average of 5 feet, and at higher elevations snow stacks up to about 7 feet. Most is gone from all elevations by mid-July. Summer temperature highs average in the 80s and 90s; winter lows average between 10 and 20 degrees.

Plants and Wildlife

Forests on the west side of the Entiat Mountains are composed of Douglas-fir, Pacific silver fir, grand fir, western hemlock, western white pine, and western red cedar, while timber on the drier eastern side is primarily Douglas-fir, alpine fir, and lodgepole pine. Large portions of the southeast end of the mountains have been burned by a succession of forest fires, and a dense lodgepole pine forest has regenerated since then.

The forest understory contains huckleberry, vine maple, mertensia, and prickly currant; in meadow breaks cheatgrass brome, starry solomonplume, heartleaf arnica, twinflower, arctic lupine, pyrola, prince's pine, wood violet, and anemone prevail. Alpine meadows at or near ridgetops are covered with arctic lupine, Sitka valerian, showy sedge, American false hellebore, and feathery miterwort. Side-slope avalanche paths support a growth of Sitka alder, mountain ash, elderberry, and trailing blackberry.

The forest is a summer range for mule deer, a small herd of elk, black bear, marten, and grouse. Spotted owls have been identified in the southern end of the mountains, and peregrine falcons have been sighted on the east side of the range.

Geology

The underlying rocks in the Entiat Mountains, primarily evident in a wedge-shaped area between Miners Ridge and the lower Mad River, are old pre-Jurassic metamorphics. A major fault line marking the eastern edge of the Chiwaukum graben runs along the west crest of the mountains in the vicinity of Miners and McDonald ridges. Chiwaukum graben rock is a pale sandstone, younger (30 million to 40 million years old) and less tightly folded than the older metamorphics on either side. Most of the folding occurred before the graben filled with sedimentary rock of volcanic origin. The remainder of the mountains between the fault line and the Entiat River are part of the Chelan batholith, a complex, massive, granitic intrusion between 60 million and 70 million years old.

Continental glaciers, which reached their maximum southern progress about 12,000 years ago, carved the valleys on either side of the Entiat Mountains through which the Entiat and Chiwawa rivers flow. Although the soils covering the mountains include glacial alluvium, they are predominately volcanic ash and pumice, ranging from 6 inches to 60 feet in depth, deposited by Glacier Peak eruptions 12,000 years ago. This light volcanic mix erodes easily when vegetation is removed.

History

Local Indian tribes were known to visit the Entiat Mountains for hunting and food gathering. There is also some evidence of early-day trappers in the Rock Creek and Blue Creek areas. By the early 1900s, sheepherders were driving their flocks to ridgetop alpine meadows for summer grazing. At the heart of the mountains, on the Mad River, is Blue Creek Meadow Campground, accessible only by trail. This was once the site of the Mad River Dude Ranch, a popular 1920s vacation spot.

When fire protection became a key mission of the Forest Service in the 1920s and 30s, fire lookout sites were placed atop many of the area's high points, including Basalt Peak, Tyee Mountain, Klone Peak, Cougar Mountain, and a knob south of Estes Butte. All of these lookouts were removed or destroyed by the 1960s, but many of the region's trails, built to access and support the lookouts, are their legacy.

ACTIVITIES

Hiking

CHIWAWA RIVER TRAILS

Trail #1523, Alder Ridge. *11 miles/m (H; S,B,M after July 15).* The lower portion of this trail leaves FR 62, crosses logging roads, and wanders up through clearcuts from the Chiwawa River near Twin Creeks (2,350 ft) to FR 6104 (3,900 ft), where the roadless area begins. Here the path continues up the ridge, covered with grand old Douglas-fir and ponderosa pine. At 5,800 feet the trail gains the crest of the Entiat Mountains, then continues north, alternating between woods and meadows, to reach its high point (6,229 ft). Rock outcrops en route offer views of Glacier Peak. The trail descends to meet Trail #1409A at the south fringe of Mad Meadow (5,810 ft).

Trail #1515, Basalt Ridge. *7.7 miles/m (H,S,B).* From Finner Campground on FR 62 (2,475 ft) the trail switchbacks up steep wooded side-slopes to a bench at the head of Minnow Creek. It resumes the climb to the summit of Basalt Peak (6,004 ft), then drops north to a rock nubbin with views of the Rock Creek drainage and the crowns of the Entiat Mountains: Garland Peak, Devils Smoke Stack, and Rampart Mountain. Switchbacks gain the crest of the ridge heading north and follow its undulations to a junction with Trail #1408 (7,348 ft) near Devils Smoke Stack.

Trail #1509, Rock Creek. *11.5 miles/m (H,S; B to the Glacier Peak Wilderness).* Near Rock Creek Campground on FR 62 (2,500 ft), the path leads up timbered slopes above the southeast side of Rock Creek. The route continues north along the creek in alternating forest and meadow, then enters the Glacier Peak Wilderness (3,650 ft). A creekside cliff forces the path high above the bank; beyond, it returns to the thickly wooded creek bottom. The forest thins to meadows as the trail climbs to the head of the drainage and switchbacks up the basin headwall. The route swings around to a saddle (5,980 ft) south of Carne Mountain, crosses it, and meets Trail #1508.

Trail #1527, Estes Butte. *2.5 miles/m (H,S,B,M).* Just north of Rock Creek Campground, spur FR 6200460 heads a short distance up the north side of Rock Creek to the trailhead (2,600 ft). Switchbacks work up the steep forested hillside, where breaks in the trees offer views down the Chiwawa River valley. The climb eases at 4,600 feet as the ridge continues north to an abandoned lookout site (5,397 ft) with views of Glacier Peak, the Entiat Mountains, and the Chiwawa River valley. The path continues north along the ridge, dipping in saddles and rising over hummocks to reach the summit of Estes Butte (5,942 ft).

MINERS RIDGE TRAILS

Trail #1411, Miners Ridge. *4.5 miles/e (H,S,B,M).* FR 52, which rides the major fault line on the east side of the Chiwaukum graben, joins both ends of this trail. The north trailhead (4,950 ft), crosses Miners Creek, then climbs gently to the broad ridgetop (5,500 ft). The track heads southeast through broad meadows, laced with lupine and Indian paintbrush, that provide wide views of Glacier Peak, Mount Stuart, and Lake Wenatchee. Just beyond a knob on the

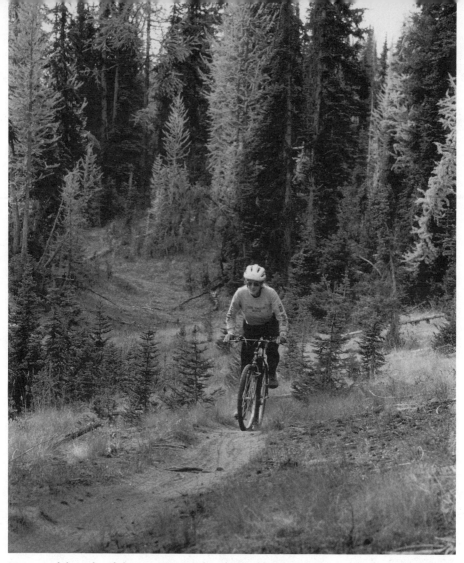

Mountain biking the Chikamin ORV Trail in the Mad River area

south end of the ridge (5,600 ft) is the west end of Trail #1410. From here the path swings downhill above the Hornet Creek Basin to rejoin FR 5200 (5,350 ft).

Trail #1410, Hornet Ridge. 6 miles/d (H,S,B,M). A route between Miners Ridge and the Mad River leaves Trail #1410 just below the high point on the south end of the ridge. An easy grade follows Hornet Ridge southeast above the steep north slope of the Hornet Creek drainage. After a saddle, a rise, and another saddle, the route traverses south slopes below the ridgetop to a narrow rib between Hornet Creek and a drainage to its north. A no-nonsense drop downhill followed by a few switchbacks leads to Trail #1409 in the Mad River canyon (1,970 ft), 1.5 miles north of Pine Flat Campground.

MAD RIVER TRAILS

Trail #1409, Lower Mad River. 14.9 miles/e (H,S,B,M). From Pine Flat Campground on FR 57 (1,620 ft) the route follows the twists of the river as it heads northwest into the canyon. Old-growth cedar and Douglas-fir frame the trail, and vestiges of a 1970s fire that devastated the area can be seen on the side-slopes above the river. The first of many side trails, Trail #1410, leaves the west side of the river at 1.5 miles, just beyond Hornet Creek. In another mile the path leaves the riverbank and zigzags up to side-slopes, where it contours for a mile before returning to the river.

At 9.8 miles the route crosses the river to avoid cliffs along the east bank. It recrosses to the east bank at 10.6 miles, just below Cougar Creek. Here Trail #1418 heads uphill to the north. For the next mile the canyon widens, then closes in again at 13 miles near Berg Creek. Another mile leads to Maverick Saddle (4,300 ft), the end point of the lower river trail, and the start of the upper one.

Trail #1409A, Upper Mad River. 12.2 miles/e (H; S,B,M after July 15). From FR 6101 at Maverick Saddle (4,300 ft) the route follows the west side of the river for a mile, crosses the river, and meets the lower end of eastbound Trail #1419. The path breaks into clearings, and at 3 miles passes the lower end of Trail #1421 to the west. Meadows continue for the next mile; the river is crossed and recrossed before meeting Trail #1415 heading east up Whistling Pig Creek. At 5 miles the south end of expansive Blue Creek Meadows is reached; its campground is another 0.5 mile farther on the bank of Blue Creek (5,430 ft).

This campground is at the heart of the upper Mad River trail system, and a favorite base camp for numerous one-day loop trips using various interconnecting paths. Trail #1426 leaves east from the campground, and Trail #1421 heads to the west. To the north the river flows through a wide basin with a string of broad meadows. Near the south end of Mad Meadow, Trail #1523 drops in from the west, and a short spur leads southwest to Mad Lake, the river's source. At 7.5 miles, in the heart of Marble Meadow, Trail #1426 takes off to the east. The track now switchbacks up the rim of Three Creek Basin, and ends at the ridgetop at 12.2 miles, where it joins Trails #1408 and #1429. Motorcycles are prohibited on trails north of here.

Trail #1418, Cougar Ridge. 6.5 miles/m (H,S,B,M). From the Mad River at Billy Creek (3,400 ft), tight, demanding switchbacks claw up the steeply pitched hillside to gain the top of a broad north-flowing ridge (5,200 ft). The route follows this undulating crest for more than 5 miles, finally breaking into meadows and rock outcrops with views of Glacier Peak. It ends on Trail #1419 (6,210 ft) just below the final rise to the summit of Cougar Mountain.

Trail #1419, Jimmy Creek. 2.9 miles/d (H,S). The trail leaves the Mad River (4,570 ft) and climbs the forested north wall of the Jimmy Creek drainage to the head of the basin at 6,100 feet. A bit farther it meets Trail #1418 (6,220 ft) arriving from the ridge to the south. The path continues along basalt slopes on the south and east sides of Cougar Mountain. It ends in another 0.2 mile on Trail #1415 (6,140 ft) as that trail crosses the mountain's north slope. A short spur climbs to the summit of Cougar Mountain (6,701 ft), a former lookout site well chosen for its unbroken views of the Cascades from Mount Rainier to Glacier Peak, as well as peaks around Mount Stuart.

Trail #1415, Tyee Ridge. 8.7 miles/m (H,S,B,M). This scenic trail atop Tyee Ridge starts from FR 5713 at the last switchback (6,400 ft) below the Tyee Mountain lookout site. The first portion of the trail wanders the ridge through the silvering snags of a large 1970s forest fire. For the next mile the route stays on south slopes just below the crest, with the Mount Stuart peaks in sight, until it reaches an open saddle (6,700 ft) on the south shoulder of Signal Peak. A slow descent along a roller-coaster ridge reaches a pocket meadow where Boiling Springs bubbles up to fill a tarn. Beyond is the head of Trail #1423 from the Entiat River valley, and in another mile the trail reaches an intersection with Trail #1419 on the northeast rib of Cougar Mountain. A descent along the north side of the mountain leads through Cougar Meadow (5,870 ft), then down Whistling Pig Creek, to the bank of the Mad River and Trail #1409A.

Trail #1421, Lost Lake. 3.9 miles/e (H,S,B,M). From the Mad River (4,800 ft), 3.2 miles south of Blue Creek Meadow Campground, a recently reconstructed trail makes a series of lazy switchbacks up the forested west slope to a 5,650-foot-high flat, then descends to tiny Lost Lake (5,550 ft). The route climbs slowly north to a 5,930-foot high point, then makes a beeline descent to Blue Creek Meadow (5,400 ft).

Trail #1426, Blue Creek. 4.8 miles/e (H,S,B,M). From the Blue Creek Campground (5,430 ft) this route heads up the west bank of Blue Creek, passes the west end of Trail #1424, then near the head of the drainage swings steeply uphill to Lake Ann (5,830 ft), the first of the Two

Little Lakes. A few hundred feet downhill is the second lake, Lake Louise (5,750 ft). The path ascends gradually north along Tommy Creek, then swings west at Klone Meadow (6,200 ft), where it meets Trail #1425. From here a gradual descent to Marble Meadow (5,930 ft) rejoins Trail #1409A.

Trail #1408, Garland Peak. 11.1 miles/m (H,S). From its junction with Trails #1409A and #1429 at the headwaters of Three Creek (6,270 ft), the route follows the rocky crest of the Entiat Mountains north, sometimes atop the ridge, other times on the west slopes, shying away from the vertical faces on its north and east sides. Views are continuous and spectacular; close at hand are the ragged summits of the Entiat Mountains, south are Rainier and the Stuart subrange, east is the Cascade crest, and north are the ice-cloaked crags of the Glacier Peak Wilderness. At its high point (7,350 ft), midway between Garland Peak and Devils Smoke Stack, the route meets Trail #1515.

From a pass on the shoulder between Devils Smoke Stack and Rampart Mountain (7,160 ft) the trail drops to timberline to round the west side of Rampart, then enters the Glacier Peak Wilderness (5,860 ft) and switchbacks up the south shoulder of Fifth of July Mountain to Cow Creek Pass (6,920 ft). Scramble routes to the mountaintop reach eye-popping views of Rainier, Glacier, Maude, Spectacle Buttes, and the ragged north end of the Chelan Mountains. The way traverses north, drops below a band of cliffs, then passes the upper end of Trail #1404 as it heads to a rocky spur above Larch Lakes (6,350 ft). It drops into the cirque (5,740 ft) enclosing the upper two lakes, where it meets Trail #1430.

ENTIAT RIVER TRAILS

Trail #1423, South Tommy. 5.7 miles/m (H,S,B,M). Two trails head west from FR 51 at Lake Creek Campground (2,215 ft); this one stays close to the west bank of the Entiat River for a short distance, then begins a torturous ascent of steep slopes in a series of switchbacks. A respite at a small bench (3,500 ft) is followed by more zigzags to the top of a spur (5,300 ft). This rib tilts abruptly upward for the final climb to a 6,485-foot-high knob on the northwest end of Tyee Ridge. The path tops the crest, then drops down the south side to join Trail #1415 (6,020 ft) west of Boiling Spring.

Trail #1424, Middle Tommy. 8.8 miles/m (H,S,B,M). The second trail from Lake Creek Campground (2,215 ft) swings up the north bank of Tommy Creek, touches a logging spur in 0.7 mile, then crosses the creek and switchbacks to a mid-ridge bench at 5,150 feet. It drops around the head of a creek basin, then resumes switchbacks up a steep rib to a saddle. The way continues west through the flower fields of East Blue Creek Meadow, then ascends to end on Trail #1426 (5,500 ft).

Trail #1425, North Tommy. 9 miles/e (H,S,B,M). FR 5605 does the first 2,000 feet of climbing up the steep north side of Tommy Creek. From the road's end (4,500 ft) the trail climbs west, switchbacking first broadly, then tightly, to maintain an easy grade for motorbikes. At a helipad knob (5,863 ft) the route swings northwest atop the ridge, undulating over hummocks to reach Three Creek Ridge. From here a short ridge romp leads to the old lookout site atop Klone Peak (6,820 ft) and great views of the summits of the Glacier Peak Wilderness, the Pyramid Mountain portion of the Chelan Mountains, and the Mount Stuart–area peaks. The route then circles the south side of Klone to end on Trail #1426.

Trail #1429, Shetipo. 4.7 miles/m (H,S,B,M). From the Entiat River's Cottonwood Campground (3,082 ft) at the end of FR 51, this route heads southwest, crosses Shetipo Creek, switchbacks up above the west bank, and stays high enough to avoid steep walls above the creek. The way crosses the creek in about 3 miles, then works up a series of side-slopes and benches to the pass at the head of Three Creek, where it meets Trails #1409A and 1408 (6,270 ft).

Climbing

There are no serious climbs in the Entiat Mountains, although several of the high points have precipitous north or east faces, ranging from 100 to 1,500 feet or more in height. The longest and most prominent faces are on Signal and Garland peaks, Devils Smoke Stack, and Rampart Mountain. All feature routes up gullies and broken rock ranging from C-3 to C-5 in difficulty.

Winter Sports

Although the interior of the Entiat Mountains is too steep and avalanche-prone to be attractive for winter sports, snows turn peripheral access roads into potential ski and snowshoe tours. They are also attractive to the wintertime cousin of the motorcycle, the snowmobile.

24

CHELAN MOUNTAINS

LOCATION: In Chelan County, south of Glacier Peak Wilderness, between the Entiat River and Lake Chelan
SIZE: 75,140 acres
STATUS: About 80 percent is designated as Roadless, but many trails are open to motorcycle use.
TERRAIN: High plateau and backbone ridge joined by numerous lateral drainages. Mountains rise steeply from deep glacier-carved valleys on either side. Ragged rocky peaks are located along the northern third of the range.
ELEVATION: 1,098 to 8,590 feet
MANAGEMENT: USFS, Wenatchee National Forest, Entiat and Chelan ranger districts
TOPOGRAPHIC MAPS: Big Goat Mtn., Brief, Lucerne, Pyramid Mountain, Saska Peak, Silver Falls, South Navarre Peak, Stormy Mtn.

The Chelan Mountains Roadless Area lies between two wide, deep, glacier-carved valleys, one containing the Entiat River, the second filled by the crystal blue waters of Lake Chelan. The side-slopes of both valleys rise abruptly to the 6,000- to 7,000-foot backbone of the range. Glaciers and creeks have carved these abrupt hillsides into a series of lateral ridges that run perpendicular to the crest of the mountains. The North Fork of the Entiat River thrusts deeply into the northwest corner of the region.

A dense pine forest climbs from the creek bottoms up the slopes to timberline meadows on ridgetops. The forest cover on the sidehills is streaked by avalanche tracks. The northern portion of the area, bordering on the Glacier Peak Wilderness, contains the region's highest and most rugged peaks, some with near-vertical faces on their north and east sides. A few tiny pocket glaciers hide in cirques below these rock bastions.

Ridgetop trails run the length of the backbone crest, fed on the east side by multiple trails that run up drainages and lateral ridges. These permit a host of loop trips that use only portions of the long crest route. The east side of the range has no maintained trails between the crest and the lake.

The mountains are not truly roadless; they are cut laterally at their midpoint by a heavily used forest road between Twentyfivemile Creek State Park on Lake Chelan and the Entiat Valley. The south and southwest borders of the roadless area have been heavily logged, and the threat of continued infringement on the present virgin forest is ever-present. Some of the ridgetops had wide fire breaks cleared to contain the massive 1970 Entiat forest fire; several decades will be required before these tracks regain their natural appearance. Unfortunately, roadless also does not mean motorless; a large portion of the trail mileage in the mountains is open to the destruction of tread and solitude by motorcycles.

Climate

Because the Chelan Mountains form a high north–south divide, weather conditions vary somewhat between the west and east sides of the range. The wetter west side receives 40 to 70 inches of precipitation annually, while on the drier east side the precipitation range is in the 25-

to 60-inch range. Sixty to 70 percent falls in the form of snow between November and May, and snow depths can vary between 6 and 15 feet, depending mostly on elevation. Temperatures in summer are warm, with highs averaging in the high 80- to 90-degree range. Lows in winter average in the teens and low 20s.

Plants and Wildlife

Forests in the Chelan Mountains are Englemann spruce, Pacific silver fir, subalpine pine, lodgepole pine, and alpine larch. Small Douglas-firs are also found in lower elevations on the west. Lodgepole pine is especially dense in old burn areas, where it is the dominant regenerative species. The forest understory includes pinegrass, ocean spray, dwarf huckleberry, and false azalea. Sheep fescue, cinquefoil, penstemon, and lupine are found in alpine meadows.

The area is used as a summer range by mule deer and a few elk. Black bear, cougar, marten, grouse, and a variety of smaller non-game birds and mammals also inhabit the forest. A few mountain goats are found in the rugged rock cliffs at the north edge of the range.

Geology

The rock on the west side of the Chelan Mountains is a portion of the Chelan Batholith, a granitic intrusion that occurred in the late Mesozoic era. The eastern flank of the mountains is a complex of pre-Jurassic metamorphic rock and migmatite, a heterogeneous mix of igneous and metamorphic rocks swirled together along the eastern boundary of the batholith. Surface soils are either granitic residuum or a combination of pumice and volcanic ash, from 6 inches to 30 feet deep, expelled during the eruption of Glacier Peak about 12,000 years ago.

The deep valleys on both sides of the mountains were carved by the last continental ice sheet. The terminus of the lobe of continental ice on the east side of the mountains stopped prior to carving through bedrock near present-day Chelan, and when the ice retreated the valley filled with the waters of Lake Chelan. The glacial lobe from the Okanogan Valley was slower to retreat and temporarily blocked the head of Lake Chelan, raising its level far above today's height, causing the waters to carve a temporary escape coulee west from Twentyfivemile Creek.

History

Long before Euro-American intrusion, the Lake Chelan area was home to the ancestors of the Chelan Indians, who lived on the margins of the lake. At least one site with pictographs has been reported along the lakeshore bordering the Chelan Mountains. The first whites in the area were trappers in the Domke Lake area who ran extensive traplines into the north end of the range. These pioneers were followed in the early 1900s by sheepherders who ran flocks up to alpine meadows for summer grazing. In the 1920s fire lookouts were constructed at several high points in the region. Among these were Duncan Hill, Big Hill, Pyramid Mountain, and Stormy Mountain. Only debris fragments and incomparable views remain today at these lookout sites.

ACTIVITIES

Hiking

ENTIAT RIVER TRAILS

Trail #1434, Duncan Hill. 10.4 miles/m (H,S; B,M to the Glacier Peak Wilderness). From the trailhead on FR 5608 (5,146 ft) at the southeast end of Duncan Ridge, this seldom-used track follows the pine-covered crest over minor knobs to reach meadows at the head of Duncan Creek. In another 0.5 mile the way gains the rocky ridge south of Duncan Hill, where views extend from distant Mount Rainier to the nearby rocky crown of the Entiat Mountains. At 7,400 feet the path traverses the west side of Duncan Hill past a spur to the old lookout site at the summit (7,819 ft). The route wiggles downhill, climbs diagonally through forest, then meadows at the head of Anthem Creek, and rises to the Glacier Peak Wilderness boundary at a pass between Anthem and Choral creeks (6,900 ft). The way drops to a small bench, then zigzags down the steep, forested slope along Choral Creek to Trail #1230A (4,915 ft).

Trail #1437, North Fork of Entiat River. 8.1 miles/m (H,S,B). This is the quickest route into the high rock summits at the north end of the Chelan Mountains. From the end of FR 5606 (4,150 ft) the trail meanders through thick forest along the east bank of the river, crosses South Pyramid Creek, and meets the lower end of Trail #1439. Avalanche tracks provide view breaks in the woods as the way climbs along the valley floor to meet Trail #1436 to Fern Lake. In another mile the route leaves the river (5,760 ft) and ascends the east side-slope to merge with Trail #1433 (6,605 ft).

Trail #1439, South Pyramid Creek. 4 miles/e (H,S,B). This is the quickest route to the expansive views from Pyramid Mountain. From the 1.3-mile point of Trail #1437 (4,110 ft), just north of South Pyramid Creek, the route climbs through dense lodgepole pine, crosses the creek three times, then meets Trail #1433 (5,849 ft) at the south base of Pyramid Mountain.

Trail #1436, Fern Lake. 1.5 miles/d (H). This primitive track leaves Trail #1437 (5,201 ft) 6.1 miles from its start. The path climbs west after a logjam scamper or a frigid wade crosses the North Fork of the Entiat. The tread becomes more rugged as it breaks into steep rock for the final ascent to Fern Lake (6,894 ft). The lake reflects the glacier-polished cliffs that rim it, and in fall the color accents of surrounding golden larch.

Remnants of the old lookout on Pyramid Peak

FR 5900 TRAILS

Trail #1433, Pyramid Mountain. 16.8 miles/m (H,S,B). This long ridgetop route extends from the heart of the Chelan Mountains north into the Glacier Peak Wilderness. From the end of FR 5900113, north of Big Hill (6,550 ft), the route follows an old firebreak along the ridge, then slides west of the crest at the confluence of Silver and Pope ridges (6,930 ft).

The path traverses the flank of Crow Hill, descends to a wooded saddle (6,442 ft), then rounds the head of Butte Creek. A climb up the open south flank of Graham Mountain leads to a traverse of the fir-dotted slope on the west side of the mountain, then across meadows to Trail #1441 (6,250 ft), the spur to the summit of Pyramid Mountain.

At South Pyramid Creek the track joins the upper end of Trail #1439 (5,849 ft), then follows the creek northwest to its headwaters. Climbing resumes, and after crossing Grouse Pass (7,190 ft) the way descends around Grouse Creek basin to the bald ridge on its north side. More downhill travel passes the intersection with Trail #1437 (6,605 ft), then a wooded traverse reaches a platform at the head of the North Fork of the Entiat, with wide views down that drainage. The way contours a rock shelf to switchbacks up the steep sidehill to Saska Pass, the wilderness boundary (7,450 ft). From the pass the trail descends through larch-rimmed meadows to pine-covered slopes and ends on Trail #1230A (5,831 ft).

Trail #1441, Pyramid Point Viewpoint. 2.9 miles/m (H,S,B). From Trail #1443 on the south slope of Pyramid Mountain (6,250 ft) the old lookout path climbs diagonally up the west side of Pyramid Mountain, then zigzags up to the summit (8,243 ft). Peer down the sheer northeast face to Lake Chelan, or turn around and admire Glacier Peak and its entourage of ice-trimmed summits.

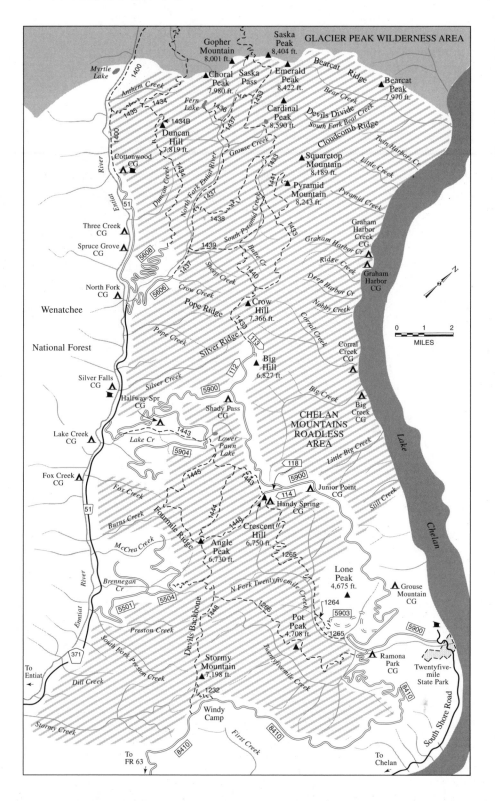

Trail #1443, Lake Creek. 7.6 miles/e (H,S,B,M). The lower sections of the original trail have been decimated by logging, and a recent logging road cuts the path midway up Lake Creek basin, but the trail still offers some forested solitude in its remaining sections. From a logging spur off FR 5900 (3,900 ft) the path ascends above the north bank of Lake Creek, mostly through lodgepole pine. It crosses FR 5904 (4,570 ft) at the base of the bowl containing Pawn Lakes and ascends the south slope of the basin. Switchbacks clamber up the wooded side-slope to ridgetop. The way proceeds east to Crescent Hill, to join Trail #1448 (6,720 ft).

Trail #1448, Devils Backbone. 13 miles/e (H,S,B,M). This motorbike racetrack follows the top of the south end of the Chelan Mountains. From the north trailhead on FR 5900118 at Crescent Hill (6,720 ft), shared with Trails #1265 and #1443, the route follows the ridge south to Angle Peak (6,720 ft). The long trek southeast runs along the backbone ridge through alpine timber and meadows. In a mile switchbacks drop below the cliffs of Point 6709, then regain the ridge east of the cliffs. Trail #1266 (6,680 ft) from Pot Peak is passed as the path continues south, following a roller-coaster ridgetop dip to a zigzag climb to the summit of Stormy Mountain (7,198 ft). Here the vista spans green orchard oases in the parched Wenatchee hills, the volcanoes of the South Cascades, the frosted cone of Glacier Peak, and the chain of North Cascade summits. The track then drops down the west slopes of the crest to end at FR 8410 (6,100 ft).

FR 8410 TRAILS

Trail #1265, North Fork of Twentyfivemile Creek. 10 miles/d (H,S,B,M). From FR 5900 on the east side of Darby Draw (2,390 ft), the path takes an easy grade west along the north bank of Twentyfivemile Creek. The route continues through riverbank fir and pine forest for another mile, then swings abruptly uphill, first in switchbacks, then just a relentless climb. The woods give way to meadows near the ridgetop (5,850 ft), and the open crest climbs arrow-straight to the northeast, with continuous views of Lake Chelan. A hook at the end of the ridge ends at Crescent Hill, where it meets Trail #1448 (6,720 ft).

Trail #1266, Pot Peak. 9.5 miles/m (H,S,B,M). From Ramona Park Campground on FR 8410 (1,920 ft), switchbacks climb the forested ridge to the southwest to a breather in a flat, mid-ridge meadow. The slope again steepens; a traverse, a swing around the shoulder of the ridge, and yet another climbing traverse gain the ridge (4,300 ft) east of Pot Peak. The way circles the peak, then begins a steady ascent of a westbound ridge. Meadows open at 6,800 feet, with views across Twentyfivemile Creek basin. Trail #1448 is met at 6,680 feet.

Climbing

Although several of the Chelan Mountain high points have sheer north faces, most have trails or easy scramble routes from other sides. Only the summits along and immediately south of the Glacier Peak Wilderness are of climbing interest. These boundary peaks (7,900 to 8,428 ft) from west to east are: Choral Peak, Gopher Mountain, and Saska, Emerald, and Bearcat peaks. Most have scramble routes from the south and steep C-3 rock ascents on the north and east faces.

Southeast of Bearcat Ridge are two companion arêtes, Devils Divide and Cloudcomb Ridge. The west end of Devils Divide is anchored by tri-topped Cardinal Peak (8,590 ft). The narrow crest on the south ridge is blocked by four near-vertical gendarmes requiring C-4 to C-5 climbing. East from Cardinal Peak, the divide is a series of craggy gendarmes with impressive rock routes up their south faces, and nontrivial ridge routes.

Cloudcomb Ridge, extending northeast from Squaretop Mountain, has four distinct summits and several intervening gendarmes along the ridgetop. Gully systems on the flanks provide summit routes up steep, friable C-3 rock.

Winter Sports

Forest roads on the fringes of the Chelan Mountains are heavily used for wintertime snowmobiling, but most backcountry trails have dangerous avalanche slopes along their routes, so winter use is limited. A possible exception is Trail #1433 between Big Hill and Pyramid Mountain. The Entiat River Road is generally open as far as Brief, and from there skis or snowshoes can be used to reach FR 5900 and climb to Shady Pass. From the pass, follow the crest trail north to the vicinity of Pyramid Mountain. The south slopes of the summit are avalanche-prone, so the trip in can be retraced from that point, or a loop trip can be made by dropping to Trail #1439 in South Pyramid Creek, then continuing to the Entiat River Road.

25

ALPINE LAKES WILDERNESS

LOCATION: In King, Snohomish, Kittitas, and Chelan counties, between US Highway 2 and I-90

SIZE: 393,360 acres

STATUS: Designated Wilderness (1976)

TERRAIN: Densely forested valleys rising to rugged rocky ridges and peaks with small glaciers and permanent snowfields. More than 700 lakes and tarns fill glacial cirques.

ELEVATION: 1,000 to 9,415 feet

MANAGEMENT: USFS, Mount Baker–Snoqualmie National Forest, North Bend and Skykomish ranger districts; and Wenatchee National Forest, Cle Elum, Lake Wenatchee, and Leavenworth ranger districts

TOPOGRAPHIC MAPS: Bandera, Big Jim Mountain, Big Snow Mtn., Blewett, Cashmere Mountain, Chikamin Peak, Chiwuakum Mountains, Davis Peak, Devils Slide, Enchantment Lakes, Grotto, Index, Jack Ridge, Lake Phillipa, Leavenworth, Mount Daniel, Mount Howard, Mount Phelps, Mount Si, Mount Stuart, Polallie Ridge, Scenic, Skykomish, Snoqualmie Lake, Snoqualmie Pass, Stevens Pass, The Cradle

The Alpine Lakes Wilderness exemplifies many of the problems faced in trying to preserve our wilderness heritage. Its jagged and irregular boundaries bespeak its history, namely that the prospectors, railroads, and loggers got here first, before recreationists and environmentalists, and staked claim to large segments of this wild and beautiful country. Long road fingers, built to support mining and logging activities, thrust up drainages into the wilderness. Patented mining claims stake out small privately owned chunks of property in the heart of the wilderness. Around the perimeter a checkerboard pattern of private and national forest land marks the alternate sections of land given to railroads under the 1862 Union Pacific Act. This property was subsequently sold to timber companies for large profits. By the time the irreplaceable beauty and natural treasures of the region were recognized and its preservation was lobbied for, these intrusions had already gnawed deeply into its periphery.

The Alpine Lakes Wilderness was created in 1976 to preserve the heart of this beautiful area. The act creating it charged the Forest Service to manage its perimeter under a common resource plan and to acquire as rapidly as feasible the private properties within the proposed wilderness boundaries. Although preservation of the land was legally assured, preservation of its wilderness nature wasn't. The 450 miles of trails, 700 lakes, and countless peaks and pinnacles are but an hour's drive from population centers of more than 4 million people, a large number of whom surge into the wilderness during summer and fall, especially on weekends, for 1-to 2-day hiking, camping, and climbing trips. The result in some places is a degree of solitude and wilderness experience similar to that found in New York's Central Park. Alpine lakes are elbow-to-elbow campsites, fragile vegetation is boot-trampled out of existence, and the natural resources the wilderness was created to protect are threatened by use-it-to-death recreation.

At the time of publication, the Forest Service was struggling with alternatives, attempting to

Opposite: *Glacier-polished Excaliber Rock in Lake Viviane, below McLellan Peak, is one of the jewels of the Enchantment Lakes.*

address overuse of this popular wilderness. Proposals would enforce strict limits on the number of people permitted to enter the wilderness at any given time, set entrance fees, severely restrict camping sites, and so on. To some these seem like draconian measures, impinging on taxpayers' God-given rights to go where and when they choose on public property—but maybe it is time for us to recognize that by overusing the wilderness we are destroying the very essence of a wilderness experience.

Climate

The variation in altitude from valley floors to the Cascade crest, as well as the barrier formed by the crest itself, creates a wide variance in local weather conditions. The western lowlands see precipitation of around 55 inches annually, while the crest averages 180 inches. At lower altitudes on eastern slopes, precipitation drops to 10 inches a year. Higher elevations are not snow-free until mid-July and often see first snowfalls by mid-October. Because of the steep gradient, summer thunderstorms often occur over the crest. Warm summer weather in the Puget Sound frequently results in temperature inversions that blanket the lowlands along the sound with fog and low clouds, while the mountains enjoy warm, sunny conditions.

On the west side of the Cascades summer temperatures are typically in the mid-70s, with occasional days in the 90s. Near the crest, days rarely exceed the mid-60s, and frosty nights are common. On the east side of the range temperatures in the 90s are the norm, and many days exceed 100. Sudden weather changes can create winterlike conditions anytime during the year. Fall and winter storms exact their toll on the forest with high winds, when steep barometric gradients generate winds as high as 75 miles per hour.

Plants and Wildlife

The wide east–west span of the wilderness, as well as its elevation extremes, encompass multiple ecological zones. Forests in lower regions on the west are mostly Douglas-fir, western hemlock, western red cedar, and red alder. Avalanche courses are coated with vine maple, and the understory includes salal, salmonberry, devil's club, and Oregon grape. With altitude the cedar and alder give way to Pacific silver fir, noble fir, and mountain hemlock, and open slopes see more Sitka alder and Douglas maple. Kinnikinnick and twinflower are introduced into the ground cover. Meadows have a profusion of blackberry, elderberry, and currant. Above 4,000 feet the dominant forest species are mountain hemlock and silver fir, with smatterings of subalpine fir. Near 6,000 feet the forest is mostly subalpine fir and dwarf juniper, and many meadows host a plethora of wildflowers, including avalanche lily, bluebells, phlox, and Indian paintbrush. Above timberline, heather, lupine, and snow lily fill spots between clumps of subalpine fir, larch, and mountain hemlock.

East of the crest occasional stands of Englemann spruce, alpine larch, and whitebark pine mix with subalpine fir, mountain hemlock, white fir, and silver fir. Lower on slopes the trees shift to Douglas-fir, hemlock, grand fir, and white fir, with the forest floor covered by pinegrass, sedge, huckleberry, elderberry, and vine maple. At the lowest elevations the forest is Douglas-fir, ponderosa pine, western hemlock, and lodgepole pine. The understory is mostly grasses and sedges decorated by rock lily, mariposa lily, hawkweed, and balsamroot.

The wilderness harbors typical wildlife species including black-tailed deer, elk, black bear, beaver, weasel, mink, bobcat, and cougar. Higher elevations are home to mountain goats, and there are reported sightings of such endangered species as gray wolf, bald eagle, grizzly bear, and spotted owl. The area also hosts 13 species of amphibians, 12 reptile species, and 177 species of birds.

Geology

The geological history of the region can be traced back about 350 million years to deposition of sedimentary and volcanic rock, probably off the shores of the North Cascades micro-continent while it was still in the mid-Pacific. Major granite batholiths intruded the crustal rocks about 80 million to 90 million years ago; today they are represented in the granite peaks of the Stuart Range and the Snoqualmie Pass area. On the south perimeter of this range is a band of serpentine rock representing older oceanic crust metamorphosed in the trench off the east coast of the micro-continent before the Stuart Range intrusions. South of this band are rocks of the Swauk Formation, sandstones that were probably deposited on the eastern edge of the North Cascades terrane during Eocene times. This formation has been folded and faulted as a result of the continental collision.

Most of the surface features recognizable today are a result of glaciation, both continental and local. Many of the hundreds of lakes for which the region is named lie in glacier-carved cirques, and exposed slabs of the granite substrate are smoothed and marked with striations from glacial erosion. The deep U-shaped valleys owe their characteristic form to glacial gouging, and many exhibit steps and hanging valleys formed by the retreat of glaciers with global warming.

History

Many central Washington Indian tribes attribute the Alpine Lake region with the source of all human life in the Cascades. Most early native visits to the high mountains were limited to hunting and gathering trips, and "vision quests," where tribal members went alone to peaks to establish contact with their guardian spirits. Trails that developed over mountain passes became essential for exchange of goods between plains- and saltwater-based Indian tribes. The first whites in the region, in the early 1800s, were trappers and fur traders. They were soon followed by missionaries and the pioneer settlers in the 1850s. Stress between the natives and immigrants culminated in the brief "Indian Wars" in 1855.

By 1853 surveys were seeking railroad routes across the Cascades. The search for routes was accelerated by the 1858 gold strikes in the Fraser River valley. Portland interests could transport goods east of the Cascades via the Columbia River, but Puget Sound merchants needed railroads to transfer goods across the range. Coal discoveries in the Roslyn area offered the cheap fuel required by railroads to run trains across the range, and the grants of alternate sections of land to railroads provided economic incentives to develop these routes. The Northern Pacific laid tracks across Stampede Pass in 1888, the Great Northern drove a tunnel through Stevens Pass in 1893, and the Chicago, Milwaukee, St. Paul, and Pacific went through Snoqualmie Pass in 1909. Most of the checkerboard sections of grant land were sold to timber companies, and this weird pattern of land holdings persists and thwarts logical management of major ecosystems today.

The Fraser River gold strikes triggered prospector searches for mineral wealth in the Alpine Lakes region, and more than 1,900 lode and placer claims and 137 patented claims were filed in the area. The minerals were mostly copper ores, with smatterings of gold and silver deposits. A presumably rich copper claim is still held in the heart of the wilderness near La Bohn Gap; it is a pain in the side for efforts to acquire all private land holdings within the wilderness.

Many east-side trails originated in the early 1900s as sheep drives. In 1905 the Forest Service was assigned management responsibility for the federal lands in the region, and during the 1930s the CCC built many of today's trails (and now-abandoned lookouts) to support the fire suppression mission of the Forest Service.

In the early 1900s, recreationists, mostly mountain climbers, recognized the unique character of the area, and by 1920 outdoor groups were strongly lobbying for its inclusion in the national park system. Formal protection was not provided until 1976, when the current wilderness area was created.

ACTIVITIES

Hiking

MIDDLE FORK SNOQUALMIE RIVER TRAILS

Trail #1002, Snoqualmie Lake. 10 miles/e-m (H; S,B on the Taylor River Road from the gate to the trailhead). Walk gated (1,225 ft) FR 5640101 up the Taylor River for 6 miles to the trailhead (1,865 ft). At a Y, Trail #1002 climbs east through old growth to Snoqualmie Lake (3,147 ft). After skirting the north shore, switchbacks reach Deer (3,583 ft) and Bear (3,610 ft) lakes. Trail #1072 continues east from Bear Lake.

Trail #1030, Dutch Miller Gap. 7.4 miles/m (H). From the end of FR 56 (2,990 ft) the

route continues northeast up the Middle Fork of the Snoqualmie River on a gentle grade with minor ups and downs. After closing to the river near a steep cascade, the way enters meadows in the broadening upper valley, with views south to Overcoat Peak and Summit Chief, Middle Chief, and Little Big Chief mountains. Passing Trail #1024, the way bends southeast to Dutch Miller Gap (4,980 ft) and an awesome view of Bears Breast Mountain. The route continues east as Trail #1362.

Trail #1024, Williams Lake. 1 mile/m (H). Beginning at a trailhead (4,360 ft) 1 mile west of Dutch Miller Gap, the way ascends heather meadows north to Williams Lake (4,600 ft). The menacing cliffs and knobby summit of Bears Breast Mountain loom to the east, and the Summit Chief group of peaks lines the south skyline. A boot-path continues through prospects to the patented mining claim at the eight small tarns of Chain Lakes (5,500 ft), then on to La Bohn Gap overlooking the Necklace Valley.

SOUTH FORK SNOQUALMIE RIVER TRAILS

Trail #1039, Talapus Lake. 3.1 miles/m (H). At the end of FR 9030 (2,640 ft) the route leaves clearcuts for forest and twists uphill through two sets of switchbacks to Talapus Lake (3,230 ft). More zigzags climb the rib to the east to Olallie Lake (3,780 ft). Campfires are not permitted at either lake.

Trail #1007, Pratt Lake. (6 miles/m (H). From FR 9034 (1,910 ft) the way swings east, then west past Trail #1016 as it climbs diagonally through second-growth forest. It bends north into the Talapus Creek drainage, passes a spur trail to Olallie Lake, then makes a horseshoe bend above the lake. The route meets Trail #1009 at a saddle (4,150 ft) with views of Mount Rainier, then twists downhill to Pratt (3,385 ft) and Lower Tuscohatchie (3,430 ft) lakes.

Trail #1016, Granite Mountain. 3.1 miles/m (H). From the 1-mile point on Trail #1007 (2,600 ft), the route wiggles up the steep wooded sidehill, breaks out of trees, and heads east diagonally across avalanche slopes (dangerous until early summer). Switchbacks reach the ridgetop and broad views south to Rainier. The way ascends slopes just north of the crest, then reaches the summit lookout (5,629 ft). Fantastic panoramic views here encompass Rainier, Stuart, Glacier, Baker, and the backbone of the Cascades.

Trail #1009, Mount Defiance. 6.8 miles/m (H). At the saddle above Olallie Lake (4,150 ft) this route leaves Trail #1007 and gradually ascends wildflower meadows west to Rainbow Lake (4,290 ft). It continues west, then rounds cliffs above Lake Kulla Kulla. The way climbs around the base of Mount Defiance, then circles the wide, open hillside above the Spider Creek basin before zigzagging down to cross a rib above Thompson Lake. More switchbacks drop to the lake (3,670 ft).

Trail #1011, Melakwa Lake. 3 miles/m (H). From Lower Tuscohatchie Lake (3,430 ft) the route crosses forested sidehills above the Pratt River before switchbacking up to Melakwa Lake (4,510 ft), where it meets Trail #1014. Above the lake are the sheer faces of Chair and Kaleetan peaks.

Trail #1014, Denny Creek. 4.3 miles/m (H). Just beyond Denny Creek Campground, a spur from FR 1021 heads west to the trailhead (2,240 ft). The way crosses Denny Creek, ducks under westbound freeway lanes, then heads upstream to recross the creek below Keekwulee Falls. The route passes Snowshoe Falls, then snakes up Denny Creek to Hemlock Pass (4,600 ft). It descends to join Trail #1011 at the outlet stream from Melakwa Lake (campfires prohibited).

SNOQUALMIE PASS TRAILS

Trail #1013, Snow Lake. 8.5 miles/m (H,S). One of the most heavily used trails in the wilderness leaves the Alpental Ski Area parking lot (3,140 ft), then traverses through forest and talus slopes above the South Fork of the Snoqualmie River. At the head of the basin a short path leads west to a viewpoint above Source Lake overlooking Chair, Bryant, and Hemlock peaks, and the Tooth. Trail #1013 switchbacks up steep slopes to a broad heather and huckleberry saddle (4,400 ft) between Chair Peak and Snoqualmie Mountain; more zigzags descend to Snow Lake (4,016 ft), where campfires are prohibited. After skirting the east shore the path descends around the steep east headwall of Rock Creek. Switchbacks drop down the forested hillside to Trail #1003 (1,620 ft) and follow it west to cross the Middle Fork of the Snoqualmie near Dingford Creek.

Trail #1033, Commonwealth Basin. *2.5 miles/m (H).* At the 2.5-mile point (3,800 ft) of the PCT out of Snoqualmie Pass, the route drops into Commonwealth Basin, meets the steep ridge leading toward Red Mountain, then begins a sharp switchback chain up its nose to a tiny tarn (4,870 feet). From here it heads up open rocky slopes to Red Pass (5,350 ft), between Red Mountain and Lundin Peak. Views from the saddle span nearby peaks, the South and Middle Forks of the Snoqualmie River, Mount Thompson, Chikamin Peak, Lemah Mountain, and Chimney Rock.

Trail #1314, Gold Creek. *4.5 miles/m-d (H).* From a spur of FR 4832142 (2,600 ft), follow the roadbed for nearly a mile before a rough tread heads upstream along the narrow, rising valley floor. Marshy meadows and beaver dams slow progress up the valley as the way struggles upstream. It passes a primitive path uphill, over rockslides and through vine maple and slide alder, to Alaska Lake (4,230 ft). The continuation of Trail #1314 up Gold Creek degrades rapidly to a bushwhack route up roots and boulders to Joe Lake (4,624 ft). Cross-country routes climb to the PCT.

Trail #1313, Rachel Lake. *4.8 miles/m (H).* The route leaves FR 4930 at Box Canyon Creek (2,770 ft) and follows the narrow wooded canyon floor upstream to a headwall where all pretense of a civilized tread ends. Switchbacks worm up cliffs, with the rough ascent mitigated somewhat by views of beautiful waterfalls. The way passes Rachel Lake (4,760 ft), then snakes up bare rock slopes to a T-junction atop Rampart Ridge. The path north leads past a spur to Lila Lake (5,195 ft), then up the knife-edge crest to the summit of Alta Mountain (6,151 ft) and outstanding views of the peaks of Chikamin Ridge. To the south the path follows the crest to the plateau bowl holding the seven Rampart Lakes (5,100 ft). Views south from here span Snoqualmie Pass, Adams, and Rainier.

Trail #1331, Mineral Creek. *5.4 miles/m (H).* From FR 46 north of Little Kachess Lake (2,365 ft), the route follows an abandoned mining road up Mineral Creek to the wilderness boundary, then continues upstream to a steep headwall climb to meadows surrounding Park Lakes (4,710 ft). Beyond, the path ascends a short distance to join the PCT (4,940 ft).

COOPER RIVER TRAILS

Trail #1309, Polallie Ridge. *8.8 miles/m (H,S).* This route leaves Salmon la Sac Campground (2,410 ft) and heads directly up the steep wooded nose of Polallie Ridge. At 4,600 feet the way traverses the northeast side of the ridge, crosses a notch, and descends to Diamond Lake (4,940 ft). The trail continues north, alternately crossing saddles and dropping into basin-top benches, then regains the crest and follows it to its high point (5,547 ft). It continues along the crest to an old lookout site, en route enjoying outstanding views of Cascade backbone peaks: Mount Daniel, Bears Breast, the Summit Chief group, Lemah Mountain, and more. Dropping north, the way follows a wooded spur down to end on Trail #1329 (4,240 ft).

Trail #1323, Pete Lake. *7.5 miles/m (H,S).* From Owhi Campground on Cooper Lake (2,788 ft), the route works through the bottomland old growth of Cooper River, passing a spur from the end of FR 4616113 (2,820 ft). The way meets Trail #1329 at Pete Lake (2,980 ft), then turns west along Lemah Creek to a fork. The northwest branch heads up to the PCT at Lemah Meadows (3,220 ft). The southwest branch either fords or crosses foot-logs over Lemah Creek, then ascends to join the PCT (3,440 ft) 1.4 miles south of the first fork.

Trail #1306, Spectacle Lake. *1.4 miles/m (H,S).* A brief route weaves up rocks and ledges from the PCT to the finger of Spectacle Point on Spectacle Lake (4,250 ft). The convoluted shoreline of this enchanting lake has vistas sweeping up cliff faces to the rugged crests of Four Brothers, Chikamin Peak, and Lemah Mountain. Trail #1339, an alternate access from the PCT to the lake, claws straight up tree roots and rocks, passing a pretty waterfall en route.

WAPTUS RIVER TRAILS

Trail #1310, Waptus River. *11.2 miles/m (H,S).* From Salmon la Sac Campground (2,410 ft) this route crosses over low, lumpy forestland to the Waptus River, then follows the southwest side of the drainage upstream. The way ascends a step to the outlet of Waptus Lake (2,963 ft), where a hiker's spur leads west to Trail #1329. The main route crosses the river, and meets Trail #1310A, a connector to the PCT. After passing the stock access to Trail #1329, the path wanders along the north shore of the lake. The trail ends as it meets the PCT (3,040 ft) 0.5 mile upstream from the head of the lake.

Trail #1329, Waptus Pass. 6 miles/m (H,S). At the southeast corner of Waptus Lake a horse route leaves Trail #1310 (3,000 ft) and crosses a ford of the Waptus River. Hiker and horse routes merge at the southwest corner of the lake, then begin a strenuous climb of more than 50 switchbacks up the Quick Creek gorge. The way flattens in broad meadows near Waptus Pass, where it meets Trail #1309. At the pass itself (4,570 ft) Trail #1329C heads off to the north. The brutal climb from Waptus Lake is now reversed; more than two dozen switchbacks drop abruptly west to meet Trail #1323 (2,990 ft) at Pete Lake.

Trail #1329C, Waptus Burn. 2.6 miles/m (H,S). This tie trail skirts the upper rim of a 1910 burn as it links Trail #1329 (4,570 ft) to the PCT (5,120 ft). The open slopes below the trail offer unblocked views of Bears Breast and Mounts Hinman and Daniel.

Trail #1362, Dutch Miller Gap. 4.7 miles/m (H,S). From the PCT (3,030 ft) near its Waptus River crossing, this route snakes back and forth up a forested slope, then climbs along a narrow bench to Lake Ivanhoe (4,652 ft). Above is a vertical wall rising 2,000 feet to the top of Bears Breast. The path then switchbacks up the cirque headwall to Dutch Miller Gap (4,980 ft), where it meets Trail #1030.

CLE ELUM RIVER TRAILS

Trail #1595A, Paddy Go Easy Pass. 3 miles/m (H,S). About 0.7 mile beyond the Fish Lake Campground, the route leaves FR 4330 (3,370 ft) and begins a gradual wooded ascent that soon shoots sharply up through dense forest, rarely using a switchback for a breather. At Paddy Go Easy Pass (6,100 ft) the way crosses the crest of the Wenatchee Mountains and enjoys views of the Cradle's cliffs. As it drops east from the pass the route becomes Trail #1595.

Trail #1345, Cathedral Rock. 4.5 miles/m (H,S). A few sweeping switchbacks climb the wooded valley wall from Tucquala Campground (3,350 ft), at the end of FR 4330, to Squaw Lake (4,841 ft). Above the lake the way climbs to a gentle bench that it follows northwest to a junction with the PCT (5,510 ft) near the fang of Cathedral Rock.

Trail #1376, Deception Pass. 5 miles/m (H,S). From the end of FR 4330, a walk along the valley floor meanders through forest to Hyas Lake (3,448 ft). After wandering along the marshy east shore, the way encounters a smaller lobe of the lake, then begins a steep switchbacked ascent of the basin headwall to Deception Pass (4,470 ft). Here it meets Trail #1059 and the PCT.

INGALLS CREEK TRAILS

Trail #1215, Ingalls Creek. 13.8 miles/m (H,S). At the end of the Valley High turnoff from US Highway 97 (1,940 ft), one of the longest valley trails in the central Cascades heads west up the narrow bottom of Ingalls Creek. The easy grade runs through forest with tantalizing avalanche-track glimpses of the stunning peaks of the Stuart Range. Steep sidehill routes rise up successive drainages on the south side of the trail: #1216 up Falls Creek, #1217 up Cascade Creek, #1218 up Hardscrabble Creek, #1219 up Fourth Creek, and #1391 up Turnpike Creek. At the head of Ingalls Creek the route climbs to just below Stuart Pass (6,270 ft), where it meets Trails #1558 and #1390.

Trail #1216, Falls Creek. 4 miles/m (H,S). At the 5.2-mile point of Trail #1215 (3,420 ft), this steep, narrow path wiggles up the Falls Creek drainage to a ridgetop saddle (6,040 ft) where it meets Trail #1210 from Negro Creek.

Trail #1217, Cascade Creek. 2.7 miles/m (H,S). Just east of Cascade Creek (3,880 ft) a thin, rough track switchbacks up the creek drainage to a notch (6,040 ft), where it meets Trails #1359 and #1226.

Trail #1219, Fourth Creek. 3.6 miles/m (H,S). A gentle grade up the wooded bottom of Fourth Creek (4,300 ft) climbs gradually to crest-top meadows and a junction with Trail #1391 (5,530 ft). Here are magnificent views of the Cashmere Crags.

Trail #1391, Beverly–Turnpike. 3.5 miles/m (H,S). Take the Turnpike—no, just Turnpike Creek; the route ascends gradually from Trail #1215 (4,600 ft) to a basin headwall, where switchbacks finish the climb to a col (5,830 ft). The way continues south down the Beverly Creek drainage.

Trail #1390, Ingalls Way. 3.7 miles/m (H). From the end of Trail #1215, south of Stuart Pass (6,240 ft), the route contours glacially polished slabs to Lake Ingalls (6,463 ft). Rock scrambles around the west shore lead up bare slopes to Headlight Creek, and on beyond to Ingalls Pass (6,500 ft). Here are outstanding views of the Mount Stuart massif, Ingalls Peak, Rainier, Adams, and the Goat Rocks. The way drops south over rocks and boulders, then switchbacks steeply down to meet Trail #1394 (4,500 ft) from the North Fork of the Teanaway.

SOUTH SIDE OF ICICLE CREEK TRAILS

Trail #1553, Snow Lake. 6.7 miles/m (H). After leaving FR 76 (1,380 ft) the route zigzags up into the Snow Creek drainage, then follows the creek south, keeping well above the brushy bottom. At Nada Lake (4,910 ft) the way crosses the creek, then follows the northwest shore. A few zigzags climb to the dam between Lower and Upper Snow Lakes (5,415 feet; 5,420 ft); after skirting the south shore of the upper lake the trail becomes #1553B.

Trail #1553B, Enchantment Lakes. 9.9 miles/m-d (H). As Trail #1553 leaves Upper Snow Lake (5,440 ft), it changes its number to #1553B and its character to just plain mean. Switchbacks work up through forest to open meadows, then polished granite slabs, as the way climbs into the fabled Enchantment Lakes. The first encounter is with Lake Viviane (6,795 ft); above is hook-shaped Leprechaun Lake (6,875 ft). Granite spires become more profuse and lake names more esoteric: Sprite Lake; Perfection (Rune) Lake (7,130 ft); Inspiration (Talisman) Lake (7,190 ft); Isolation (Brynhild) Lake (7,700 ft); and Tranquil Lake (Lake Freya) (7,795 ft). Scattered to the sides are the Troll Sink and Gnome Tarn. The rough, primitive track continues uphill westward to Aasgard Pass (7,850 ft).

Trail #1599, Stuart Lake. 5.5 miles/m/ (H; S, closed to stock from May 1 to the first weekend after Labor Day). From FR 7601 (3,430 ft) the route heads up the wooded bank of Mountaineer Creek on an easy grade, then switchbacks up a valley step past Trail #1599A. A marshy path wends upstream to Lake Stuart (5,064 ft) and awesome views up to the imposing north wall of Mount Stuart.

Trail #1599A, Colchuck Lake. 1.6 miles/m (H). A strenuous route from Trail #1599 (4,890 ft) zigzags up through open forest and granite nubbins to Colchuck Lake (5,570 ft) below steep cliffs leading to Aasgard Pass.

Trail #1552, Eightmile Lake. 3.3 miles/m (H,S). The 1.5-mile road/trail from FR 7601 (3,280 ft) travels through balding clearcuts to the wilderness boundary. There the way wiggles upstream past Little Eightmile Lake (4,404 ft), where Trail #1554 heads uphill to the northwest, then on to Eightmile Lake (4,641 ft).

Trail #1554, Eightmile–Trout Creek. 8 miles/m (H,S). The route climbs from Little Eightmile Lake (4,410 ft) through a series of wooded switchbacks that break into flower meadows before reaching the final step to Lake Caroline (6,190 ft). Here are impressive views southwest to the Enchantments and Mount Stuart. The trail strolls up past Little Caroline Lake (6,300 ft), then climbs through subalpine meadows to Windy Pass (7,230 ft) and even broader views of the Stuart Range and Cashmere Mountain. From the pass the route traverses north through meadows into forest, then switchbacks down to join Trail #1555 (4,600 ft) at Trout Creek.

Trail #1556, Icicle Gorge. 3 miles/e (H). From the start of Trail #1558 on FR 7600615 (2,800 ft), follow this spur northeast to a new trail along the banks of Icicle Creek. This path continues east through old-growth forest on the south bank of the creek, with Cascades views and access to small beaches. About 1.5 miles downstream it crosses Icicle Creek (2,680 ft), where a companion path follows the opposite bank upstream for a pleasant loop trip.

Trail #1558, Jack Creek. 10.5 miles/m (H,S). From FR 7600615 (2,800 ft) the route crosses Jack Creek and switchbacks up past Trail #1555. The side-slope path continues into the Jack Creek drainage to meet the rising creek. Upstream are muddy creekside sections as the way passes Trail #1557 and ascends to a Y (3,760 ft). The west fork, Trail #1559, heads up Meadow Creek, while Trail #1558 continues south up the bottom of Jack Creek. The way plows through forest and dense brush as it follows the creek uphill, crosses avalanche chutes, then reaches flower meadows and rocky slopes leading to Stuart Pass (6,400 ft). At the pass, rugged ridges rise east to the cliffs of Mount Stuart and west to the summit of Ingalls Peak. The way then drops over the pass to join Trail #1215 (6,240 ft).

Trail #1555, Trout Creek. 4 miles/m (H,S). From Trail #1558 (3,400 ft) the way heads east across sidehills, then bends south into the Trout Creek drainage. It continues upstream to join Trail #1557 and the west end of Trail #1554 (4,600 ft).

Trail #1557, Jack Ridge. 4 miles/m (H,S). From the junction with Trails #1555 and #1554 (4,600 ft) the way continues to Trout Lake (4,790 ft), then swings uphill to the west. Switchbacks climb steeply to the ridge crest (5,700 ft). After a brief sojourn in ridgetop meadows, knee-jarring switchbacks drop down the wooded slopes west to the 3-mile point of Trail #1558 (3,640 ft).

Trail #1559, Meadow Creek. 6 miles/m (H,S). From the junction with Trail #1558 (3,640 ft) the route branches west and passes Trail #1560 as it heads up the flat, wooded bottom of the Meadow Creek drainage. The easy grade is mostly in forest, but periodically breaks into meadows with views north to the walls of the Cradle. An imperceptible pass is crossed (5,350 ft) and the way drifts down to join Trail #1595 near the head of the French Creek drainage (4,900 ft).

Trail #1560, Snowall–Cradle Lake. 12.6 miles/m (H,S). One mile from the east end of Trail

A lakelet in Snow Creek, in the Upper Enchantment area: Mount Temple Ridge is in the distance, with Prusik Peak on the left and The Temple on the right.

#1559 (3,980 ft), this route snakes steeply uphill. After topping wooded cliff bands it heads diagonally to Cradle Lake (6,180 ft). The way climbs through meadows above the lake to a col (6,400 ft) with impressive views of the precipitous south face of the Cradle, then drops abruptly through cliffs, and switchbacks down to soggy meadows at the head of Snowall Creek. An easy creek-bottom grade continues north, then in sweeping switchbacks breaks down the canyon wall to French Creek and Trail #1595 (3,350 ft).

Trail #1551, Icicle Creek. 11.5 miles/e-m (H,S). At the end of FR 76 (2,840 ft) the route heads through old-growth forest along the valley floor of Icicle Creek. The way passes a succession of side trails: #1595 up French Creek, #1592A into Frosty Creek, #1566 into Leland Creek, #1568 up Lorraine Ridge, #1569 to Chain Lakes, and #1582 down Whitepine Creek. For most of its length the way slowly creeps up the creek bottom, but near the confluence of Trapper, Basin, and Icicle creeks it is forced abruptly uphill to the headwaters of the creek at Josephine Lake (4,681 ft). After circumnavigating the ridge above the lake, the route ends on the PCT (4,950 ft).

Trail #1595, French Creek. 9.3 miles/m (H,S). This creek-bottom route through dense old-growth forest sees few scenic breaks along its entire length. Beginning 1.25 miles up Trail #1551 (2,900 ft), the way turns into French Creek and traces its sometimes muddy banks upstream past Trail #1560 as it makes a long sweep west, then south, to meet Trail #1559 near the headwaters of French Creek. An uphill burst via numerous switchbacks leads to Paddy Go Easy Pass (6,100 ft), where it continues as Trail #1595A.

Trail #1566, Leland Creek. 5.3 miles/d (HS, but not recommended for stock). At 6 miles up Trail #1551 (3,220 ft) this path fords Icicle Creek, passes Trail #1568, then fords Leland Creek. It makes a gradual ascent up the wide valley bottom to Prospect Creek. Leland Creek bends south and narrows, and the route continues up the muddy valley floor. Steep canyon walls close in as the trail climbs steeply upstream to Lake Leland (4,461 ft).

Trail #1568, Lorraine Ridge. 4 miles/m (H,S). From Trail #1566 between Icicle and French creeks (3,220 ft), the route tilts up the nose of a wooded ridge. As the slope becomes increasingly steeper, a straight-on attack relents to switchbacks. Near the crest the forest cover breaks to rock outcrops with views across and down the Icicle Creek valley. The way contours just below the top of Lake Lorraine Point, an old lookout site, then follows the ridgetop bench to a break in cliff bands, where it heads down to Lake Lorraine (5,056 ft).

NORTH SIDE ICICLE CREEK TRAILS

Trail #1570, Icicle Ridge. 26 miles/m (H,S). This long, scenic ridgetop route starts east of the wilderness from FR 76 (1,180 ft), 1.5 miles south of Leavenworth. The inevitable series of more than three dozen switchbacks reaches the east end of Icicle Ridge; then the way continues its relentless ascent straight up the wooded ridge to the first meadow breaks at about 6,200 feet. At 8.7 miles it hits a high point (6,900 ft), and 0.5 mile farther enters the wilderness. The tread fades in and out on a roller-coaster route along the meadowed crest with continuous great views into deep flanking valleys and south to Cashmere Mountain and the Stuart Range.

From a saddle the path zigzags down a steep wooded canyon wall, crosses Cabin Creek (4,990 ft), then reverses the pattern as it scales the north drainage slopes and regains a crest (6,400 ft) that parallels Icicle Ridge. This ridge is followed west to a meadow meeting with Trail #1577. The track drops west from the ridge into the upper valley of Cabin Creek, then twists up to its headwaters at Lake Augusta (6,854 ft). From there it heads west over a rocky saddle (7,300 ft), then drops to Carter Lake (6,150 ft). Once again it climbs to a notch (6,650 ft), then switchbacks down to Index Creek (4,890 ft).

The way swings back and forth out of the basin to reach a slabby shoulder of Icicle Ridge and pass Trail #1580. The path, obscure in places along the rock and meadow crest, climbs to Lake Edna (6,750 ft), then ascends glacier-smoothed slabs around the nose of Cape Horn to Ladies Pass (6,790 ft), where it meets Trail #1571. The route contours a cliffy basin to a 6,900-foot notch where the twisting path heads northwest, up and down through the meadows and rocks above Lakes Mary and Margaret, to end at Frosty Pass (5,960 ft). There it joins Trails #1592, #1547, and #1592A.

Trail #1577, Hatchery Creek. 6.5 miles/m (H,S). From a spur off FR 7905 (2,800 ft), switchbacks charge up the broad wooded ridge, pause briefly at a bench junction with Trail #1576, then climb to a broad crest at 6,050 feet. A long contour through meadow and flower fields around the Fall Creek headwaters reaches Trail #1570 (6,700 ft).

Trail #1576, Badlands. 5 miles/m (H,S). A link between Trail #1571 (5,170 ft) and Trail #1577 (5,340 ft) crosses the broad grassy top of the Badlands (6,200 ft). The start and finish of the trail are steep, but the central highland portion is a moderate grade.

Trail #1571, Chiwaukum Creek. 12.2 miles/m (H,S). Starting at a gate on FR 7908 (2,020 ft), hike the road 1.5 miles to the start of the trail. The way continues through old growth up the deep, narrow bottomland beside Chiwaukum Creek to a Y; Trail #1591 continues upstream, and Trail #1571 follows the south fork of the creek. As the path heads upstream past Trail #1576, the valley widens and forest cover opens at Timothy Meadow. The gradual ascent through forest and across avalanche meadows reaches a cliff-rimmed cul-de-sac. Switchbacks snake up the south end of the headwall past meadow-draped Lakes Flora (5,700 ft) and Brigham (5,830 ft), then the path zigzags up rocky slopes to Ladies Pass (6,790 feet) to meet Trail #1570.

Trail #1591, North Fork Chiwaukum. 6.2 miles/m (H; S as far as junction with Trail #1573). From Trail #1571 (3,320 ft) this route continues up the main fork of Chiwaukum Creek, where walls force switchbacks up to the base of cliffs. A traverse over talus and boulders reaches Chiwaukum Lake (5,210 ft). The way follows the shore, enters meadowed Ewing Basin above the lake, then fishhooks around the head of the basin as it climbs to Larch Lake (6,078 ft).

Trail #1580, Chatter Creek. 5 miles/m (H,S, but not recommended for stock). Starting off FR 76 (2,760 ft), 0.2 mile above Chatter Creek Campground, the route slithers up the brushy, rocky canyon wall beside Chatter Creek to a flat pocket at 5,000 feet. Steep walls, including the vertical east face of Grindstone Mountain, surround the basin. The track picks its way up through talus and boulders to a notch (6,660 ft) in Icicle Ridge, then contours above cliffs to a junction with Trail #1570 (6,140 ft).

Trail #1592A, Frosty Creek. 5.9 miles/m (H,S). From Trail #1551 (3,050 ft), just past the upper crossing bridge, the way traverses uphill into Frosty Creek. Avalanche paths and meadows open near 5,000 feet as the way climbs to Lake Margaret (5,430 ft), then on beyond to Frosty Pass (5,760 ft) to meet Trails #1592, #1570, and #1547.

Trail #1569, Chain Lakes. 4 miles/m (H,S). As Trail #1551 begins its valley-head climb, this route (3,770 ft) climbs up east slopes in 17 tight switchbacks, then begins a long diagonal ascent to Chain Lakes (5,628, 5,679, and 5,690 ft). The cliff face of Bulls Tooth rises above the lakes to the east, and an unnamed spike on the north side of the lakes towers 1,000 vertical feet above. A rugged path climbs northeast up talus slopes to a rocky col (6,200 ft), then drops abruptly to Doelle Lakes (5,775 and 5,635 ft).

US HIGHWAY 2 TRAILS

Trail #1582, Whitepine Creek. 8.1 miles/m (H,S). From the end of FR 6950 (2,800 ft) the track follows the brushy bottom of the Whitepine Creek drainage southwest. The easy-grade route lies mostly in old-growth forest, with occasional avalanche tracks affording glimpses of flanking ridges. The path passes Trail #1592 as it continues upstream through muddy spots to the creek's headwaters. After crossing a low wooded saddle (4,650 ft) it descends to meet Trail #1551 (4,390 ft) below Josephine Lake.

Trail #1592, Wildhorse Creek. 6.5 miles/m (H,S). At the confluence of Whitepine and Wildhorse creeks the route leaves Trail #1582, switchbacks quickly up the wooded lower canyon wall, then begins a long diagonal ascent to timberline. Views open north to Nason Ridge and the distant cone of Glacier Peak. The way continues up headwall slopes to Frosty Pass (5,750 ft) and Trails #1570, #1547, and #1592A.

Trail #1060, Surprise Creek. 4.7 miles/m (H). From FR 6090 (2,250 ft) near Scenic, the route follows the wooded bank of Surprise Creek upstream, then zigzags steeply up the basin wall to Surprise Lake (4,508 ft). Here Spur #1060A twists up 500 vertical feet to join the PCT just below Trap Pass. The main trail climbs an easy rib beyond the lake to meet the PCT near

Glacier Lake (4,806 ft). Cliffs rise above to Thunder and Surprise mountains.

Trail #1063, Surprise Mountain. 1.5 miles/d (H,S). An old lookout trail leaves the PCT at the largest of the Deception Lakes (5,053 ft). It follows the old route of the Crest Trail to Surprise Pass (6,400 ft), and climbs south, then north to the lookout site atop Surprise Mountain (6,330 ft). Panoramic views of the Cascades from Glacier to Stuart provide a counterpoint to the sheer north face, which drops 1,500 feet to Glacier Lake.

Trail #1059, Deception Creek. 10.3 miles/m (H; S south of Trail #1059.1). This densely forested creek-bottom route leaves FR 6088 (2,000 ft) and wanders upstream above the banks of Deception Creek. At 5 miles a cheater's shortcut, Trail #1059A, drops 0.5 mile to FR 6830 in Fisher Creek. The way climbs high above the creek to a brief link, Trail #1059B, that snakes uphill to join the PCT just south of the Deception Lakes. The main trail drops back down to Deception Creek and follows it to Deception Pass (4,480 ft) to meet Trails #1066 and #1376 and the PCT.

FOSS RIVER TRAILS

Trail #1058, Tonga Ridge. 6 miles/m (H,S). At the west end of Tonga Ridge the route leaves FR 6830310 (4,320 ft), traveling in second growth, then in meadows along the crest. The way slips to the south side of the ridge below Mount Sawyer. At a broad wooded saddle (4,760 ft), a spur climbs south over a bench, then descends to Fisher Lake (4,763 ft). The main trail continues east, then drops to FR 6830 at Fisher Creek (3,650 ft).

Trail #1062, Necklace Valley. 7.5 miles/e-d (H). An enchanting and very popular trail leaves FR 68 (1,650 ft) to follow the old bed of a narrow gauge railroad through forest up the East Fork Foss River. The way crosses the river and strikes abruptly up a narrow drainage as it presses relentlessly on to tiny, cliff-rimmed Jade Lake (5,442 ft). Heather and glacier-smoothed rock accompany the path up Necklace Valley past Emerald (4,700 ft) and Opal (4,790 ft) lakes. Numerous angler tracks seek out other small lakes in the valley.

Trail #1064, West Fork Foss River. 6.8 miles/e-m (H). At the end of FR 6835 (1,640 ft), the route heads up the rapidly narrowing valley of the West Fork Foss River as it climbs to Trout Lake (2,030 ft). Above the lake switchbacks grind up open slopes beside a tributary stream to Copper Lake (3,961 ft). En route a spur climbs 0.2 mile to Malachite Lake (4,089 ft). From Copper Lake the way weaves up to Little Heart (4,204 ft) and Big Heart (4,545 ft) lakes. Bootpaths explore another half-dozen alpine lakes in the vicinity.

MILLER RIVER TRAILS

Trail #1072, Lake Dorothy. 4.5 miles/e-m (H). From the end of FR 6412 (2,240 ft), a heavily used track climbs through forest to Lake Dorothy (3,058 ft), then winds along its east shore and across its soggy inlet marsh. Switchbacks grind west up a steep wall to the basin holding Bear (3,610 ft) and Deer (3,583 ft) lakes, and meet Trail #1002.

Pacific Crest National Scenic Trail. 67 miles/m (H,S).

PCT: Snoqualmie Pass to Park Lakes. 2.5 miles. From the Snoqualmie Pass parking lot (3,000 ft) the route heads into Commonwealth Basin, passing Trail #1033. A pair of sweeping switchbacks reach the ridgetop (5,400 ft) north of Kendall Peak, where the trail crosses the crest and picks its way gingerly along the Kendall Katwalk, a narrow path blasted from the side of a rock cliff. The route descends a bit to heather meadows, then contours high above Alaska Lake. It twists around the base of Alaska Mountain, swings along the ridge above Joe Lake, then contours flower meadows below Huckleberry Mountain. The trail traverses along the base of the 600-foot-high cliffs of Chikamin Peak and Four Brothers, crosses a col (5,600 ft), and descends to Trail #1331 (4,950 ft) above Park Lakes.

PCT: Park Lakes to Waptus Lake. 19.7 miles. A few switchbacks reach the top of Chikamin Ridge (5,350 ft) northwest of Three Queens, then the path wiggles down past Trails #1306 and #1339. A long traverse passes Trail #1323 en route to Lemah Meadow (3,200 ft), to meet Trail #1323B. Compensating for the grueling switchbacks that climb out of the meadow are striking views of Lemah Mountain and Chimney Rock. After gaining the top of the ridge (5,600 ft) south from Summit Chief Mountain, the way contours basin walls above Escondido Lake, then begins its descent into the Waptus River drainage. After a few switchbacks Trail #1329C is met; next, a traverse across an old burn, with a view of the impressive face of Bears Breast, leads to two more series of zigzags descending to the Waptus River (3,030 ft) and Trail #1362. The way bends southeast and traverses the side-slope above Waptus Lake, passing Trail #1310.

PCT: Waptus Lake to Deception Pass. 14.7 miles. The route heads away from Waptus Lake up Spinola Creek, passes Trail #1310A, and climbs once again to meadow country and Deep Lake (4,382 ft). Trail #1345 is met near the base of the sharp vertical thumb of Cathedral Rock. The way dips into the Cle Elum River basin to 3,700 feet before climbing again to Deception Pass (4,470 ft) to meet Trails #1066, #1376, and #1059.

PCT: Deception Pass to Trap Pass. 8.3 miles. A long, gradual ascent reaches Deception Lakes (5,053 ft), joining Trail #1059B just below the lakes and Trail #1063 at the lakes themselves. The way continues a gradual ascent along the west flank of Surprise Mountain, crosses its north shoulder (5,550 ft), then switchbacks down to Glacier Lake (4,806 ft). To save a miserable drop and climb, the trail has been rerouted horizontally across the slope east of Slippery Slab Tower to join Trail #1060A for the final half-dozen switchbacks to Trap Pass (5,800 ft).

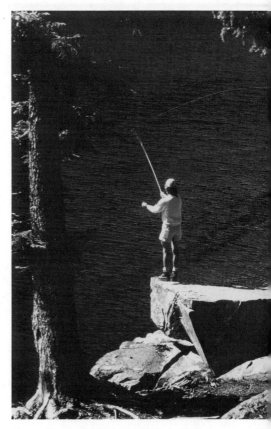

An angler tries his luck in Big Heart Lake.

PCT: Trap Pass to Stevens Pass. 12.3 miles. The way slips east of the pass, contours through a cliff band, then follows a forest and meadow sidehill northeast before descending to Hope Lake and Trail #1061 (4,400 ft). The route wraps around tiny Mig Lake (4,661 ft) and weaves up to a saddle (5,200 ft) above Swimming Deer Lake. Contouring above cliffs, the way reaches the ridge (4,950 ft) above Josephine Lake, where it meets Trail #1551. A few zigzags descend to Lake Susan Jane (4,595 ft), then a short ridgetop run leads to FR 6960. Final switchbacks climb an easy rib to the head of the ski lifts, then descend the groomed ski area slopes to Stevens Pass (4,056 ft).

Climbing

Although there are hundreds of individual peaks and towers in the Alpine Lakes, the tops of many are simple scrambles, possibly overlooking terrifying faces dropping away from easily attained summits. Others, however, are true climbing challenges. The solid, stable granite walls of the Stuart batholith offer some of the best and most challenging rock climbing in the Cascades. By virtue of their ease of access, many difficult alternative routes have been placed up otherwise easy peaks; here attaining the top is not so much the achievement, how you get there is.

On the west flank of the wilderness is isolated, difficult, and dangerous Mount Garfield (5,510 ft). Its height belies its challenge since it rises nearly 4,000 feet from its low-lying base in a complex structure of spires, gullies, and faces. Route finding is almost as challenging as climbing, and most routes score in the mid- to high C-5 range.

The most popular climbs are those in the vicinity of Snoqualmie Pass (5,168 to 6,554 ft), all easy 1-day assaults from the highway. The more interesting, with C-4 to C-5 plus routes, are the

Tooth, Chair Peak, the north ridge of Kaleetan Peak, the west face of Guye Peak, and Lundin Peak. A bit more north is Mount Thompson (6,554 ft), a particularly striking peak with sheer faces; most routes are no more difficult than C-4.

Farther north along the crest are the isolated spire of Chikamin Peak (7,000 ft) and the tri-topped summit of Three Queens (6,678 ft). Lemah Mountain (7,480 ft) has five sharp summit pinnacles ranging between C-3 and C-5.5. Nearby companions north along the crest are Chimney Rock (7,680 ft), with multiple routes rated C-5 and C-5.8; the castlelike top of Overcoat Peak (7,432 ft), and the Summit Chief group (7,120 to 7,464 ft): Summit Chief, Middle Chief, and Little Big Chief, all rated between C-3 and C-4. One of the most imposing peaks in the Waptus Lake area is Bears Breast Mountain (7,197 ft), a huge tower with vertical faces, multiple spires and crags, and no routes below C-5.4. North from Waptus Lake is massive multi-summited Mount Daniel (7,899 ft) and companion Mount Hinman (7,492 ft). Both have large glaciers on their north flanks, but easy summit routes. The distinctive rock thumb of Cathedral Rock (6,724 ft) is skirted by the PCT; it offers various C-3 and C-5.7 routes.

The crown jewels of climbing in the central Cascades are the Cashmere Crags in the Enchantment Lakes region. Dozens of solid, distinctive granite spires, ranging from one to two leads to 1,500-foot faces, spike ridgelines throughout the area. Provocative names such as Crocodile Fang, Razorback Spire, Prusik Peak, Bloody Tower, Cruel Thumb, and Cynical Pinnacle proclaim their challenge. Almost all of the climbs are in the high C-5 range, with some rated as high as an unbelievable C-5.11. They are grouped geographically into the Rat Creek group at the northwest corner of the plateau; Mount Temple Ridge on the northeast side; Three Musketeers Ridge to the far northeast; McClellan Ridge on the southeast; the Knitting Needles, low on the southeast flank; Nightmare Needles on the south slopes; Flagpole Needles, near Little Annapurna; and the Dragontail Plateau group. The northwest face of Dragontail Peak is one of the most challenging walls in the Cascades, with a dozen routes rated from C-5.6 to C-5.11.

The highest peak in this portion of the wilderness is massive Mount Stuart (9,415 ft). Its fractured buttresses and enormous 2,000-foot-high faces are distinctive from 50 miles away. There are a dozen or more routes on the mountain, the simplest rated C-3, the most difficult C-5.10. Surrounding this impressive peak are comparably challenging companions: Ingalls (7,662 ft), Sherpa (8,605 ft), and Argonaut (8,453 ft) peaks.

Winter Sports

Winter visitors can follow the summer trail up Gold Creek and the gentle valley floor for 2 miles from a Sno-Park before the slopes above become steep avalanche hazards. East from the pass the Mount Margaret Trail is a popular winter tour, especially when the maze of logging roads are snow-covered, and more direct up and downhill routes become available.

On the east side of the wilderness the valley-floor route to Cooper and Pete lakes makes an easy tour, given proper discretion during avalanche conditions. Trips can also be made up the Ingalls Pass Trail. For a long northside trip, leave Stevens Pass and follow the Crest Trail south to Lake Susan Jane and Lake Josephine; extend the trip either by a descent down Whitepine Creek or continue on to the Surprise Creek valley and Glacier Lake.

Opposite: Edith Creek splashes down heather and rock slopes below Mount Rainier.

THE SOUTH CASCADES

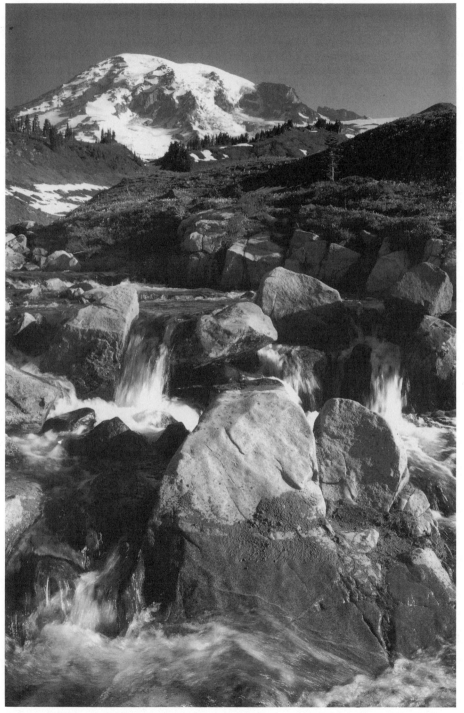

26

CLEARWATER WILDERNESS

LOCATION: In Pierce County, on the northwest corner of Mount Rainier National Park, 15 miles southeast of Enumclaw

SIZE: 14,300 acres

STATUS: Designated Wilderness (1984)

TERRAIN: A jumble of high, narrow ridges dissected by headwater branches of the Clearwater River and South Prairie Creek

ELEVATION: 2,000 to 6,089 feet

MANAGEMENT: USFS, Mount Baker–Snoqualmie National Forest, White River Ranger District

TOPOGRAPHIC MAPS: Bearhead Mtn., Clear West Peak, Old Baldy Mtn.

This small vestige of unlogged federal land on the perimeter of Mount Rainier was saved from the saw in 1984 when it was designated a wilderness. Private land on the north and west sides, by contrast, is heavily logged, as is national forest land along its west side. Fortunately, this island of west-side Cascade old-growth forest, its dozen small lakes, and its exceptional viewpoints were preserved from a similar fate.

Climate

The weather picture in the area can be summarized as mild and wet. Total annual precipitation ranges between 59 and 80 inches, depending on elevation, 90 percent of which falls between October and May, much in the form of snow. The average annual snowfall is between 6 and 25 feet, and snow often persists in higher elevations until late July. Winter temperatures are relatively warm, with midwinter lows averaging in the low 20s; summers are comfortable, with highs averaging in the lower 70s.

Plants and Wildlife

The forest is typical of the west side of the Cascades: the major tree species are Douglas-fir, western hemlock, and western red cedar. The moist understory is made up of swordfern, deerfern, ladyfern, Oregon oxalis, deerfoot vanillaleaf, wild ginger, white inside-out flower, and a variety of liverworts and mosses. The animals found here are the usual black-tailed deer, black bear, cougar, bobcat, a few elk, squirrels, skunks, raccoons, and marmots. In the skies you are likely to see golden eagles, goshawks, and sharp-shinned hawks, and flitting about the forest are bluebirds, flycatchers, jays, and nutcrackers.

Geology

The base upon which all of the Mount Rainier vicinity is built is the Ohanapecosh Formation, sedimentary deposits laid down about 40 million years ago. Folding and faulting created a syncline that ran northwest through the park and continued through the heart of the Clearwater Wilderness. About 25 million years ago the base layers were overlaid by the rhyodacitic ash flows of the Stevens Formation, which covered the southeast side of the wilderness. The heart of the area is a large pluton, the Carbon River Stock, which intruded into the older formations

some 10 million to 15 million years ago. This pluton is composed mainly of granodiorite, quartz diorite, and quartz monozonite. Clear West Peak, at the southeast corner of the wilderness, is a huge plug of flow-banded vitrophyre and welded tuff, which may have been extruded contemporaneously with the pluton intrusion. The current surface features of the area were carved by a number of local glaciers that flowed northward from the area's east–west backbone ridge between 15,000 and 20,000 years ago.

History

Although the Puyallup Indians undoubtedly hunted and gathered berries in the area, there is no evidence of any extended habitation by these natives. In the 1930s lookouts were built on two of the wilderness high spots, Bearhead Mountain and Clear West Peak; both buildings were removed in the 1960s.

ACTIVITIES

Hiking

CARBON RIVER TRAILS

Trail #1177, Summit Lake. 2.5 miles/e (H,S). From a road-end clearcut on FR 7810 (4,400 ft), the route heads into the old-growth forest of the wilderness and switchbacks up to Twin Lake (4,810 ft). Here it meets the west end of Trail #1179, then weaves up a small rib before starting a long, gradual ascent to Summit Lake (5,439 ft). In meadows on the northwest shore, enjoy a striking view of Mount Rainier's Willis Wall

Trails of the Clearwater Wilderness traverse flower-filled meadows.

mirrored on the surface of the lake. The meadows have suffered badly from inconsiderate use, so please treat them gently. A footpath leads to the top of a 5,740-foot-high knob on the west side of the lake, with an even better mountain view.

WHITE RIVER TRAILS

Trail #1178, Clearwater. 8.1 miles/d (H,S, but not recommended for stock). From the east the route leaves Trail #1179, just beyond its trailhead at the end of FR 7450 (4,140 ft), and descends northwest around the head of a basin densely covered with old-growth forest. Switchbacks drop sharply to a long, gradual descent to the Clearwater River (2,110 ft). The route heads west, crosses Lily Creek, then climbs determinedly above its west fork to a small lake in Celery Meadows. After a short ascent to a flat, the path continues west to the wilderness boundary and crosses into private land. A few switchbacks lead south through clearcuts to FR 7720 (4,320 ft).

Trail #1179, Carbon. 9.4 miles/d (H,S, but not recommended for stock). Leaving the end of FR 7450 at Martin Gap (4,140 ft), the trail twists down around basins and ridges to the Clearwater River (3,140 ft), then crosses it. After switchbacking up above the brushy river bottom, the way follows the drainage south to its head, where more switchbacks surmount the steep wall leading to Hurricane Gap (4,960 ft). The track heads west in a gentle ascent around the steep south and southwest sides of the long massif of Bearhead Mountain, en route passing over an open knob with outstanding views of Mount Rainier. Trail #1179.1 to the old lookout is passed at 8.1 miles, and the path ends as it meets Trail #1177 at Twin Lake (4,810 ft).

Trail #1179.1, Bearhead. 0.8 mile/m (H,S). This spur leaves Trail #1179 (5,430 ft) and zigzags up to the northwest summit of Bearhead Mountain (6,089 ft), a former lookout site. The way passes through meadows spackled with wildflower color to reach the fantastic mountaintop viewpoint; to the south Mount Rainier's Willis Wall looms up, below the wilderness's Summit Lake and Twin Lake sparkle like blue gems—and to the west is a sea of logged hillsides.

Trail #1181, Clear West Peak. 0.8 mile/m (H,S). This short path leaves the end of FR 7430 (4,720 ft) and follows the top of a narrow rib uphill to the site of a former fire lookout (5,644 ft). The open summit offers great views up the tongue of the Winthrop Glacier to the summit of Mount Rainier and down the deep valley of the White River drainage.

27

NORSE PEAK WILDERNESS

LOCATION: In Pierce and Yakima counties, on the north and east sides of Highway 410 between Chinook and Naches passes

SIZE: 50,923 acres

STATUS: Designated Wilderness (1984)

TERRAIN: Steep, rocky ridges at higher elevations enclosing narrow valleys, and open parkland basins holding mountain lakes

ELEVATION: 3,200 to 6,858 feet

MANAGEMENT: USFS, Mount Baker–Snoqualmie National Forest, White River Ranger District; and Wenatchee National Forest, Naches Ranger District

TOPOGRAPHIC MAPS: Goose Prairie, Mount Clifty, Noble Knob, Norse Peak, Raven Roost

The Norse Peak Wilderness straddles the Cascade crest on the east side of Mount Rainier National Park. The historic Naches Pass Trail, cut across the Cascades in 1853 by pioneer immigrants to the Puget Sound, lies just north of the wilderness boundary; the leg of Highway 410

Fife Peak in the Norse Peak Wilderness

east of Chinook Pass marks its southern limits. The southwest corner of the area is flecked with prospects, mine shafts, and moldering remnants of old cabins, memorials to the search for elusive mineral wealth that embraced the area in the late 1800s to early 1900s. Deep, narrow drainages—the Greenwater River west of the crest, and, on the east, Union and Crow creeks and the South Fork of the Little Naches River—cut into the heart of the wilderness. Nearly two dozen lakes and tarns, only half with names, dapple flats and pockets at mid- and upper altitudes.

Climate

Climate varies somewhat, depending on location and elevation. In general, the annual precipitation runs about 100 inches, 80 to 90 percent of which falls as snow, accumulating to depths of more than 6 feet. Most snow is generally gone from higher elevations by late July. Winter low temperatures average between 10 and 20 degrees, and summer highs are in the mid-70s.

Plants and Wildlife

The area's ecology incorporates transitions from western Cascades to eastern Washington forests, and from mid-altitude valley bottoms to subalpine ridgetops. At lower altitudes west of the crest, the forest is Douglas-fir, true fir, western hemlock, and western red cedar. The understory includes swordfern, deerfern, ladyfern, white inside-out flower, Oregon oxalis, wild ginger, deerfoot vanillaleaf, liverworts, and a variety of mosses. At higher elevations mountain hemlock and subalpine fir become more prevalent, and the forest frequently breaks into mead-

ows with a covering of huckleberry, Indian paintbrush, luetkea, woolly everlasting, cinquefoil, lupine, and sedges. On the eastern rim of the wilderness, some larch and Englemann spruce appear, as well as larger stands of lodgepole pine and white pine.

Wildlife found in the wilderness includes mule deer, black-tailed deer, elk, black bear, cougar, lynx, fisher, wolverine, mountain goat, and several species of grouse. Bald and golden eagles have been seen in the Green–water River drainage.

Geology

The bulk of the area is composed of the Fifes Peak Formation, a composite of lava flows, mud flows, and volcanic clastic rock, from 50 to 500 feet thick. Rhyolite flows are exposed in the Fifes Peak–Fifes Ridge area at the head of Falls Creek, and on Castle Mountain, along the western rim of the wilderness. This formation is thought to be about 25 million years old, and lies on top of the earlier Stevens Ridge Formation, a slightly thicker layer of ash flows and volcanic clastic rock. About 10 million to 15 million years ago these lava flows were intruded by granitic plutons along the southwest side of the wilderness; the mineralized contact zone along the perimeter of the plutons has been heavily prospected for both placer and lode gold.

History

Names such as Bullion Basin, Gold Hill, Placer Lake, and Pickhandle Gap all attest to the early-day gold fever that drew prospectors to the southwest corner of the wilderness in the 1880s. Although the Summit Mining District recorded nearly 50 active claims in the headwaters of Morse and Silver creeks, and extensive hydraulic mining on Morse Creek recovered some nuggets, the gold extracted never covered the costs of recovery. A large fire swept the northwest section of the wilderness around 1900, creating alpine meadows that were later leased by the government for cattle and sheep grazing. After the Washington Forest Reserves were created, the Forest Service built fire lookouts atop Noble Knob, Norse Peak, and Raven Roost, and cut trails into the region to support the lookouts and fire patrols. The 1950s and '60s saw the creation of Washington's largest ski resort, Crystal Mountain, in the Silver Creek basin along the west boundary of the wilderness; this in turn has increased interest in winter use of the adjoining wilderness backcountry.

ACTIVITIES

Hiking

GREENWATER RIVER TRAILS

Trail #1176, Greenwater. 11.9 miles/e-m (H,S). From the junction with the historic Naches Trail near the beginning of FR 7033 (2,480 ft), the route follows the banks of the Greenwater

River southeast through dense Cascade forest past Greenwater (Meeker) Lakes (2,860 and 2,906 ft) and Trail #1185. The way continues upstream between encroaching forest walls, then climbs to the wooded pocket enclosing Echo Lake (3,819 ft). The path continues upstream to Hidden Lake (4,190 ft) as Trail #1176.1. A pair of switchbacks climb to a steep side-slope traverse to the west end of Trail #1188. A long switchback then climbs to FR 7174 at Corral Pass (5,550 ft).

Trail #1185, Lost Lake. *5.1 miles/m (H,S).* At the 3.2-mile point on Trail #1176 (3,070 ft), this path heads south into the Lost Creek drainage. A brief ascent out of the basin floor bypasses Quinn Lake (3,890 ft); the way then continues to Lost Lake (3,985 ft). Here the route heads west and a strenuous climb tops the divide between Lost and George creeks (5,240 ft). A traverse of the steep, open, rocky face of Noble Knob meets Trail #1184 (5,700 ft) on the rib south of that high spot.

CORRAL PASS TRAILS

Trail #1155, Rainier View. *2.2 miles/m (H,S).* From the FR 7174 trailhead (5,550 ft) the route starts southwest, then winds south as it slowly climbs to the elongated summit ridge of Castle Mountain (6,100 ft). Once atop the crest, hikers are rewarded by a horizon-filling view of the White River side of Mount Rainier. In a short distance the way drops west atop a minor rib to join Trail #1188 (5,900 ft).

Trail #1188, Castle Mountain. *5.1 miles/d (H,S).* This route heads southwest from Trail #1176.1 (5,000 ft) at its second major switchback below Corral Pass. A gradual ascent around a small basin leads to switchbacks over a rib into the forested bowl above the main fork of the Greenwater River. It sags into the headwater basin, then works up the opposite side toward the divide between the Greenwater and Crow Creek. A winding traverse joins the PCT at Martinson Gap (5,750 ft). The trail is still under construction and may be hard to follow in places.

SILVER CREEK TRAILS

Trail #1191, Norse Peak. *5.2 miles/m (H,S).* The trail leaves FR 7190410 (3,990 ft) north of the Crystal Mountain Ski Area and switchbacks up a steep sidehill. The tread has been reconstructed at an easy grade to combat erosion problems caused by its steeper predecessor. At 4 miles a spur leads to the top of Norse Peak (6,856 ft), once the site of a fire lookout. Panoramic views include the Puget Sound basin, Snoqualmie Pass summits, the rolling hills east to the Columbia Plateau, Mount Adams, and the icy bulk of close-at-hand Mount Rainier. The way tops the ridge (6,040 ft), and drops east into Big Crow Basin to join the PCT (6,280 ft).

AMERICAN RIVER TRAILS

Trail #956, Union Creek. *7.1 miles/m (H,S).* The trail leaves a roadside pull-off (3,410 ft) from Highway 410 east of Chinook Pass, and crosses Union Creek below an impressive waterfall. The way tightly switchbacks up the wooded rib along the east side of the falls, then follows Union Creek upstream, staying a few hundred feet above the dense creek-bottom brush. At the North Fork of the creek, the trail crosses a bridge over another foaming waterfall, then continues east, dropping to creek level at 4 miles. A gradual ascent into the widening basin leaves the creek and swings up the headwall to meet Trail #987 (5,920 ft).

Trail #953, Crow Lake Way. *12.7 miles/m (H,S).* The trail leaves Highway 410 (3,390 ft) east of Chinook Pass, heads northwest along Miners Creek, and grinds uphill in a succession of 30 switchbacks. It tops the divide between Miners and Survey creeks, then traces it uphill, staying near the edge of its sheer southwest face. At 5,800 feet the way swings west around the head of Survey Creek, then bends north to broad meadows and a tiny tarn at Grassy Saddle (5,600 ft). From the saddle a leisurely wooded descent meets Trail #951 (4,580 ft), 0.5 mile west of Crow Creek Lake. The way now wanders west along the broad bottomland to the headwaters of Crow Creek, then switchbacks up a steep headwall to join the PCT in Big Crow Basin (6,230 ft).

Trail #954, Fifes Ridge. *8.8 miles/m (H,S).* From Highway 410 (3,360 ft) east of Chinook Pass, the route makes a steady ascent up Walsh Creek to near its headwaters. Switchbacks claw up the wooded basin headwall to a saddle on Fifes Ridge (5,190 ft) just east of Fifes Peaks. Trail

#954 heads east along the crest and shortly tops a bare knob with views west to the vertical battlements and sharp pinnacles of Fifes Peaks. The route traces the convolutions of the ridge east down the descending ridge to end on Trail #952 (5,100 ft), off FR 1920.

RAVEN ROOST TRAILS

Trail #951, Cougar Valley. 5.2 miles/m (H,S). The old road west of Raven Roost has been converted to trail. In a mile it splits; the section heading south winds down Cougar Valley to the meadows beside Crow Creek Lake (4,550 ft), then continues up Crow Creek another 0.5 mile to end on Trail #953 (4,580 ft). The segment heading west wanders through meadow and forest near the top of the east–west ridge to meet the PCT (5,830 ft) near the head of the South Fork of the Little Naches River.

Trail #945.1, Louisiana Saddle. 3.2 miles/m (H). After leaving Trail #945 (4,200 ft) this route soon enters the wilderness and traces the ridgetop west in a gradual ascent, interrupted once by a short face requiring switchbacks to surmount. The path then wends through wild-flower meadows to meet the PCT at Louisiana Saddle (5,210 ft).

Pacific Crest National Scenic Trail. 26.6 miles/m (H,S). From Highway 410 at Chinook Pass (5,432 ft) the route runs northeast on the sidehill above the highway for a little more than a mile. It then rounds a hogback and turns north, climbing to Sheep Lake (5,750 ft). A weaving path up a steep, rocky side-slope crosses Sourdough Gap (6,410 ft). After a short descent east of the gap, the path traverses the treeless head of Morse Creek Basin to Bear Gap (5,882 ft), site of the junction with Trails #1192 and #1193 from the west, and #967 from the east. Swinging north around Pickhandle Point, with views down the Silver Creek Basin, the way drops briefly east of the crest at Pickhandle Gap (5,980 ft).

After passing Trail #987, on the southeast side of Crown Point, a switchback returns the

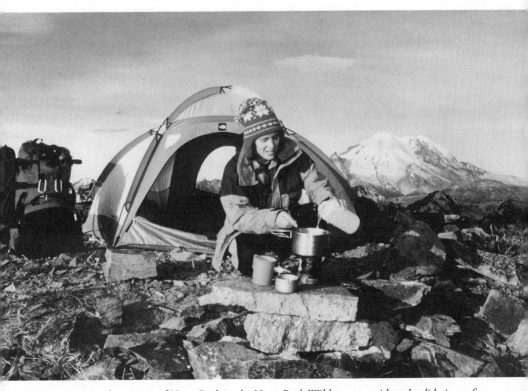

A campsite on the summit of Norse Peak in the Norse Peak Wilderness provides splendid views of Mount Rainier.

path west of the crest for the next segment of the trek. Trail #1156 is joined at the head of Bullion Basin, and a long, gradual ascent recrosses the crest at Scout Pass (6,550 ft). A traverse above the rocky slopes of Lake Basin leads to a flat wooded track around the head of Big Crow Basin, passing Trails #1191 and #953. A gradual wooded descent meets Trail #1188 at Martinson Gap (5,780 ft), then the way weaves back and forth across the crest, passing Trail #951. The path now follows the ridgetop to Louisiana Saddle (5,210 ft), where it meets Trail #945.1. The wooded west side of the crest is followed to Rods Gap (4,850 ft), where the track descends to Government Meadow (4,730 ft) on the west side of Naches Pass.

Climbing

The main climbing interests in the wilderness are the multiple andesite summits of Fifes Peaks, most with high vertical walls, and a collection of crags and spires that line the ridge between them (6,375 to 6,917 ft). Although the peaks have challenging faces, the rock is very loose and friable. The defined summits are the Far East Peak, with nearby Teddy Bear Pinnacle and Mainmast; the East Peak, the largest and most imposing of the summits, with adjoining Cannonhole Pinnacle; the West Peak, sheer on three sides, but easy from the east; and the Northwest Peak, the highest and easiest of the summits, with a detached tower close by.

On the ridge east of Sourdough Gap is Cupalo Rock (6,593 ft), part of the granitic intrusion at the southwest corner of the area. The east face has a number of two- to three-lead, solid rock climbs in the C-5 to C-5.7 range.

Winter Sports

One of western Washington's major ski resorts, Crystal Mountain, lies adjacent the southwest corner of the wilderness, and several strenuous cross-country ski/snowshoe treks fan out from there into the Norse Peak Wilderness and adjoining roadless areas. One of the more popular of these tours is to Bullion Basin, east of Crystal Mountain. Extensions of this tour head north along the crest to the summit of Norse Peak, and on to Lake and Big Crow basins east of the peak, or south to Crown Point. Expert-level tours cross Bear Gap and head east down Morse Creek, or follow the Pacific Crest Trail southwest from the gap to make a loop trip around Threeway Peak.

A less demanding trip follows the snowbound road toward Corral Pass, then at timberline swings south up the ridge to the top of Castle Mountain. A second route continues on to the pass, then heads north, following the route of Trail #1184 to the top of Mutton Mountain.

28

MOUNT RAINIER NATIONAL PARK

LOCATION: In Pierce and Lewis counties, surrounding Mount Rainier
SIZE: Park: 235,612.5 acres; wilderness: 228,480 acres
STATUS: National Park (1899), Designated Wilderness (1988)
TERRAIN: High, heavily glaciated, dormant volcano surrounded by alpine parks framed between rugged, precipitous canyons
ELEVATION: 1,950 to 14,411 feet
MANAGEMENT: National Park Service
TOPOGRAPHIC MAPS: Chinook Pass, Cougar Lake, Golden Lakes, Mount Wow, Mt. Rainier East, Mt. Rainier West, Mowich Lake, Ohanapecosh Hot Springs, Sawtooth Ridge, Sunrise, Tatoosh Lakes, Wahpenayo Peak, White Pass, White River Park

Just as the summit of Mount Rainier marks the highest point in the state of Washington (and the fifth-highest spot in the Lower 48 states), the park abounds with other superlatives. It contains 382 lakes and ponds, 470 rivers and streams, and 9 major watersheds. Its 27 named glaciers cover a surface area of about 37 square miles, the largest glacial system on a single peak in the coterminous U.S. The forests and alpine meadows around the mountain are habitat for 787 plant species, 54 mammal species, 130 bird species, and 17 species of reptiles and amphibians.

The park is also a recreationist's paradise. There are more than 300 miles of maintained trails within its borders; one, the Wonderland Trail that encircles the mountain, is 93 miles long. Five standard campgrounds in the park contain nearly 600 campsites, and the 41 backcountry camps can accommodate more than 1,000 wilderness hikers and climbers. Each year from 6,000 to 8,000 people attempt to climb the mountain, some in private parties, others using the Rainier Mountaineering Service. Fewer than half succeed in reaching the summit.

Climate

Both temperature and precipitation vary markedly with altitude and location. At lower elevations, midsummer temperatures range between 48 and 80 degrees; at Paradise (5,400 ft), the range is between 44 and 64 degrees; and at the summit of Rainier, summer temperatures have been recorded between minus 10 and 32 degrees. Average midwinter temperatures at Longmire are in the upper 20s to low 40s; at Paradise, lower

Climbers negotiate a deep glacier crevasse on Mount Rainier.

20s to lower 30s At the summit, temperature records are sketchy, but a low of minus 80 has been recorded. Valleys below 5,000 feet are frequently draped in local clouds or fog when the high country is clear and sunny. Winds increase with elevation; on the summit they are almost nonstop at about 30 mph, and are known to reach as high as 100 mph.

Rain or snow starts falling in October, and there are only intermittent sun breaks until mid- to late April. Total annual precipitation at lower elevations is about 80 inches; at Paradise, 100 inches. There are no reliable figures for the summit, however, because cold, high-altitude air has less moisture-carrying capacity, it is safe to assume that precipitation levels there are somewhat less than on the slopes below. A substantial portion of this moisture falls as snow that accumulates to depths of 2 to 4 feet at lower elevations, grading up to 20 feet or more at the altitude of Paradise. July, August, and September are generally dry and pleasant, with only two to four rainy days a month.

The mountain is said to "generate its own weather," which to a certain extent is true. The 14,411-foot peak is both high and massive enough to significantly disrupt area wind flows (witness the lenticular cloud cap that often forms above the summit).

Plants and Wildlife

The 12,000-foot altitude differential within the park spans multiple forest zones. The portions of the park below 4,000 feet are covered with a dense old-growth forest consisting of Douglas-fir, western hemlock, and western red cedar. Grand fir, cottonwood, and maple are

found in drainage bottoms, and avalanche-stripped slopes are blanketed with red alder and vine maple. Understory elements include devil's club, huckleberry, oxalis, skunk cabbage, twin-flower, trillium, and many other flowers. Swordfern, deerfern,ladyfern, licorice fern, bracken, 100 species of mosses, and 200 species of fungi flourish in the shady, damp environment.

Between 4,000 feet and 6,500 feet, the forest constituents change to mountain hemlock, Alaska cedar, whitebark pine, and subalpine fir, spaced more openly with increasing altitude. This woodland cover is broken by meadows stippled with a spectrum of wildflower color: lu-pine, Indian paintbrush, western anemone, penstemon, mountain bistort, aster, pedicularis, cinquefoil, and Sitka valerian, to name but a few.

Above timberline are broad subalpine meadows with only a few short, gnarled tufts of mountain hemlock and subalpine fir. Between late June and early September, these meadows are a sea of multihued wildflowers. More than 76 species have been identified, among them beargrass, heather, avalanche lily, goldenrod, monkeyflower, shooting star, fireweed, larkspur, buttercup, Jacob's ladder, and columbine. The harsh alpine zone at the lower fringes of the gla-ciers has mosses, lichens, sedges, moss campion, and phlox, hardy plants uniquely adapted to this environment.

Among the 54 mammal species found in the park, the most often seen are elk, black-tailed deer, black bear, mountain goat, raccoon, pine marten, beaver, porcupine, skunk, cougar, bob-cat, hoary marmot, pika, snowshoe hare, golden mantled ground squirrel, and yellow pine chip-munk. Of the 130 species of birds that live or nest in the park, or pass through in migratory travel, the more common residents are blue grouse, jays, Clark's nutcracker, flickers, Vaux's swift, thrushes, kestrels, rough-legged and red-tailed hawks, Steller's jay, red-breasted nuthatch, red-winged blackbird, mountain chickadee, hummingbirds, and yellow-bellied sapsucker.

Geology

The geological story of Mount Rainier begins some 40 million years ago, when the base Puget Group of siltstones and arkoses, probably deposited in a shallow inland sea, was gradually overlaid by layers of lava flows, mudflows, ash flows, and rhyolites of the Ohanapecosh Forma-tion. The interleaving of tuff breccias with laminated siltstones and thin-graded sandstone indi-cates that most of these eruptions occurred underwater. As eruptive material accumulated, parts of the basin may have risen above water level. The only identified centers for this volcanic activ-ity are the Mount Wow and the Cowlitz Chimney–Sarvent Glacier areas. The Ohanapecosh Formation built to a thickness of about 10,000 feet over a period of 8 million to 10 million years. After its deposition the formation was subjected to folding along a north–northeast axis.

The next phase of volcanic activity started some 25 million to 30 million years ago when the ash flows and volcanic clastic rocks of the Stevens Formation overlaid the Ohanapecosh Forma-tion and its erosion debris to a depth of 450 to 3,000 feet. This volcanic activity occurred mostly in the southern part of the park, although smaller outcrops have been identified in the north and northwest sections.

About 5 million years later a third phase of volcanism began. The lava flows, mudflows, and clastic rocks of the Fifes Peak Formation were layered over the Stevens Ridge formation to a depth of 1,000 to 3,000 feet. These lava streams appear to have radiated from vents just east of the present park boundary. Continued deformation along the old fold axes deepened and dis-torted the Ohanapecosh Formation, and this syncline was partially filled by flows of the Stevens and Fifes Peak formations.

The last geological element to impact the area prior the volcanism that built the present peak occurred 8 million to 15 million years ago. The huge Tatoosh Pluton intruded the overlying formations, slicing through them and warping and distorting their structure. As the top of the pluton forced through the other formations, a spider's web of sills and dikes radiated from its dome, especially along the base of the Stevens Ridge Formation. In places the pluton magma broke through the surface in volcanic explosions; the eroded plugs of these vents make up Sour-dough Mountain and the Palisades.

About 3 million years after the Tatoosh Pluton intruded, a general uplift of the whole Cascade Range began; the three older formations were raised to an altitude of about 4,000 feet, and were heavily eroded by rivers and streams that cut deep canyons through their layers. The birth of the current volcano began about 1 million years ago with a rapid outpouring of lava flows, the oldest occurring in the north and west sections of the park. This lava filled the deep canyons first, inverting the ancestral drainages of the White, Carbon, Mowich, and Puyallup rivers, which were forced to find new courses along the sides of these new masses of lava. Today those canyon-filling flows comprise the alpine plateaus of Grand Park, Sunset Park, and Burroughs Mountain.

Continuing eruptions built up successive layers of lava flows interspersed with breccias from pyroclastic flows. Strata on lower slopes included mudflows triggered by steam explosions when hot lavas mixed with snow or meltwater. Smaller lava flows that reached the base of the new stream-cut canyons banked against the older lava to form a series of terraces. The cone of the volcano continued to build over succeeding centuries to reach an estimated height of about 15,500 feet.

Two satellite volcanoes appeared on the mountain's north flank during the Pleistocene glaciation period, erupting olivine andesite that flowed into the valleys below, flooding the headwaters of the Carbon and North Mowich rivers. Dissected remnants of these two cones form Observation and Echo rocks. The blunt summit of Rainier then lost nearly 1,000 feet of its height, either because the core of the volcano subsided due to diversion of magma to the two satellite volcanoes, or because the core, softened by meltwater, found breaches in the rim and flowed down the volcano's sides in massive mudflows. Approximately 5,800 years ago, something triggered the massive Osceola mudflow; nearly half a cubic mile of debris swept down the White River valley to the site of present-day Auburn. The three current summits—Liberty Cap, Point Success, and Columbia Crest—lie on the lip of the older summit cone.

Rainier's last known volcanic activity, minor pumice eruptions, occurred 500 to 600 years ago and briefly between 1820 and 1854. More recent historical changes have taken the form of floods and mudflows. Major floods from the Nisqually Glacier occurred in 1926, 1932, 1934, and 1955; a large slurry flood surged down the Kautz River in 1947; in 1963 a massive debris avalanche peeled off the north side of Little Tahoma and raced down the Emmons Glacier to the White River Campground; 20 debris flows have moved down Tahoma Creek since 1967; and more recent South Tahoma debris flows have washed out portions of the West Side Road.

History

Indians living on the perimeter of the park hunted, fished, and gathered berries within its boundaries for centuries. Their legends are rich with stories of Takhoma, as they called the imposing volcano centerpiece, and some of its satellite peaks. Although portions of the park were at one time claimed by the Muckleshoot, Nisqually, Yakima, Puyallup, and Taidnapum tribes, there is no solid evidence of any permanent native residence within the current boundaries.

The first European explorers to see Mount Rainier were members of the 1792 Vancouver expedition; its leader, Captain George Vancouver, named the peak for a friend, Rear Admiral Peter Rainier of the British Navy. The next recorded sighting of the mountain was by the Lewis and Clark Corps of Discovery in 1806. In 1833, William Tolmie, the physician at the Hudson's Bay Company's Fort Nisqually, made the first attempt to approach the peak. With five Indian guides he made his way up the Puyallup and Mowich rivers to Mowich Lake, on the mountain's northwest flank. He pressed higher and climbed an intermediate peak, possibly Hessong Rock, for close views of the rugged north face of the mountain.

In the 1850s settlers began trickling into the Puget Sound area. One of them, James Longmire, made the second thrust into the park area as he followed the Nisqually River upstream, searching for an alternative to troublesome Naches Pass across the Cascades. Longmire blazed a trail into the southwest corner of the park in 1861, and for the next 20 years he guided approach marches of many of the first climbing parties. In 1870 he discovered a mineral spring in a meadow in the Nisqually River valley, filed a claim there, and later constructed a rough tourist resort at Longmire Hot Springs.

An old Indian guide recounted having taken a party of two unnamed white men, purportedly Indian Treaty boundary surveyors, to the summit in 1855 by way of the Emmons and Winthrop glaciers. Although his description of the crater's features seems to verify this story, the men remain unknown. Lieutenant. A. V. Kautz made the first reported summit attempt in 1857 via Wapowety Cleaver; the party turned back near Point Success, a few hundred feet short of the summit in elevation, and a half mile away in distance. The first recorded successful ascent of the peak was made in August 1870 by General Hazard Stevens and Philemon Beecher Van Trump. They approached from south of the present park, crossed the Tatoosh Range, descended to Mazama Ridge, and climbed from there to the present site of Camp Muir, where they used the Gibraltar Rock route to reach the summit.

The surge of prospecting in the late 1800s also hit Mount Rainier; by the turn of the century more than 300 mining claims had been filed in the park. Copper was the only mineral of significance found, and most mining rapidly folded. Three mines became producers: the Eagle Peak Copper Mining Company's mine in the Tatoosh Range, the North Mowich Glacier Mine at the base of Eagle Cliff, and the Mount Rainier Mining Company's mine at Starbo, in Glacier Basin. All mining ceased in 1948.

The mountain rapidly became a major tourist attraction, featuring Longmire's resort in the Nisqually Basin, where an inn opened in 1906; a tent lodging business at Paradise, which operated between 1898 and 1915; and the Ohanapecosh Hot Springs Resort, which was in full swing by the late 1920s. In 1893 the striking beauty of the mountain and its outstanding natural features led to intensive lobbying by several national scientific and outdoor organizations for its preservation. Congress established the national park in March 1899, the fifth such area in the U.S. to be so designated. Further protection for its unique backcountry was assured in 1988, when all undeveloped portions of the park became a designated wilderness.

ACTIVITIES

Hiking

WESTSIDE TRAILS

Because of repeated washouts, the West Side Road is closed at Dry Creek, 3.1 miles up the road. This means that additional road hiking is required to reach the following west-side trails.

Gobblers Knob Trail. 2.5 miles/m (H). From the West Side Road at Round Pass (3,900 ft), an easy grade ascends 1 mile to Lake George (4,292 ft). Most visitors stop here to camp or fish, but the trail continues more steeply up the forested slope west to the lookout atop Gobblers Knob (5,485 ft), where views of the Tahoma Glacier and Sunset Amphitheater reward the extra effort.

Kautz Creek Trail. 5.7 miles/m (H). The trail leaves the Nisqually–Longmire Road (2,410 ft) near the Kautz Creek bridge, passing initially along the top of the 1947 mudflow, amid regenerating forest. The near-level grade ends in a mile after crossing the creek, and more than two dozen switchbacks weave up the steep, densely forested, northwest wall of the drainage to a forest-and-meadow bench. One more steep open stretch of trail, followed by gentle parkland, leads to the Wonderland Trail at Indian Henrys Hunting Ground (5,450 ft).

Mirror Lakes Trail. 0.7 mile/m (H). At Indian Henrys Hunting Ground (5,450 ft) a path ascends northeast to the four tiny Mirror Lakes (5,400 ft). At this classic photo spot the lakes reflect the rocky headwall of Success Cleaver rising above the South Tahoma Glacier. Stroll through flower fields above the lakes to the base of Pyramid Peak.

South Fork Puyallup Trail. 1.6 miles/m (H). The trail heads east from the West Side Road (3,500 ft) through the deep forest on the sidehill above the South Fork of the Puyallup River. Just before reaching the Wonderland Trail (4,070 ft) it passes one of the most distinctive and photogenic examples of columnar basalt in the park.

St. Andrews Trail. 2.2 miles/m (H). This route departs the West Side Road (3,770 ft) for the steep wooded hillside north of St. Andrews Creek. Switchbacks reach the top of Klapatche Ridge (4,600 ft), then the way follows the crest east to Aurora Lake (5,500 ft) and the Wonderland Trail. The lake, at the edge of Klapatche Park, reflects the icy west side of Rainier.

North Puyallup Trail. 2.75 miles/e (H,S). The last 3 miles of the West Side Road (4,000 ft) have been blocked and converted to a trail that runs along the steep wooded hillside, 600 to 800

Mount Rainier shows off her beauty in Reflection Lake.

feet above the North Fork of the Puyallup River. It follows the drainage upstream to meet the Wonderland Trail at river's edge (3,700 ft).

MOWICH TRAILS

Spray Park Trail. *8.7 miles/m (H).* The path to the outstanding flower fields of Spray Park leaves the south end of Mowich Lake (4,929 ft) and descends through subalpine forest along the west flank of Fay Peak to the rim of Eagle Cliff (4,640 ft). Switchbacks climb up along the edge of the cliff to a short viewpoint spur (4,900 ft) near the base of the 400-foot-high ribbon of Spray Falls. More than 20 tight switchbacks now scale the wall along Grant Creek to reach the lower fringes of Spray Park. This flower-covered meadow is but a sample of those to come. The way ascends eastward into expansive fragrant meadows that blend upwards into snowfields below Observation and Echo rocks. Above, narrow, fragmented Ptarmigan Ridge sweeps up beside the Mowich Face for 6,000 feet to Liberty Cap. The way, marked by cairns, crosses a permanent snowfield (6,360 ft), then descends the ridge framing the west side of Seattle Park. At timberline the route zigzags down the steep wooded bank of Marmot Creek to Cataract Creek (4,000 ft). A gradual descent of this drainage meets the Wonderland Trail at the Carbon River (3,190 ft).

Tolmie Peak Trail. *2.8 miles/m (H).* This path leaves the Wonderland Trail at Ipsut Pass (5,140 ft), eases up past Eunice Lake (5,354 ft), then in a pair of long switchbacks gains the top of Tolmie Peak (5,920 ft). The lookout here has around-the-compass views of Mount Baker, the Olympic Range, Mount St. Helens, the northwest face of Rainier, and the Cascades.

CARBON RIVER TRAILS

Northern Loop Trail. *10.6 miles/m (H).* A long swing through the lightly visited north segment of the park leaves the Wonderland Trail (2,860 ft) as a switchback chain up a steep, forested wall to a flat at the base of Yellowstone Cliffs (5,200 ft). A climb through steep meadows past pretty little lakes reaches Windy Gap (6,020 ft), overlooking the ragged top of nearby Sluiskin Mountain. A short side trail heads north along the meadowed east flank of Independence Ridge, then drops to Natural Bridge, a 100-foot-long, 100-foot-high andesite arch carved by stream erosion.

The way drops east from the gap, first in meadows, then forest, as it descends to Lake James (4,430 ft). It then zigzags down precipitous wooded slopes near Van Horn Creek to cross the West Fork of the White River (3,160 ft). The trail immediately regains all of its recently lost altitude. The wooded uphill haul climbs to an open promontory (5,696 ft) with wide views of Grand Park, Mount Fremont, Skyscraper Mountain, the West Fork drainage, Redstone Peak, and Lake James. The Grand Park Trail to Lake Eleanor is passed as the path skirts the southwest edge of Grand Park. It descends to the head of Cold Basin (5,380 ft), then heads up the upper Lodi Creek basin, squeezed between Mount Fremont and Skyscraper Mountain. A steeper grade reaches Berkley Park and rejoins the Wonderland Trail (6,400 ft).

Grand Park Trail. *3.3 miles/m (H).* Splitting from the Northern Loop Trail (5,650 ft) at Grand Park, the route skirts the northwest fringe of this broad, meadowed plateau, then gradually descends through woods to secluded Lake Eleanor (4,985 ft).

SUNRISE TRAILS

Palisades Lakes Trail. *3.5 miles/e (H).* From the Sunrise Road at Sunrise Point (6,120 ft), the path drops past a short spur to Sunrise Lake (5,725 ft), then wanders by Clover Lake (5,732 ft). It crosses a low notch, meanders near Tom Dick and Harry Lakes (5,500-5670 ft), and passes a boot-path to Hidden Lake (5,915 ft). After crossing a meadowed bench, it ends at Upper Palisades Lake (5,805 ft), perched below the rock cliff of the Palisades

Fremont Lookout Trail. *1.3 miles/e (H).* From the west end of the Sourdough Ridge Trail (6,500 ft), continue west to Frozen Lake (6,850 ft). This trail leaves the lake and ascends parkland to Fremont Lookout (7,140 ft), where in clear weather hikers can scan the Cascades, Olympics, Rainier, and downtown Seattle.

Burroughs Mountain Trail. *4 miles/m (H).* From Sunrise Campground (6,350 ft), the way passes the spur to the Emmons Overlook before heading up steep snow slopes to First Burroughs

Mountain (7,170 ft). The route continues west across the delicate tundra crest to Second Burroughs Mountain (7,402 ft). An easy downslope to a broad saddle leads to 28 tightly linked switchbacks that drop abruptly to the Glacier Basin Trail (5,530 ft). An alternative route from First Burroughs Mountain heads northeast down a steep snowbank to the Wonderland Trail, just west of Frozen Lake.

WHITE RIVER TRAILS

Glacier Basin Trail. 3.5 miles/e (H). An easy grade from White River Campground (4,310 ft) follows an old wagon road past the Emmons Moraine Trail to mining ruins at Starbo in Glacier Basin. Near the head of the basin is the lower end of the Burroughs Mountain trail (5,530 ft).

EAST-SIDE TRAILS

Crystal Lakes Trail. 3 miles/m (H). Leaving Highway 410 opposite the Highway Department maintenance sheds (3,530 ft), the route heads up the heavily forested hillside in a series of tight switchbacks. The twisting trail continues uphill, crosses avalanche slopes, passes Lower Crystal Lake (5,460 ft), and breaks into alpine meadows as it arrives at Upper Crystal Lake (5,828 ft). Elk and mountain goat are often seen in the vicinity.

Naches Peak Trail. 3 miles/m (H,S). From Highway 410 at Chinook Pass (5,432 ft), a gentle path drops to Tipsoo Lake (5,294 ft), crosses the highway, and contours east through meadows on the south flank of Naches Peak to a small unnamed lake near the Cascade crest. The old Crest Trail continues east into the William O. Douglas Wilderness to Dewey Lake (5112 ft).

Eastside Trail. 16.5 miles/e-m (H,S). A long hike with shortcut options leaves Highway 410 (5,340 ft) southwest of Chinook Pass, weaves down to cross Highway 123 at 4,560 feet, then dives into deep forest at the head of Chinook Creek. The first 2 miles drop steeply along the sidehill above the creek to the intersection with the Owyhigh Lakes Trail (2,850 ft) near the mouths of Kotsuck and Deer creeks. From here a gentle grade follows the wooded bank of Chinook Creek to its confluence with the Ohanapecosh River. The way continues south on the low slopes above the river, crosses the east end of the Stevens Canyon Road (2,200 ft), passes the Olallie Creek trailhead, and ends at the Ohanapecosh Campground (1,850 ft).

Olallie Creek Trail. 1.3 miles/m (H,S). From the east end of the Stevens Canyon Road (2,320 ft) the route slips into dense old-growth forest as it heads north up the sidehill to the Olallie Creek drainage. Here it bends west, continuing its wooded ascent to the creek's headwaters. Switchbacks climb the basin headwall to a junction with the Wonderland Trail at the ridgetop (4,760 ft).

Laughingwater Creek Trail. 7 miles/m (H,S). From Highway 123 (2,150 ft), south of the park's Stevens Canyon entrance, the track climbs up a wooded sidehill and over a ridgetop knob to a bench and a small marshy lake beside Laughingwater Creek. The way follows the creek upstream to where the lilting waters break into a crescendo at a waterfall, then climbs upslope away from the creek to Three Lakes (4,650, 4,650, and 4,678 ft), straddling the park boundary. The route continues east, weaving back and forth across the border of the park, to a junction with the PCT (5,700 ft).

PARADISE VALLEY TRAILS

Lakes Trail. 2.3 miles/e (H). The easy-grade path passes through the alpine meadows of Mazama Ridge, from the Skyline Trail (6,010 ft) near Sluiskin Falls to Reflection Lakes (5,600 ft).

Pinnacle Peak Trail. 1.5 miles/e (H). From the Stevens Canyon Road (4,870 ft) at Reflection Lakes, the easy grade steepens as it twists uphill through open woods, meadows, snowfields, and talus to the saddle (5,940 ft) at the west base of Pinnacle Peak. Here is an awesome view of the south side of Rainier; turn around to a complementary scene to the south that includes Mount Adams and the Goat Rocks.

LONGMIRE TRAILS

Eagle Peak Trail. 3.5 miles/m (H). The route heads south from Longmire (2,800 ft) wrapped in dense old-growth forest. It soon bends east and climbs steep wooded slopes using easy-grade switchbacks. Trees give way to a steep meadow, splashed with wildflower color, as the path nears a saddle (5,740 ft) on the south ridge of Eagle Peak. The reward is great views of the sweep of the Nisqually Glacier from Paradise to the summit of "The Mountain."

Rampart Ridge Trail. 3 miles/m (H,S). Starting from the Trail of the Shadows Nature Loop at Longmire (2,800 ft), the way snakes up a steep forest slope at the southwest end of the Ramparts. After topping the ridge, the route continues up the crest to an open viewpoint (4,100 ft) with a wide view up the Nisqually River valley. The track continues along the ridge to a junction with the Wonderland Trail (3,870 ft), which can be used as a return leg to Longmire.

Van Trump Park Trail. 6.4 miles/m (H). From the Wonderland Trail atop Rampart Ridge (3,830 ft), this path ascends the gentle wooded crest northeast to a short, steep, switchbacked slope that breaks to the alpine meadow bench of Van Trump Park (5,400 ft). A spur climbs to Mildred Point (5,935 ft) and great views of the steep-walled snout of the Kautz Glacier. From the parkland the track contours to cross Van Trump Creek, then begins a zigzag descent past the spray-crowned ribbon of 250-foot-high Comet Falls. More falls are passed as the way drops down the narrow canyon cut by Van Trump Creek, then crosses a bridge above Christine Falls to return to the Longmire–Paradise Road (3,610 ft).

THE WONDERLAND TRAIL

This 93-mile-long loop encircles the mountain, alternately climbing to high alpine meadows dotted with lakes and carpeted with wildflowers, then dropping swiftly into deep river canyons carved into the Mountain's lava slopes. Scenery is varied and breathtaking throughout its length, as every profile of Rainier's upper slopes is presented. Access trails from the perimeter provide opportunities for loop hikes, as well as resupply points for around-the-mountain hikers. Only a few segments of the trail are open to pack stock.

Wonderland Trail: Longmire to Rampart Ridge. 2 miles/m (H,S). From Longmire (2,800 ft) the route zigzags up steep wooded slopes to top Rampart Ridge, where it meets the Van Trump Park (3,850 ft) and Rampart Ridge (3,870 ft) trails.

Wonderland Trail: Rampart Ridge to Indian Henrys Hunting Ground. 5.1 miles/m (H). After crossing Rampart Ridge, the way descends gradually to cross Kautz Creek (3,500 ft), then wanders through regenerating forest atop the thick deposits of the 1947 Kautz mudflow. Switchbacks that climb the steep wall out of the drainage near Fishers Hornpipe Creek are followed by a diagonal wooded ascent to the deep cleft of Devils Dream Creek. The path swings through marsh meadows past Squaw Lake (5,070 ft) before entering the flowered park of Indian Henrys Hunting Ground. Here the Kautz Creek (5,250 ft) and Mirror Lakes (5,230 ft) trails are passed.

Wonderland Trail: Indian Henrys Hunting Ground to North Puyallup River. 13.3 miles/m (H). A steep switchbacked drop leads to a suspension bridge crossing Tahoma Creek (4,250 ft). A bouldery grade east atop a lateral moraine is followed by a zigzag climb to the base of cliffs at the east end of Emerald Ridge. Open slopes overlook the west wall of Glacier Island—watch for mountain goats. After crossing a narrow saddle (5,620 ft) with views of the Tahoma Glacier, Puyallup Cleaver, and Tokaloo Spire, the way slinks down the rim of a 200-foot-high cliff before dropping to the South Puyallup River (4,070 ft) and its parallel access trail.

It's uphill once more as switchbacks work up the drainage wall to St. Andrews Park and St. Andrews Lake (5,886 ft). The way then descends to Aurora Lake (5,500 ft), embraced by the flower fields of Klapatche Park. Here the head of the St. Andrews Trail is met. The way drops abruptly northeast below Aurora Peak, then wiggles precipitously down to the old end of the West Side Road (now trail) at the North Puyallup River (3,700 ft).

Wonderland Trail: North Puyallup River to Mowich Lake. 14.9 miles/m (H,S). A gradual ascent through cool, pleasant forest passes an old burn, then climbs more steeply into the meadowland of Sunset Park (5,250 ft). A twisty contouring path arrives at Golden Lakes, a group of lakes and tarns scattered along the rim of Sunset Park between 4,230 and 5,000 feet. The path traces a ridgetop arc west to a saddle (4,677 ft) just inside the park boundary, then heads down again through two dozen wooded switchbacks to the South Mowich River (2,710 ft). The path through broad bottomland woods crosses both forks of the Mowich River; an uphill grind, mitigated by switchbacks, finally reaches Mowich Lake (4,929 ft), just beyond the junction with the Spray Park Trail.

Wonderland Trail: Mowich Lake to Carbon River. 5.5 miles/m (H,S). A gentle grade north from Mowich Lake reaches Ipsut Pass and the start of the Tolmie Peak Trail. The way snakes down the steep basin headwall northeast of the pass to follow Ipsut Creek down through huge old-growth cedar to the Carbon River and Ipsut Creek Campground (2,340 ft).

Wonderland Trail: Carbon River to Sunrise. 13.3 miles/m (H). An easy grade from the campground traces the bank of the Carbon River through broad bottomland to two river-crossing alternatives. The first, at the junction with the Northern Loop Trail (2,860 ft), is a sometimes washed-out log bridge. Farther upstream at the base of Echo Cliffs (3,230 ft), just beyond the Spray Park Trail, a bouncy, swaying suspension bridge has a better survival record, but adds thrills for the nervous. A parallel path on the opposite side of the river links the two crossing points. A short distance beyond the upper bridge the trail reaches a viewpoint at the snout of the Carbon Glacier below Northern Crags (3,600 ft), then ascends along the moraine for another 2 miles. A steep climb through woods crosses the saddle at the south end of Old Desolate, then descends through tree clumps and meadows to Mystic Lake (5,700 ft).

West of the lake the path wanders down the bank of the West Fork of the White River, rounds the snout of the Winthrop Glacier (4,720 ft), and threads below Garda Falls. Switchbacks climb along Granite Creek to Skyscraper Pass (6,730 ft), where the view west encompasses the Winthrop Glacier, Old Desolate, Vernal Park, and Sluiskin Mountain. The route heads across meadows and pumice slopes around the head of Berkeley Park, passes the east end of the Northern Loop Trail, then reaches a major intersection at Frozen Lake (6,850 ft). Here the Burroughs Mountain Trail goes southwest, the Fremont Lookout Trail heads north, and the Wonderland Trail splits, with one leg descending to the Sunrise Campground (6,350 ft) and a second to the Sunrise Ranger Station (6,430 ft).

Wonderland Trail: Sunrise to White River. 4.2 miles/m (H). One of the less popular segments of the Wonderland Trail is the brief civilization-to-civilization link that zigzags down from Sunrise to the White River Campground (4,300 ft).

Wonderland Trail: White River to Indian Bar. 9.8 miles/m (H). The trail resumes east of White River Campground at the junction of the White River and Sunrise roads (3,950 ft), then follows the wooded south edge of the road to Fryingpan Creek, where there is an alternative access from the road. The next woodland stretch traces the creek upstream for 3 miles before breaking into meadows where Rainier and Little Tahoma appear. The way wiggles uphill to Summerland (5,950 ft), a popular alpine park below the Fryingpan Glacier and Little Tahoma. The track southeast crosses snowfields that persist until August, passes frigid tarns, then climbs to Panhandle Gap (6,750 ft). Here are great views of the Sarvent Glaciers and the Cowlitz Chimneys, jagged remnants of an old volcanic plug, and Mounts Adams and Hood; above are glaciers sliding from the rock pyramid of Little Tahoma.

Avalanche lilies create a spectacular display in Spray Park on Mount Rainier.

Beyond the gap is the highest and most remote stretch of the trail; it crosses smooth, glacier-polished rock, steep snowfields, and windswept benches reaching 6,700 feet before heading down a skinny ridgetop to Indian Bar (5,100 ft). Near the shelter here is unpronounceable Wauhaukaupauken Falls.

Wonderland Trail: Indian Bar to Cowlitz Divide. 4.2 miles/m (H). Rocks, slabs, and meadows accompany the ascent southeast to a bald viewpoint (5,930 ft) at the north end of Cowlitz Divide, featuring Rainier, the Tatoosh peaks, Adams, St. Helens, Shriner Peak, the Cascade crest, and the Cowlitz Chimneys. The way rolls along the minor ups and downs atop the narrow divide, gradually descending through trees to the junction with the Olallie Trail (4,760 ft).

Wonderland Trail: Cowlitz Divide to Reflection Lakes. 10.2 miles/m (H,S). From the top of the divide, 16 switchbacks drop to Nickel Creek (3,310 ft). After crossing the creek, the trail continues down to the Stevens Canyon Road at Box Canyon (3,140 ft). From the south side of the road the route swings down around a forested nose, then begins a gradual ascent of Stevens Canyon, en route passing several waterfalls. (The most striking are Sylvia and Martha falls.) The Stevens Canyon Road is crossed at 4,150 feet, and met again at 4,600 feet, where the trail parallels the road to Lake Louise (4,597 ft) and Reflection Lakes (4,854 to 4,865 ft).

Wonderland Trail: Reflection Lakes to Longmire. 5.6 miles/m (H,S). The route leaves the lakes after crossing the Stevens Canyon Road, swings back and forth down past the Narada Falls Trail, then continues a descent of the narrow Paradise River canyon. After crossing the river and passing Carter Falls, the way runs beside remnants of a decaying wooden pipeline that funneled water to a powerhouse that once delivered electricity to mines high on Eagle Peak, and later to the park at Longmire. Passing the powerhouse ruins (3,250 ft), the way crosses the Nisqually River and continues parallel to its bank to Longmire (2,800 ft).

Climbing

The obvious climbing attraction within the park is "The Mountain" (14,411 ft), which attracts thousands of summit aspirants every year; however only 40 percent of the parties, both guided and private, reach the summit. Weather and the rapid transition in altitude eliminate a major portion of the climbers; unfortunately, Rainier has also claimed many climbers' lives. Routes have been put up every side of the peak, and most have one or more variations, either to attack new challenges or to accommodate seasonal changes in crevasse patterns, sloughing off of ledges, and so on. The easiest routes are on the south and east sides of the mountain, while those on the west and north sides range from difficult to terrifying.

The easy to moderate routes, all less than G-III are, Ingraham Glacier–Disappointment Cleaver, Gibraltar Ledge, Nisqually Ice Cliff, Nisqually Ice Fall, Furher Finger, Wilson Glacier Headwall, Kautz Glacier, Kautz Glacier Headwall, Kautz Cleaver, Success Cleaver, Tahoma Glacier, Russell Cliff, and Emmons–Winthrop glaciers.

The more difficult or dangerous routes, all G-III to G-V, include South Tahoma Headwall, Tahoma Cleaver, Sunset Amphitheater–Tahoma Glacier, Sunset Amphitheater Headwall, Edmunds Headwall, Central Mowich Face, North Mowich Headwall, North Mowich Face Icefall, Ptarmigan Ridge, Liberty Wall, Liberty Ridge, Willis Wall, and Curtis Ridge.

The second-highest peak in the park (and the third-highest in the state) is Little Tahoma (11,138 ft), a subsidiary partner of Rainier. The rocky summit pyramid is normally climbed via combination rock-and-glacier routes out of Summerland that range from C-3 to C-4 in difficulty. The loose north and northeast faces are rated at C-4 to C-5, and the west ridge has been climbed in winter when ice glues the C-5.7 rock leads together.

South of Paradise is an arc of striking rock peaks (the Tatoosh Range), most of whose 5,900- to 6,900-foot summits are just a few leads of solid rock above cross-country hikes from easy access trails. Among the most interesting of these are Unicorn Peak, C-3 to C-4; the Castle, C-3; Pinnacle Peak, C-3 to C-4; and Eagle Peak, C-4. The rest of the summits are scrambles or easy walk-ups.

Although there are a number of interesting, distinctive summits on the west and northwest sides of the mountain, few offer any serious climbing challenge. One exception is Tokaloo Spire (7,480 ft) on the Puyallup Cleaver, a 70- to 150-foot-high dike with two vertical faces. A C-4 crack-and-chimney route reaches the top from its east rib.

Sluiskin Mountain, between Windy Gap and Vernal Park, is a scraggly crest with some challenging climbing on the major summit, the Chief (7,026 ft), C-3. The secondary high spot, the Squaw (6,960 ft), and the Papooses, a series of pinnacles to the ridge on the west, are easy scrambles.

The eroded volcanic plugs that make up the pinnacles of the Cowlitz Chimneys and Governors Ridge, on the east side of the park, are more strenuous rock climbs. In the Cowlitz Chimneys, the Main Chimney (7,605 ft) has a contorted, hard-to-follow C-3 route to its top; the North Chimney (7,105 ft), one of the most inaccessible spots in the park, has pitches ranging from C-5 to C-5.8 in difficulty. Governors Peak (6,600 ft) is a steep pyramidal C-3 to C-4 summit, and nearby Governors Needle (6,500 ft) is a slender, friable C-5 pinnacle.

Winter Sports

The road from the Nisqually entrance to Paradise is the only one presently open in the winter. Sledding, snowshoeing, tubing, and cross-country skiing are the winter activities at Paradise. Depending on year-to-year budgets the sledding and tubing areas may or may not be groomed. Three marked but ungroomed trails run from Paradise to Nisqually Vista, Paradise to Narada Falls, and Narada Falls to Reflection Lakes.

Cross-country skiing and ski mountaineering reach other untracked areas. Among the more popular 1-day trips are the broad open snowfield ridge between Paradise and Camp Muir, Paradise to Reflection Lakes via Mazama Ridge, Narada Falls to Reflection Lakes, and Reflection Lakes to the Castle Peak saddle in the Tatoosh Range. On the north side of the mountain is the road trek to Mowich Lake, and on the east side is the advanced tour into Crystal Lake Basin.

Longer ski/snowshoe trips involving multiday snow camps and mountaineering skills head into Seattle Park and the Russell Glacier, Steamboat Prow, the Carbon Glacier, Van Trump Park, the Nisqually Glacier, the Wilson Glacier, and the traverse from Paradise to White River via the Ingraham and Emmons glaciers.

In recent years there has been increased interest in winter climbs, both of Rainier and Little Tahoma. The easier routes often become simpler as crevasses are filled by snow. Some of the most difficult, hazardous in summer because of loose muddy pumice and constant rockfall, have faces that are thankfully glued together by ice; alas, avalanches become a new hazard.

29

GLACIER VIEW WILDERNESS

LOCATION: In Pierce County, on the southwest corner of Mount Rainier National Park
SIZE: 3,080 acres
STATUS: Designated Wilderness (1984)
TERRAIN: A high U-shaped ridge with two long north–south fingers encloses meadows and
    alpine lakes in the headwaters of a fork of the South Puyallup River.
ELEVATION: 3,320 to 5,507 feet
MANAGEMENT: USFS, Gifford Pinchot National Forest, Packwood Ranger District
TOPOGRAPHIC MAPS: Mount Wow

Nine lakes, some small or intermittent, lie in cirques or on benches in a pleasant little basin shielded from outside noise and distraction by long ridges on either side. A trail paralleling the western boundary of the wilderness offers access to the area's highest points, with breathtaking views east of Mount Rainier and the thin rock dikes separating the long frozen tongues of the Tahoma, Puyallup, and South Mowich glaciers; above them is the frigid bowl of the Sunset

Amphitheater. To the west the view is another story: miles and miles of clearcuts—denuded slopes along winding, caterpillar-like logging roads that have nibbled up to within inches of the wilderness boundary.

Climate

The precipitation in the area averages around 85 to 90 inches annually, with a large portion of that falling as snow. More than 30 feet of snow falls during the winter months, but most is gone by mid-July. Winter temperatures are generally in the low 20s, and summer highs average between 65 and 70 degrees.

Plants and Wildlife

The area is forested with Pacific silver fir, western hemlock, noble fir, Douglas-fir, western red cedar, white pine, and true fir. Typically found in the understory are oakfern, ladyfern, white trillium, queencup beadlily, deerfoot vanillaleaf, twinflower, white inside-out flower, purple twisted stalk, bunchberry dogwood, starry solomonplume, dwarf blackberry, a variety of huckleberries, three-leafed coolwort, devil's club, and a wide assortment of mosses. The basin is an important summer range for elk and mountain goats.

Geology

The rock exposed in the wilderness is that of the Ohanapecosh Formation, which is the original base on which the entire Mount Rainier area is built. It consists of multiple layers of volcanic breccias, sandstone, and siltstone more than 9,000 feet thick that resulted from volcanic epiclastic and pyroclastic flows. Best evidence indicates that this succession of thick volcanic

The west side of Mount Rainier from the summit of Glacier View in the Glacier View Wilderness

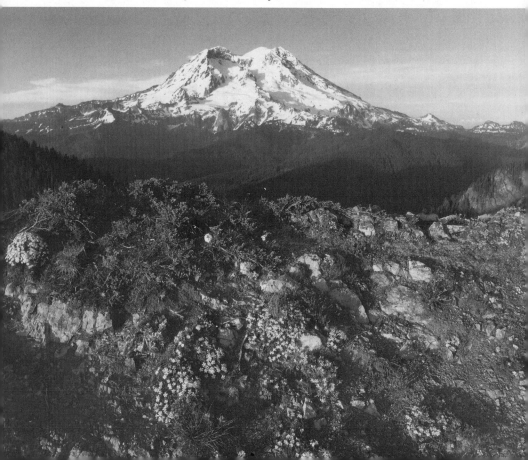

mudflows, with intervening sedimentary sheeting, occurred underwater in a relatively placid lake or bay about 36 million years ago. The strata of the Ohanapecosh Formation in the Glacier View Wilderness tilt upward to the west at a 25- to 30-degree angle along a north–south strike. The small cirques notched in the basin walls were carved by local glaciation some 12,000 to 15,000 years ago.

History

In support of the Forest Service fire-suppression mission in the 1920s and '30s, a fire lookout was built atop Glacier View; it was removed in the 1960s. A temporary lookout (a telephone and a toolshed) was placed atop Mount Beljica. Maps in the early 1960s show the typical one-section checkerboard pattern of private and federal land reaching all the way to the national park boundary. In subsequent years the Forest Service consolidated a dozen contiguous sections of forest under federal ownership, and the virgin portion of that land was designated as the Glacier View Wilderness in 1984.

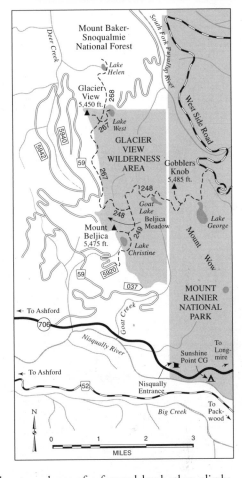

ACTIVITIES

Hiking

The only road open to the public that approaches the area is FR 59, which leaves Highway 706 between Ashford and the park boundary.

Trail #249, Lake Christine. 1.8 miles/e (H,S). From the end of FR 5920 (4,420 ft) the route rises out of a clearcut to traverse the steep slopes of a forested knob, then climbs abruptly along an outlet stream to Lake Christine (4,802 ft). After circling the east side of the lake, the trail ascends north through virgin timber to a rib (5,080 ft) east of Mount Beljica, where a faint boot-path leads west to its summit (5,475 ft). The way now descends to Beljica Meadow, and meets Trail #248 (4,580 ft).

Trail #248, Puyallup. 2.5 miles/m (H,S). From the junction with Trail #267, this route traverses south to Beljica Meadow, rounds the north side of a finger ridge, then descends gradually to Goat Lake (4,343 ft). A long diagonal ascent up slopes to the east reaches the park boundary (4,700 ft), where the trail continues on to Gobblers Knob, Lake George, and Round Pass.

Trail #267, Glacier View. 2.9 miles/d (H,S). At a low saddle (4,550 ft) a shortcut drops 100 feet down to FR 59. The route heads north, sometimes atop the boundary ridge, sometimes skirting the west side of ridgetop knobs. At a notch south of Glacier View, a short spur climbs to the summit (5,450 ft) and meditation-worthy views of Mount Rainier. From the notch the way drops northeast, passes the end of Trail #268, and continues down through the woods to the tiny pocket holding Lake West (4,582 ft).

Trail #268, Peak Two. 1.3 miles/m (H,S). After leaving Trail #267 (5,040 ft) on the east slopes of Glacier View, the way crosses the northern wilderness boundary and continues a long gradual descent to Lake Helen (4,612 ft), just a few hundred yards south of the clearcuts that mark the national forest boundary.

30

TATOOSH WILDERNESS

LOCATION: In Lewis County, along the southern boundary of Mount Rainier National Park
SIZE: 15,800 acres
STATUS: Designated Wilderness (1984)
TERRAIN: An area framed by two long, steep, rugged ridges, with forested lower slopes leading up to subalpine and alpine parklands
ELEVATION: 1,230 to 6,310 feet
MANAGEMENT: USFS, Gifford Pinchot National Forest, Packwood Ranger District
TOPOGRAPHIC MAPS: Tatoosh Lakes, Ohanapecosh Hot Springs, Wahpenayo Peak

The steep flanks, formidable ridges, and high-altitude meadows of this southern end of Mount Rainier's Tatoosh Range had not yet been ravaged by logging, as had all adjoining forest, before it was saved by wilderness designation in 1984. The only accesses to the area are a pair of trails with a few short spurs to lakes and the high point of the wilderness. The steep, rough terrain does not abet easy cross-country travel, and the trails are tedious and demanding in their climb to the more pleasant ridgetop treks. Once in the high-country parkland, the flower fields, berry patches, and views of the major Cascade volcanic summits reward the effort to get there. Of the half-dozen lakes in the backcountry, only three are more than tiny tarns, and these have so delicate an ecology surrounding them that camping is not permitted there.

White beargrass blossoms catch the early morning light.

Climate

Precipitation and temperatures vary between the lower elevations of flanking drainages and the ridge crest that dominates the wilderness. The following information applies to the higher heart of the region, since this is the area of most interest to recreationists. Precipitation is heavy, averaging about 100 inches annually, a large part falling as snow. A total of about 40 feet of snow is dropped on the area each winter, some of which persists on the ground until late July. Midwinter lows average in the mid- to high teens, and summer highs are a comfortable 70 degrees.

Plants and Wildlife

The lower-level forest is made up of Pacific silver fir, western hemlock, noble fir, Douglas-fir, and western red cedar. The understory includes oakfern, ladyfern, deerfoot vanillaleaf, white trillium, twinflower, queencup beadlily, bunchberry dogwood, various huckleberry species, dwarf blackberry, devil's club, and mosses. Higher elevations see the addition of mountain hemlock, pyrola, and beargrass. Parklands have a ground cover that includes blue-leaf huckleberry, dwarf blackberry, luetkea, woolly everlasting, Indian paintbrush, and, in varying locations, pedicularis, lupine, sedge, cinquefoil, and alpine aster. A 560-acre RNA has been established in the Butter Creek drainage, in conjunction with an adjoining one in the national park, for the study of watersheds, stream biology, and subalpine plant communities.

Black bear, cougar, bobcat, black-tailed deer, elk, and mountain goat are found at upper elevations in summer and early fall, and the bottom of the Muddy Fork of the Cowlitz River drainage serves as a winter range for these animals. In addition, hikers are likely to see marmots, pikas, white-tailed ptarmigans, snowshoe rabbits, golden eagles, and Swainson's hawks.

Geology

The geology of the Tatoosh area is among the more complex in the Mount Rainier vicinity. At the far west side of the area, exposed rock is a part of the Ohanapecosh Formation, composed of volcanic breccia, sandstone, and siltstone resulting from underwater volcanic epiclastic and pyroclastic flows some 36 million yeas ago. The formation was folded on a northwest to southeast line, and a major syncline follows the Butter Creek drainage, on the west side of Tatoosh Ridge. A vertical fault along the east side of the ridge marks a sharp delineation between the exposed Ohanapecosh Formation on the west, and the Stevens Ridge Formation, which overlaid it, on the east. Tatoosh Ridge itself is multilayered, and the lowest layer is the Ohanapecosh Formation. The next layer of basaltic andesite flows was overlaid by the Stevens Ridge Formation, consisting of rhyodactic ash flows deposited about 30 million years ago. This is topped by the Fifes Peak Formation, a heterogeneous composite of lava flows, mudflows, and volcanic clastic rock about 25 million years old. The Stevens Ridge Formation that pervades the east side

Mount Rainier rises above ridges of the Tatoosh Wilderness.

of the wilderness has been intruded by numerous east–west trending basalt dikes and sills from roughly the same period

History

The Taidnapam Indians, who had summer fishing camps near the confluence of the Muddy and Clear forks of the Cowlitz, would head to Tatoosh Ridge in the fall to hunt, gather materials for making baskets, and harvest and dry huckleberries. According to legend, Coyote visualized a mountain named "neq'u't," where there would be a thick growth of berries for the tribe to pick and dry; this mountain was Tatoosh Ridge. The major trail through the area was put in by the Forest Service to reach and support the Tatoosh fire lookout, which stood atop the ridge between the 1920s and 1960s.

ACTIVITIES

Hiking

Trail #161, Tatoosh. 8.6 miles/d (H,S). Starting from the northwest at FR 5270 (2,920 ft), switchbacks climb an abrupt 1,000 feet through thick forest. A sidehill ascent continues east to just below a notch on Tatoosh Ridge (5,530 ft), where Trail #161B heads northeast. The route contours the west side of the ridge, twisting around the heads of basins, most of the time in subalpine meadows ablaze with the colors of wildflowers in early summer. The tread may be indistinct; hold a level grade to reach a ridgetop saddle (5,760 ft), the start of Trail #161A. The way swings to the east side of the crest as it continues south and, with the ridge, starts a gradual descent toward Butter Peak, at its southern end. The trail bends east 0.4 mile from that peak and heads downhill in steep switchbacks. It crosses Hinkle Tinkle Creek and, swinging back and forth, finally reaches FR 5290 (2,355 ft).

Trail #161A, Tatoosh Lookout. *1 mile/e (H,S).* From the saddle junction with Trail #161 (5,760 ft), follow the crest north to reach the former fire lookout site at the highest point on the ridge (6,310 ft) outside the national park. Views are spectacular; Mount Adams looms to the southeast, the Paradise side of Mount Rainier is close at hand to the north, and to the south is the gaping maw of Mount St. Helens.

Trail #161B, Tatoosh Lake. *0.5 mile/d (H).* The way leaves Trail #161 (5,530 ft), climbs a short distance to a ridgetop notch, then stumbles down an indistinct, rough, eroded tread to Tatoosh Lakes (4,822 ft). The lakes are cuddled in a tight north-facing cirque with views of Mount Rainier above the outlet stream. Camping is prohibited.

31

WILLIAM O. DOUGLAS WILDERNESS

LOCATION: In Lewis and Yakima counties, mostly east of the Cascade crest, between the American and Tieton rivers
SIZE: 167,195 acres
STATUS: Designated Wilderness (1984)
TERRAIN: Two broad, high ridge complexes, deeply cut by lateral streams, rise abruptly on either side of the Bumping River drainage to a crest of subalpine meadows and rocky summits. The two ridges meet on the Cascade crest at the Bumping River headwaters in a wide, flat plateau, lightly timbered and covered with numerous meadows, lakes, and ponds.
ELEVATION: 3,200 to 7,766 feet
MANAGEMENT: USFS, Gifford Pinchot National Forest, Packwood Ranger District; and Wenatchee National Forest, Naches Ranger District
TOPOGRAPHIC MAPS: Bumping Lake, Chinook Pass, Cougar Lake, Goose Prairie, Meeks Table, Norse Peak, Old Scab Mtn., Rimrock Lake, Spiral Butte, Timberwolf Mtn., White Pass

The William O. Douglas Wilderness is named for the conservation-minded Supreme Court justice who had a cabin here at Goose Prairie, hiked extensively throughout the area for years, and wrote about it in the book *Of Men and Mountains.* The wilderness contains a magnificent spectrum of geological, biological, botanical, scenic, and recreational treasures. Its geography includes deep drainages at the headwaters of four major rivers, high rugged ridges topped by subalpine meadows and rocky crags, dense old-growth forests, juvenile volcano cinder cones, and a broad, lightly forested parkland plateau with 59 named lakes of various sizes and more than 250 unnamed lakes, ponds, and puddles. (Who can count?) The eastern portions of the wilderness drop to open ridges and stands of ponderosa pine.

The area's 66 trails, totaling more than 250 miles, offer similar variety. The Pacific Crest National Scenic Trail runs north–south along its western backbone, crossing the meadow-and-lake parkland with a spider's web of interlinked paths leading from one scenic spot to another. The route along the top of American Ridge is the longest continuous trail in the Naches Ranger District, twisting, climbing, and diving along the contorted crest for nearly 27 miles. On the southeast side of the wilderness is Nelson Ridge, a narrow, bald, alpine rib reached by grueling, straight-up switchback chains that only a miner could build.

Climate

Since the wilderness stretches east from the Cascade crest for more than 17 miles, there is a significant difference in the precipitation falling on its east side versus its west side. On the west it totals nearly 120 inches, while the east, in the rain shadow of the Cascades, sees only 24 inches. The bulk of the moisture falls during winter months as snow, with accumulations of 7 to 10 feet at upper elevations. Winter minimums throughout the area are in the 15-degree range; summer highs on the west side are in the low 70s, while the east side enjoys significantly more sunny days, with highs averaging in the upper 70s to lower 80s. The lower east side of the wilderness is generally snow-free by early June, but snow patches linger on the west, and at higher elevations, until mid-July; first flakes fall early in November.

Plants and Wildlife

By virtue of its location astride the Cascade crest, the William O. Douglas Wilderness has a diverse group of plant communities representing both the wet west side of the Cascades and the drier east slopes. On the west, the dense old-growth forest at lower elevations typically consists of Douglas-fir, western hemlock, and western red cedar. With a gain in altitude the forest composition shifts to western hemlock, Pacific silver fir, noble fir, western white pine, and Englemann spruce. At the upper elevations along the crest, and across the parklands of the Tumac Plateau, Alaska cedar, mountain hemlock, and subalpine fir predominate. Many of these species are also found on the east side of the wilderness, but they are joined by whitebark pine at upper elevations and ponderosa pine lower down. A 64-acre RNA at Meeks Table, on the eastern rim of the area, has a representative ecology of the ponderosa pine–pinegrass community in combination with Douglas-fir. A second RNA of 2,205 acres with a mixed old-growth and shrub forest and a Pacific silver fir forest has been proposed in the Cedar Creek drainage.

The eastern portion of the wilderness has substantial herds of elk and mule deer that winter in the meadows of the Bumping River drainage. Other species found in the area include cougar, fisher, lynx, wolverine, Cascade red fox, mountain goat, and blue and ruffed grouse.

A wildflower garden of beargrass, lupine, and hellebore brightens a subalpine meadow of the William O. Douglas Wilderness.

Geology

For a region of its size, the geology of the area is relatively complex. The base structure, exposed in only a few sites along the south edge, is old pre-Miocene sandstone and pillow basalt formed on the east coast of the North Cascades subcontinent prior to its becoming attached to the North American continent. The northern half of the region has been overlaid with Eocene andesite and rhyolite, while the southern portion of the wilderness, immediately north of White Pass, is covered by a thick layer of High Cascade volcanic flows between 10 million and 30 million years old.

Several granodiorite plutons, or perhaps several exposures of the same pluton, intruded through the lava flows about 10 million years ago. One lobe of this pale gray granite runs up the Bumping River drainage and hooks back along Miners Ridge; an arm also slices through American Ridge near Sunrise Creek. A second outcrop is found at the northwest corner of American Ridge, a third is in the vicinity of Carlton Pass, and a fourth lies adjacent to US Highway 12 at Cortright Creek. Mineralization along the pluton borders, typical of such intrusions, has led to extensive prospecting in some of these areas.

Continental ice sheets later covered the area, smoothing the high plateau along the Cascade crest and carving the deep drainages in the center of the wilderness and on its north and south flanks. More recent volcanic activity, probably contemporary with the last glaciation some 10,000 to 15,000 years ago, is represented by the cinder cones of Spiral Butte and Tumac Mountain.

History

For centuries the Yakama Indians hunted, fished, and gathered berries in the wilderness region, and trod paths across Cowlitz Pass to trade with Puget Sound tribes. The first white surveyors followed these trails over the pass in 1861, and a railroad survey party cut a path from Summit Creek over Cowlitz Pass to Bumping River in 1867. An 1881 map shows a trail from the Nisqually River to the upper Cowlitz, across Cowlitz Pass, then down Indian Creek to the Tieton River and on to Yakima, a route apparently used as a cattle drive.

Bumping Lake and Bumping River were discovered in the 1850s; they were also known by their Indian names of Tanum Lake and Tanum River well into the 1880s. The Northern Pacific Railroad attempted, unsuccessfully, to dam the river in 1894, a feat that was finally accomplished by the Bureau of Reclamation in 1910. The Bumping Lake area was the site of prospecting in the late 1880s as prospectors, operating out of the Copper City mining camp at the head of the lake, burrowed into quartz sulphide veins in search of gold and copper ores.

By 1897 the present wilderness area was incorporated in the Pacific Forest Reserve, and the early 1900s saw herds of sheep annually grazing in the high meadows. The availability of CCC crews, and the increased emphasis on fire suppression in the 1930s, led to an extensive trail system in the area and construction of fire lookouts at Goat Peak, Little Bald Mountain, Miners Ridge, Mount Aix, Tumac Mountain, Timberwolf Mountain, and Clover Springs.

ACTIVITIES

Hiking

SOUTHEAST OF BUMPING RIVER TRAILS

Trail #975, Soda Springs. 5.2 miles/m (H,S). From Soda Springs Campground (3,000 ft) a footbridge crosses the Bumping River to a fork; Trail #975 heads south, #975A north. After a no-nonsense climb to a wooded saddle (3,670 ft) the trails merge and head up a broad steep ridge toward Old Scab Mountain. The way becomes even steeper as it attacks a finger northeast of the summit, then grudgingly eases at a marsh and meadow flat (5,500 ft) below the peak's east face, where it meets Trail #985 (5,670 ft).

Trail #985, Windy Ridge. 3.2 miles/m (H,S) Not capriciously named, this route leaves FR 16 (5,900 ft) for a short ascent to Flat Iron Lake (5,605 ft), where it joins the southeast end of Trail #975. The way climbs south through forest to a meadow (6,435 ft), then descends briefly to touch FR 16 at Clover Spring (6,351 ft). It drops across exposed, breezy east slopes, then descends a steep forested nose, turns southwest, and continues down to meet Trail #973 on the North Fork of Rattlesnake Creek (4,400 ft).

Trail #973, Richmond Mine (Thunder Creek). 10.2 miles/m-d (H,S). A miner's track, redirected out of a soggy creek bed by the Forest Service, departs a road spur (3,365 ft) northeast of Bumping Crossing Campground. It winds up a rib north of Thunder Creek, crosses the creek twice, attacks a seemingly vertical face head-on to gain a saddle (6,200 ft), then descends to Richmond Lake (5,990 ft). From the lake the way drops southeast to meet Trail #985 (4,500 ft) above the North Fork of Rattlesnake Creek, then switchbacks south up the drainage wall to a narrow col (6,405 ft) west of Nelson Butte. The trail drops downhill one more time into the Dog Creek drainage, where it continues downstream to end on Trail #982 (4,430 ft).

Trail #982, Mount Aix. 13.8 miles/m-d (H,S). An uphill grind from FR 1800395 (3,667 ft) climbs through 36 switchbacks before relaxing to a steep sidehill diagonal climb to the top of Nelson Ridge (7,100 ft). Here views of Rainier, Adams, and the Goat Rocks reward the tongue-dragging climb. A scramble east up a narrow rock-and-heather ridge reaches the top of Mount Aix (7,766 ft). The trail traverses the steep, rocky south slopes of the peak, follows a narrow, barren crest east, then drops to the headwaters of Lookout Creek. The way snakes across subalpine meadows, dives to Dog Creek to meet Trail #973 (4,430 ft), then climbs past Buck Lake (4,740 ft) to end at FR 1502695 (4,780 ft).

Trail #979, Pear Butte. 8.2 miles/d (H,S). From FR 1800395 (3,660 ft) the route climbs into the wooded slopes of the Copper Creek drainage to 20 puckered switchbacks that gain a ridge nose (5,200 ft) leading south to Pear Butte. Once atop the ridge the way flows through alternating forest and meadows to the north flank of Pear Butte. It then drops southwest to a broad saddle (5,220 ft), where it eases downhill to meadows around Apple Lake (5,365 ft), then meets Trail #1105.

Trail #1114, Rattlesnake. 13 miles/m-d (H,S). Like to wade streams? This is the trail for you. Leaving Trail #981 at the confluence of Dog and Rattlesnake creeks (3,235 ft), the path crosses Rattlesnake Creek nine times as it follows it upstream. The route meets several side trails en route. At 4,180 feet the way turns southwest up McNeil Creek, then switchbacks up the drainage headwall to join Trail #1141 (5,270 ft).

Trail #1141, Ironstone Mountain. 10.6 miles/m-d (H). From the end of FR 1500199 at Cash Prairie (6,335 ft), the route follows the ridgetop west to the bald top of Burnt Mountain (6,536 ft) and great views of Goat Rocks and Mount Adams. The way undulates up and down along the ridge, contours a steep sideslope, then bends around the south side of Ironstone Mountain. At Russell Ridge (5,990 ft) it follows the crest north to a steep, rough switchback chain across McNeil Peak (6,650 ft), where there are good views down the Indian Creek drainage to Rimrock Lake. A rugged track slides off the northwest side of the peak to meet Trail #1114 at the divide between the McNeil Creek and Indian Creek drainages. From here the way crosses a shallow saddle, then descends through forest to end on Trail #1105 at Indian Creek Meadow (4,930 ft).

NORTHWEST OF BUMPING RIVER TRAILS

Trail #958, American Ridge. *26.8 miles/m-d (H,S).* The northeast end of the trail leaves County Road 1050 (Bumping River) 0.7 mile from Highway 410 (2,800 ft). After a brief climb, a gentle grade heads southwest across a wooded bench to the sharp end of American Ridge. Switchbacks climb the forested face, and after a brief ridge romp (4,300 ft) more switchbacks drop to a wooded shelf that is followed southwest to Fifes Creek. A gradual ascent above the creek headwaters regains the ridge (5,0505 ft) above Goat Creek basin. In another mile the fun is over; 43 tight switchbacks grind up to the top of Goat Peak (7,473 ft), a former lookout site. The upper end of Trail #958C is passed about halfway to the summit. Here are dramatic views across the American River valley to the spikes of Fifes Peaks, farther west to Rainier, and south to Adams.

More switchbacks drop west to a diagonal descent to the saddle junction with Trail #959 (5,690 ft). The way now twists, turns, and rolls up and down through alternating forest and meadows atop the ridge. After passing Trail #972 (6,020 ft) from Goose Prairie, the route zig-zags down the east face of the ridge to little Kettle Lake (5,670 ft). A gentle ascent around the upper Kettle Creek basin then crosses a saddle (6,340 ft) to a traverse below cliffs at the head of Timber Creek. Switchbacks regain the crest of American Ridge (6,880 ft); the way crosses the ridge, then contours the head of Big Basin (6,350 ft). It regains the ridgetop and tracks its ups and downs southwest past Trail #969 to an overlook of the cirque holding Cedar Lake. After more bends and jogs on the forested slopes above Swamp Lake, the way descends to a broad woods-and-meadow flat where it meets Trail #970. Trail #958 climbs west to meadow-wrapped American Lake (5,260 ft) and its end on the PCT (5,360 ft).

Trail #958C, Goat Peak. *2.8 miles/m (H).* From Hells Crossing Campground on Highway 410 (3,320 ft), the route makes a relentless climb south up a steep hogback ridge, sometimes in forest, sometimes in meadow. It joins Trail #958 (5,900 ft) for that trail's final thrust to the summit of Goat Peak (7,373 ft).

Trail #999, Pleasant Valley Loop. *13 miles/e (H,S).* Pleasant indeed is this long, gentle loop that leaves Hells Crossing Campground (3,320 ft) and parallels the north side of Highway 410 west for 6 miles. It crosses the American River above Union Creek (3,440 ft). On the south side of the river the way heads back downstream, sometimes near the riverbank, but mostly in nearby forest. The downstream leg passes the starting points of Trails #957 and #958C before returning to Hells Crossing. The way is well maintained, and footbridges are present at the many stream crossings.

Trail #959, Goat Creek. *3.7 miles/m (H,S).* The way leaves County Road 1050 (3,100 ft) near Cougar Flat Campground and heads up the steep forested hillside with determination. The grade tempers somewhat at 4,500 feet, but in another mile the trail resorts to switchbacks to surmount a final face and reach Trail #958 at the ridgetop (5,690 ft) west of Goat Peak.

Trail #972, Goose Prairie. *5.1 miles/m (H,S).* Northeast of Bumping Lake Campground, Trail #972 leaves County Road 1050 (3,340 ft) for a steady ascent west, augmented by a few switchbacks. It weaves up forested hillsides to join Trail #958 (6,020 ft) north of Kettle Lake.

Trail #957, Kettle Creek. *6.2 miles/m (H,S).* A gradual valley-bottom trail departs Trail #999 (3,460 ft) to follow the bank of Kettle Creek upstream to its headwaters. Here it switchbacks up the steep drainage headwall and joins Trail #958 on the shore of Kettle Lake (5,670 ft).

Trail #969, Mestachee. *5.3 miles/m (H,S).* At the end of FR 1700460 (3,640 ft) the route crosses Morse Creek and the American River, then begins a rapid zigzag ascent to gain the steep wooded slopes above the east bank of Mestachee Creek. A steady climb leads to a creek crossing (4,900 ft), then a long switchback works up the sideslope to meet Trail #958 at the head of the basin (5,850 ft).

Trail #971, Bumping Lake. *10.1 miles/e (H,S).* From the end of FR 1800394 (3,460 ft), on the northwest side of Bumping Lake, the track follows the lakeshore west to its input stream, then heads upstream through an ever-broadening valley, browsing ground for elk and deer. The way crosses Red Rock Creek, passes an unnamed lake, then follows the bank of the Bumping River to meet the PCT (4,090 ft) just east of Fish Lake.

Trail #970, Swamp Lake. 4.6 miles/m (H,S). At the end of FR 18 (3,550 ft) the trail cuts quickly to a tenuous crossing of Bumping River, crosses Trail #971, then climbs steadily up forested slopes to Swamp Lake (4,795 ft). The way weaves through flowers and blueberry fields to end on Trail #958 (5,040 ft).

CASCADE CREST TRAILS

Trail #1105, Indian Creek. 8 miles/m (H,S). At the end of FR 1308 (3,380 ft) this path heads up the lower Indian Creek gorge to meet Trail #1109 a few footsteps away from a gorgeous 150-foot-high waterfall. The way continues upstream to Indian Meadows, where it meets Trail #1141, then Trail #979, before bending west to Blankenship Lakes (5,270 ft). The trail continues north through Blankenship Meadows and Mosquito Valley before descending to Trail #980 (4,660 ft) and FR 1800395 at Deep Creek.

Trail #1104, Sand Ridge. 8.5 miles/m (H,S). At the end of Spur #488 on the north side of US Highway 12 (3,400 ft), the route ascends Sand Ridge, then heads northwest to meet Trail #1142 on the east side of Spiral Butte. The gentle grade continues north through the forest and meadows of the Tumac Plateau, rounds the east side of Tumac Mountain, passes the north end of Trail #44, and ends on Trail #980 on the shore of the smaller of the Twin Sisters Lakes (5,190 ft).

Trail #980, Twin Sister. 4.2 miles/m (H,S). The trail leaves Deep Creek Campground (4,270 ft) at the end of FR 1800395 (a stock trailhead is 0.5 mile east) to head up wooded slopes above Deep Creek. In 1.5 miles the way meets Trail #1104 on the north shore of the smaller of the Twin Sisters Lakes (5,190 ft). After crossing a wooded neck to the larger lake (5,152 ft) the route descends through pond-and-pothole meadows to the PCT (4,950 ft).

Trail #1142, Shellrock Lake. 4.4 miles/m (H,S). Taking off northwest from Trail #1104 (4,600 ft), the route follows the east base of Spiral Butte past Trail #1108, then enters the lake country of the Tumac Plateau. It skirts Shellrock Lake (4,926 ft), then passes Trail #1106, which leads to more of the area's lakes. The route ends on Trail #44 (5,190 ft), just east of the PCT (5,145 ft).

Trail #1108, Spiral Butte. 2.2 miles/d (H,S). From Trail #1142 (4,800 ft) this rough route winds around the rim of Spiral Butte to its summit (5,940 ft). The trail was originally built in the 1930s to serve a proposed lookout, never built, atop the peak. The cinder cone was created by one of the more recent volcanic eruptions in the region, scarcely 10,000 years ago. Terrific views here peer down to Dog Lake and White Pass, and northwest across the many lakes and meadows of the Tumac Plateau.

Trail #1106, Cramer Lake. 5.4 miles/m (H,S). From the Dog Lake Campground on US Highway 12 (4,240 ft) this popular route starts up the marshy North Fork of Clear Creek drainage, then makes a diagonal climb up a steep forested slope west of Spiral Butte. An easier grade leads north to Cramer Lake (5,025 ft). Above the lake the way bends east and weaves past Otter Lake (5,030 ft) and a smattering of other ponds, to end on Trail #1142 (5,075 ft).

Pacific Crest National Scenic Trail. 13.5 miles/m (H,S). From US Highway 12 at White Pass (4,470 ft), the PCT passes the east shore of Leech Lake, then climbs steeply to the wilderness boundary. It passes a marshy meadow near Deer Lake (5,206 ft), then heads north to meet Trail #60 at shallow Sand Lake (5,295 ft). The way wanders up to a saddle (5,480 ft) with glimpses through open timber stands to Spiral Butte and the Goat Rocks.

The route winds down to Buesch Lake (5,100 ft), then twists north past Pipe Lake (5,210 ft). It now heads northwest and winds through a maze of meadows, ponds, and puddles to Snow Lake (4,935 ft); 0.6 mile north it meets Trail #980. The way starts a long, uninterrupted descent past Trail #43 to Trail #971 on the bank of the Bumping River. About 0.3 mile upstream is Fish Lake (4,112 ft), and a junction with Trail #22.

Switchbacks climb a precipitous south-facing slope to a contour path above Buck Lake, then bend around a rib to Crag Lake (5,010 ft). A flower-meadow basin is traced west to a pair of lazy switchbacks that gain the Cascade crest (5,740 ft) with views of Rainier, Adams, and St. Helens. The path meets Rainier Park's Laughingwater Trail just west of the crest, then swings to east-

A pack string crosses a meadow on a trail ride through the William O. Douglas Wilderness. Tumac Mountain is in the distance.

side slopes above the Red Rock Creek drainage. The way now recrosses the crest (5,700 ft) to wildflower meadows and a knockout picture of Mount Rainier. West-side slopes are contoured northwest across lateral ribs to a col (5,340 ft); the way crosses east to Trail #958, then climbs to another saddle (5,580 ft). A descent of wooded west-side slopes leads to Anderson Lake (5,350 ft), and yet another crest crossing. Sideslopes are descended gradually to Dewey Lake (5,112 ft) and Trail #968. The route then climbs northwest to meet Highway 410 at Chinook Pass (5,432 ft).

Trail #60, Sand Lake. 3 miles/m (H,S). From US Highway 12 (3,860 ft) west of White Pass, the route winds up a steep forested slope, crosses FR 1284, then makes several switchbacks to gain a near-flat bench (5,200 ft). It wanders through open forest past small meadows below Cortright Point to reach the PCT at Sand Lake (5,290 ft).

Trail #44, Cowlitz. 5.2 miles/m (H,S). The route leaves Soda Springs Campground (3,220 ft; the stock trailhead #44A is on FR 4510) to follow Summit Creek upstream to its headwaters. The way heads east to Penoyer Lake (5,005 ft), then wanders up through meadow hummocks and ponds to the PCT (5,180 ft), whose tread it shares for a short distance. After passing the end of Trail #1142 the route ascends the south side of Tumac Mountain (5,700 ft). At the top are sweeping views of the entire plateau with its myriad meadows and tiny lakes, as well as a tiny pond below in the heart of the crater. The way drops through subalpine forests and meadows to join Trail #1104 near Twin Sisters Lakes.

Trail #22, Carlton Creek. 4 miles/m (H,S, but not recommended for stock). From the end of FR 44 (3,200 ft), the route follows the twists of Carlton Creek upstream to Carlton Pass (4,140 ft), then wanders down to Fish Lake (4,112 ft) to meet the PCT.

Trail #968, Dewey Lake. 6.5 miles/m (H,S). Just beyond the point where Trail #969 crosses the American River (3,630 ft), this route heads south along the east bank of the river and follows it upstream for 4 miles. The way crosses the main river course to track a tributary up steep forested slopes to Dewey Lake (5,112 ft), where it joins the PCT at the lake's south shore. The trail was reconstructed in 1993.

Winter Sports

Although the rugged ridge country framing the Bumping River drainage is either inaccessible or dangerous for winter travel, excellent ski and snowshoe trips are available along the north and south borders of the wilderness and into the heart of the west-side plateau. Sno-Parks at Hells Crossing and Pleasant Valley campgrounds on Highway 410 east of Chinook Pass offer two access points to Trail #999, an easy, near-flat, 13-mile-long loop on both sides of the highway. Although the trail is not groomed, there is enough traffic to make it easy to follow.

Across the highway from the White Pass Ski Area, a groomed track around Leech Lake links up with the south end of the PCT. The trail can be followed west to Deer Lake, a short easy tour. With careful navigation, the trail can be followed north past Sand and Beusch lakes to Cowlitz Pass. A base camp here permits tours of the meadow- and lake-pocked plateau. An extended tour can continue east to the summit of Tumac Mountain and Blankenship Meadows. Aside from possible bad weather and the ease of getting lost in the look-alike maze of meadows, this trip is relatively danger-free. Tours farther north along the crest are unwise, because slopes quickly become steep and avalanche-prone.

32

BLUE LAKE

LOCATION: In Lewis and Skamania counties, between the Cispus River and its North Fork
SIZE: 10,000 acres
STATUS: The core area is Semiprimitive Motorized; the remainder of the periphery is managed for Timber Harvest.
TERRAIN: A high northwest-to-southeast tending ridge with an even-gradient, steep-sided southwest slope, and a northeast slope dissected into lateral ridges by deep stream drainages
ELEVATION: 1,600 to 5,738 feet
MANAGEMENT: USFS, Gifford Pinchot National Forest, Randle Ranger District
TOPOGRAPHIC MAPS: Blue Lake, East Canyon Ridge, Tower Rock

The dichotomy in the names of the area's creeks, Doe Creek and Buck Creek, Cat Creek and Mouse Creek, Slickrock Creek and Smoothrock Creek, is perhaps reflected in man's view of the area: exploitation versus preservation. Ten years ago the Blue Lake Roadless Area was nearly double its present size and had a splendid buffer of old-growth forest along slopes leading up to the top of its backbone ridge. Today the flanks of the area are a maze of logging roads connecting clearcut patches. Unfortunately, without a shift in the management direction of the Forest Service, there is scant hope that this "harvest" concept will change. At best the basin holding the azure gem of Blue Lake may be spared, with perhaps a narrow strip along the very crest of Blue

Lake Ridge. Even if logging slows down (or, to dream, ceases), many old trails and abandoned logging roads have been reconstructed to ATV standards, assuring little solitude and wilderness experience for the foot-bound visitor. Perhaps a trip into the area will rekindle memories of what once was, and what could have been, in time to salvage what little wild country is left.

Climate

Blue Lake is on the wet side of the Cascades, so it enjoys about 90 to 100 inches of precipitation annually. Most falls as snow between November and April, and the trails are generally not snow-free until early July. Mid-winter lows average around 15 degrees, and summer highs range in the mid-70s.

Plants and Wildlife

The forest spared from chain-saws is typical of the west side of the Cascades. Principle tree species are Pacific silver fir, Douglas-fir, western hemlock, western red cedar, and white pine.

Mule deer, elk, and black bear are found in the area.

The Blue Lake Butte Trail leads through fields of beargrass.

Geology

The base rock of the area is composed of volcanic andesite flows that form a thick cover over the continental crust. Most of the rock is of Oligocene or Miocene age, about 25 million years old. Some older Eocene andesite and rhyolite are also found in the vicinity.

ACTIVITIES

Hiking

Trail #271, Blue Lake Ridge. 11.2 miles/m (H,S,B,M). From FR 23 (1,916 ft) the route climbs diagonally up the steep southwest slope of Blue Lake Ridge, crossing FR 2317 several times en route. After a breath-catching pause at a bench above Blue Lake Creek, the way climbs to yet another bench and splits. The motorized expressway, Trail #271A, continues uphill to join Trail #272 (4,960 ft). The segment of trail that passes the camp area at the outlet from Blue Lake (4,058 ft) and continues uphill to meet Trail #272 southeast of the lake is restricted to hikers. From the Trail #272 junction the path wanders along the northeast side of the ridge, passes the upper end of Trail #119, climbs to a high of 5,040 feet, then descends a forested drainage to Mouse Lake (4,475 ft). A newly constructed section, rerouted to avoid logging, rounds the lake and drops southwest to FR 7812. It descends the road for about a mile before rejoining the original trail route down to FR 21 (2,790 ft).

Trail #274, Blue Lake Hiker. 2.5 miles/d (H). A rugged new route that avoids motorized congestion in the area leaves the end of FR 2300171 to climb along the north bank of Blue Lake Creek. Crossing steep exposed sidehills and climbing rock stairways, the way passes below a striking 250-foot-high wall of columnar basalt before it meets Trails #271 and 271A at Blue Lake (4,058 ft).

Trail #272, Bishop Ridge. 8.7 miles/m (H,S,B,M). After leaving FR 23 (1,540 ft) the way climbs a steep bank, then turns up the southwest slopes of Bishop Mountain. The track weaves back and forth to avoid steeper spots before finally switchbacking to the ridgetop south of the mountain's summit. Open timber and a few small meadows offer broad views of the Cispus River valley. The way follows the 5,000-foot-high crest southeast past the junction with Trail #271A, to end on Trail #271 southeast of Blue Lake (4,520 ft).

Trail #119, Blue Lake Butte. 3.5 miles/m (H,S,B,M). This old sheepherder's route from FR 78 (4,166 ft) heads up a lateral ridge running east from the area's backbone. A grade wanders up through alternating forest and meadow to its junction with Trail #271, at the head of the Blue Lake basin (4,610 ft).

—33—

GOAT ROCKS WILDERNESS

LOCATION: In Lewis and Yakima counties, astride the Cascade crest south of US Highway 12
SIZE: 105,633 acres
STATUS: Designated Wilderness Area (1964, 1984)
TERRAIN: A series of moderately high summits, with north slope glaciation, that run north–south along the Cascade crest. Deep lateral drainages are separated by steep ridges that rise to timberline meadows and parklands.
ELEVATION: 2,200 to 8,201 feet
MANAGEMENT: USFS, Gifford Pinchot National Forest, Packwood Ranger District; and Wenatchee National Forest, Naches Ranger District
TOPOGRAPHIC MAPS: Hamilton Buttes, Jennies Butte, Ohanapecosh Hot Springs, Old Snowy Mtn., Packwood Lake, Pinegrass Ridge, Spiral Butte, Walupt Lake, White Pass

The Goat Rocks represent what today's Cascade volcanic giants, Rainier, Adams, and St. Helens, will look like (barring further eruptions) 2 million to 5 million years from now. The present-day Goat Rocks are remains of a volcano cone (or cones) that once stood more than 12,000 feet high. Glacial and stream erosion since Pliocene times has reduced this ancient giant to a string of moderate summits linked by ridges capped with short pinnacles of more resistant basalt.

Much of the area's 120 miles of trails travel high ridges near or above timberline, passing through beautiful alpine meadows that flame with wildflower color as soon as the snow melts. There are two large lakes on the western edge of the wilderness, and the high-altitude parklands are sprinkled with dozens of smaller ponds and lakes (and accompanying mosquitoes).

Climate

Climatic conditions vary dramatically with altitude in the Goat Rocks; warm summer days at lower elevations are a sharp contrast to the possibility of sudden near-blizzard conditions at higher elevations, even in midsummer. Higher trails may be impassable due to snow until early August, and September can see the first flurries of winter storms. In general, the area receives between 90 and 110 inches of precipitation annually, over 90 percent of which falls as snow between October and May. Total snowfall averages more than 25 feet, with accumulated depths of 10 feet or more. Temperatures are mild; winter minimums average in the lower teens, and summer maximums rarely rise above the balmy lower 70s.

Plants and Wildlife

Because of its altitude differential, the Goat Rocks Wilderness spans three separate vegetation zones. Dense low-level forests, primarily found in the area's deep stream drainages, are composed of Pacific silver fir, Alaska yellow cedar, western white pine, and noble fir, with associated plants such as boxwood, princess pine, mountain blueberry, pipsissewa, and bunchberry dogwood. Higher slopes have forests of mountain hemlock, subalpine fir, and whitebark pine. Here broad meadows are covered by golden fleabane, sandwort, sheep fescue, penstemon, sibbaldia, cinquefoil, and sedges. When the snow melts the meadows are painted with wildflower color; look for prairie lupine, goldenrod, saxifrage, aster, arnica, paintbrush, phlox, marigold, and avalanche lily. Surrounding the highest peaks are areas of barren rocky soil, talus slopes, lingering snowfields, and small glaciers. Even here, Lyall lupine, mountain hare sedge, white heather, and other small hardy plants find ways to survive in the short growing season.

Among the animals of the wilderness are black-tailed deer, elk, black bear, coyote, pine marten, and cougar. In alpine country hikers can find pikas, and hear the shrill whistle-welcomes of hoary marmots. Mountain goats are frequently seen near Nannie Basin, in the Upper Lake Creek valley, and around the area's highest summits. Several species of grouse are found, and among the sensitive species in the wilderness are the three-toed woodpecker and great horned owl.

Geology

During the Pliocene epoch, volcanic vents erupted at Hogback Mountain, Old Snowy, Ives, and Lakeview Mountain, spewing flows of basalt, andesite, and rhyolite into adjoining river drainages formed from folds of crustial bedrock. Over time erosion from streams and glaciers cut away the older soft rock, exposing sharp ridges composed of these volcanic flows. Further erosion ground volcanic summits down to the present form of the Goat Rocks. On the southwest edge of the region, the younger Mount Adams laid new lava over the ancient basalt. Deposits of glacial till and volcanic detritus were recently overlaid with a thick ash cover from the 1980 eruption of Mount St. Helens; the process of blending this latest of many such volcanic deposits into surface soil can be traced in the alpine meadows of the wilderness.

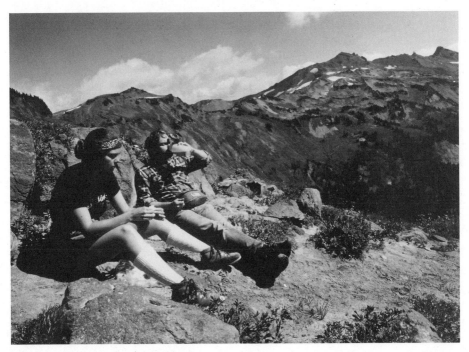

Lunch break in the Goat Rock Wilderness

History

Both the Klickitat and the Cowlitz Indians visited the area for hunting game and gathering herbs and roots. Elk Pass was one of the routes regularly used for trading between Columbia Plateau and Puget Sound tribes. In 1931, 44,500 acres at the heart of the area were dedicated as the Goat Rocks Primitive Area. This was expanded to 72,440 acres in 1935, and in 1940 to 82,680 acres, when it was designated as the Goat Rocks Wild Area. Official wilderness protection was bestowed on the area in 1964, and in 1984 the most recent addition increased its size to 105,633 acres. In the 1930s CCC crews built several trails here to support new fire lookouts atop Lakeview Mountain, Goat Ridge, Hawkeye Point, Nannie Peak, Lost Lake, Round Mountain, and Bear Creek Mountain. None of these lookouts survives today.

ACTIVITIES

Hiking

FR 21, FR 48, FR 1260, and FR 46 all originate on US Highway 12 within 5 miles of Packwood.

FR 21 TRAILS

Trail #98, Nannie Ridge. 4.5 miles/d (H,S). From Walput Lake (3,950 ft) this route heads north via grinding switchbacks and a rough tread to reach the ridgetop (5,880 ft) south of Nannie Peak. An unmarked path leads to the top of the peak (6,106 ft), a former fire lookout site with great views of Adams, St. Helens, and the heart of the Goat Rocks. The trail drops east of the ridge to skirt cliffs on the peak's east face. The ridge is regained northeast of the peak, and the path contours around an intervening knob to the flower meadows surrounding Sheep Lake (5,710 ft), to join the PCT.

Trail #96, Snowgrass. 5.3 miles/m (H,S). There are two trailheads, 0.5 mile apart, one on FR 2150405 (4,660 ft) designated for hikers, and one at Berry Patch on FR 2150040 (4,680 ft) for horses; both join a short distance uphill. The way ascends gently through dense forest to a swampy, mosquito-laden crossing of Goat Creek. A climb up the wooded wall to the east leads to a trail reroute that swings the path west, away from Snowgrass Flat. The famous flower fields of the flat, buried in 1980 by ash from the St. Helens eruption, are being carefully nurtured to assist their comeback. The way climbs through open meadows to a junction with Trail #86 at Alpine Camp (5,930 ft). A 0.5-mile talus and heather scramble uphill meets the PCT (6,440 ft).

Trail #90, Angry Mountain. 9.4 miles/m (H,S). Not for the lazy, this trail leaves FR 2120 (2,700 ft), leans back, and heads for the sky. Eighteen sweaty switchbacks later, the way tops the west end of Angry Mountain (4,950 ft). An easy grade wanders 2 miles east along the crest to a reality check, 23 more switchbacks that grind uphill to the crest east of the mountaintop (5,800 ft). Finally, a pleasant respite, as an open, flower-decked alpine ridge leads east toward the imposing mass of Johnson Peak. Trail #86 is met (6,150 ft) atop the rib west of the summit.

FR 48 TRAILS

Trail #86, Lily Basin. 11.4 miles/m (H,S). A long, long ridgeline route, with endless breath-taking scenery, leaves FR 48 (4,220 ft) on a long gentle grade to the top of the divide (5,200 ft) between Upper Lake and Glacier creeks. Here is the first glimpse down to the broad blue-glass surface of Packwood Lake and, on the horizon above, the glacier-clad summit of Rainier. The route follows the ridge east, first on one side, then the other, then contours around the head of Glacier Creek, skirting the base of cliffs rising to Johnson Peak. The upper end of Trail #90 is passed (6,150 ft) on the ridge west of the peak, and the horizon view now shifts to Mount

Conrad Creek and Gilbert Peak in the Goat Rocks Wilderness

Adams. The way contours the steep barren slope on the south side of the peak around the cirque above Heart Lake (5,700 ft). It continues through alpine parkland at the head of the Middle Fork of Johnson Creek to Goat Ridge (6,600 ft). A traverse of talus slopes to the east reaches Goat Lake (6,430 ft), often ice-clad until late summer. A long gradual descent of alpine meadows meets Trail #96 (5,950 ft) above Snowgrass Flat.

FR 1260 TRAILS

Trail #78, Packwood Lake. 9.6 miles/m (H,S). The section of trail outside the wilderness is blessed with a parallel route to Packwood Lake for motorcycles, leaving a degree of solitude for the foot trail as it ascends through old-growth forest from FR 1260 (2,700 ft) to the lake (2,857 ft). A mass of humanity is rejoined briefly at the Packwood Lake Campground and Resort. The trail heads along the north shore, then leaves the lake and climbs through dense forest to Mosquito Lake (4,853 ft). An uphill grade past the north end of Trail #79 reaches the flower-trimmed shores of Lost Lake (5,165 ft). A stiff climb from here breaks onto an open ridge to meet Trails #65 and #76 (6,250 ft), just below the former site of the Lost Lake lookout.

Trail #79, Coyote. 6.8 miles/m (H,S). About 0.5 mile before Trail #78 reaches Lost Lake (5,150 ft), this route splits off for a long gradual ascent on the west side of the ridge above Upper Lake Creek, with frequent glimpses down the deep valley to Packwood Lake. After skirting the base of Chimney Rock, the track makes an easy descent along the top of a southeast-tending ridge to Packwood Saddle (5,530 ft). Switchbacks negotiate the ridge to the southeast to reach the PCT at Elk Pass (6,700 ft).

FR 46 TRAILS

Trail #65, Bluff Lake. 6.6 miles/m (H,S). A long grinding climb begins (2,840 ft) on FR 4612, and continues relentlessly through old-growth forest to Bluff Lake (3,841 ft). A steep grade clambers uphill to the 5,000-foot level of Coal Creek Mountain, then the way makes a long, diagonal ascent just below the crest of the deep, dark Coal Creek valley. Timber opens to alpine meadows with views north to Rainier as the track climbs to meet Trails #76 and #78 (6,250 ft) just below the summit that once bore Lost Lake lookout.

Trail #61, Clear Fork. 9.6 miles/m (H,S). A long forested ascent leaves the end of FR 46 (3,150 ft), passes Lily Lake (3,660 ft), crosses Trail #76, and wanders gradually up through dense timber above the Clear Fork of the Cowlitz River. At 6.5 miles the way fords the river to begin an uphill thrust to Tieton Pass (4,780 ft), where it meets the PCT and Trail #1118.

US HIGHWAY 12 TRAILS (WEST OF WHITE PASS)

Trail #76, Clear Lost. 6.8 miles/m (H,S). Heading west from US Highway 12 (3,750 ft), the trail descends to cross the Clear Fork of the Cowlitz, then works gradually uphill to cross Trail #61. The way heads up a very steep forested hillside, climbing through ragged palisades to Lost Hat Lake (5,590 ft). A diagonal climb up talus slopes reaches the site of the Lost Lake lookout (6,376 ft), and, just below, meets Trails #65 and #78.

WHITE PASS TRAILS

Pacific Crest National Scenic Trail. 31.1 miles/m-d (H,S).

PCT: White Pass to Elk Pass. 13.2 miles/m. From US Highway 12 opposite the Leech Lake Campground (4,390 ft), the trail makes long lazy switchbacks south to Ginnette Lake (5,420 ft). Passing the upper end of Trail #1144 above the lake, the way heads southwest up the easy ridge, then follows the open rib southwest to Hogback Ridge. A traverse of the shale slopes of the Miriam Lake basin reaches a saddle where Trail #1117A drops into the Shoe Lake basin. Camping is prohibited in the basin.

The way descends into the upper Scatter Creek basin, then climbs, crosses to the west side of the crest, and winds down to Tieton Pass (4,790 ft), where it joins Trails #61 and #1118. The route recrosses the crest at Lutz Lake (5,100 ft), then climbs back over the crest and traverses meadows and talus slopes to Elk Pass (6,500 ft), where it meets Trail #79 from the west.

PCT: Elk Pass to Snowgrass Flat. 3.8 miles/d. The trail segment between Elk Pass and Snowgrass Flat is the highest portion of the PCT in the state (7,100 ft), and the most dangerous section to cross. The track tiptoes along the top of a steep, narrow ridge, not wide enough for horses and hikers to pass each other safely, and exposed to the rake of sudden dangerous storms at any time of the year. At the south end of this catwalk the route traverses between the upper end of the Packwood Glacier and the slopes below the top of Old Snowy, then gradually descends to the parkland above Snowgrass Flat, where it meets Trail #96 (6,440 ft).

PCT: Snowgrass Flat to South Wilderness Boundary. 14.1 miles/m. The route contours east above the headwaters of the Cispus River to Cispus Pass (6,450 ft). After a brief sojourn east of the crest, the way returns to the west side and works down into the Nannie Creek drainage to meet Trail #98 at Sheep Lake. The track descends into the forested hillside above Walupt Creek and swings west on easy slopes above the flower fields of the Coleman Weedpatch. After a slow ascent along alpine ridges, the trail leaves the wilderness.

FR 12 TRAILS (FROM US HIGHWAY 12 EAST OF WHITE PASS)

Trail #1144, Round Mountain. 5.5 miles/d (H,S, but not recommended for stock). Starting at the end of FR 1200830 at Indian Spring (4,310 ft), a wooded uphill slog on a rough, rutted tread climbs past a spur to the top of Round Mountain (5,970 ft), a former lookout site with commanding views of the Tieton River basin. The way continues to the bare, sharp point of Twin Peaks (5,843 ft), with views across the valley to Spiral Butte, down to White Pass, and up the Tieton River drainage into the heart of the wilderness. The route follows the ridge west to meet the PCT (5,400 ft) near Ginnette Lake.

Trail #1118, North Fork Tieton. 4.9 miles/e (H,S). The trail leaves the end of FR 1207 (3,330 ft) at an easy grade up wooded slopes on the west side of the North Fork of the Tieton River. It continues a gradual ascent to Tieton Pass (4,780 ft), where it ends at a junction with the PCT and Trail #61.

Trail #1128, Tieton Meadows. 4.7 miles/m (H,S). After leaving the end of FR 1207 (3,330 ft), the trail spends a brief period on the gentle valley floor along the east side of the North Fork of the Tieton, then lets it rip as 17 switchbacks twist up a wooded hogback to the east. A long diagonal climb winds around three stream headwater basins to meet Trail #1130 (6,230 ft).

Trail #1130, Bear Creek Mountain. 7.4 miles/m (H,S). From the end of FR 1204 at Section Three Lake (6,030 ft), the route heads southwest to a saddle, then slowly ascends to alpine meadows as it winds around the head of Bear Creek basin. From the midpoint of the trail (6,250 ft), a spur switchbacks up the rocky face of Bear Creek Mountain to the old lookout site (7,337 ft) and knockout views of Devils Horn, Tieton, Old Snowy, Ives, and Curtis Gilbert. The way then drops to a forested bench and contours west for more than 2 miles to the west rim of the South Fork of the Tieton drainage. Switchbacks drop down the steep hogback to Conrad Meadows and a gate barring further vehicle traffic up FR 1000776 (4,030 ft).

Trail #1120, South Fork Tieton Loop. 10.1 miles/m (H,S). From the gate on FR 10 at Conrad Meadows (4,030 ft), the way follows the South Fork of the Tieton upstream, and at 4 miles splits into a loop high above the headwall of the basin. A clockwise course zigzags up a steep wooded wall to Surprise Lake (5,255 ft), where a bench (5,700 ft) between cliff bands is followed north to the upper headwater trickle of the South Fork. An unmarked path climbs north up a raw rock slope to another alpine bench below Curtis Gilbert Peak; this can be wandered north as far as Conrad Creek. The loop trail continues around the north side of the basin rim, then switchbacks abruptly down to the trail split point.

Climbing

Although the highest peaks of the Goat Rocks range around 8,000 feet and support a band of glaciers along their north sides, all are relatively easy ascents over mixed rock and snow routes. The northernmost, Old Snowy Mountain, is a large gentle summit only a scramble away from the PCT. Ives Peak has easy routes from either east or west. Although the summit ridge of Curtis Gilbert Peak (8,184 ft), the highest point in the Goat Rocks, is an easy scramble, there are interesting climbs via rock on the south, or glaciers on the north. A number of basalt horns (7,750 to 7,960 ft) on the ridge west of Curtis Gilbert offer a few pitches of C-4 climbing. Among these are Big Horn, Little Horn, and Black Thumb.

Winter Sports

The ridges south of the White Pass Ski Area are popular with cross-country skiers and snowshoers, partly because much elevation can be gained by using the area's main chairlift. From the top of the lift tours head west through bizarre sculptures of snow-plastered trees to the open ridge of Hogback Mountain and great views of the Goat Rocks. With due caution for avalanche conditions, some parties push on to snow camps at Shoe Lake, or even as far as Tieton Pass. The summer route to Round Mountain is another vigorous tour out of the White Pass area. Those willing to put up with a long snow-covered road approach can also enjoy a pleasant trip into Packwood Lake, peaceful without its motorized summer crowds.

34

POMPEY PEAK

LOCATION: In Lewis County, wrapping around the Smith Creek drainage south of Packwood

SIZE: 23,530 acres

STATUS: Semiprimitive Nonmotorized, and Mountain Goat Habitat

TERRAIN: A high divide between the Cowlitz River and the North Fork of the Cispus River, with steep, rugged north-tending ridges cut by the deep canyons of Burton, Dry, and Smith creeks

ELEVATION: 1,030 to 5,900 feet

MANAGEMENT: USFS, Gifford Pinchot National Forest, Packwood and Randle ranger districts

TOPOGRAPHIC MAPS: Blue Lake, Packwood, Packwood Lake, Purcell Mountain, Tower Rock

On the south side of US Highway 12 between Randle and Packwood, densely wooded hillsides climb abruptly from the Cowlitz River valley to a cockscomb rim of rock-faced cliffs. Dark, V-shaped valleys drive deep into this mountain mass, and for a brief moment one can imagine what the surrounding country must have looked like before it was logged. Only the horseshoe-shaped ridges surrounding the Smith Creek drainage are currently managed by the Forest Service as semiprimitive areas, and all of their periphery, as well as the thrust of Smith Creek into their heart, has been heavily harvested. The historic old cross-Cascades Indian trade route along the south rim of the area is only a stone's throw from clearcuts in places, but fading unmaintained tracks atop two north-tending crests still offer real solitude, route-finding challenges, and unsurpassed scenery.

Climate

Due to nearly 4,000 feet of vertical elevation difference, the area's climate differs significantly with altitude. In general, precipitation levels are high, averaging around 100 inches per year, with the bulk of this falling as snow between November and April. The snowpack at lower elevations ranges between 2 and 4 feet, while upper elevations see snow depths of 10 feet or more. Most trails are clear of snow by mid-July. Temperatures are relatively mild, with winter lows averaging between 10 and 20 degrees, and midsummer highs in the mid-70s.

Plants and Wildlife

The altitude differential in the Pompey area spans three separate forest zones. The lower valley floors are covered with western hemlock, Douglas-fir, and Pacific silver fir; red alder, western red cedar, and bigleaf maple are also found in damper locations. The understory in cool, moist areas includes swordfern, Oregon oxalis, oakfern, and devil's club; white foamflower, vanillaleaf, Oregon grape, salal, and oceanspray are found in drier spots. With elevation the forest mix shifts to mountain hemlock, Alaska yellow cedar, subalpine fir, and (in old burns) lodgepole pine. Queencup beadlily, huckleberry, Cascade azalea, and beargrass occur in the ground cover. On the highest ridgetops, clusters of small subalpine fir fringe parklands covered by sedges, beargrass, mountain blueberry, partridgefoot, and heathers, as well as floral displays of asters, shooting star, lupine, Indian paintbrush, and cinquefoil.

Among forest inhabitants are black-tailed deer, elk, black bear, bobcat, pine marten, cougar, raccoon, mink, snowshoe hare, marmot, and a variety of squirrels, chipmunks, and mice. Frequently seen members of the bird community are gray jays, Clark's nutcracker, blue and spruce grouse, and white-tailed ptarmigan. The valley floors are winter range for the deer and elk, and mountain goats have both summer and winter ranges in the area.

Geology

The base rock in the area, common throughout the region, is mostly thick volcanic flows of andesite and rhyolite laid down over a period between 15 million and 35 million years ago. The surface features, the hills and valleys, were shaped by glacial and stream erosion over the last 15,000 years.

History

The area has been visited by local Indian tribes for perhaps as long as 6,000 years. The

A meadow in the Pompey Peak Roadless Area, from Cispus Point

Taitnapam Indians headed into the higher elevations in summer and fall to hunt game and gather berries, medicinal plants, roots, and bark. A major Indian trade route between the Puget Sound tribes and tribes east of the Cascades ran through the area; Trails #7 and #128 follow portions of this route. In the late 1920s to early 1930s, the Forest Service built fire lookouts at area high spots, including South Point, Dry Creek Point, Pompey Peak, and Cispus Butte. None of them remains today. The most obvious activity throughout the region over the past 50 years has been logging, and miles of roads snake up the slopes of every drainage to link the never-ending clearcut scars.

ACTIVITIES

Hiking

Trail #7, Klickitat. 17.1 miles/m (H,S,B). This trail follows an old Indian trade route across the Cascades. Much of the original west end of the trail has been obliterated by logging; the route now starts at the end of FR 5508024 (4,320 ft), atop the divide between the North Fork of the Cispus River and Kilborn Creek. The crest is followed east for over a mile, where a gradual ascent across the south side of Twin Sisters reaches the east end of Trail #128 (5,260 ft). The way bends southeast, crossing alpine parklands below Castle Butte, to reach a spur trail to the top of Cispus Butte (5,450 ft). Here are great views of Rainier, Adams, St. Helens, and

Hood, and (unfortunately) an endless succession of clearcuts hacked from the valley walls of the North Fork of the Cispus River. A diagonal descent southeast skirts rock walls to logging on either side of Jackpot Lake (4,551 ft). This spot can also be reached via FR 20 up Smith Creek.

To the east the original trail has been rerouted out of the Smith Creek drainage to avoid logging; it rejoins the old route at the divide between Smith and Deception creeks. After skirting clearcuts at the head of Deception Creek, the way makes a diagonal climb up the hillside between Cold Springs Butte and St. Michael Lake, then descends to St. John Lake (5,110 ft). A sidehill traverse and a climb to the ridgetop meadows leads to the top of Mission Mountain (5,698 ft). The route now starts a long, gradual descent of the forested rib arcing to the south to reach its present east end at FR 22 (4,400 ft).

Trail #128, Pompey Peak. 5.5 miles/d (H,S,B). From the end of FR 2304 (3,520 ft), a short, gentle grade northwest swings up the forested west shoulder of Pompey Peak, then skirts its steep south side to the gentler east ridge, where a spur leads up the shoulder of Pompey Peak to the summit (5,180 ft), an old lookout site. All other faces of the peak drop away sharply. An impressive view spans the broad Cowlitz River valley, the vertical east face of Goat Dike, the Twin Sisters, and on the horizon the ice-clad summits of Rainier and Adams, and the blast-opened face of St. Helens. The way continues along the narrow ridge around the head of Kilborn Creek to break into alpine meadows. The route then traverses beneath the rocky cliffs of Twin Sisters to a saddle between them and Castle Butte, where it meets Trail #7 (5,260 ft).

Trail #125, Dry Creek. 3.5 miles/m (H,S,B,M). From the Cowlitz River valley the forested slopes rise with neck-craning abruptness beside the deep dark gash of Dry Creek. From FR 20 (1,060 ft), endless long switchbacks work up an imposing hillside to its northernmost point (3,815 ft), once a fire lookout site. Here are great views north across the broad Cowlitz River valley to Mount Rainier.

Trail #123, South Point Lookout. 4.5 miles/d (H,S,B). The route leaves FR 20 (2,740 ft), deep in the Smith Creek drainage, and begins a grueling climb up the forested west side of South Point Ridge, mitigated by ceaseless switchbacks. Two long diagonal sweeps lead to final zigzags to the top of South Point (5,980 ft), a former fire lookout, now a microwave relay station site. The lookout's views remain, including Rainier and Adams, the Goat Rocks, and the rocky face of Smith Ridge across the valley.

35

DARK DIVIDE

LOCATION: In Lewis and Skamania counties, between the Cispus and Lewis rivers on the north and south, and Mounts Adams and St. Helens on the east and west

SIZE: 55,000 acres

STATUS: Unroaded Recreation; Semiprimitive, part Nonmotorized, part Motorized. Includes the Shark Rock Special Scenic Area and the Table Mountain Special Wildlife Area

TERRAIN: Two narrow north–south ridgelines rise abruptly more than 4,000 feet above the adjoining valley floors to form the northern lobes of the area. Twelve peaks over 5,000 feet are scattered along these craggy crests. In the broad southern portion of Dark Divide, ridges frame the headwaters of several creeks that have cut deeply into bedrock as they flow south to the Lewis River.

ELEVATION: 1,550 to 5,880 feet

MANAGEMENT: USFS, Gifford Pinchot National Forest, Mount Adams and Randle ranger districts

TOPOGRAPHIC MAPS: Blue Lake, East Canyon Ridge, French Butte, McCoy Peak, Quartz Creek Butte, Spencer Butte, Steamboat Mtn., Tower Rock

As logging gnaws at the periphery of Dark Divide and old trails are consumed, the Forest Service has tried its best to redirect these paths to avoid, or at least accommodate this disruption. Unfortunately, the voracious appetite for old-growth timber continues to decimate these historic old routes and severely impact both the scenic beauty of the region and access to it. The two northern lobes of the region, which frame the McCoy Creek drainage, rise with neck-popping abruptness to narrow, twisting crests. For the most part these are topped by alpine meadows and rugged rocky outcrops. Ridgetop trails offer splendid views throughout their length, down to creeks and rivers more than 4,000 feet below, and across to the giant ice-clad Cascade volcanoes on the horizon. Although crowded by logging activity, the lower southern portion of Dark Divide still retains prime examples of old-growth forest that can wrap one in a blanket of wilderness solitude. The major creeks that drain the area have cut deep, narrow gorges along much of their courses, and play a rushing-water symphony as they drop steeply down cascades and roll over waterfalls.

Climate

Average annual precipitation runs about 90 inches, varying somewhat with location and altitude. Less than 5 percent of this falls in peak summer months; much of it makes up the 23 feet of snow that drops on the area each year. Except for shaded gullies and north slope pockets, snow is gone at most elevations by July, and the first flakes don't generally fall until November. Temperatures are relatively mild—midwinter lows average 24 degrees, and summer highs run in the low 70s.

Plants and Wildlife

The forests in the Dark Divide Roadless Area are predominately Pacific silver fir and western hemlock, with lesser occurrences of noble fir, Douglas-fir, and western red cedar. In the

ground cover are huckleberry, prince's pine, bunchberry dogwood, rhododendron, queencup beadlily, twinflower, salal, rustyleaf, and dwarf blackberry. The lower southern portion of the area is noted for occurrences of fringed pinesap, on the state Sensitive Plant Species list. Higher on the ridges, subalpine fir and mountain hemlock gain prominence. Old fires are generally credited as the source of the meadows, pastures, and prairies that cover the remainder of the area. These clearings are covered with beargrass and huckleberries, complemented by a wide variety of wildflowers that bloom in early summer.

Small meadows and ponds at lower elevations are important elk calving habitats. The forest also contains black-tailed deer, black bear, marten, and northern spotted owl. The subalpine communities support northwestern salamander, western toad, northern pigmy owl, northern goshawk, evening grosbeak, Clark's nutcracker, and mountain chickadee.

Geology

The bedrock underlying the area is Eocene andesite and rhyolite, from volcanic flows about 50 million years ago. In the middle to north portions of the roadless area are a number of small Miocene dunite intrusions with

Huckleberries are a trailside treat.

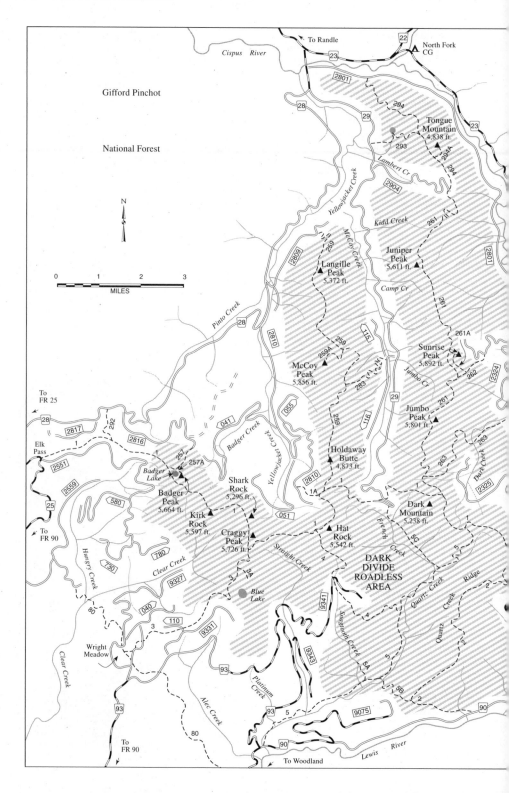

mineralization along their edges. These have led to placer gold mining along McCoy and Camp creeks. Low-grade copper ores have also been found in the area. Continental, then local, glaciers, carved and shaped ridges, sharp arêtes, and cirques enclosing lakes and tarns are found throughout the area. Ridgetop soils are shallow and insecure, while those in the valley bottoms are deep and stable. The 1980 eruption of Mount St. Helens overlaid portions of the region with a layer of fine pumice that will take decades to merge with native soils.

History

Dark Divide contains sites with stone fragments and peeled cedars that would indicate the region was used by natives for hunting and gathering before recorded history. Trail #1, the

Boundary Trail, marked the border between the Rainier Forest Reserve, established in 1897, and the Columbia National Forest, which was created from it in 1908. The latter was redesignated the Gifford Pinchot National Forest in 1949. During the 1930s, fire lookouts were built atop McCoy Peak, Tongue Mountain, Sunrise Peak, Summit Prairie, and Badger Peak; many of the area's trails were put in to support the lookouts and associated fire patrol activities. All of these lookouts were removed, vandalized, or burned by the late 1960s; only the views remain. Many of the trails have been consumed by the region's omnivorous logging, although some were preserved and rerouted by the Forest Service once chain saws had gorged themselves full.

ACTIVITIES

Hiking

Trail #1, Boundary. 31.5 miles/m (H,S, B,M). This historic old trail runs east to west across the region. The path has been cut by logging roads and nibbled on the fringes by clearcuts, but it still retains a modicum of its former stature. On the east side of Dark Divide the route begins on FR 2334 (4,320 ft) and proceeds southwest along the base of Table Mountain. The way winds up to Summit Prairie, where it meets Trail #2 (5,070 ft) north of a former lookout site. A gradual descent northwest reaches a pair of shallow lakes at Dark Meadows (4,360 ft) and finally joins Trail #261.

A jagged contour west crosses clearcuts at the head of McCoy Creek, joins the south end of Trail #259, passes spur Trail #1A to FR 2810 (3,980 ft), then swings around the basin at the headwaters of Yellowjacket Creek. After slinking below the sheer north face of Hat Rock, the route switchbacks down to Yellowjacket Pass (4,350 ft). The way follows the

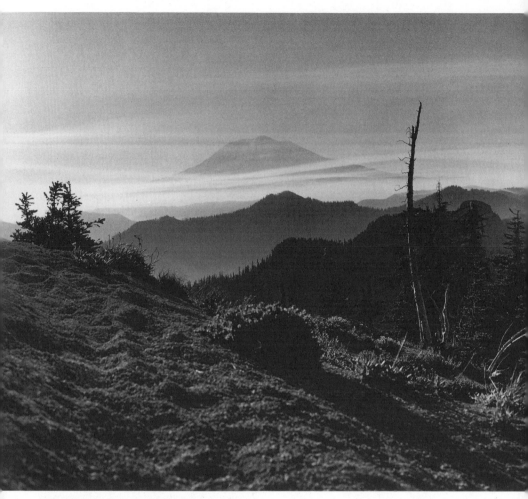

Mount Adams from the Badger Mountain Trail

narrow ridge west toward Craggy Peak, contours its southeast side to meet Trail #3, then turns north along the west base of the peak.

The route snakes up the steep, bare east face of Shark Rock, then traces a narrow ridge west to Kirk Rock. A ridgetop path continues northwest, traverses below Badger Peak, then swings down to a fringe of meadows at Badger Lake (4,940 ft). From here the way follows undulations of the ridge west, between logging incursions from both sides, to Elk Pass (4,080 ft) on FR 25.

Trail #257, Badger Ridge. 0.9 mile/m (H,S,B). The shortest approach to Badger Lake and Badger Peak leaves the end of FR 2816 (4,880 ft) atop Badger Ridge. In early summer the meadowed crest is carpeted with wildflowers, and fall brings a feast of huckleberries. All seasons offer great views of the truncated cone of Mount St. Helens and Pinto Rock, a rugged old volcano core. The path crosses a notch (5,300 ft), passes a spur to Badger Peak, and circles down a basin wall to meadows west of Badger Lake.

The unsigned path to the top of Badger Peak (5,664 ft) leads to a final 300-foot gully to the summit that can be dangerous until snow melts out. This rocky point had its top blasted off for a onetime lookout cabin. The view here is stupendous; close by is the ragged Shark Rock Scenic Area, and Cascade volcanoes—Hood, St. Helens, Adams, and Rainier—glisten on the horizon.

SOUTH-SIDE TRAILS

Trail #2, Summit Prairie. 9 miles/m (H,S,B,M). Starting on FR 90 (2,310 ft), the relocated lower end of this route begins with a deceptively easy diagonal ascent up wooded slopes to a clearcut near the end of FR 9075 (3,220 ft). Here the fun is over, as switchbacks twist uphill to a broad, forested ridgetop (4,520 ft). The way heads north along the top of steep-walled Quartz Creek Ridge, the divide between Quartz and Deer creeks. Most of the time is spent atop the narrow crest, but occasionally the track drops to talus slopes on its east side. The route wiggles east atop the ridge, then north to the former lookout site (5,238 ft) above Summit Prairie, before it descends north to Trail #1 (5,235 ft).

Trail #5, Quartz Creek. 10.6 miles/m (H,S,B). This is the premiere trail on the south side of Dark Divide. It leaves FR 90 near the mouth of Quartz Creek (1,770 ft) on an ancient mining road, then winds along the steep-walled creek bank to cross Platinum Creek. The way climbs out of the narrowing gorge past mining relics, crosses a clearcut, then drops to a shaky log crossing of Straight Creek. A few switchbacks regain a shelf above the deep, narrow course of Quartz Creek. After skirting another clearcut the way enters magnificent old-growth forest as it continues upstream along the rim of the creekbed wall.

The route crosses Straight Creek (2,270 ft), where an unmarked path works uphill for a peek at a beautiful, wide, 50-foot-high falls. The way gradually climbs away from the stream, meets the east end of Trail #4, then drops again to cross Quartz Creek at a wider spot in the drainage. The route recrosses the creek just above French Creek, where Trail #5C heads up that drainage. The path switchbacks up out of the upper Quartz Creek gorge, then climbs to join Trail #1 (4,280 ft) on the divide above Dark Creek.

Trail #3, Craggy Peak. 4.4 miles/m (H,S,B,M). A well-maintained trail from FR 9327 (3,840 ft) ascends through clearcuts, the last of which can also be reached by FR 9331110 (4,280 ft). Logging activity is skirted for another mile, then the route swings around the head of Alec Creek with glimpses down into the cirque containing Blue Lake. Ridgetop meadows are followed to join the southern sweep of Trail #1 (5,200 ft) south of Craggy Peak.

NORTHWEST LOBE TRAILS

Trail #259, Langille Ridge. 8 miles/d (H,S,B,M). This trail, which runs the length of the northwest lobe of Dark Divide, leaves FR 2809 (2,630 ft) in switchbacks up a densely forested slope. The path passes the west base of Langille Peak, then gains the open, meadowed crest at 5,200 feet. Beargrass, wildflowers, and huckleberries (depending on season) accompany the route south along the high narrow ridge, which is broken by weird rock outcrops. The way contours above Bear Creek, then climbs its headwall. It follows the east side, then the top of the ridge south to join Trail #1 (4,525 ft) south of Holdaway Butte.

NORTHEAST LOBE TRAILS

Trail #294, Tongue Mountain. 5.4 miles/m (H,S,B,M). There are two ways to reach the top of Tongue Mountain. The long, tedious route leaves FR 2801 (1,380 ft) to puff and pant through endless switchbacks up a broad ridge (2,800 ft), then continues southeast to Trail #294A (4,020 ft) to the top. A second path leaves FR 2904 at 3,580 feet and ascends north along a broad, wooded ridge for 1 mile to Trail #294A. Both offer breathtaking views from the ridgetop down precipitous wooded slopes to the Cispus River, 3,000 feet below.

Trail #294A, Tongue Mountain. 0.7 mile/d (H). A spur from Trail #294 (4,020 ft) slithers up a difficult, fractured, washed-out path through crumbling rock to the onetime lookout site atop Tongue Mountain (4,838 ft). The weathered trail, not for the faint-hearted, rewards its conquerors with outstanding views of Adams and Rainier.

Trail #261, Juniper Peak. 13 miles/m (H,S,B,M). From FR 2904 (3,640 ft), along the headwaters of Lambert Creek, the way switchbacks up to the ridgetop and follows the crest south to the base of Juniper Peak (5,611 ft). This old sheep drive picks its way along narrow huckleberry meadows atop Juniper Ridge, then slips up cliffs to the crest south of Sunrise Peak. A 0.3-mile spur leads to the top of the peak, an old lookout site with impressive views of Hood, Adams, St. Helens, and Rainier. The way then descends an open berry-field hillside to the broad saddle of

Old Cow Camp (4,707 ft). Next the trail strikes up along the rock cliffs northwest of Jumbo Peak, skirts the west side of this summit, then drops south along the ridge past Trail #263 to meet Trail #1 at Dark Meadows (4,400 ft).

Trail #263, Dark Meadows. 3.2 miles/m (H,S,B,M). From FR 23 (2,500 ft) the way heads southwest through second-growth forest, then heads for the sky up the wooded cliffs of the lower Dark Creek drainage. After crossing the creek it climbs through old-growth timber to meet Trail #261 at meadows near the head of Dark Creek (4,480 ft).

Trail #262, Sunrise. 1.1 miles/m (H,S,B,M). From the end of FR 2324063 (4,200 ft) the route climbs southwest in open flower-covered meadows to end on Trail #261 at the Old Cow Camp saddle (4,740 ft).

Climbing

Although there are no major peaks of climbing interest in the area, several solid and interesting rock outcrops (5,000 to 5,725 ft) offer near-vertical 200- to 400-foot solid rock faces for challenging short climbs. Those along Trail #1 include Kirk Rock, Shark Rock, Craggy Peak, Hat Rock, and Table Mountain. Similar rock faces are found on peaks along Trails #261 and #294. Among these are Tongue Mountain (4,838 ft), Jumbo Mountain (5,801 ft), and three nearby unnamed summits (5,445 to 5,610 ft).

36

MOUNT ST. HELENS NATIONAL VOLCANIC MONUMENT

LOCATION: In Cowlitz, Lewis, and Skamania counties, surrounding Mount St. Helens
SIZE: 110,330 acres
STATUS: National Volcanic Monument (1982)
TERRAIN: The shattered crater of Mount St. Helens is surrounded by steep, rugged ridges denuded by the 1980 eruption, and numerous unique geological features reflecting the effect of this and past eruptions.
ELEVATION: 800 to 8,365 feet
MANAGEMENT: USFS, Gifford Pinchot National Forest, Mount St. Helens National Volcanic Monument Ranger District
TOPOGRAPHIC MAPS: Cougar, Cowlitz Falls, Elk Rock, Goat Mountain, Hoffstadt Mtn., Mount St. Helens, Mt. Mitchell, Smith Creek Butte, Spirit Lake East, Spirit Lake West, Vanson Peak

Mount St. Helens gained worldwide fame on May 18, 1980, when an earthquake triggered a massive landslide, releasing the forces within the mountain in a catastrophic eruption that blew away the north side of the peak, leveled more than 230 square miles of forest with a hot lateral blast, and filled rivers as far as the Columbia with a surge of hot mudflows.

In 1982 Congress created the 110,000-acre Mount St. Helens National Volcanic Monument to preserve this unique environment for research into ongoing volcanism, the natural process of recovery from the eruptive destruction, and visitor education and recreation.

Climate

Climate in the monument varies with altitude; precipitation ranges from 65 inches in the valleys to more than 140 inches on the upper portions of the mountain. Snow, much of which falls between October and March, accounts for most of this precipitation. Lower-level snowpacks are between 2 and 4 feet; mid-altitudes accumulate 7 to 14 feet. July and August are the

Shattered trees, remnants of the 1980 eruption, frame the view from Norway Pass. In the distance are the log-covered Spirit Lake, Mount St. Helens, and its lava flow.

driest months; only 5 percent of the total annual rainfall occurs during those two months. Midsummer temperatures run between 45 and 72 degrees, and winter averages are between 24 and 33 degrees. Extreme temperatures, most occurring with continental easterly winds, can drive winter minimums to minus 15 degrees and raise summer highs above 90.

Plants and Wildlife

The May 1980 eruption drastically altered the biosphere within the monument. The debris avalanche, pyroclastic flows, and mudflows covered an area of 24 square miles on the north side of the summit, in the headwaters of the North Fork of the Toutle, with a layer of debris between 150 and 640 feet thick. Mudflows also wiped out the forest around the South Fork of the Toutle River, and in the Swift Creek, Pine Creek, and Muddy River drainages. The lateral blast

and pyroclastic flows leveled the forest as far as 23 miles north of the crater, and scorched trees on the perimeter of this area.

With a few exceptions, all wildlife in the blast zone was killed, including the entire mountain goat and ptarmigan populations, and an estimated 5,000 deer, 1,500 elk, and 200 black bear. The only mammal survivors on the north side of mountain were those underground at the time of the eruption: gophers, deer mice, Pacific jumping mice, and moles. Where still covered by snow, young trees and plants were unharmed, as were amphibians and fish in secluded snow-covered lakes.

Since the eruption, recolonization has started, first with fireweed, thistles, bracken fern, huckleberry, and willow. Over time a typical conifer forest will once again develop in the area. Toads, frogs, and salamanders have returned to the region, as have elk, black-tailed deer, beaver, and coyote. Birds now seen are ravens, flickers, juncos, bluebirds, sandpipers, killdeer, and several species of ducks.

Some areas were untouched by the eruption; the deep Green River Valley on the northern border of the monument has a dense forest of old-growth Douglas-fir, and the area on the west side of the mountain near Blue Lake has one of the largest known stands of old-growth noble fir. The southwest corner of the monument was touched only by ashfall, and there a healthy forest is dominated by Douglas-fir, Pacific silver fir, western hemlock, and lodgepole pine. The understory contains red huckleberry, rustyleaf, kinnikinnick, salal, creambush oceanspray, oval-leaf huckleberry, beargrass, western fescue, swordfern, penstemon, and silver hairgrass.

Among the mammals in the undisturbed area are elk, black-tailed deer, black bear, cougar, snowshoe hare, porcupine, coyote, bobcat, river otter, beaver, weasel, muskrat, raccoon, skunk, and marten. Birds seen here are grouse, ptarmigan, several species of woodpeckers, sparrows, finches, swallows, vireos, thrushes, wrens, blackbirds, nutcrackers, crows, ravens, spotted owls, screech owls, great horned owls, red-tailed hawks, sharp-shinned hawks, goshawks, osprey, and bald eagles.

Geology

Ancestral Mount St. Helens probably formed about 40,000 years ago, when eruptions of andesite and dacite formed a relatively small cone at the present site of the peak. This primordial mountain was later modified, about 19,000 years ago, by mudflows, lava flows, and pyroclastic eruptions. Some of these flows are evident in the Kalama, Lewis, and North Fork of the Toutle River drainages. About 10,000 years ago, further eruptions were accompanied by pyroclastic flows and ash deposits that can be traced as far east as central Washington.

Some 3,500 years ago, a series of explosive eruptions, accompanied by surges of pyroclastic flows and mudflows into the North Fork of the Toutle River, created a dam that formed the original Spirit Lake. Five hundred to 700 years later, smaller eruptions resulted in pyroclastic flows on all sides of the mountain, and a number of small dacite domes formed.

About 2,000 years ago, ejected materials shifted from dacite to andesite and basalt, and the more recent cones began to form. The Dogs Head dome emerged from the northeast side of the mountain; basalt flows on the south side of the mountain created the lava tube caves and dammed the Kalama River to create Merrill Lake.

Around 1,000 years ago, a lateral blast on the north side of the mountain dumped lava boulders and thick ash deposits north and east of the peak, and two new domes formed, Sugar Bowl on the northeast side of the mountain, and East Dome on the east side.

The once-familiar symmetrical cone was built 300 to 500 years ago in a series of andesite and pyroclastic flows on the west, north, and south sides of the mountain. The most recent eruptions (prior to 1980) were in the Goat Rocks, where a dome formed and lava flowed down both the northeast and south sides of the mountain.

May 1980 marked the cataclysmic event that created the current Mount St. Helens. Two summit fumeroles formed and merged, and the north side of the mountain took on an ominous bulge. A magnitude 5.1 earthquake triggered the total collapse of the north flank, and 0.65 cubic mile of debris surged from the north face at speeds greater than 200 miles per hour, blocked the mouth of Spirit Lake, and drove over intervening ridges at the headwaters of the North Fork of the Toutle. The collapse of the north side of the mountain released pressure on the underlying lava tubes. A huge lateral blast cloud of hot gases and pulverized mountain fragments raced north at speeds to 250 miles per hour and temperatures up to 680 degrees, leveling and destroying anything in its path. A column of powdered ash rose more than 15 miles high, floated east with prevailing winds, and blanketed eastern Washington, Idaho, Montana, and southern British Columbia. Rapid melting of snow and ice, as well as water squeezed from the debris avalanche, caused mud to race down Smith and Pine creeks, the Muddy River, and the North and South Forks of the Toutle River, in hot flows as much as 12 feet above normal river levels. Hot pyroclastic flows followed, depositing lava blocks and pumice on top of debris and mudflows.

The lava dome inside of the crater has since had several eruptive cycles and grown to its present size of 1,400 feet wide and 876 feet high. In view of the history of St. Helens, the present quiescent state of the mountain is certain to give way to similar violent episodes at some time in the next few centuries.

History

Indians probably lived in the vicinity of Mount St. Helens since prehistoric times; at the time the first Euro-Americans arrived, the Klickitats and Cowlitz, along with a half-dozen other minor tribes, inhabited the area.

The mountain was initially seen by Europeans when it was named by Captain George Vancouver during his northwest coastal surveys between 1792 and 1794. The first overland explorers to note the mountain were the Lewis and Clark Corps of Discovery, who visited the area in 1805–06. White settlers were introduced to the violent nature of St. Helens during an eruptive cycle between 1842 and 1853. There were eyewitness reports of steam plumes rising from the summit, lava flowing from a crater on the south side of the mountain, a new smoking crater on its northwest flank, and sporadic heavy ashfall. By 1860 the mountain had entered a temporary dormant period.

Homesteaders, loggers, and miners soon probed the mountain's flanks; the community of Toutle was established in 1876, and a trading post was opened near Spirit Lake in 1876. A logging railroad was extended into the North Fork of the Toutle in 1895, and two years later major logging also began in the South Fork. Miners arrived in 1891, and shortly thereafter claims were staked near Spirit Lake and in the Green River Valley. In 1901, the county completed a wagon road into Spirit Lake to support mining efforts, but mineral wealth proved illusory, and most mines folded by 1911.

St. Helens was included in the first forest reserves in the 1890s, and became a part of the Columbia National Forest in 1908. A ranger station was established at Spirit Lake in 1913, and a fire lookout was built on the summit of the mountain between 1918 and 1921. Although the lookout was abandoned in 1929, lumber fragments from the building were still visible on the site in the late 1970s. Most of the area's trails not destroyed in the 1980 eruption were built by the CCC in the 1930s.

ACTIVITIES

Hiking

HIGHWAY 504 TRAILS

Trail #211, Lakes. 9.3 miles/m (H). The route leaves the boat launch area at the southwest end of Coldwater Lake (2,490 ft), or from an alternate path at the Coldwater Ridge Visitor Center, and follows the northwest shore past fishing spurs. Above is a blast-bared 1,400-foot-high wall. After wandering along the flat valley bottom above the lake, the way climbs into the narrowing drainage of Coldwater Creek, where it meets Trail #230 (2,880 ft). A new trail extension continues upstream, switchbacks up the steep north valley wall past Snow Lake (4,700 ft), then weaves east along the ridge crest to Shovel Lake (4,700 ft).

Trail #230, Coldwater. 4.5 miles/m (H). A strenuous grind leaves Trail #211 (2,880 ft) and weaves uphill, following onetime roads past destroyed logging equipment. It snakes through ridgetop notches to join Trail #1 (5,050 ft) above St. Helens Lake.

NORTHEAST TRAILS

Trail #213, Green River. 7.5 miles/m (H,S,B). In sharp contrast to the devastation in most areas north of St. Helens, the Green River Valley was protected from the eruption (and, equally astonishing, from encroaching chain saws). From FR 2612036 (2,640 ft), negotiate 0.5 mile of blast-leveled timber, then enter huge old-growth Douglas-fir as the way traces the deep, steep-walled river course downstream. The path passes the Minnie Lee Mine, then at 5 miles meets the lower end of Trail #213A. In slightly more than a mile the way reaches the monument boundary and ends on a private logging road (1,879 ft).

Trail #213A, Vanson Ridge. 3.3 miles/m (H,S,B). This link between Trail #213 (2,330 ft) and Trail #217 (4,110 ft) heads east through deep forest, wiggles uphill to the base of wooded cliffs, then sweeps northwest in a bold diagonal climb of the face. On reaching the bench above (3,400 ft), it winds uphill in a more leisurely fashion to join Trail #217 west of Vanson Peak.

Trail #217, Goat Mountain. 8.6 miles/m (H,S,B). After leaving FR 2600130 (3,320 ft), a rugged switchback chain gains the ridgetop (5,000 ft), where the way breaks out of timber to rock and pumice studded with patches of wildflowers and huckleberry bushes. The next 2 miles of open crest have horizon views of Rainier and St. Helens complemented by vistas below of both blowdown and lush old-growth forest. The route drops off the ridgetop to a saddle junction with Trail #218 (4,400 ft), where a spur descends to the shore of Deadmans Lake (4,352 ft). Surrounding woods survived the 1980 blast, but the bottom of this clear, shallow lake is coated with a heavy cover of pumice from the eruption.

Trail #217 continues northwest, regains the crest, follows it a way, then descends to a saddle to meet Trail #205 and the southeast end of loop Trail #217A (4,700 ft). The route drops into a wooded basin to join Trail #213A and a brief path to Vanson Lake (4,190 ft), tucked in a forested bowl on the southwest side of Vanson Peak. A short distance farther is the other end of Trail #217A, and beyond that the monument boundary, well defined by private logging clearcuts.

Trail #217A, Vanson Peak. 1.25 miles/m (H,S,B). A short loop leaves Trail #217 (4,700 ft) on the south side of Vanson Peak, crosses its summit (4,948 ft), then rejoins Trail #217 northwest of the peak (4,140 ft). A foundation is all that remains of a fire lookout once located atop the peak. From the top look down into the deep Green River and Cowlitz River valleys, and along the horizon to Rainier, Adams, St. Helens, and Hood.

Trail #218, Tumwater. 9 miles/m-d (H,S,B). The route leaves Trail #217 (4,400 ft) near Deadmans Lake to follow a ridge crest, first east, then north along the monument boundary. The grade is gentle, with easy ups and downs over ridgetop knobs. At 5 miles a spur scrambles up a narrow ridge to the summit of Tumwater Mountain (5,250 ft) and great panoramic views. The way drops west into a pocket meadow where elk are often seen. It then swings north around a finger rib, diagonals down its cliffy west face, then switchbacks down to reach Goat Creek. A short distance downstream it joins Trail #205 (2,560 ft).

Trail #205, Goat Creek. 6 miles/m (H,S,B). From the end of FR 2750 (2,400 ft) the route traverses the steep, forested hillside to Leona Falls. Here it ducks into a 300-foot-long hollow behind the 100-foot-high falls. Another mile upstream the way meets Trail #218, then bends up the west fork of Goat Creek and climbs steeply to a pocket meadow near its source. It weaves westward up a ridge through another meadow, and across the south face of Vanson Peak to the saddle, where it joins Trail #217 (4,700 ft).

EAST-SIDE TRAILS

Trail #1, Boundary. 20.2 miles/m (H,B). The western segment of this 70-mile-long east–west trail is picked up on FR 99 (4,100 ft) west of Bear Meadow. It climbs west through dense forest, then contours a creek-head basin. Bending around a ridge, the way enters the monument and descends to Clearwater Creek (3,700 ft), where clumps of surviving trees are intermixed with blast-downed forest. Trail #1B wends upstream through blast-flattened trees and clumps of smaller conifers to Ghost Lake (3,785 ft), where downed trees along the shoreline support its name. Trail #1 ascends west to a saddle, then drops through flattened forest to cross FR 26 (3,680 ft). The route weaves up westward through blowdown to Norway Pass (4,500 ft) to meet

Trail #227, and a spectacular view of the crater and lava dome glaring down on Spirit Lake.

After swinging north to Bear Pass (5,600 ft) the way snakes along the bare, convoluted ridge west to Mount Margaret (5,858 ft), where a short spur gains the summit for great views of St. Helens and Spirit Lake. The bald crest is followed west of Margaret and around the west side of the St. Helens Lake basin to Trail #1G, a steep switchback path to the former lookout site atop Coldwater Peak (5,700 ft). Here are impressive views of the crater, the lava dome, St. Helens Lake, Johnson Ridge, and the Coldwater Creek basin.

After passing Trail #230 the way ducks under a natural arch framing Adams in one direction and St. Helens in the other. A contour of the headwaters of Coldwater Creek then passes Trail #207. It heads west to the Johnston Ridge Observatory, en route crossing the fractured, barren landscape of the debris avalanche that overrode the ridge. From the first road switchback west of the observatory, the way descends west to the debris and lahar plain south of Coldwater Lake (2,580 ft).

Trail #227, Independence Pass. *3.5 miles/m (H,B).* From Independence Pass on FR 99 (4,030 ft), the way climbs to a grand viewpoint of St. Helens and Spirit Lake. It continues uphill through blowdown, then bends west to the barren slopes 1,000 feet above the lake, where it heads north toward Norway Pass. En route it passes basalt monoliths, once hidden by forest, now exposed rock-climbing challenges. The route ends on Trail #1 at Norway Pass (4,500 ft).

Trail #224, Harmony. *1.1 miles/m (H).* This is the only access to the shoreline of Spirit Lake. It drops from FR 99 (4,100 ft) to the lake (3,406 ft), passing through blowdown and bleached, blast-sanded stumps. Note the scoured high-water mark formed as waves surged up the shoreline following the eruption, and the mat of dead trees still floating on the lake's surface.

Trail #207, Truman. *7 miles/m (H.B).* From the Windy Ridge parking lot (4,040 ft) the route begins on a gated jeep road used by researchers to access the Pumice Plain below the crater. From the road end (4,550 ft) the way heads north across a desolate, multilayered product of the 1980 eruption. Buried deepest are portions of the massive debris avalanche that obliterated portions of old Spirit Lake and created a huge dam at the outlet of new Spirit Lake. Overlaying this debris are pyroclastic flows and mudflows whose heat sterilized the Pumice Plain. The route wanders across this bleak area, then climbs a portion of the debris avalanche that overrode Johnston Ridge to end on Trail #1 (4,010 ft).

SOUTHEAST TRAILS

Trail #225, Smith Creek. *9 miles/d (H,B).* Starting on FR 99 (4,320 ft) 1.5 miles north of the Windy Ridge Viewpoint, the route follows a twisting, bald, pumice-covered ridge down to the headwater canyon of Smith Creek. It continues atop the broad mudflow that surged down the creek, leveling everything in its path. Near the halfway point the creek, 3 to 4 feet deep, must be forded. The trail leaves the blast area near the creek dropping from Ape Canyon, then continues atop the broad mudflow along the stream course. The way ends on FR 8322 (1,680 ft) at the confluence of Smith Creek and the Muddy River, as it meets Trail #184.

Trail #234, Ape Canyon. *5.5 miles/m (H,B).* From the end of FR 83 (2,860 ft) the route climbs northwest through old-growth forest as it snakes along a ridge on the northeast side of the Muddy River lahar. It occasionally breaks from the trees for glimpses of this broad mudflow plain. At 4,150 feet the trail reaches the deep, narrow defile of Ape Canyon, sliced through 3,600 years of lava flows by the grainy, rasping water. A short distance farther it ends on Trail #216.

Trail #184, Lava Canyon. *2.4 miles/m-d (H).* From a geological point of view this is one of the most interesting trails in the monument. The 1980 mudflows scoured all vegetation from the walls of this narrow canyon, exposing lava flows depicting nearly 2,000 years of the mountain's eruptive history. From the end of FR 83 (2,860 ft), a barrier-free boardwalk leads to the top of a beautiful waterfall. The trail beyond gets a bit dicey, with wet slippery areas and ladders on short cliff faces. The trip is worth it, as it passes more falls and huge columns of basalt that were hard enough to resist the savage carving of the mudflow. The trail ends as it meets Trail #225 and FR 8322 (1,680 ft) at the confluence of Smith Creek and the Muddy River.

SOUTHWEST TRAILS

Trail #238, Toutle. 13.4 miles/e-m (H,S,B). The lower end of this route leaves FR 81 at Kalama Horse Camp (2,030 ft) and follows the north bank of the Kalama River in a gradual ascent east to FR 8100600 (2,670 ft). After passing McBride Lake (2,677 ft) the route climbs to a wooded side-slope traverse to Redrock Pass (3,100 ft), where it crosses FR 81. The way ascends north across an open lava flow into trees to reach the lower end of Trail #238A. The path gradually ascends along the base of Butte Camp Dome, then swings west across a mudflow to reach FR 8123 (3,213 ft).

The trail continues due north along wooded slopes above Blue Lake (3,346 ft), then enters one of the largest stands of old-growth noble fir in the Cascades. It descends into Sheep Canyon to cross a creek, mudflow, and Trail #240 in the drainage bottom. The track climbs out of the canyon, crosses another small mudflow, bends around a minor rib, and drops steeply to the South Fork of the Toutle. After crossing the river it hooks around the sharp nose of Crescent Ridge, to end on Trail #216 (3,300 ft).

Trail #238A, Butte Camp. 3.7 miles/m (H,B). The second most popular climbing route on St. Helens leaves Trail #238 (3,300 ft) and heads north up a steep, wooded slope. The path twists up around the east base of the Butte Camp Dome, zigzags up a steep lava wall, and ends on Trail #216 (4,720 ft) with a sweeping view of the rock and snow slopes leading up to the crater's rim. Climbing permits are required to travel higher.

Trail #239, Ape Cave. 1.5 miles/m (H,B). This link between the two entrances to Ape Cave leaves the main entrance parking lot (2,090 ft) and stumbles uphill over lava blocks to the upper entrance (2,480 ft).

Trail #221, Castle Lake. 3.2 miles/m (H). A maze of private logging roads leads to other trail accesses, but the only route to Castle Lake through the monument leaves Trail #216G and heads north along the line between a barren ridge and the mudflow that filled the North Fork of the Toutle. The route follows this demarcation line northeast to the mouth of Castle Lake (2,510 ft), formed when the debris avalanche dammed the South Fork of Castle Creek.

ROUND-THE-MOUNTAIN TRAIL

Trail #216, Loowit. 28 miles/m-d (H; B on the south side of the mountain between Windy Pass and South Fork of Toutle). This rugged trail, bearing the Indian name for Mount St. Helens, wraps around the mountain between the 4,000- and 4,700-foot levels. Starting from the northeast corner of the crater, at the end of access Trail #216E (3,960 ft), the route contours the rugged jumble of the pyroclastic flow and debris avalanche to a spur trail up to a hot-water falls tumbling from the yawning mouth of the blown-away crater. Farther west the trail becomes very difficult, often washed out, as it weaves through rough moonscape gullies below the open gap in the crater wall. When it reaches the precipitous rim of the South Fork of the Toutle, Trail #216G breaks off to the west, and the main route snakes down to the river bottom to meet Trail #238 (3,300 ft).

The route ascends tight switchbacks east up Crescent Ridge along the fringe of the blast zone, then crosses a mudflow to meet the upper end of Trail #240 (4,600 ft). It then snakes southeast at timberline to Butte Camp Dome, where it joins Trail #238A (4,750 ft). A timberline traverse, difficult because of numerous stream-cut gullies, continues across old lava flows. Trail #216A (4,700 ft) is met after crossing the Swift Creek lava flow. The way now follows the treeline downhill, scrambling in and out of stream-washed gullies with poor tread. At the wall above June Lake, Trail #216B is joined (3,400 ft).

Lost altitude is regained in a very difficult ascent across the Worm Flows and the deep, unstable gashes cut by the headwater forks of Pine Creek and the Muddy River. After negotiating the upper edge of the Muddy River mudflow, the route joins Trail #234 (4,180 ft) near the Ape Canyon overlook. Scenery here is outstanding; Adams and Hood are on the horizon, and above is the breach in the crater wall at the head of the Shoestring Glacier. Below is the broad Muddy River lahar and the narrow cleft carved through old basalt by Ape Canyon Creek.

The grade becomes easier; after fording Ape Canyon Creek the track is nearly flat as it crosses the Plains of Abraham (4,400 ft), swept and leveled by eruption mudflows. After passing Trail #216D at the north end of the Plains, the path turns west and climbs abruptly to Windy Pass (4,850 ft). A gradual downhill grade completes the circuit at the junction with Trail #216E.

Trail #216A, Ptarmigan. 2.1 miles/d (H,B). Part of the most used climbing route on the south side of the mountain, this trail leaves FR 8100830 (3,720 ft) in noble fir forest and climbs, gradually at first, then more steeply, to break out on the Swift Creek lava flow as it meets Trail #216 (4,700 ft).

Trail #216B, June Lake. 1.4 miles/e (H,B). A popular trail, both in summer and winter, leaves the end of FR 8300250 (2,700 ft) and gradually ascends through second-growth forest to the walled pocket holding tiny June Lake (3,150 ft). A beautiful waterfall cascades over cliff walls into the northeast end of the lake. A pair of switchbacks climb to join Trail #216 (3,400 ft) on a bench above the lake.

Trail #216D, Abraham. 2 miles/m (H). This route heads south from Trail #207 at the end of the gated road section of that trail (4,100 ft). It follows a narrow, eroded pumice ridge south to 4,600 feet, then traverses the headwater basin of Smith Creek to meet Trail #216 at the north end of the Plains of Abraham (4,430 ft).

Trail #216G, Castle Lake. 2 miles/m (H,B). This path leaves Trail #216 (4,000 ft) on the rim of the South Fork Toutle River canyon, heads west along the ridge past a junction with Trail #221 (4,240 ft), then traces the monument boundary northwest to Weyerhaeuser Road #3000 (4,200 ft).

Caving

There are at least 56 known caves, all lava tubes, located in the long basalt flow on the south side of Mount St. Helens. Many of these caves have unique, delicate geological features, as well as a varied collection of vegetation, mammals, insects, and invertebrates, many of which are rare and vulnerable species. Casual cave visitors can severely damage this precarious environment by carelessness, ignorance, or vandalism, and the caves' geological features are not likely to be reproduced short of another major basalt flow like the one that created these. Even then, if ever, centuries would pass before the diversity of biota would be replicated. By their very nature caves force even the most careful explorers to trace the same routes, and each visit further disturbs surface features. For this reason, only one of these caves, Ape Cave, is open to monument visitors. The locations of other caves, and paths to their entrances, are not publicized; experienced cavers should contact local speleological groups for more information regarding them.

Ape Cave is the longest known lava cave on the North American continent: 12,810 feet. It was first discovered in 1947, and mapped in detail in 1978. During summer months the Forest Service operates an information center on FR 8303, near the main entrance. The cave has had no artificial development except metal staircases at the main and upper entrances. When visiting the cave, visitors must bring their own lanterns, or rent some at the information center. The cave extends 4,000 feet downslope from the main entrance and 8,000 feet upslope. The upper end of the cave has a stairway exiting a skylight entrance; Trail #239 leads from there back to the information center. Portions of the upper cave are rough going due to breakdown, and there are dropoffs up to 8 feet that must be climbed. The downslope portion of the cave has a sand floor, and is the easiest section for most visitors.

Climbing

The south side of Mount St. Helens was reopened to climbing in 1987, however, permits are required between May 15 and October 31 to climb above 4,800 feet on the mountain. The permit system restricts the number of climbing parties to help preserve the fragile alpine vegetation. The mountain is no longer a technical climb, just a long, dusty, 6-hour uphill slog once the snow has melted off. The view from the rim down to the crater and the lava dome is impressive, and worth the effort, but use extreme caution near the lip, as it is still unstable. There are three commonly used approaches for climbing the mountain: the Butte Camp route, via Trails #238 and 238A; the Monitor Ridge route, via Trail #216A; and the Worm Flows route, via either Trail #244 or #216B. The latter is primarily used in the winter.

Winter Sports

The popular winter recreation area at Spirit Lake disappeared in the 1980 eruption, but it has been replaced by new recreation areas on the south side of the mountain. Two Sno-Parks are located here: Cougar, at the junction of FR 81 and FR 83, and Marble Mountain, at the junction of FR 83 and FR 8312. The latter has a log cabin warming hut, and both have several groomed snowmobile routes. Since the area is popular with both snowmobilers and cross-country skiers, the Forest Service provides separate trails strictly for skiers. Shared trails are marked by orange diamonds, skier-only trails by blue diamonds.

Although a number of winter trails simply follow summer roads, others have been constructed primarily for winter use. The Wapiti Ski Loops, near Marble Mountain, are five trails of varied length, all flat and relatively easy. More difficult are the Sasquatch Ski Loops, three loop trails, totaling 6.7 miles, that climb higher on the mountain. The June Lake and Swift trails climb to timberline following summer Trails #244 and #216B. All of the Cougar routes trace snowbound roads, some as long as a 15-mile round trip. There are several excellent views of snow-mantled St. Helens en route.

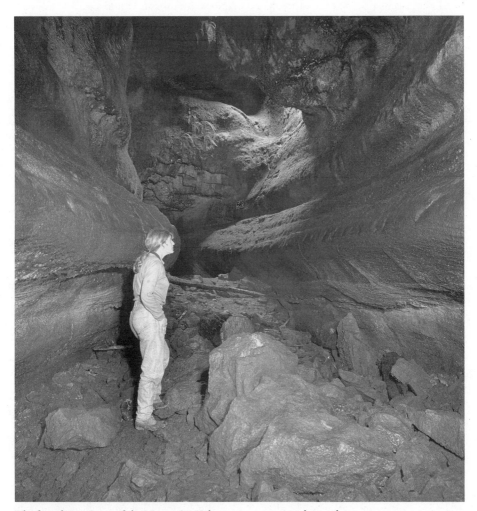

The famed Ape Caves of the Mount St. Helens area are ancient lava tubes.

■────────────────────**37**────────────────────■

MOUNT ADAMS WILDERNESS

LOCATION: In Yakima and Skamania counties, surrounding Mount Adams
SIZE: 42,280 acres; 12,100 acres of adjacent roadless areas
STATUS: Designated Wilderness (1964, 1984); South Midway and West Adams, Semi-primitive Nonmotorized; Gotchen Creek, Unroaded Recreation
TERRAIN: Rising above forested slopes and subalpine meadows is the massive volcanic peak of Mount Adams, with steep rock faces and several large glaciers radiating from the summit.
ELEVATION: 3,300 to 12,276 feet
MANAGEMENT: USFS, Gifford Pinchot National Forest, Mount Adams Ranger District; Yakama Indian Nation
TOPOGRAPHIC MAPS: Glaciate Butte, Green Mountain, Jungle Butte, King Mountain, Mount Adams East, Mount Adams West, Steamboat Mountain, Trout Lake

The second-highest and the most massive of the Cascade volcanoes in the state, Mount Adams, is the focal point and namesake of the wilderness. Forested slopes climb gradually to a timberline level of about 6,600 feet, above which ten major glaciers cloak the mountain to its 12,276-foot summit. The low gradient of the mountain's south side contrasts with the steep icefalls and arêtes on the west side, and the sheer cliffs, precipitous hanging ice, and deep rugged valleys on the east. Most of the wilderness's 64 miles of trails lie at or below timberline. Three link to encircle three-fourths of the base of the mountain; the rest serve primarily as feeder routes to these three. The east side of the mountain, which lies in the Yakama Indian Reservation, has no path along its base, and the few short trails in Tract D of the reservation are open only on a permit basis.

Presently there are three Semiprimitive Roadless areas on the periphery of the wilderness, all deserving protection before they are consumed by logging. South Midway is a wedge-shaped piece of meadow and forest at the northeast corner of the wilderness; West Adams is a thin strip of woodland along the west boundary; Gotchen Creek, on the south side of the mountain west of the Tract D boundary, is a timbered section that includes the geologically and botanically important A. G. Aiken Lava Beds, one of the most recent and accessible lava extrusions on the mountain.

Climate

Average annual precipitation in the area ranges from 90 to 100 inches, almost all of which falls between September and May, mainly in the form of snow. The annual snowfall ranges between 10 and 25 feet, dependent on elevation. Midwinter lows average between 10 and 20 degrees, and summer highs are a mild 70 to 80 degrees.

Plants and Wildlife

Mount Adams's diversity of trees, shrubs, and flowers represents both the wet west side and the dry east side of the Cascades; its wide elevation range also spans several ecological zones. On lower slopes the forest is made up of Pacific silver fir, western hemlock, noble fir, Douglas-fir, western red cedar, and western white pine, with less frequent occurrences of grand fir, Englemann spruce, and lodgepole pine. The understory is composed of huckleberry, salal, prince's pine, rhododendron, queencup beadlily, dwarf blackberry, and twinflower. Higher up the slopes, whitebark pine, mountain hemlock, and subalpine fir are more common, with a groundcover of huckleberry and beargrass. Wet meadows and bogs in subalpine regions host a variety of unique species such as water sedge, bog willow, tall cotton grass, pale laurel, horsetail, elephant's head pedicularis, western tofieldia, and Oregon saxifrage. Among the flowers found in alpine meadows are avalanche lily, white marsh marigold, monkeyflower, Indian paintbrush, gentian, phlox, lupine, mountain red heather, cinquefoil, and penstemon. The harsh environ-ment of lava flows supports rugged plant communities, mostly mosses and lichens.

Common animal species are black-tailed deer, elk, and coyote. Less frequently seen are black bear, pine marten, and mountain goat. At higher elevations, pika and hoary marmot abound. Among the avian population are blue, ruffed, and spruce grouse; white-tailed ptarmigan; moun-tain chickadee; Clark's nutcracker; prairie falcon; red-tailed hawk; gray jay; golden-crowned kinglet; and gray-crowned rosy finch.

Geology

The broad summit of Mount Adams was built from the eruptions of several cones over a wide span of time, rather than through a series of peak-building eruptions forming a single cone, as is common in other Cascade volcanoes. Its lower slopes are pocked with eroded cones and lava flows from numerous other minor eruptive vents. Underlying most of the Mount Adams area is 10-million- to 15-million-year-old Yakima basalt. The earliest eruptions in the immediate vicinity occurred in Pleistocene times, about 450,000 years ago, when andesite flows created most of the mass of the present mountain. More recent additions to the south side of the mountain are a result of eruptions between 12,000 and 25,000 years ago. These occurred during the last advance of the continental ice sheets, which shaped and polished the ragged lava surface of the mountain. The most recent eruptions happened somewhere between 2,000 and 6,000 years ago. A vent near Red Butte extruded the blocky andesite that forms the 10.4-square-mile Muddy Fork flow, one of the largest lava fields in the Cascades. A similar eruption in the vicinity of South Butte also created the A. G. Aiken Lava Beds on the south side of the mountain.

The mountain continues to be sculpted by its active glaciers. Four of these, the White Salmon, Adams, Lyman, and Klickitat glaciers, originate from the summit; the Mazama, Avalanche, Pinnacle, Lava, Wilson, and Rusk glaciers all lie on lower slopes below steep rock headwalls. With the exception of the Rusk and Klickitat glaciers, which have cut deep canyons on the east face of the peak, these lower glaciers are in broad, shallow cirques and fan out to low gradients near their terminuses.

The combination of hydrogen sulfide and glacial meltwater, forming sulfuric acid, has weakened rock faces, causing huge avalanches to break off rocky headwalls. About 5,000 years ago one such avalanche peeled from the west side of the summit above the White Salmon Glacier to form the sheer face of the Pinnacle. More recent avalanches broke off the same area in 1921 and 1983. Other such avalanches have been noted near Devils Garden, Avalanche Valley, and Battlement Ridge.

History

There is evidence of Indian visitation to Mount Adams as long as 9,000 years ago. According to Yakama and Klickitat tribal legends, Pah-to (Mount Adams), one of five wives of the Sun, became jealous of other wives, Wahkshum and Plash-Plash (the Goat Rocks), because each day they were touched by the Sun before Pah-to. She fought with the other two wives and broke their heads off, leaving them the less significant summits of today.

The egotistical Pah-to then went south of the Columbia River and brought back all of the forest plants and animals there to flourish on her slopes. Klah-Klahnee (Oregon's Three Sisters) convinced Wy-east (Mount Hood) to fight Pah-to; in the ensuing battle Pah-to's head was knocked off and scattered to the north (today's Muddy Fork Lava Beds); all of the animals and plants returned south, and the slopes of Pah-to became barren. Since the Great Maker knew that people waiting to be born near Pah-to would need plants and animals to survive, he gave her a new head, the Great White Eagle from the Land Above, who caused her slopes to once again be fruitful and populated with game. The mountain is considered sacred by local Indian tribes.

The 1792 Vancouver expedition to Puget Sound failed to notice the mountain, perhaps because of its more easterly location. The first explorers to note seeing it were the Lewis and Clark expedition in 1805, although observations at the time often confused it with Mount St. Helens. An 1839 proposal to call the Cascades the Presidents Range and name its summits after past presidents, recommended renaming Hood and St. Helens as Adams and Jefferson. Amid confusion in surveys, the name Mount Adams was given to the present peak (and, fortunately, the rest of the renaming scheme fell from favor).

The first verifiable ascent of the mountain took place in 1854, and the second (the first by women) occurred in 1867. In 1897 Mount Adams was included in the newly created Mount Rainier Forest Reserve, and its slopes were opened to grazing leases. As many as 100,000 sheep grazed on the mountain in the early 1900s; this use gradually tapered off until the last permit expired in the 1970s. Between 1918 and 1921 the Forest Service constructed a fire lookout atop

Mount Adams as seen from Adams Glacier Basin

the summit, but frequent poor visibility and the arduous supply route caused it to be abandoned as an active lookout in 1924.

A mining claim was filed on the broad summit in 1929, and sulphur mining began in 1932. A wagon road and pack trail route to support the mining operations saw as many as 168 pack trains a year during the height of operations. Today's South Spur climbing route follows this old path. Sporadic mining occurred here until 1959.

In 1908 the Columbia National Forest, which included Mount Adams, was cut from the Mount Rainier Forest Reserve; the forest was renamed for Gifford Pinchot in 1949. Mount Adams was initially designated as a wild area in 1942; when the 1964 Wilderness Act was signed, 36,356 acres around the mountain became one of its first units. When an old survey error defining the border with the Yakama Indian Reservation was corrected in 1972, 1,000 acres of the wilderness were returned to the tribe, who manage it as a primitive area. The Washington Wilderness Act of 1984 added 6,914 acres along the north and west borders to the wilderness, bringing it to its present size.

ACTIVITIES

Hiking

The east side of Mount Adams, including Tract D along the southeast side of the wilderness, lies in the Yakama Indian Reservation. Permits are required to use trails and campgrounds and to fish within Tract D; the rest of the reservation is closed to the public. Fees are charged for such use; the amount varies with the duration of the stay. During summer months permits may be obtained from the Tract D ranger stationed at Bird Lake.

SOUTH-SIDE TRAILS

Trail #9, Around the Mountain. 8.3 miles/m (H,S). Somewhat misnamed, this trail does not go "around the mountain," but only skirts its south flank. Starting on the west from the PCT at Horseshoe Meadow (5,900 ft), the route meanders southeast through subalpine forest and intermittent wildflower-splashed meadows just below timberline. The path rolls up and down, passes Trail #16 at the head of Crofton Creek (6,160 ft), and crosses Trail #183 at the head of Hole in the Ground Creek (6,280 ft). After crossing the upper edge of the A. G. Aiken Lava Beds (6,250 ft), the way meets Trail #11 at the Tract D boundary, then continues to Bird Creek Meadow (6,100 ft).

Trail #11, Snipes Mountain. 5.7 miles/m (H,S; B to the junction with Trail #71). From its start on FR 8225150 (3,800 ft), the trail climbs through open pine forest along the east side of the A. G. Aiken Lava Beds. At 4,800 feet the path meets the west end of Trail #71, then veers away from the lava beds to follow Gotchen Creek northeast to the Tract D boundary, where it meets Trail #9 (6,290 ft) at the wilderness boundary.

Trail #183, South Climb. 3.4 miles/m (H,S). Once part of the old trail used by pack strings serving the sulfur mines at the summit of Mount Adams, this trail today is the most popular and heavily used route for summit climbs. Starting at Cold Springs Campground (5,600 ft), the route heads uphill, crosses Trail #9 (6,380 ft), then climbs the rib west of the Crescent Glacier to 8,200 feet. Here the maintained trail ends, and a footpath continues up to the "Lunch Counter" (9,000 ft). Above this point the climbing route to the summit follows névé slopes to the false summit (11,500 ft), and then on to the top of the mountain (12,276 ft).

Trail #71, Pine Way. 2.7 miles/m (H,S,B). This old cattle drive leaves FR 8290 at the Tract D boundary (4,270 ft) to climb northwest along a rocky path through second-growth timber before reaching Trail #11 at the edge of the A. G. Aiken Lava Beds (4,800 ft). Bikes are not permitted on Trail #11 above this junction.

Trail #16, Shorthorn. 2.8 miles/d (H,S). After leaving Morrison Creek Campground (4,790 ft), the way follows the Morrison Creek drainage north through thin forest stands and over rocky slopes as it climbs to meet Trail #9 at timberline (6,120 ft). Meadows en route are ablaze with wildflowers in midsummer, and offer glimpses up the Avalanche Glacier to the summit.

Trail #12, Stagman Ridge. 4.3 miles/d (H,S). From a clearcut at the end of FR 8031120 (4,400 ft), the way enters the wilderness and old-growth forest as it proceeds up the crest of Stagman Ridge. To the southeast cliffs drop abruptly nearly 1,000 feet to Cascade Creek. In 1.5 miles the path swings west from the drainage wall to broader slopes with open timber broken by small meadows. The trail jogs west, then climbs a short distance to join the PCT (5,800 ft) west of Horseshoe Meadow.

WEST-SIDE TRAILS

Pacific Crest National Scenic Trail. 20.8 miles/m (H,S). After crossing FR 23 (3,854 ft) east of Swampy Meadows, the PCT climbs north to the wilderness boundary. It then swings east for a gradual ascent through dense old-growth timber to the headwaters of the White Salmon River. A recent relocation of the trail weaves uphill to meet the upper end of Trail #12 (5,800 ft). From there the way contours north to Sheep Lake (5,768 ft), and a short distance farther meets Trail #64. After a brief journey across a lava-bed moonscape at the head of Mutton Creek, the way bends northeast, crosses meadows and forks of the Lewis River, then meets the upper end of Trail #112 (6,020 ft). Crossing rocky slopes at Adams Creek, the way wends through open forest and meadows to meet Trails #113 and #10 (6,110 ft). The trek continues northeast past the west end of Trail #114 (5,910 ft) near a splattering of small ponds and marshes. The way now descends gradually north through thick forest to cross Trail #13 (5,231 ft), then weaves around the south and west sides of the Muddy Fork Lava Beds before descending to FR 5603 (4,750 ft) north of the wilderness boundary.

Trail #112, Divide Camp. 2.8 miles/m (H,S). This route starts on FR 2329 (4,720 ft) southeast of Takhlakh Lake, then climbs gradually southeast up forested slopes interspersed with small meadows. At 5,678 feet a spur leads southwest to Divide Camp on the West Fork of Adams Creek. The main trail ascends another 0.8 mile to meadows to meet the PCT (6,020 ft).

NORTH-SIDE TRAILS

Trail #113, Killen Creek. 3.1 miles/m (H,S). From FR 2329 (4,584 ft) south of Killen Creek Campground, the route ascends south-southeast through timber and small meadows. It breaks into a meadow with a wildflower carpet as it meets the PCT (6,084 ft).

Trail #13, Muddy Meadows. 4 miles/m (H,S). From the end of FR 2329087 (4,410 ft), the route slogs through Muddy Meadows, with glimpses of the north side of Adams soon wiped out by dense old-growth forest. The way now heads seriously uphill over rough, rocky footing through open timber to cross the PCT (5,231 ft). An easy grade heads east, then swings south as it ascends a wooded wash to end on Trail #114 (5,860 ft).

Trail #114, Highline. 7 miles (5.3 miles to the Yakama Reservation Boundary)/m (H,S). From the PCT at the head of Killen Creek (5,900 ft), this route heads east on a roller-coaster course across forested slopes on the north side of Mount Adams. After passing the upper end of Trail #13, it ascends to a pleasant little meadow at Foggy Flat (6,000 ft). The way swings south and gets down to serious climbing as it scrambles up through the jumble of the terminal moraines of the Lava and Lyman glaciers. The icefalls of these two glaciers tower above, and below are the huge Muddy Fork Lava Beds. The indistinct tread, marked by large rock cairns, continues up to top a barren, wind-swept ridge (7,750 ft) just below the Devils Garden (the Yakama Reservation boundary). Switchbacks drop down rock slopes, then the track skirts the lower end of the Wilson Glacier to reenter subalpine forest at a saddle (7,020 ft) between Adams and Goat Butte. The path weaves through open timber and meadows as it descends into Avalanche Valley and a pleasant campsite (6,600 ft) at a tarn above Rusk Creek.

Climbing

Mount Adams (12,276 ft), the second-highest peak in the state, is the only summit in the wilderness. At least 25 routes have been put up this popular mountain, ranging in difficulty from nontechnical to very challenging ice and rock climbs. The 6,000-foot elevation gain from timberline to the summit, the possibility of sudden storms, whiteouts, and below-zero wind-chill temperatures require good physical conditioning, proper equipment, and navigation skills for a safe ascent, even on the easiest routes.

The easiest routes—Mazama Glacier, South Spur, Southwest Chute, and Avalanche–White Salmon Glacier—are on the long, mild-gradient south slope. Routes on the west and north sides of the mountain, up the Pinnacle, Adams, Lava, and Lyman glaciers and intervening cleavers, are more difficult, and all are rated at G-II. They often involve heavily crevassed glacier segments, up to 1,000 feet of 40- to 50-degree ice or narrow exposed ridges. The most challenging routes, ranging from G-II to G-III, are found on the remote east side of the mountain, where vertical headwalls tower above the steep, narrow cleavers dividing the long narrow icefalls of the Wilson, Rusk, and Klickitat glaciers.

Winter Sports

Sno-Parks are maintained south of the wilderness (north of Trout Lake) at Pine Side and Smith Butte. Sixteen miles of groomed, signed ski trails follow snowbound logging roads from these two locations. The South Spur climbing route is a popular spring skiing or snowshoeing trek, but it may involve several miles of approach march, depending on how high the roads have melted out. The climb is crevasse-free, but it can be avalanche-prone and very hazardous in stormy weather or whiteout conditions. The summer route must be followed meticulously, and wanding to mark a descent route is advisable.

38

SIOUXON CREEK

LOCATION: In Clark and Skamania counties, south of Yale Lake and the Swift Reservoir
SIZE: 26,800 acres
STATUS: Mostly Semiprimitive Nonmotorized and Semiprimitive Motorized; smaller portions are Roaded Natural and Roaded Modified
TERRAIN: A broad creek basin, including low-elevation watercourses and high, forested bordering ridges
ELEVATION: 600 to 4,169 feet
MANAGEMENT: USFS, Gifford Pinchot National Forest, Wind River Ranger District; Washington State Department of Natural Resources; some private logging company lands
TOPOGRAPHIC MAPS: Bare Mountain, Cougar, Mount Mitchell, Siouxon Peak

The Siouxon Creek basin is a bastion of uncut forest land amid an otherwise heavily logged-off region. The multiple forks of the creek flow from high, bounding ridges down deep, quiet canyons covered with a canopy of second-growth trees, not replacements for logged generations, but the rebuilding of a forest destroyed by fires over 90 years ago. The creek and its tributaries are famous for the numerous flashing waterfalls, plunge pools, and rippling cascades that mesmerize visitors along trails through the area.

Climate

The local climate varies with elevation, but in general the area receives between 90 and 100 inches of precipitation annually, 95 percent of which falls between September and May as snow. Annual snowfall varies between 8 and 20 feet depending on altitude. Temperatures are quite mild; winter lows average in the mid-20s, and summer maximums range in the upper 70s. Lower-elevation trails are generally usable from the end of May to the end of November; those on the ridgetops are open from July through October.

Plants and Wildlife

Although the Siouxon Creek basin is mostly forested, its near-uniform tree cover is less than 100 years old. The Yacoult burn of 1902 denuded much of the old-growth forest, and the current forest is mostly second-growth Douglas-fir. Other significant timber species include western hemlock, western red cedar, and bigleaf maple. The understory brush is made up of vine maple, Pacific rhododendron, western yew, Oregon grape, salal, red huckleberry, and trailing blackberry. Herbs and forbs here include evergreen violet, twinflower, swordfern, sweetscented bedstraw, and cutleaf goldthread; berries and mushrooms are abundant.

The creek bottom is a winter range for elk and black-tailed deer, and black bear are also found in the vicinity. Much of the area surrounding Horseshoe Ridge has been identified as spotted owl habitat. The snags that remain standing from the Yacoult burn also provide homes for cavity-dwelling mammals and birds.

Geology

The entire area is underlain by thick, multilayered volcanic flows of andesite breccia of the Ohanapecosh Formation. These range from 25 million to 50 million years in age. The surface soil is an eroded volcanic mix that tends to be unstable along Siouxon Creek. The highest summits in the basin have rock outcrops atop broad talus slopes.

History

The higher ridgelines of Siouxon are rumored to contain prehistoric artifacts, indicating they were probably used by native tribes for berry and herb gathering for several thousand years. The large September 1902 forest fire that swept the region completely destroyed the forest cover, with the exception of isolated pockets of trees along the creek bottoms. When the Forest Service intensified its fire-prevention efforts in the 1930s, most of the present trails were put into the area, several by CCC crews. Hickman's Cabin, alongside Trail #130, was built in the same period for use as a fire-crew base camp; it is one of the few standing artifacts of that era. Fire lookout sites were manned at times atop Horseshoe Ridge, Huffman Peak, and Mount Mitchell.

ACTIVITIES

Hiking

Trail #130, Siouxon. 12 miles/m (H,S,B). The lower end of the trail can be accessed from two points on FR 5701. From the westernmost of the two (1,820 ft), the way gradually descends the forested slopes on the south side of Siouxon Creek, passes Hickmans Cabin and the lower end of Trail #129, then meets FR 5701 again at the road's end (1,360 ft), the second access point. The route crosses West Creek and passes near the first of several delightful cascades and waterfalls that enrich the trip upstream. In less than a mile the west end of Trail #140 is passed. Shortly, the way crosses Horseshoe Creek at yet another waterfall, then bends away from the creek to bypass a narrow steep-walled section of the streambed. In another mile the route returns to water's edge to meet the east end of Trail #140 and the lower end of Trail #156. After passing the start of Trail #130A, the way crosses beneath a foaming falls on Chinook Creek (1,540 ft), then swings southwest up the ever-steepening walls of the Siouxon Creek canyon. It's all uphill from here, first in a long diagonal sweep up the east slope above the creek, then in

A frothing cascade on Siouxon Creek

rugged switchbacks to a bluff above the west drainage rim. More switchbacks surmount the final rib and reach FR 58 (3,500 ft).

Trail #129, Huffman Peak. *6.9 miles/m (H,S,B).* Just east of Hickmans Cabin, the route leaves Trail #130 (1,340 ft), zigzags down to a challenging wade of Siouxon Creek (1,190 ft), then starts a haul up the steep, forested sidehill to reach a saddle on the ridgetop (2,000 ft). The cliff-rimmed crest is followed northeast for 2 miles to a talus slope below a rocky knob, then swings around the north side of Huffman Peak. The summit (4,106 ft) can be reached by a rock-and-meadow scramble. The track stays atop a narrow, wooded crest to the northeast, passes the upper end of Trail #156, and continues on to the summit of Siouxon Peak (4,169 ft), with great views of Rainier, St. Helens, and Hood, as well as Swift Reservoir and Mount Mitchell, to the north. Just north of the summit the track meets FR 6403216 (4,050 ft).

Trail #140, Horseshoe Ridge. *6.9 miles/d (H,B).* At its west end the route leaves Trail #130 (1,290 ft) 1 mile from the end of FR 5701. Switchbacks work up through dense forest to the northwest end of Horseshoe Ridge (2,600 ft). The way continues east atop the narrow steep-walled ridge, enjoying breaks of tiny meadows clad in beargrass and huckleberries. After reaching the ridge high-point (3,495 ft) the path merges with FR 5700320 for 0.1 mile at the toe of the horseshoe, then starts down its north web. After a long diagonal descent, a few switchbacks complete the drop back to Trail #130 (1,400 ft).

Trail #156, Wildcat. *2.5 miles/d (H,S,B).* From Trail #130 on the bank of Siouxon Creek (1,410 ft), this route struggles through 21 switchbacks up a wooded nose before the grade tempers somewhat (2,800 ft). The way then continues up the ridge to join Trail #129 (3,600 ft). A major reward for the effort is the view of tumbling 75-foot-high Wildcat Falls near the start of the climb.

Trail #130A, Chinook. *2.1 miles/m (H,S,B).* The way leaves Trail #130 near the confluence of Chinook and Siouxon creeks (1,600 ft) to climb steeply up the side of the Chinook Creek drainage, passing beautiful cascades en route. It ends on FR 6403 (2,640 ft).

Winter Sports

The lower portions of Trail #130 can be reached in early winter or late spring for short periods of cross-country skiing. The snowy solitude of the valley floor makes a good 1-day tour with no avalanche danger.

39

INDIAN HEAVEN WILDERNESS

LOCATION: In Skamania County, between the White Salmon and Wind rivers
SIZE: 20,960 acres
STATUS: Designated Wilderness Area (1984)
TERRAIN: A 4,500-foot-high bench with forest, open meadows, a plethora of ponds and small lakes, and several alpine ridges and volcanic cinder cones
ELEVATION: 3,020 to 5,927 feet
MANAGEMENT: USFS Gifford Pinchot National Forest, Mount Adams Ranger District
TOPOGRAPHIC MAPS: Gifford Peak, Lone Butte, Sleeping Beauty

Indian Heaven Wilderness, which in early summer could justly be known as Mosquito Haven Wilderness, covers a mid-altitude plateau spattered with over 150 small lakes, marshes, and ponds amid meadows and open forest. The meadows lie at the base of many wooded warts and knobs, as well as the area's highest summits, all bearing the easily identified shape of old volcanic cones. Summer visitors up to the challenge posed by biting bug hordes will find a sea of color as the meadow wildflowers burst into bloom. A more pleasant time to visit, however, is fall; the pests have mostly died off, and the palette of early frosts mixes brilliant scarlets and golds displayed on huckleberry bushes and other deciduous plants. A feast of ripe purple huckleberries is an added attraction.

Climate

Indian Heaven receives moderately heavy precipitation, in the order of 90 to 100 inches annually. Most falls between November and April as snow, with 4 to 6 feet accumulating by midwinter. Fortunately for recreationists, the snow is mostly gone by mid-July. Temperatures in the winter are relatively mild, with minimums ranging in the low 20s. Summer highs average a pleasant 74 to 78 degrees.

Plants and Wildlife

The forested segments of the wilderness contain Pacific silver fir, noble fir, and subalpine fir, with less frequent occurrences of Douglas-fir, mountain hemlock, white pine, and lodgepole pine. The extensive meadow communities on the plateau support a wide variety of plants including water sedge, cotton grass, bog willow, western aster, marsh horsetail, camas, willow weed, shooting star, elephant's head pedicularis, marsh violet, northern starflower, and several species of sphagnum mosses.

The area is a summer and fall habitat for black-tailed deer and elk; black bear love to feast on its huckleberries. Most lakes over three acres in size have some rainbow and eastern brook trout, and several are stocked regularly.

Geology

The entire Indian Heaven Plateau is made up of recent volcanic rock, dating from Pleistocene times. Virtually every knob and high spot along the crest was once a volcanic cone that released basalt and andesite flows and scattered bursts of volcanic fragments on the surrounding landscape. These eruptions were mainly one-shot affairs, building a cone of only a few hundred feet. Two larger cones are East Crater, with 600-foot-high walls and a small pond in its depressed center, and Lemei Rock, whose broad, fractured crater now contains Wapiki Lake.

History

Native tribes regularly visited the Indian Heaven area for more than 9,000 years. The area's rich huckleberry fields resulted from periodic fires that cleared off the encroaching forest. These fires were either intentionally set by Indians, accidentally triggered by berry-drying fires, or caused by lightning. During the early 1900s, Indian Heaven saw large groups from the Yakama,

Klickitat, Cascade, Wasco, Wishram, and Umatilla tribes meet here annually to pick and dry huckleberries, fish the lakes, hunt and dry meat, tan hides, make baskets, and engage in trading and social rituals. The Indian Race Track, in the southern part of the wilderness, was the site of one such gathering. The track, 10 feet wide and about 2,000 feet long, was used by the Indians to race horses; fast, strong horses were prized possessions.

ACTIVITIES

Hiking

Pacific Crest National Scenic Trail. 16.4 miles/m (H,S). The trail leaves FR 60 at Crest Horse Camp (3,490 ft) to ascend through forest to the southern wilderness boundary. The path wanders down a broad bench between two wooded volcano cones, past Trail #171A, to the Indian Race Track. Switchbacks climb to the long, flat top of Berry Mountain (5,000 ft) and views of Hood, St. Helens, and Adams. More switchbacks drop off the north end of the mountain to a contour of the southeast side of Gifford Peak. The path arrives at Blue Lake (4,630 ft), meeting Trail #111. A rerouted segment of trail continues north, winds around the base of East Crater, and arrives at Junction Lake (4,730 ft), where it meets Trail #48.

The new trail, uphill from the boggy old pond-and-puddle route, continues north to Bear Lake (4,750 ft). A short distance farther is Deer Lake (4,770 ft) and an intersection with Trail #33. The way picks up the 5,000-foot contour line along the southwest side of Bird Mountain, passes the upper end of Trail #29, then ascends to a saddle (5,237 ft) on the north side of the mountain, where it is joined by Trail #108. After skirting a small knob, the route traces the crest north to Sawtooth Mountain.

The PCT stays on the west side of the mountain; those wishing to climb along its summit can take Trail #107, a rugged 2-mile parallel route along a narrow ridge. Cautious scrambles over loose rock to its top (5,353 ft) give acrophobic views down the sheer east face. Just north of the mountain, the trail leaves the wilderness and descends gently to the berry fields straddling FR 24 (4,238 ft) just south of Surprise Lake Indian Campground.

WEST-SIDE TRAILS

Trail #171, Race Track. 3.1 miles/m (H,S). At Falls Creek Horse Camp on FR 65 (3,490 ft), the way heads southeast through second-growth forest, crosses the creek, and climbs a rocky tread to reach flatland forest (4,200 ft). In another mile, a shallow pond at the edge of the receding meadow marks the Indian Race Track. Trees are rapidly reclaiming most of the 2,000-foot-long path over which Indians held riding competitions for half a century. The route continues south from the meadow as it climbs toward the Red Mountain lookout (4,965 ft) at the end of FR 6048.

Trail #111, Thomas Lake. 3.3 miles/d (H,S). Starting from a clearcut on FR 65 (4,450 ft), the way heads uphill through thick timber to a passage between Dee, Heather, and Thomas lakes (4,300 ft). It continues uphill east past Brader Lake (4,470 ft), several smaller ponds, and Naha Lake (4,740 ft), to the west shore of Rock Lake (4,780 ft). Here the way wends southeast past more small lakes and ponds to the narrow path between Lake Sahalle Tyee (4,670 ft) and Blue Lake, where it joins the PCT (4,640 ft).

Trail #29, Placid Lake. 3.5 miles/m (H,S). Leaving FR 3000420 (4,120 ft), the path descends gradually through old-growth forest to Placid Lake (4,042 ft). It skirts the north end of the lake, passes a spur to Chenamus Lake, then weaves up the steepening wooded slopes to the east. Subalpine meadows are entered on the west flank of Bird Mountain, where the way joins the PCT (4,980 ft).

EAST-SIDE TRAILS

Trail #108, Cultus Creek. 1.5 miles/d (H,S). Originating at Cultus Creek Campground (3,988 ft) on FR 24, the route switchbacks up through steep, lightly timbered slopes, then into huckleberry meadows and talus to a saddle (5,237 ft) on the north end of Bird Mountain. Here enjoy views of Adams and Rainier before crossing west of the crest to meet the PCT (5,150 ft).

Trail #33, Indian Heaven. 3.3 miles/m (H,S). From Cultus Creek Campground (3,988 ft), the way heads southwest through dense forest as it works up the steep east flank of Bird Moun-

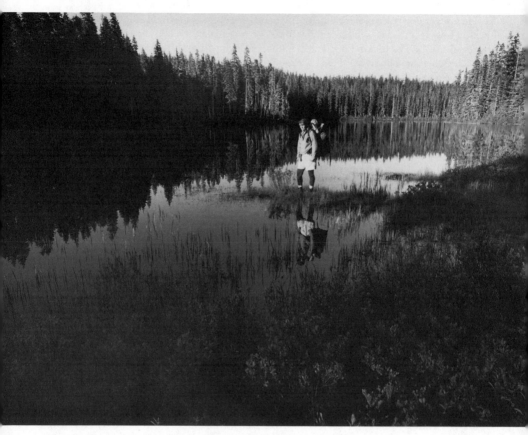

Placid Lake, in the Indian Heaven Wilderness, is well named.

tain. It swings south past cliffs on the upper portion of the mountain, then passes a short spur to Deep Lake (5,087 ft). At Cultus Lake (5,070 ft) the way meets Trail #34 at a saddle (5,100 ft) between Bird Mountain and Lemei Rock. The path descends 0.3 mile south, turns west along a shoreside meadow at Clear Lake (4,950 ft), and ends on the PCT at Deer Lake (4,770 ft).

Trail #34, Lemei. 5.3 miles/d (H,S). The way leaves FR 24 (3,650 ft) on an abandoned road-bed on the north side of Smoky Creek. It then starts a long gradual ascent due west through thick second-growth forest. The path plods uphill through older and less dense timber, then passes a spur to Lake Wapiki (5,250 ft), tucked in a pocket that was once part of the crater cone of Lemei Rock. Trail #34 breaks into meadows and steepens as it climbs to a saddle (5,600 ft) on the north shoulder of Lemei Rock, a scenic spot with views of Wapiki Lake and the cliff face of the rock. The way descends west to Cultus Lake, where it joins Trail #33 (5,100 ft).

Trail #48, East Crater. 2.5 miles/m (H,S). From FR 6035 (4,080 ft) the route starts in forest and wiggles uphill to meadows spattered with a dozen or more small lakes and ponds. A gradual ascent around the east base of East Crater leads to Junction Lake (4,730 ft), where the way meets the PCT.

Winter Sports

With some of the adjoining forest roads now being plowed in winter, the gentle terrain of the wilderness, relatively avalanche-free, is becoming more popular as a ski-touring destination. Check with the Mount Adams Ranger Station to find which roads are clear when planning such a trip.

40

TRAPPER CREEK WILDERNESS

LOCATION: In Skamania County, between the Wind River and Siouxon Creek
SIZE: Wilderness, 6,050 acres; adjacent Bourbon area, 4,540 acres
STATUS: Designated Wilderness (1984); Bourbon, 30 percent Semiprimitive Nonmotorized, 70 percent Roaded Natural
TERRAIN: Steep, heavily forested ridges make a horseshoe wrap around the deep Trapper Creek drainage.
ELEVATION: 1,200 to 4,268 feet
MANAGEMENT: USFS Gifford Pinchot National Forest, Wind River Ranger District
TOPOGRAPHIC MAPS: Bare Mountain, Termination Point

This major creek drainage, and its delightful variety of ecological zones, have been preserved from omnipresent chain saws by a 1984 grant of wilderness status. An equal amount of virgin territory that borders the northeast side of the region begs for the same protection. Trapper Creek runs nearly the length of the wilderness; it and its clear, sparkling tributaries dive steeply downhill, cutting deep canyons and rolling tumultuously over waterfalls before settling down to a valley-floor meander to the Wind River. A single lake is captured in a cliff-walled cirque at the southwest corner of the wilderness. The high enclosing ridges offer spring wildflower displays, fall huckleberry feasts, and horizon-stretching scenic views.

Climate

Although the wilderness receives annual precipitation of 90 to 100 inches, fortunately for recreationists only 5 percent of this falls between June and August. The amount dropping as snow varies with altitude, ranging from 8 feet at lower levels to 20 feet at upper elevations. Low temperatures in midwinter are around 24 degrees, and midsummer highs average a mild 74. Most trails are accessible to hikers from May to November, although in the highest areas snow clings through June, and flurries can be expected in October.

Plants and Wildlife

Lower-level forest cover is made up of Pacific silver fir, western hemlock, noble fir, western red cedar, Douglas-fir, and western white pine. The understory includes salal, rhododendron, rustyleaf, prince's pine, queencup beadlily, twinflower, bunchberry dogwood, huckleberries, and dwarf blackberry. Higher subalpine ridges see whitebark pine, mountain hemlock, and subalpine fir. Meadows here have a carpet of beargrass and huckleberries, along with a wide assortment of wildflowers that appear as soon as the snow melts.

Among the woods' residents are black-tailed deer, elk, black bear, cougar, bobcat, and pine marten. Pikas and whistling marmots inhabit higher-elevation rock outcrops. Grouse, white-tailed ptarmigan, northern spotted owl, barred owl, goshawk, pileated woodpecker, gray jay, and Clark's nutcracker all make their homes here.

At the northwest corner of the wilderness is the Sister Rocks Research Natural Area. The RNA is preserved for the study of subalpine forests and soils, as well as the ecology of the Pacific silver fir, which occurs in the area in a variety of vegetation communities.

Geology

The base rock of the Trapper Creek area is a thick series of basalt and andesite flows dating between 25,000 and 50,000 years ago. The region has numerous basalt outcrops that fracture and drop to talus slopes.

History

In 1910 a Portland brewing company built a hotel and resort at Government Mineral Springs, a half-mile upstream from the mouth of Trapper Creek. Guests were brought 15 miles by horse-drawn wagon from Carson to this vacation spot. The resort was elegant for its day, with flower gardens, mineral baths with purported curative powers for all sorts of ailments, a dance pavilion, and a riding stable. A campground, very popular with families, was built east of the hotel. The resort flourished in the Prohibition era, when it was said to have been a haven for liquor and gambling. The hotel burned to the ground in 1935, but the campground, enhanced by the work of CCC crews in the 1930s, remains today. The Trapper Creek Wilderness has the resort to thank in part for its existence. Early forest plans required non-logged buffer zones beside roads and near places such as the resort. Because the property, plus its buffer space, effectively sealed off any easy access to the Trapper Creek basin, the forest there escaped cutting.

Although the path to the top of Observation Peak predates Forest Service activity in the area, most of the area's trails were built in the 1930s to support fire-suppression activities. Fire lookout sites were once manned atop Observation Peak and Sister Rocks.

ACTIVITIES

Hiking

Trail #133, Soda Peaks Lake. 5.6 miles/d (H). From the 1.5-mile point on Trail #192 (1,450 ft), the way drops 100 feet southwest to a bridge over Trapper Creek, then heads west up a steep, forested hogback. It weaves and bobs up the crest at the edge of the steep north face to

Trapper Creek streams through moss-covered rocks in the Trapper Creek Wilderness.

reach a tiny saddle (3,250 ft). The ridgetop widens for 0.5 mile, then in a final uphill thrust arrives at the cirque holding Soda Peaks Lake (3,760 ft). From the lake the way ascends the north and west sides of the cirque to a gap between Soda Peaks (4,250 ft). Here it drops northwest down a narrow, wooded finger ridge to meet FR 54 at its junction with FR 5400331 (3,670 ft).

Trail #192, Trapper Creek. *6 miles/e-d (H,S).* This long route traces Trapper Creek from its mouth to its headwaters. From a common trailhead with Trail #194 on FR 5401 (1,150 ft), the gentle, wooded grade parallels the road to Government Mineral Springs. Here Trail #132 takes off to the northeast, and in another 0.5 mile Trail #133 leaves to the southwest. The way now steepens as it ascends diagonally up the slope on the east side of Trapper Creek. It climbs into second-growth forest and maintains its distance above the creek as it snakes up the drainage. The route crosses Trapper Creek, then abruptly climbs the 700-foot basin headwall to a spectacular view of 100-foot-high Trapper Falls. A gentler grade above the basin ends as it joins Trails #132 and #158 (3,800 ft).

Trail #132, Observation. *7.4 miles/m (H,S).* One mile from the start of Trail #192 (1,300 ft) this route climbs 200 feet, then begins a steady diagonal ascent of the west flank of Howe Ridge.

The path swings through the steep Lush Creek drainage, then heads up through old-growth forest to the crest (3,200 ft). It crosses the ridge to continue the ascent across rocky slopes on the east flank of Observation Peak. At a saddle northwest of the summit, a spur heads to the top of the peak (4,207 ft), a former lookout site, and what a sight indeed! The tops of St. Helens, Adams, Rainier, and Hood are seemingly a touch away, and on a clear day vistas stretch across a vast sea of forested ridges as far north as Mount Baker, and south to Mount Jefferson.

Trail #132 continues northwest to a saddle junction with Trails #158 and #192 (3,800 ft). A gentle climb north leads to the shoulder of Sister Rocks where an 0.5-mile cross-country scramble southwest gains their summits (4,261 ft and 4268 ft), a former lookout site. An easy descent north through huckleberry-laden meadows arrives at the junction of FR 58 and FR 5800224 (3,550 ft).

Trail #194, Dry Creek. 4 miles/m (H,S). From the joint trailhead with Trail #192 on FR 5401 (1,150 ft), the route meanders along the west bank of Dry Creek, passing through intermittent old-growth groves. After crossing Bourbon Creek, the path ends on Trail #158 (1,550 ft).

Trail #158, Big Hollow. 3.2 miles/d (H,S). The way leaves FR 64 (1,480 ft), crosses Dry Creek, passes the north end of Trail #194, and climbs due west up an ever-steepening spur from Howe Ridge. A sometimes testy wade of a fork of Hollow Creek leads to huckleberry meadows and the junction with Trails #132 and #192 (3,800 ft) northwest of Observation Peak.

41

SILVER STAR MOUNTAIN

LOCATION: In Clark and Skamania counties, between the East Fork of the Lewis River and the Washougal River

SIZE: 12,545 acres

STATUS: Semiprimitive Nonmotorized; Washington State Department of Natural Resources and private timber production

TERRAIN: Sharp ridges with rocky outcrops radiate in all directions from the top of Silver Star Mountain. Deep stream drainages cut steep-gradient slopes between ridge crests.

ELEVATION: 1,200 to 4,390 feet

MANAGEMENT: USFS Gifford Pinchot National Forest, Wind River Ranger District; Washington State Department of Natural Resources; portions of one section privately owned

TOPOGRAPHIC MAPS: Bobs Mountain, Dole, Gumboot Mtn., Larch Mtn.

This bald, rocky summit, more than 4,300 feet high, looms above the Columbia foothills northeast of the Portland–Vancouver area. It was heavily wooded prior to a 1902 forest fire; subsequently its burn-bald summit was made a fire lookout site. Although its forest cover has never regenerated to its former stature, the remaining rock and meadow slopes nurtured a variety of plant species that adapted to the new environmental conditions. Today these are diverse and unique enough that the area is a highly prized botanical reserve. In addition to its flora, the treeless ridgetops offer horizon-filling views of surrounding volcanic peaks and the urbanized lowlands along the Columbia River. Roads that invaded the western portion of the area in the 1940s were placed off-limits to motorized traffic in 1984, and have gradually degenerated to trails. The net result, barring intrusive logging efforts, is a wonderfully scenic semi-wilderness within sight and easy hiking distance of Columbia River population centers.

Climate

The average annual precipitation ranges between 75 and 85 inches. Temperatures are mild;

midwinter lows run in the mid- to upper 20s, and summer highs are usually a comfortable 80 degrees. The area is free of snow by May, and remains so until November. This area is one of the earliest to enjoy wildflowers, which generally begin blooming by the end of May.

Plants and Wildlife

The bottoms of some creek drainages have pockets of old-growth Pacific fir, western hemlock, noble fir, and western red cedar, and some upper slopes have open stands of second-growth Douglas-fir. More than a third of the area has not recovered its forest cover since the 1902 Yacoult burn, and it remains meadows and rock outcrops. Common meadow species are beargrass, vine maple, salal, Oregon grape, big huckleberry, red huckleberry, and twinflower. The wide variety of bushes, herbs, and wildflowers found here, as well as several uncommon species such as the endangered Clackamas corydalis, has made Silver Star a candidate to be made a Biological Special Interest Area.

A large number of black-tailed deer live in the region's forests, as do black bear, cougar, Lewis woodpecker, blue grouse, and Larch Mountain salamander.

Geology

The entire area lies atop a granitic pluton that intruded Eocene oceanic basalt, andesite, and rhyolite sometime in mid- to late-Tertiary times. Typical of such intrusions, the periphery became mineralized and has been the scene of intensive prospecting. Over a hundred unpatented mining claims were filed within the area's boundaries, and placer gold, some platinum, and low-grade copper have been found.

History

The Silver Star region has attracted archaeological interest with the discovery of at least ten sites of prehistoric human activity. Among these are pits dug on a ridge near the top of the mountain. The purpose of these pits is unknown; speculation is that they were used either as spots for ritual isolation during a guardian spirit quest or possibly as blinds for hunting animals flushed upslope.

Placer gold was discovered in the East Fork of the Lewis River, the Washougal River, and their tributaries in the 1890s, and the Washougal Mining District was soon the site of heavy prospecting. No significant lode ores were found.

In 1902 the massive Yacoult burn consumed 283,000 acres of timber, including that in the Silver Star area; only isolated stands deep in creek drainages survived. Aged silver snags from the burn are still found today in open meadows and second-growth patches of trees on the mountain. In the years following the fire, the Forest Service intensified its fire-control effort in the area. In the 1930s, CCC crews constructed a road to a lookout site atop Silver Star Mountain, and several ridgetop trails were put in to support fire suppression.

ACTIVITIES

Hiking

Trail #180, Silver Star. 2.5 miles/m (H,S). FR 4109 climbs south from Copper Creek to a gate (3,080 ft) where it is closed to motorized traffic and becomes Trail #180. The route continues up the old rocky roadbed through meadows bedecked with wildflowers, swaying stalks of beargrass, and huckleberries. It ends as it meets Trail #172 (4,130 ft); a short spur continues to the summit of Silver Star Mountain (4,390 ft) and wide views to Rainier, St. Helens, Adams, and Hood, as well as down to the Columbia River Gorge and segments of metropolitan Vancouver and Portland.

Trail #175, Starway. 3.3 miles/d (H,S). The trail departs from rough, difficult FR 4107 (1,620 ft) in a switchback chain up the steep, rugged, wooded ridge on the east side of Star Creek. The never-ceasing grind continues up the narrowing ridge backbone to talus and brush, where the route becomes obscure and poorly marked in places. As the south-tending ridge merges with another from the east, the way ends on Trail #172 (3,800 ft).

Trail #172, Bluff Mountain. 7.8 miles/d (H,S). From the end of torturous FR 4100502 (3,070 ft), the path descends to a saddle, then contours through old burns beneath cliffs on the north side of Bluff Mountain. At a col west of the mountain the path shifts to the south side of the ridge and heads west below Little Baldy. West of this knob, the path traces the narrow, rocky crest past the upper end of Trail #175, then skirts the north flank of Silver Star Mountain to meet the spur to the top and Trail #180 (4,130 ft). Abandoned FR 4107 is followed south to an X-junction with the Sturgeon Rock Trail and Trail #174. In 0.4 mile the way leaves FR 4107 to head west down another rocky, eroded roadbed. It descends through old-burn meadows, thick with a carpet of beargrass and wildflowers, passes below Pyramid Rock, and drops to DNR Road 1200 at Grouse Creek Vista (2,375 ft).

Tarbell Trail. 2.5 miles/m (H,S). This DNR trail leaves a common trailhead with Trail #172 at Grouse Creek Vista (2,375 ft), contours through second-growth into the Rock Creek basin, and passes above a beautiful 100-foot-high waterfall. The way switchbacks up to cross the Sturgeon Rock Trail at a narrow saddle (3,040 ft) east of the rock itself. Nine long switchbacks drop north to Coyote Creek (1,950 ft), then the route works its way uphill around the head of the basin. A traverse west along the side of Squaw Butte at 2,500 feet leads to a broad northwest-

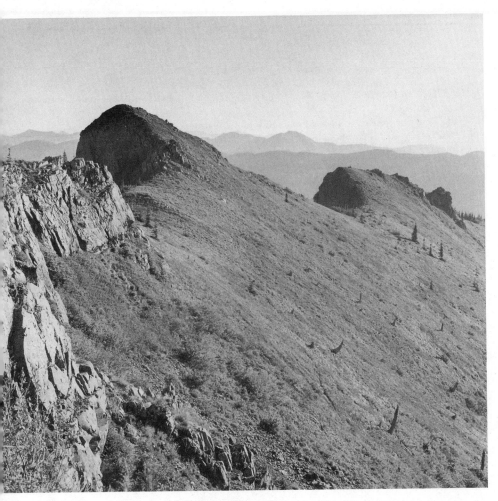

The view east along the crest of Silver Star Mountain

directed ridge. The way descends the gentle wooded rise to the Tarbell Picnic Area (1,700 ft).

Sturgeon Rock Trail. *4.5 miles/m (H,S).* From DNR Road 1210 southwest of its crossing of Coyote Creek (1,350 ft), this abandoned roadbed wanders east, then north to a 2,000-foot saddle where it crosses into the Rock Creek drainage. The track continues uphill past Sturgeon Rock to a saddle junction with the Tarbell Trail. An ascent from here through open fire-cleared meadows meets Trail #172 (4,060 ft) west of the summit of Silver Star Mountain.

Climbing

Sturgeon Rock (3,100 ft), at the west side of the area north of Rock Creek, has a few leads of technical rock climbing on its north face.

Winter Sports

FR 4109 into Silver Star from the north is generally driveable in winter to within a mile or so of the start of Trail #180. A ski or snowshoe trip the remainder of the way to the top of Silver Star is easy and hazard-free, and offers excellent wintertime views of Portland, Vancouver, and the nearby volcanic summits of the Cascades.

42

BIG LAVA BED

LOCATION: In Skamania County, between Indian Heaven Wilderness and the Columbia River
SIZE: 19,300 acres
STATUS: Semiprimitive Nonmotorized, and Roaded Natural
TERRAIN: The area is composed of two sections, the Big Lava Bed and the Big Huckleberry Mountain–Grassy Knoll area. The former is a lightly forested jumble of huge lava blocks that once flowed from a crater at its north end; the latter is a sharp Y-shaped group of ridges that meet at the summit of Big Huckleberry Mountain.
ELEVATION: 2,400 to 4,202 feet
MANAGEMENT: USFS Gifford Pinchot National Forest, Mount Adams and Wind River ranger districts
TOPOGRAPHIC MAPS: Big Huckleberry Mtn., Gifford Peak, Little Huckleberry Mtn., Willard

The unique feature of this roadless area is the 12,500-acre lava bed that covers a 9-mile-long by 1- to-4-mile-wide swath on its east side. The eruption that generated the lava flow occurred 3,000 years ago—a few moments ago, geologically speaking. As a result, it has not succumbed to inevitable erosion, but instead has a vast jumble of sharp rock towers, intriguing fractures in the lava surface, short caves, and a moonscape appearance. The crater that vented this eruption is at the north end of the area, rising about 600 feet above the surrounding landscape. A fairly uniform stubble of lodgepole pine combined with the scrambled landscape makes the lava bed an excellent place to get lost during cross-country explorations.

The western portion of the area consists of a trio of ridges radiating from Big Huckleberry Mountain. The crests are a combination of light forest and open subalpine meadows with excellent views and an interesting diversity of botanical features. Unfortunately, logging activity has gnawed right up to the base of these ridges and threatens to consume what little is left of their virgin forest.

Climate

The mean annual precipitation for the area is 100 inches, with a substantial portion of that occurring as snow; average annual snowfall is about 8 feet. Winter low temperatures average in the mid-20s. Summers are dry and comfortably warm; average summer highs range in the lower 80s. Less than 5 percent of the precipitation falls between June and August, and the area is mostly snow-free between May and October.

Plants and Wildlife

With only nominal soil, and no known source of underground water, the lava beds are still about 70 percent rock, although vegetation from the surrounding forests is slowly populating the area. Sparse stands of lodgepole pine have spread across most of the lava bed, and an occasional isolated Douglas-fir can also be found. The only shrub unique to the area is trailing juniper. In the surrounding forest, and making some inroads into the lava beds, are communities of Sitka willow, white alder, black cottonwood, mountain wormwood, and subalpine fir. Understory members include hedge nettle, figwort, beargrass, vine maple, salal, Oregon grape, queencup beadlily, western prince's pine, bunchberry dogwood, deerfoot vanilla fern, various species of huckleberry, and a number of mosses and herbs. The ridge area between Big Huckleberry Mountain and Grassy Knoll has a typical forest of Pacific silver fir, western hemlock, noble fir, western white pine, western red cedar, and Douglas-fir. Grassy slopes along the crests have dense growths of huckleberries.

Animals found in the region are black bear, black-tailed deer, a few elk, and marten. Larch Mountain salamanders hide in the lava bed, and the forested section of the area is also habitat for blue grouse, Lewis woodpeckers, and pileated woodpeckers.

Forest covers much of Big Lava Bed. In the center of the photo is the cinder cone that was the source of the flow.

Geology

The base rock beneath the area consists of several layers of mid-Tertiary pyroclastic volcanic flows. The unique surface formation of the Big Lava Bed is of far more recent origin; the cone at the north end of the area ejected one or more lava flows to create this bed less than 3,000 years ago. The lava is fractured by many cracks and folds, and has not suffered any significant smoothing erosion. Soil layers are sparse or nonexistent.

History

The volcanic cone that created the Big Lava Bed erupted within historical times, but little is known about the area since then. Two primitive trails once crossed the area, possibly made by Indians, since they predated any Forest Service presence in the region. Big Huckleberry is thought to be a summer campsite used by the Klickitat tribe when gathering herbs, roots, and huckleberries. Peeled cedars, whose bark was used to form baskets to carry the harvest, have been reported near the trail to the mountain. Grassy Knoll was also once a fire lookout site. The meadows between Grassy Knoll and Big Huckleberry Mountain were used for sheep grazing between 1920 and 1940.

ACTIVITIES

Hiking

There are no maintained trails in the Big Lava Bed, and because of the jumble of lava blocks, the uniform thin cover of lodgepole pine, and the lack of unique identifiable features, it is very easy to get lost when exploring the area. The most interesting feature of the beds is the crater from which they erupted. The forested walls rise about 400 feet above the surrounding lava beds, and the 200-foot-deep depression in its center holds a tiny meadow where a profusion of wildflowers grows in early summer. Also of interest is a deep T-shaped trough with near-vertical sides, located a half-mile west of the crater. The nearest cross-country approach is from FR 60 south of the junction with FR 6000240.

Trail #146, Grassy Knoll. *5.5 miles/m-d (H,S).* From the junction of FR 68 and FR 6800511 (2,850 ft), the route heads uphill in swatches of forest between clearcuts to the top of a long northwest–southeast trending ridge (3,600 ft). The way follows the crest northwest to Grassy Knoll, then continues along ridgetop meadows with brilliant spring wildflower displays, fall huckleberries, and fantastic views of Mounts Hood and Adams, the Big Lava Bed, Mount Defiance, and the Columbia Gorge. The trail then contours the forested west slopes just below the ridgetop to intersect the PCT (4,000 ft) west of the summit of Big Huckleberry Mountain.

Pacific Crest National Scenic Trail. *11.7 miles/m (H,S).* After crossing FR 68 east of Panther Creek (2,786 ft), the PCT heads into the Big Lava Bed area atop the divide between Cedar and Mouse creeks. It continues a gradual winding ascent through forest and subalpine meadows to the west shoulder of Big Huckleberry Mountain, where it meets Trail #146 (4,000 ft). A spur pops up to the top of the mountain (4,210 ft) and great views of the Columbia River Gorge and nearby volcanic summits in Washington and Oregon. The way now heads north through ridgetop meadows, then descends to the west edge of the Big Lava Bed (3,200 ft). The route traces the winding perimeter of the bed north for 3 miles before arriving at FR 60 and Crest Horse Camp (3,510 ft).

Opposite: *The view from Copper Pass into the Lake Chelan-Sawtooth Wilderness Area*

CENTRAL WASHINGTON

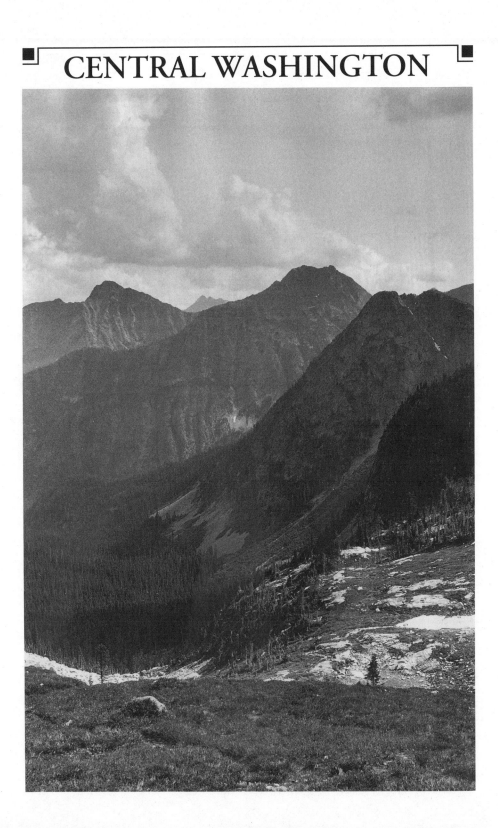

■┌────────────────────**43**────────────────────┐■

PASAYTEN WILDERNESS

LOCATION: In Whatcom and Okanogan counties, along the Canadian border between Ross Lake and Toats Coulee Creek

SIZE: 530,000 acres

STATUS: Designated Wilderness Area; 505,000 acres designated in 1968, 25,000 acres added in 1984

TERRAIN: High rugged ridges and peaks in the west and subalpine parkland plateaus in the east, both cut by deep, densely wooded drainages

ELEVATION: 2,550 to 9,066 feet

MANAGEMENT: USFS, Okanogan National Forest, Winthrop and Tonasket ranger districts

TOPOGRAPHIC MAPS: Ashnola Mtn., Ashnola Pass, Bauerman Ridge, Billy Goat Mtn., Castle Peak, Coleman Peak, Crater Mountain, Frosty Creek, Horseshoe Basin, Hozomeen Mtn., Hurley Peak, Jack Mtn., Lost Peak, McLeod Mountain, Mount Lago, Mt. Barney, Pasayten Peak, Pumpkin Mtn., Remmel Mtn., Robinson Mtn., Shull Mtn., Slate Peak, Sweetgrass Butte, Tatoosh Buttes

"Immense" is the only adjective to appropriately describe the Pasayten Wilderness. It is 54 miles across, east to west, and from 10 to 23 miles deep, north to south. It contains more than 160 lakes, and at least as many creeks and rivers, a dozen of which flow through deep steep-walled canyons. Nearly 150 of its summits exceed 7,500 feet in elevation. More than 600 miles of trails wander the wilderness; the longest runs 73 miles, from the eastern boundary to the Cascade crest.

Climate

The climate varies markedly across the vast expanse of the wilderness. Annual precipitation averages 106 inches on the west and 31 inches on the east. Average midwinter minimums swing from 15 degrees on the west to 8 degrees on the east; temperatures drop much lower with altitude and storms. Summer highs in the west are in the balmy 70s, while the east side sees average highs in the 80s and occasional days 10 to 15 degrees warmer. Eastern trails are generally snow-free by early July; high trails in the west often don't melt out until early August. Most snowfall occurs between October and May, but the entire area is susceptible to sudden storms.

Plants and Wildlife

The forest communities in the wilderness are diverse, varying with both altitude and east–west location. At lower altitudes in the west the forest is mostly Pacific silver fir, Alaska cedar, and western hemlock, shifting with altitude to subalpine fir, Englemann spruce, and subalpine larch. On the east slope of the Cascades the dominant species are grand fir, Douglas-fir, western white pine, and, at higher elevations, western larch and subalpine fir. Lodgepole pine is the first species to regenerate in burn areas, which are scattered throughout the wilderness. Subalpine parklands have growths of lupine, sedge, and cinquefoil.

The high steppes in the eastern portion of the wilderness have a varied cover of low sagebrush, fescue, Sandberg's bluegrass, tufted phlox, sedges, penstemon, cinquefoil, and alpine pussytoes. Lodgepole and ponderosa pine are the most common trees.

Wilderness inhabitants include white-tailed and mule deer, moose, marten, black bear, wolverine, gray wolf, grizzly bear, cougar, mountain goat, bighorn sheep, and the largest lynx population in the Lower 48 states.

Geology

According to plate tectonic theory, the western half of the wilderness was once part of a continental shelf on the east side of the North Cascades micro-continent originally located in the mid-Pacific. Thick layers of sandstone laced with marine fossils built up on this submerged shelf between 100 million and 140 million years ago. About 100 million years ago the shelf was raised above sea level, and plate movements brought this terrane and the North American continent closer together in the vicinity of Southern California. Over the next 40 million years the new coastal plain was intruded by several granitic plutons along a north–south arc. The microcontinent slid north along the coast of North America to finally dock firmly in its present position about 50 million years ago. The crushing meeting of the two pieces of continental crust was followed by faulting and folding along the line of contact. The section between the Pasayten Fault (on a line roughly northwest from Eightmile Creek to the Pasayten River) and the Ross Lake Fault (along the east side of that lake) dropped, forming the Methow graben.

The eastern half of the wilderness is underlaid by a vast granite batholith, which intruded somewhere between 80 million and 100 million years ago on the coast of another terrane that had merged earlier with the west coast of North America. The waves of ice sheets that moved south across the area up to 15 million years ago scraped and smoothed this granite to the large basins and broad saddles found in that area today. The glaciers also carved the deep channels throughout the wilderness, forming the characteristic U-shaped north–south valleys through which its major rivers and creeks flow. In post-glacial times the lower portions of several of these drainages have been incised by rapidly moving water to form deep, narrow gorges with near-vertical walls.

Local alpine glaciers that remained after the retreat of the continental ice sheet further molded the landscape to sharpen ridgelines and cut the cliff-walled cirques that contain many of the area's lakes. The largest glacier in the wilderness today is the Nohokomeen Glacier on the northwest side of Jack Mountain. Several other higher peaks also have small pocket glaciers clinging to their north faces.

History

There is some evidence of prehistoric Indian travel in the upper Lost River area, and nomadic tribes are thought to have roamed the region as early as 6,500 B.C. The late 1800s saw the first contacts between natives and whites entering the region. By 1871 the question of Indian-versus-settler land ownership demanded resolution, and the US government assigned the tribes to various reservations. In 1879 the Moses Reservation, encompassing most of the present-day Pasayten Wilderness, was established for the Columbia tribe under Chief Moses. The tribe, whose traditional lands were farther southeast near the Columbia, refused to move to the re-

The Pasayten Wilderness hosts the largest lynx population in the Lower 48 states.

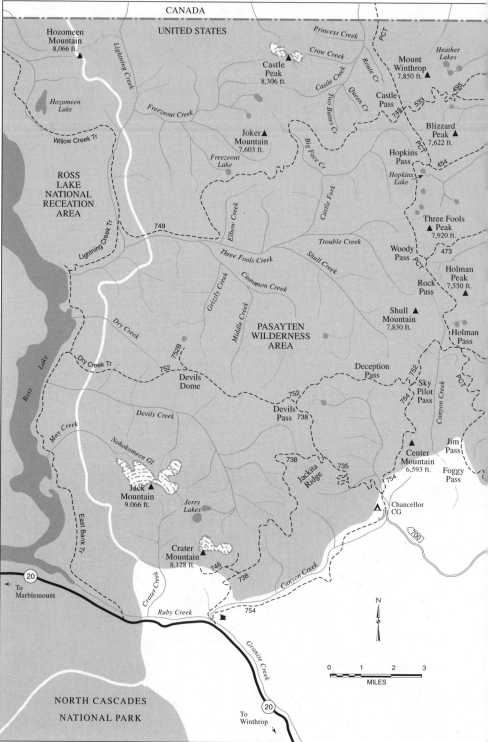

CANADA

UNITED STATES

Hozomeen
Mountain
8,066 ft.

Lightning Creek

Princess Creek

PCT

Crow Creek

Castle
Peak
8,306 ft.

Mount
Winthrop
7,850 ft.

Heather
Lakes

Route Cr

Castle Creek

Queen Cr

Two Buttes Cr

Castle
Pass

749

533

495

Hozomeen
Lake

Freezeout Creek

Willow Creek Tr

Joker
Mountain
7,603 ft.

Big Face Cr

Blizzard
Peak
7,622 ft.

Hopkins
Pass

454

ROSS
LAKE
NATIONAL
RECEATION
AREA

Freezeout
Lake

Hopkins
Lake

PCT

Elbow Creek

Castle Fork

Three Fools
Peak
7,920 ft.

Lightning Creek Tr

749

Trouble Creek

Woody
Pass

473

Three Fools Creek

Shull Creek

PCT

Rock
Pass

Holman
Peak
7,550 ft.

Grizzly Creek

Cinnamon Creek

Dry Creek

Middle Creek

PASAYTEN
WILDERNESS
AREA

Shull
Mountain
7,830 ft.

Holman
Pass

Ross Lake

Dry Creek Tr

752B

752

Devils
Dome

Deception
Pass

752

Sky
Pilot
Pass

PCT

Canyon Creek

May Creek

Devils Creek

752

Devils
Pass

738

754

Jim
Pass

738

Nohokomeen Gl

738

735

Jackita
Ridge

Center
Mountain
6,593 ft.

Foggy
Pass

East Bank Tr

Jack
Mountain
9,066 ft.

Jerry
Lakes

754

Chancellor
CG

Crater
Mountain
8,128 ft.

746

738

Canyon Creek

700

20

To
Marblemount

Crater Creek

Ruby Creek

754

N

Granite Creek

0   1   2   3
MILES

NORTH CASCADES

NATIONAL PARK

20

To
Winthrop

serve. The few white miners and stockmen in the area were unhappy with the reservation designation and demanded that a 10-mile-wide strip along the Canadian border that held their mines and pastures be withdrawn from the reservation. In 1883 a 15-mile-wide strip here was restored to public domain. The remainder of the reservation was changed to public domain in 1884, and opened to settlement two years later.

Prospectors found promising placer deposits in the Canyon Creek and Slate Creek areas in the early 1890s. The search changed from placer to lode gold later in the 1890s, and camps with over 2,000 miners grew at Chancellor and Barron, on the southwest fringe of the wilderness, to exploit rich gold-bearing quartz veins.

The first forest reserves in the state, established in 1897, were converted to national forests by the early 1900s. The Chelan National Forest, which encompassed most of the area between the Canadian border and the Entiat River, was divided in 1911; the portion in Okanogan County became the Okanogan National Forest. The forest lands were initially used for grazing,

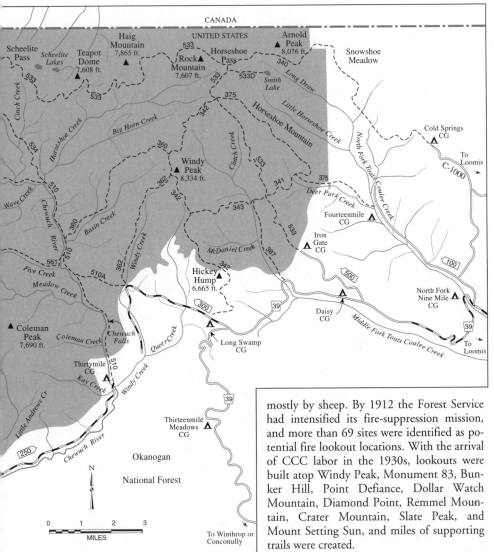

mostly by sheep. By 1912 the Forest Service had intensified its fire-suppression mission, and more than 69 sites were identified as potential fire lookout locations. With the arrival of CCC labor in the 1930s, lookouts were built atop Windy Peak, Monument 83, Bunker Hill, Point Defiance, Dollar Watch Mountain, Diamond Point, Remmel Mountain, Crater Mountain, Slate Peak, and Mount Setting Sun, and miles of supporting trails were created.

Tungsten deposits were found near Sheelite Pass in 1904, and World War I demands triggered active mining here that peaked by 1916. The long, difficult trip to the mines, and the discovery of cheaper sources of the ore elsewhere, finally ended production by the 1930s.

The first logging in the area occurred in the 1920s, but many of the old-growth timber losses were due to large forest fires in 1929. Over 500,000 acres of the Pasayten were designated as a wilderness area in 1968, and another 25,000 acres along the south and east borders were added to the wilderness in 1984.

ACTIVITIES

Hiking

ROSS LAKE NRA TRAILS

Trail #749, Elbow Basin. 18.1 miles/m (H,S). From the Lightning Creek Trail at Deer Lick Cabin (1,960 ft), the way swings into the Three Fools Creek drainage. A near-flat grade continues upstream to cliffs above the mouth of Elbow Creek. No fun now, as 47 switchbacks labor uphill northwest through second-growth timber, then meadows, to the divide (5,950 ft) between Elbow and Freezeout creeks. The track, sketchy in places, heads east on or just below the open grassy crest. On the horizon are ragged peaks: Hozomeen, the Chilliwacks, the Pickets, and Jack and Crater mountains.

After crossing a pass (6,350 ft) at the head of Elbow Basin, a spur follows the ridge north to a minor summit (6,898 ft) with knockout views to Castle Peak and Joker, Jack, and Crater mountains. The main route drops steeply across avalanche tracks to Big Face Creek (4,830 ft), then switchbacks up to a long diagonal ascent of the opposite side of the basin to the ridgetop (6,400 ft). The crest and trail bob up and down as they head east above Castle Fork and Two Buttes Creek. After a gradual descent of meadowed sidehills, switchbacks drop into the Castle Fork Basin. A brief ascent reaches Castle Pass (5,451 ft) and the PCT.

Trail #752, Devils Ridge. *17.6 miles/m (H,S).* From Devils Junction on Ross Lake (1,850 ft), the way climbs steadily through forest to enter the wilderness (3,400 ft). The uphill grade continues to top the ridge at Dry Creek Pass (5,860 ft). The path crosses open parkland as it ascends to the top of Devils Dome (6,982 ft), a broad bald knob and former lookout site, with an awesome view across the deep gulf of Devils Creek to the glacier-clad face of Jack Mountain (9,066 ft), the highest point in the wilderness. Switchbacks down a narrow rib east from the summit lead to a more gradual descent, first in meadows, then in forest, to Devils Pass (6,130 ft) and the north end of Trail #738.

The route contours the head of the North Fork of Canyon Creek to wooded, nondescript Deception Pass (5,300 ft). A brief ascent leads to Sky Pilot Pass (6,300 ft) to meet Trail #754. The way slowly descends the wooded Canyon Creek slopes, zigzags down to meet the rising creek (4,910 ft), then turns uphill to end on the PCT at Holman Pass (5,060 ft).

HIGHWAY 20 TRAILS

Trail #738, Jackita Ridge. *15.2 miles/m-d (H,S).* From the Granite Creek Guard Station (1,904 ft), this route crosses Canyon Creek for a steep, switchback climb through big old-growth forest to the subalpine meadows of McMillan Park (5,500 ft). Here unmaintained Trail #746 climbs to two abandoned lookout sites on the summit of Crater Mountain. The gentle grade to the head of Nichol Creek steepens to gain a broad, wildflower-smothered ridge leading to Devils Park. A gradual ascent north across meadows offers great views of Jack and Crater mountains. The way snakes around ribs and basins on the west side of Jackita Ridge, where tread slippage makes travel difficult. The route descends east, contours open grassy slopes at the head of the North Fork of Devils Creek (6,200 ft), then drops to Devils Pass (6,130 ft) to end on Trail #752.

HARTS PASS TRAILS

Trail #754, Chancellor. *15.5 miles/e-m (H,S). (The segment of the trail between Granite Creek and Chancellor Campground is covered in the Liberty Bell section.)* From the campground at the old Chancellor mining camp site (2,870 ft), the route heads north up Canyon Creek. Strenuous switchbacks climb 2,000 feet up a broad wooded rib, then the way tapers to a steep uphill grade to a saddle (6,340 ft) north of Center Mountain. The crest, sometimes wooded, sometimes meadow, is followed north to Sky Pilot Pass (6,300 ft) and Trail #752.

Pacific Crest National Scenic Trail. *32.5 miles/m (H,S).* This major north–south trail leaves FR 5400600 (6,780 ft) at a switchback south of Slate Pass, then contours northwest above Barron. A mining town with a population of thousands in the late 1880s, it is now just a few shacks fading into the forest. The way climbs to Windy Pass (6,280 ft), zigzags northwest to Foggy Pass (6,190 ft), then crosses Jim Pass (6,280 ft) to contour east-side slopes around Devils Backbone. A gradual ascent northwest rounds a wooded shoulder, then switchbacks drop to Holman Pass (5,060 ft) to meet Trail #752.

The way traverses slopes above Canyon Creek, then climbs the open southwest flank of Holman Peak to Rock Pass (6,550 ft). It crosses east of the crest to scree slopes below Powder Mountain, passes the west end of Trail #473, then climbs to Woody Pass (6,624 ft). The way contours the west side of the crest below Three Fools Peak, tops Lakeview Ridge (7,200 ft), then descends Devils Stairway. Switchbacks down an open sidehill to Hopkins Pass (6,122 ft) pass a way-trail dropping to Hopkins Lake (6,171 ft). A long gradual descent north through forest and across avalanche tracks reaches Castle Pass (5,451 ft) to meet Trails #479 and #533. Route Creek is followed north to the Canadian border (4,360 ft) and into British Columbia's Manning Park.

Trail #473, Rock Creek. *7.1 miles/m (H,S).* From the PCT (6,400 ft) the path traverses steep, side-slopes east of Woody Pass, with views of the abrupt north faces of Holman Peak and Powder Mountain. It then crosses numerous avalanche-track meadows as it descends into Rock Creek to meet Trail #472 (4,300 ft) above the Pasayten River.

White-winged crossbills are commonly found in conifer forests such as those of the Pasayten Wilderness.

Trail #472, West Fork Pasayten. *14 miles/m (H,S).* Just beyond the gate (7,200 ft) on FR 5400600 near Slate Peak, the way heads northeast across meadows and open timber to the west side of Haystack Mountain. It swings down the West Fork of the Pasayten, traversing past old prospects, before descending to the riverbank. The route follows the wooded drainage downstream, then wanders away from the river along the valley floor. It ends on Trail #473 (4,390 ft) at Rock Creek near the confluence of the West and Middle forks of the Pasayten.

Trail #498, Buckskin Ridge. *15.7 miles/m (H,S).* From the second switchback on FR 5400600 (6,860 ft), the route heads north and ascends meadows on the east side of Haystack Mountain. It weaves around several creek basins to Silver Lake (6,256 ft), drops to cross Silver Creek, then climbs to Silver Pass (6,500 ft). Switchbacks descend into the headwaters of Threemile Creek, then climb up east bank slopes. A traverse north rounds a sharp rib from Buckskin Ridge, then climbs east to cross Buckskin Ridge at a narrow, rocky col (7,300 ft). The way drops into the upper Point Creek basin, where a traverse north leads to Buckskin Lake (6,492 ft). After an ascent northwest below the rocky cliffs of Buckskin Point, the way makes a long drop down a broad wooded ridge to join Trail #478 at the Pasayten River (4,290 ft).

Trail #478, Robinson Creek. *23.2 miles/m (H,S).* From the Robinson Creek Campground (2,520 ft) the way traces the banks of Robinson Creek through old-growth forest and across avalanche slopes to flower-covered meadows near Robinson Pass (6,220 ft). It descends to the Middle Fork of the Pasayten River, then wanders north through large valley-bottom old-growth. After leaving the river bottom to traverse side-slopes for 4 miles, en route passing trails #484A, and #485, the track rejoins the river, crosses it, and meets Trail #498. Farther north it passes Trail #472, then Trail #473 near the south end of the abandoned Pasayten airstrip. The way ends at the north end of the strip, where it meets Trail #533 (4,279 ft).

Trail #484, Monument Creek. *17.8 miles/e-d (H,S, but not recommended for stock beyond Eureka Creek bridge).* Near the mouth of the Lost River, the route leaves FR 54 (2,400 ft) and heads north upstream through old-growth cedar and Douglas-fir along the base of cliffs framing the deep U-shaped drainage. At the bridge across the mouth of Eureka Creek (2,640 ft), one can peer upstream into the impressive gorges of Eureka Creek and the Lost River. Vertical faces more than 2,000 feet high frame both of the narrow watercourses. Work begins at the bridge— more than 80 switchbacks gnaw up parched talus slopes to the north to the 5,800-foot-high crest. The ascent continues along the crest for another mile, then traverses steep side-slopes through vestiges of a large 1986 fire. Another switchback chain gains narrow Pistol Pass (7,100 ft) and dramatic views of the peaks flanking Monument Creek. The way drops to the creek (4,650 ft), then follows the drainage upstream to a headwater junction with Trail #484A (6,560 ft).

Trail #484A, Shellrock Pass. 8 miles/d (H,S). A trail with plenty of vigorous ups and downs heads west from Trail #484 (6,560 ft) south of Butte Pass. It climbs talus slopes to Shellrock Pass (7,500 ft), then switchbacks west down a rocky face and the basin headwall of Eureka Creek. The path climbs sidehills to a col (7,120 ft), then twists down into the small cirque enclosing Freds Lake (6,507 ft). A side-slope descent reaches a rib above Berk Creek, where switchbacks drop to Trail #478 (4,960 ft).

EIGHTMILE CREEK TRAILS

Trail #477, Hidden Lakes. 21.9 miles/m (H,S). The route leaves the end of FR 5130 (4,650 ft) for a gradual climb northwest across Eightmile Pass (5,440 ft). It descends Jinks Creek to meet Trail #502 (4,650 ft) at Drake Creek. One long switchback leads to Lucky Pass (5,780 ft); beyond, the route descends steep sidehills to Diamond Creek, then drifts down along the Lost River to Cougar Lake (4,270 ft). The way follows the glacier-cut valley northwest to First Hidden Lake (4,303 ft), then crosses a subtle divide, meets Trail #485, and slips down to Big Hidden Lake (4,316 ft). At the north end of the lake, Trail #451 heads east; Trail #477 continues down the East Fork of the Pasayten to end on Trail #533 (4,000 ft).

Trail #485, Tatoosh Butte. 12 miles/m (H,S). At the imperceptible divide between Middle

Remmel Mountain is one of the highest peaks in the Chewuch River area of the Pasayten.

and Big Hidden Lakes (4,318 ft) the track switchbacks up through big old-growth forest north of Gunbarrel Creek to break into the flowered meadows of Tatoosh Buttes (7,100 ft). Miles of bare ridges open to the south. The way descends through forest to Lease Creek, then continues west to cross the Pasayten River and meet Trail #478 (4,500 ft).

Trail #502A, Billy Goat. 6 miles/m (H,S). From the end of FR 5130 (5,000 ft) the route climbs north through old-growth forest to Billy Goat Pass (6,600 ft), where it passes Trail #538. North of the pass it drops past Trail #532, then joins Trail #502 near the mouth of Two Bit Creek (5,600 ft).

Trail #502, Larch Creek. 16.2 miles/m (H,S). From Trail #477 (4,700 ft), this route follows Drake Creek upstream past Trail #502A, then bends north through an old burn to cross Three Fools Pass (6,101 ft). It descends through woods to Diamond Creek (5,500 ft), then swings into the Larch Creek drainage. The tread follows the creek upstream, passes Trail #532, then crosses Larch Pass (7,150 ft). It passes Trail #451 as it climbs to a saddle (7,490 ft) at the head of McCall Gulch, where flower-splashed meadows offer broad views across the Ashnola River valley. Rolling parkland continues north to Peeve Pass (6,880 ft), where the route ends on Trail #533.

Trail #532, Fool Hen. 12 miles/d (H,S). Although poorly maintained, this twisting, curving, up-and-down route covers a major north–south segment of the wilderness south of Ashnola Pass. From Trail #502A (5,900 ft) north of Billy Goat Pass, the way follows Drake Creek upstream through meadows, then switchbacks abruptly up east slopes to the ridgetop (7,250 ft). It wanders north along the sinuous crest, traverses the basin above Fool Hen Lake (7,301 ft), then descends past more lakes to a bench (6,960 ft) south of Diamond Point. Switchbacks climb steep talus to the summit of Diamond Point (7,916 ft), a former fire lookout with great views of the Ashnola River valley. The bare crest is traced northwest, then the way drops abruptly to a pass (6,850 ft) at the head of Diamond Creek before descending to Trail #502 (6,400 ft).

Trail #451, East Fork Pasayten. 8.5 miles/m (H,S). A long valley-bottom path leaves Trail #477 at the north end of Big Hidden Lake (4,350 ft) and climbs east through lodgepole pine along the riverbank into McCall Gulch to meet Trail #502 (7,180 ft) north of Larch Pass.

CHEWUCH RIVER TRAILS

Trail #500, Lake Creek. 18.9 miles/e (H,S). From the horse camp at the end of FR 5160100 (3,162 ft), the track follows the bottom of the broad, glacier-cut Lake Creek drainage northwest to Black Lake (3,982 ft). It continues up the narrowing valley, with wooded walls rising as much as 2,000 feet on either side of the stream course. The route becomes steeper by the mile as it climbs to Ashnola Pass. At the pass it skirts the shore of Fawn Lake (6,201 ft), then descends north into the Spotted Creek drainage. The way follows the creek downstream to meadows at the confluence with the Ashnola River (5,800 ft). The route then flows down to join Trail #533 on the banks of the Ashnola (5,081 ft).

Trail #504, Andrews Creek. 15.5 miles/m (H,S). Another long north–south thrust into the heart of the wilderness leaves the Chewuch River at Andrews Creek Campground (3,050 ft). After a brief jump up the sidehill to cross Little Andrews Creek, the way settles to a gentle ascent through old-growth forest along Andrews Creek. Traces of a 1984 fire are evident between Little Andrews and Blizzard creeks. At Ram Creek, Trail #505 leaves to the east, and Trail #525 heads west at Peepsight Creek. The way climbs steadily to Andrew Pass (6,690 ft), where glimpses open to the east face of Andrew Peak and Trail #525 is rejoined. Meadows open to views of other peaks as the way descends from the pass along Spanish Creek. The path ends on Trail #533 (6,730 ft) at Spanish Camp.

Trail #505, Coleman Ridge. 12.7 miles/m (H,S, but sections are impassable by stock). At the mouth of Ram Creek the route leaves Trail #504 (4,590 ft) and switchbacks up the lodgepole pine–covered slope to the head of the creek, where it threads through a wooded notch to Meadow Lake (6,361 ft). The way follows a gentle ridge north over a 6,827-foot knob, then continues northwest across meadows and through open timber to the south end of Coleman Ridge. It rises steadily across the west side of the ridge, dips briefly into a wooded basin, then climbs to a saddle (7,200 ft) between Coleman Ridge and Remmel Mountain. The way worms over scree and boulders below a cliff to reach Four Point Creek (7,100 ft). Good backcountry sleuths can find the old route up the gully at the head of creek that once led to a lookout perched on the tip of Remmel Mountain (8,685 ft). The rocky track contours the basin wall northeast past the way-trail to Four Point Lake (6,850 ft), then drops abruptly through switchbacks to the Chewuch River and Trail #510 (5,240 ft).

Trail #525, Peepsight. 8.1 miles/d (H,S, but sections are impassable by stock). This loop trail on the west side of the Andrews Creek drainage initially leaves Trail #504 (5,310 ft) 0.5 mile north of the mouth of Peepsight Creek. It ascends through timber on the north side of the creek, then climbs steeply north to Crazy Man Pass (7,260 ft). Here are great views of rugged surrounding peaks—Peepsight Mountain, Andrew Peak, and Remmel Mountain. The way slides down scree and boulders to the north to reach Rock Lake (7,170 ft). From here it meanders up, down, and around gullies and ribs before settling to a northward climb to Trail #504 at Andrew Pass (6,690 ft).

Trail #510, Chewuch. 18.1 miles/m (H,S). Starting at Thirtymile Campground (3,440 ft) this route traces the banks of the Chewuch River to its headwaters deep in the heart of the wilderness. Two miles from the trailhead is the first attraction, Chewuch Falls. The way continues through river-bottom lodgepole pine to pass Trails #561 and #360. As the river makes a sharp bend west at 4,650 feet, Trail #534 heads off to the north. The way maintains its river-bottom slog, passes Trail #505, and reaches the junction of Remmel and Cathedral creeks (5,600 ft). As it heads up Remmel Creek, trees slowly thin and the way breaks out to rumpled meadows painted with the reds and blues of paintbrush and lupine. The trail skirts Remmel Lake (6,871 ft), with the ragged summits of Remmel and Amphitheater mountains in view. The path wanders west across rolling parkland to end on Trail #533 (6,910 ft).

Trail #360, Basin Creek. 6 miles/m (H,S). The way climbs steeply up the east wall of the Chewuch River drainage from Trail #510 (4,360 ft), then bends north away from Basin Creek. It climbs through lodgepole pine to larch and subalpine fir as it skirts the northwest edge of Topaz Mountain, then joins Trail #342 (7,340 ft) north of Windy Peak.

Trail #534, Tungsten Mine. 6.2 miles/m (H,S). At the westward bend of the Chewuch River (4,660 ft), this route climbs north through lodgepole forest, crosses Cinch Creek, then traces Tungsten Creek upstream to the Tungsten Mine (6,800 ft), where crumbling mining debris clutters the junction with Trail #533.

TOATS COULEE CREEK TRAILS

Trail #342, Windy Peak. 11.5 miles/m (H,S). Starting at Long Swamp Campground (5,500 ft), the route heads north through lodgepole pine along the east side of Hickey Hump, then continues sharply uphill through Englemann spruce and subalpine fir to Two Bear Camp (6,970 ft). The way plugs uphill across alpine meadows, where a spur continues uphill to the top of Windy Peak (8,334 ft), once the site of a fire lookout. Here are horizon-sweeping views of the entire east side of the Pasayten wilderness. Trail #342 descends grassy slopes past the east end of Trail #360, then dips northeast through swampy meadowland before climbing to end on Trail #533 (6,910 ft) west of Sunny Pass, at the south side of Horseshoe Basin.

Trail #533, Boundary. 73.1 miles/m (H,S). The longest trail in the wilderness leaves its southeast corner, winds up and down west along the U.S.–Canada border, and ends on the PCT 15 miles from the west side of the wilderness. The east end starts at Iron Gate Campground (6,120 ft), then climbs through a young lodgepole pine forest that opens to flower meadows at Sunny Pass (7,215 ft), where it meets Trails #342 and #375. The way continues north across broad parkland to Horseshoe Pass (7,000 ft).

The trail now bends west past shallow Louden Lake (7,070 ft) and below the north-face cliffs of Rock Mountain. The path then contours around the south sides of Haig Mountain, Teapot Dome, and Bauerman Ridge. Heading northwest along the lower slopes of that ridge, the trail crosses Scheelite Pass (6,713 ft), worms west to the remains of the Tungsten Mine, where it meets Trail #534. The path rounds parkland slopes at the head of Tungsten Creek, then bends west to broad Apex Pass (7,300 ft). A long sweep to the northwest turns the head of Cathedral Creek, then climbs to Cathedral Pass (7,570 ft), where ghostly silver snags of trees burned in a 1920s fire haunt young growths of lodgepole pine. The path drops from the pass to the larch-lined shore of Upper Cathedral Lake (7,390 ft). The lake, below the imposing cliffs of Amphitheater Mountain, is one of the most photographed spots in the wilderness, especially when decorated by brilliant fall colors. The Boundary Trail ducks southwest through a flat meadowland pass and descends gradually to Spanish Camp (6,720 ft), passing the north end of Trail #510 en route.

From here to the Ashnola River, the original route, high on the slopes of Bald Mountain, has been replaced by a lower and gentler grade that includes long sweeping switchbacks down forested slopes to meet Trail #500 and cross the Ashnola River (5,020 ft). The way climbs the west side of the broad U-shaped valley, then breaks into meadows. An easy grade reaches Peeve Pass (6,860 ft) where Trail #502 heads south.

At a narrow slot (6,750 ft) between Sand Ridge and Quartz Mountain, a short spur contours to the cirque enclosing Quartz Lake (6,741 ft). A swing across a long parkland slope on the southwest side of Quartz Mountain has continuous breathtaking views west to the peaks of the Cascade crest. The way twists around basins and wanders up and down in open timber to reach meadowland atop Bunker Hill (7,239 ft), an old lookout site, with even closer views of the crest peaks. The route now makes a long, tempered descent through forest to the Pasayten River.

Trail #477 is joined just before the Pasayten Bridge (3,910 ft), and the vague remains of Trail #461 head north just across the river. An easy grade follows the broad river valley southwest to reach the abandoned Pasayten airstrip (4,290 ft). Trail #478 continues south, but this route crosses the north end of the airstrip into densely wooded Soda Creek Canyon. At a stream fork the way bends northwest past Dead Lake (5,062 ft), then heads west up the wide, heavily forested Frosty Creek drainage past Frosty Lake (5,343 ft). The trail switchbacks up an avalanche slope, contours an open basin below Mount Winthrop, then climbs to Frosty Pass (6,500 ft). It then descends to Castle Pass (5,451 ft), where it ends on the PCT.

Trail #375, Albert Camp. 8.6 miles/m (H,S). One of the most scenic trails on the eastern rim of the wilderness leaves Fourteenmile Campground and follows Deer Park Creek northwest through state forest land to the wilderness boundary. The first 3 miles of tread through Deer Park have been rebuilt into lazy, easy-grade switchbacks to the ridgetop (6,890 ft). A traverse northwest through subalpine forest crosses a pair of saddles, then finally climbs to broad parkland (7,700 ft) with good views southwest of the high, rugged face of Windy Peak. The path then switchbacks down to end on Trail #533 north of Sunny Pass (7,220 ft).

Climbing

Although more than 50 peaks in the wilderness are listed in climbing guides, and over 100 have sheer rocky north or west faces ranging between 200 and 1,000 vertical feet, simple scramble routes lead up south and east slopes or along north–south ridges. Only a handful of peaks demand any technical skill to reach their summits.

West of the Cascade crest is Jack Mountain (9,066 ft), the highest point in the wilderness, and one of the ten peaks in the state over 9,000 feet that are not volcanoes. Easy, although steep, routes work up a south-face gully to a single C-4 pitch. The north ridge and northeast glacier have C-4 routes, and the most challenging approach via the southeast ridge has one C-5.6 pitch.

One of the few north-face challenges that has been attacked is Castle Peak (8,306 ft) west of the Cascade crest near the Canadian border. Routes up the wall rate between C-5 and C-5.8. The route to the top of Shull Mountain (7,830 ft), northwest of Holman Pass, is not difficult, but several pinnacles on the long north–south ridge that makes up the summit are worthy of a lead or two of interesting climbing. Holman Peak (7,550 ft), just east of the crest, has a few hundred feet of pleasant rock on the summit block.

Two other summits in the north-central portion of the wilderness that have seen development of north-face routes are Amphitheater Mountain (8,358 ft) and Apex Mountain (8,279 ft). The former has routes that range from C-5.3 to C-5.9. The latter has multiple pitches between C-5.7 and C-5.9. Just north of Cathedral Pass, Cathedral Peak (8,601 ft) has solid C-5.6 to C-5.9 routes, and other pinnacles on the ridge northeast at the Canadian border appear to have equally challenging crags.

44

LONG SWAMP–SHERMAN PEAK

LOCATION: In Okanogan County, on the southeast rim of the Pasayten Wilderness
SIZE: 86,660 acres
STATUS: Roadless; motorized recreation permitted on some trails
TERRAIN: Creeks and rivers run through deep canyons with moderately steep side-slopes, topped by benches and rounded ridgetops. At the northwest corner is the steep rugged Isabella Ridge–Craggy complex of rocky peaks.
ELEVATION: 2,500 to 8,470 feet
MANAGEMENT: USFS, Okanogan National Forest, Winthrop Ranger District
TOPOGRAPHIC MAPS: Billy Goat Mtn., Coleman Peak, Doe Mountain, Mt. Barney, Spur Peak, Sweetgrass Butte, Tiffany Mtn.

Long Swamp, a large wedge-shaped roadless area south of the Pasayten Wilderness, is bisected by the Chewuch River Road. The Sherman Peak area is a smaller section of roadless territory on the northwest side of Long Swamp. Logging has encroached on the south fringes of both areas and may continue to. Long Swamp's topography primarily consists of high rounded ridges cut by deep peripheral stream drainages. Slopes are covered mostly by a terminal succession of lodgepole pine, with larger Douglas-fir, ponderosa pine, and Englemann spruce growing in drainages and draws. The latter are rapidly being reduced by selective logging. Extensive meadows line ridgetops and wider valley floors, and these have colorful wildflower displays in spring. The Sherman Peak area consists of partially forested parkland leading up the barren, craggy rock walls of the highest peaks in the area.

Climate

A relatively dry eastern Washington climate pervades the area, with mean annual precipitation between 19 and 26 inches, much falling as winter snows. The mean midwinter minimum temperatures are 8 to 12 degrees, and mean midsummer maximums range from 77 to 84.

Plants and Wildlife

Lower elevations support stands of Douglas-fir and ponderosa pine, with Englemann spruce in draws. Higher elevations are covered mostly by lodgepole pine, with some occurrences of western white pine. The highest section, in the vicinity of Sherman Peak, has mountain hemlock, whitebark pine, and subalpine fir giving way to tundra-like meadows and barren rocky slopes. The ground cover on open ridgetop meadows includes sedges, bluegrass, fescue, Indian paintbrush, lupine, columbine, valerian, and pussytoes. The upper Chewuch River drainage has been proposed as a 10,000-acre RNA because of its unique ecosystem, which includes riparian hardwoods, black cottonwood, and willow along the river; Englemann spruce and subalpine fir on lower slopes; an upwelling spring; and lodgepole pine forest with subalpine meadows at higher altitudes.

The forest is home for mule deer, black bear, marten, fisher, grouse, and one of the largest lynx populations in the country. Mountain goats are also found in the high rocky Isabella Ridge area. The Chewuch River corridor is a wintering ground and spring fawning habitat for the large Methow mule deer herd. Among threatened or sensitive species in the area are grizzly bear, golden eagle, northern bog lemming, water vole, wolverine, and three-toed woodpecker.

Geology

The base rock of the region was created over 100 million years ago when the west side of the Okanogan micro-continent fractured and was subducted by oceanic crust, leaving its cover of sedimentary rock in a trench along the west side of the tiny plate. Hot basalt rising above the sinking slab and magma from newly emerging volcanoes along the continental rim transformed this trench rock into the granitic base of the area. The principal drainages of the area display the characteristic U-shaped form of glacier-carved valleys, created when the last continental ice sheets overrode the area 15 million years ago. Base rock is covered in most places with a layer of glacial till and volcanic ash from the last series of eruptions of Glacier Peak. Base rock outcrops can be seen in the Isabella Ridge–Craggy area and in the steep side-slopes of the upper Chewuch River.

History

The Chewuch River and its main tributaries were identified on maps dated as early as 1873, so some exploration had been done prior to that time. Prospecting in the area began around 1910, and mines in the vicinity of Isabella Ridge and Billy Goat Pass produced limited amounts of gold, silver, and copper ore between 1914 and 1935. Low-grade tungsten, molybdenum, and zinc ores have also been found in that area. Ridgetop meadows were opened to grazing in the early 1900s, and several existing and abandoned trails are old stock or sheep drives into the Pasayten. During the 1920s, the Forest Service put fire lookouts atop Burch and Doe mountains and North Twentymile Peak, and built trails to serve them. The original lookout on North Twentymile Creek still stands, with its unique cupola atop a log-cabin ground house. It is believed to be one of the last lookouts of this style still in existence. As is obvious around the perimeter of the roadless area, logging has been the dominant industry in the area over the past 50 years.

Carrying water for the lookout on North Twentymile Peak. The lookout is no longer manned, although the structure still stands.

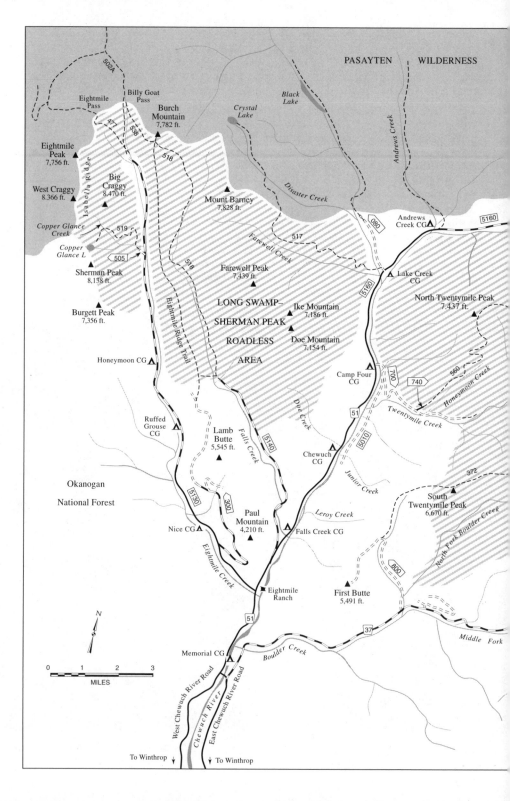

PASAYTEN   WILDERNESS

Black Lake

Crystal Lake

502A

Eightmile Pass

Billy Goat Pass

Burch Mountain 7,782 ft.

477

508

Disaster Creek

Andrews Creek

5160

Andrews Creek CG

080

Eightmile Peak 7,756 ft.

518

Isabella Ridge

Big Craggy 8,470 ft.

Mount Barney 7,828 ft.

West Craggy 8,366 ft.

Copper Glance Creek

519

517

Farewell Creek

5160

Lake Creek CG

North Twentymile Peak 7,437 ft.

Copper Glance L

505

518

Farewell Peak 7,439 ft.

Sherman Peak 8,138 ft.

LONG SWAMP–SHERMAN PEAK

Ike Mountain 7,186 ft.

Burgett Peak 7,356 ft.

Eightmile Ridge Trail

ROADLESS

Doe Mountain 7,154 ft.

560

Honeymoon Creek

AREA

Honeymoon CG

Camp Four CG

700

740

Twentymile Creek

Ruffed Grouse CG

Doe Creek

51

Lamb Butte 5,545 ft.

Falls Creek

5140

5010

372

Chewuch CG

Okanogan

National Forest

5130

300

Paul Mountain 4,210 ft.

Leroy Creek

Junior Creek

South Twentymile Peak 6,670 ft.

North Fork Boulder Creek

Nice CG

Falls Creek CG

800

Eightmile Creek

First Butte 5,491 ft.

N

Eightmile Ranch

51

37

Middle Fork

0 1 2 3
MILES

Memorial CG

West Chewuch River Road

Chewuch River

East Chewuch River Road

Boulder Creek

To Winthrop   To Winthrop

ACTIVITIES

Hiking

EIGHTMILE CREEK TRAILS

Trail #519, Copper Glance. 3.3 miles/m (H,S,B,M). From the gate at the start of FR 5130505 (3,850 ft), hike this old road north for 1.5 miles to a mine shaft, the start of the true trail. The route ascends west to a meadow, then climbs into forest after crossing Copper Glance Creek. The path stumbles up a rough rocky slope to a ridge shoulder (6,250 ft), then drops down to the bouldery shore of tiny Copper Glance Lake (6,110 ft). Southwest of the lake, cliffs rise 2,000 feet to the crags atop Isabella Ridge.

Trail #538, Burch Mountain. 2 miles/m (H). An unmaintained trail, once used to support a lookout atop Burch Mountain, heads southeast from Trail #502A at Billy Goat Pass (6,600 ft). The tread may be washed out or it may disappear in places, but it is relatively easy to follow. The long traverse of an open southwest-facing sidehill has continuous views of the vertical rock faces of the Craggy group of peaks, and beyond, Isabella Ridge. After a few switchbacks at the end of the traverse, the path rounds a small rib to a bench, reverses direction, and climbs to the former lookout site atop the mountain (7,782 ft). In addition to the Craggys, the Pasayten Wilderness now comes into view.

Eightmile Ridge Trail. 5.7 miles/m-d (H). This old ridgetop sheep drive starts at the end of FR 5140300 (5,400 ft). At a saddle in 2 miles a spur drops east, crosses Falls Creek, and follows it downstream to the end of FR 5140 (5,030 ft). From the saddle the route follows the open crest of Eightmile Ridge north 3.7 miles to Burch Mountain (7,782 ft). It has an easy grade and great views en route of Isabella Ridge and the Craggy Peaks.

CHEWUCH RIVER TRAILS

Trail #517, Crystal Lake. 3.3 miles/m (H,S). After leaving FR 5160080 (2,800 ft) the trail makes long lazy switchbacks up the forested slopes north of Farewell Creek, then follows the valley west, keeping high above the creek. In 3.5 miles, the way bends north into a marshy basin and climbs across a 6,100-foot saddle into the Pasayten Wilderness. It drops to cross Disaster Creek, then follows it upstream to Crystal Lake (7,114 ft), a beautiful little alpine lake hidden in tall timber stands. Cross-country scrambles can reach two other lakes over the ridge to the north.

Trail #560, North Twentymile. 11 miles/m (H,S,B,M). After starting on abandoned FR 5010740 (3,200 ft), the track turns into the Honeymoon Creek drainage for a long, gradual ascent up the west bank of the creek. Near the steeper head of the basin, switchbacks climb to the broad ridge crest (6,800 ft), where meadows escort the path to the top of North Twentymile Peak (7,437 ft). Here are a pair of fire lookouts, an ancient cupola-style one built in 1923, and a more modern one completed in 1948. A sea of timbered ridges rolls west to Silver Star Mountain, southeast to Tiffany Mountain, and north to the Pasayten Wilderness. A seldom-maintained section of trail continues east in ridgetop meadows, then slowly descends the broad crest to join Trail #371 at the head of the Smarty Creek basin (6,480 ft).

Trail #371, Smarty Creek. 11.7 miles/m (H,S). From FR 39, at the point it crosses the South Fork of Twentymile Creek (5,840 ft), the route heads downstream to the northwest, along boggy South Twentymile Meadows. At 2.5 miles (5,450 ft) the path crosses Twentymile Creek to reach the mouth of Smarty Creek, then follows the latter creek upstream to a saddle (6,480 ft) where it meets Trail #560 from North Twentymile Peak. The route heads east, ascends a broad gentle ridge to 6,890 feet, then drops down a steep hillside to the West Fork of Twentymile Creek. It follows meadows northeast along the West Fork, then turns north to Thirtymile Meadows.

Climbing

The only peaks of climbing interest are in the northwest corner of the area along ragged Isabella Ridge. The long rocky ridge has precipitous north and northeast faces, but much gentler slopes on the south side. North along the ridge from Burgett Peak (7,365 ft) is Sherman Peak (8,138 ft). Although it has a vertical 1,600-foot north face, an easy southwest slope reaches the summit. Other possible routes along flanking ridges must bypass a number of ridgetop gendarmes. The arête northwest of Sherman has several crags just over 8,100 feet.

The north end of Isabella Ridge ends in the wishbone crest capped by the Craggy Peaks. Big Craggy (8,470 ft) has rock faces on either side of a northern buttress, but its south slope is a steep, nontechnical scree climb. West Craggy (8,366 ft) is gentle on its hard-to-reach southwest slope; its precipitous north ridge has one difficult C-5.8 route up the east face.

45

TIFFANY

LOCATION: In Okanogan County, bordered by the North and West Forks of Salmon Creek and the North Fork of Boulder Creek
SIZE: 24,027 acres
STATUS: Semiprimitive Roadless, Nonmotorized
TERRAIN: A cluster of high mountain summits atop a long ridge dividing the Chewuch and Okanogan river drainages. Small streams flow down all sides of the main ridgeline.
ELEVATION: 4,000 to 8,250 feet
MANAGEMENT: USFS, Okanogan National Forest, Winthrop Ranger District
TOPOGRAPHIC MAPS: Conconully West, Coxit Mountain, Old Baldy, Tiffany Mtn.

The forested flanks and open parklands of the north–south backbone of this compact area are a utopia of leisurely hikes. The longest single trail is just over 6 miles, and almost all of the routes can be linked in different ways to form day-hike loops. Although logging continually chews around the borders of Tiffany, old-growth stands remain untouched in the lower portions of the area. Once above timberline, both dry and damp meadows are covered by multiple species of grasses, forbs, flowers, and shrubs. Although the area has only four lakes, two are in beautiful subalpine settings. The open ridges and two timber-free summits that once held fire lookouts provide sweeping views of both distant snow-clad peaks and dry rolling plateaus.

Climate

The region is subject to the continental weather systems of central Washington, so the mean annual precipitation averages only 19 to 20 inches, much falling as snow. Temperatures are more extreme, with midwinter minimums averaging 12 degrees, and midsummer highs averaging 85 degrees. Extended periods in which temperatures exceed these averages are not uncommon.

Plants and Wildlife

A dense forest cover of Douglas-fir, lodgepole pine, and Englemann spruce occurs mainly on

The open summit of Tiffany Mountain provides sweeping views of the wilderness.

damper north slopes and in creek drainages. Old-growth stands are found on Middle Tiffany Mountain and along Isabel, Clark, Pelican, and the North Fork of Salmon creeks. On mid-altitude slopes, the forest is thinner, composed of lodgepole pine, Englemann spruce, subalpine fir, and some western larch. Ridgetops are mostly treeless, covered only with grasses and heathers. These meadows, as well as those at lower altitudes, may contain combinations of fescues, needlegrass, wheatgrass, buckwheat, gilia, penstemon, saxifrage, stonecrop, lupine, and paintbrush. Ground cover in any specific meadow depends upon soil depth, moisture, and prior grazing history.

Tiffany has been proposed as a Research Natural Area by virtue of several unique ecosystems represented here. The specific ecological cells are: an Englemann spruce–subalpine forest, an alpine community mosaic, an oligothorpic lake, a permanent pond, a vernal pond, and subalpine sagebrush parkland.

The common forest inhabitants of mule deer, black bear, fisher, marten, and assorted species of small rodents are joined in this area by large numbers of blue grouse, black-backed woodpecker, pileated woodpecker, flammulated owl, golden eagle, and members of the largest lynx population in the coterminous United States.

Geology

Tiffany is mostly underlaid by granite, formed 60 million to 150 million years ago, covered with glacial alluvium and an upper layer of volcanic ash from the last eruptions of Glacier Peak. Base rock is highly mineralized in the upper Bernhart Creek drainage, at the southwest corner of the area, and near Rock Mountain, on its north border. Lode ore consists of veins of silver and lead; some low-grade surface uranium deposits also exist.

History

In 1879 all of present-day Okanogan County was designated as a reservation for the Columbia tribe headed by Chief Moses. The reservation was opened to homesteading in 1886, but only a few settlers dribbled into the area. Prospectors soon thronged to the hills north and west of Conconully to engage in hard-rock mining of its silver deposits. Prosperity was short-lived, and most mines closed when the bottom dropped out of the silver market in 1893.

Tiffany Mountain, and its present surrounding roadless area, are thought to be named for Perry and William Tiffany, brothers who came to the area at the height of the mining boom. Although the brothers were rumored to be members of the wealthy Tiffany Jewelry Company family, archive searches indicated that they were probably just distant relatives of the founder of that firm.

The first forest reserves in Washington were established in 1897, and they rapidly became grazing ranges for cattle and sheep as newly arriving settlers began claiming and fencing the fertile valley floors. In 1911 the huge Chelan National Forest was partitioned, and the portion in Okanogan County became today's Okanogan National Forest. Throughout its early history the forest was used mostly for grazing, and several of today's trails are old stock driveways. Fire suppression became a priority mission for the Forest Service in that period, and lookouts were placed atop Tiffany and Muckamuck mountains in 1932, in a flurry of building and trail construction by the Depression-born CCC.

ACTIVITIES

Hiking

Trails in the Tiffany area can be reached from forest roads originating either at Winthrop, to its southwest, or Conconully, to its southeast. FR 37, a portion of which forms the south border of the area, connects these two towns.

Trail #373, Tiffany Lake. 6.5 miles/m (H,S). This route runs east–west across the north end of the Tiffany area. From Tiffany Spring Campground on FR 39 (6,750 ft), the trail descends a short distance east to Tiffany Lake (6,550 ft). From the lake, it climbs through forest and a succession of meadows to Honeymoon Pass (7,150 ft). A short scramble through the woods to the southwest reaches cliff-bound Little Tiffany Lake (7,370 ft). From Honeymoon Pass the track drops briefly into the headwaters of the North Fork of Salmon Creek, then climbs diagonally up a cliff face to a ridge-crest meeting with Trail #345 (7,300 ft). The route follows the narrow rib east to meadows along the broadening crest above Peak Creek. A descent of the forested ridge nose leads to FR 3820 (4,920 ft).

Trail #345, Freezeout. 3.5 miles/m (H,S). The trail leaves FR 39 at a saddle (6,580 ft) and heads up the forested ridge to the east to break into meadows at 1.5 miles. A steady ascent of the broad open shoulder of Tiffany Mountain works around its steeper south side to meet Trail #369 at Whistler Pass (7,600 ft). The track ends 0.5 mile farther east where it joins Trail #373 (7,300 ft).

Trail #367, Bernhart. 3 miles/m (H,S). From FR 39 (5,740 ft) this old miner's route heads east through woods along the bank of Bernhart Creek. It follows a fork of the creek to the southeast past boggy meadows, then swings north up the basin wall to the Bernhart Mine (6,640 ft). From the mine the trail shoots up steep slopes, with nary a switchback, to a parkland junction with Trail #369 (7,360 ft).

Trail #369, North Summit. 5.5 miles/m (H,S). This old stock driveway heads into the woods north of FR 37 (5,840 ft) and follows the ridge to the northeast, sometimes in forest, sometimes in meadow. After skirting several ridgetop knobs, the way reaches a narrow saddle with views north to the long, meadow-capped crest between Clark and Tiffany mountains. The route heads east up a narrow ridge, traverses past two knobs, and meets Trail #363 on the south rib of Clark Peak. A long sidehill contour of meadows on the east flank of Clark passes the head of Trail #367, then the way ascends to Whistler Pass (7,600 ft) where it meets Trail #345. A short spur switchbacks northwest to the top of Tiffany Mountain (8,245 ft), an abandoned lookout site. Here are broad views across a rolling sea of forested ridges to the distant North Cascades on one side, and the thirsty brown Okanogan Highlands on the other.

Trail #363, Clark Ridge. 4.8 miles/m (H,S). A hundred yards beyond the east end of Trail #373 (5,030 ft), this route turns southwest into the Peak Creek drainage, descends to a creek crossing, then climbs to the divide between Peak and Isabel creeks. The way follows this wooded crest west, then traverses south around the head of Isabel Creek to Clark Ridge. A gradual ascent on south slopes below the ridgetop reaches the rocky headwall below the south face of Clark Peak. A few switchbacks gain a saddle at the head of the basin where Trail #369 is joined (7,320 ft).

Winter Sports

The west flank of the Tiffany area is inaccessible in the winter except for long snowmobile approaches over snowbound forest roads. FR 38, up the North Fork of Salmon Creek, is generally plowed as far as Salmon Meadows Campground, so east-side trails are within easy reach of cross-country skiers, and there are few avalanche hazards along the paths of summer trails.

46

LAKE CHELAN–SAWTOOTH WILDERNESS

LOCATION: In Chelan and Okanogan counties, along the east side of Lake Chelan, the Lake Chelan National Recreation Area, and North Cascades National Park, and south of Washington Pass

SIZE: 145,667 acres

STATUS: Designated Wilderness Area (1984)

TERRAIN: A high backbone ridge runs northwest to southeast the length of the wilderness. Several creeks originate high on the central rib, then drain through steep-sided lateral valleys separated by subalpine ridges whose outer ends drop abruptly to Lake Chelan or the Twisp River.

ELEVATION: 1,098 to 8,974 feet

MANAGEMENT: USFS, Wenatchee National Forest, Chelan Ranger District; Okanogan National Forest, Twisp and Winthrop ranger districts; and a few patented private mining claims

TOPOGRAPHIC MAPS: Big Goat Mtn., Gilbert, Lucerne, Martin Peak, Mazama, McAlester Mtn., Midnight Mountain, Oval Peak, Prince Creek, Rendevous Mountain, Silver Star Mtn., Sun Mountain, Thompson Ridge, Washington Pass

On the west the wilderness rises abruptly from Lake Chelan to the subalpine crest of the Sawtooth Range, which runs northwest–southeast through the wilderness. On the northeast side of the crest, the terrain drops to the wide glacier-carved valley of the Twisp River. Another steep subrange rises on both sides of Wolf Creek between the head of the Twisp and Winthrop rivers, in the Methow Valley. Creeks cut deep, narrow lateral drainages northeast and southwest

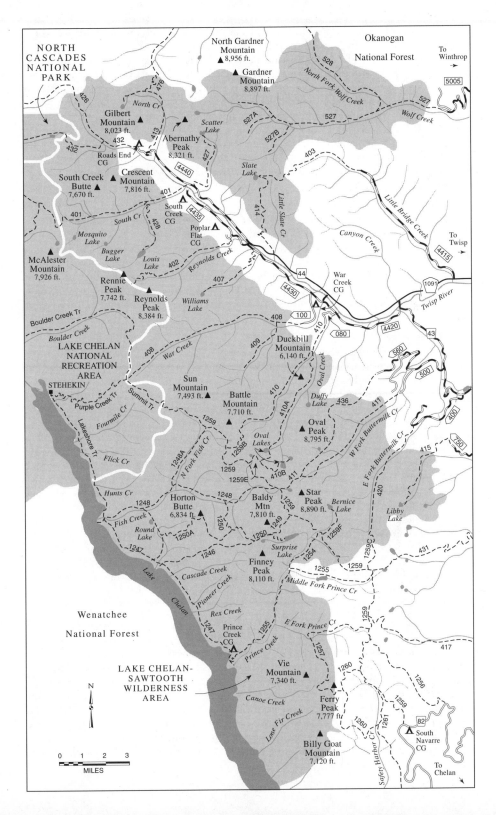

from the summit backbone. The range is capped by pyramid-shaped summits, most with gentle slopes to the southwest and vertical rock faces on the north.

High cirques hold 63 lakes, more than half so small that they don't even bear names. Most are in rugged alpine settings, and only a dozen or so are reached by trails. In many cases this is not a deterrent to visiting them, as cross-country travel is relatively easy in the open timber and parkland at upper elevations on the southeast side of the crest.

A diverse group of biological communities can be found in the wilderness, and the trails here climb through the spectrum of east Cascade timber, bushes, grasses, herbs, and flowers. The sunny drier climate of eastern Washington means that flowers bloom earlier and trails open sooner than in wilderness areas in the heart of the Cascades. These favorable climatic conditions bring with them certain negatives, including an increased likelihood of encountering such annoyances as rattlesnakes and ticks.

Climate

The Methow Valley is influenced more by continental weather patterns than by the Pacific Ocean weather systems that dominate the climate west of the Cascades. As a result, winters are colder and clearer, and summers drier and hotter, than the same seasons in regions 50 miles to the west. Midwinter temperatures average in the 20s, with lows from minus 30 to 10 degrees. Average summer temperatures are in the 70s, and the summer highs are over 90. Annual precipitation is a sparse 18 to 23 inches in the Methow Valley, and up to 75 inches at the crest, mostly falling as snow during winter months. Snow depths reach 4 to 5 feet at mid-level elevations, and as deep as 12 feet at the crest.

Plants and Wildlife

Because of the wide elevation differential in the Lake Chelan–Sawtooth Wilderness, several east-slope ecological zones are represented within its boundaries. Its lower-level forests are mostly ponderosa pine, Douglas-fir, lodgepole pine, and western larch. The understory varies with soil composition: the finer-textured soils support snowberry, oceanspray, sedges, arnica, and woods rose; the rockier areas grow fescue, wheatgrass, balsamroot, dwarf mountain fleabane, and needle and thread. Above 3,500 feet, pinegrass is added to this mix.

With another 500 to 1,000 feet of altitude, subalpine fir, Englemann spruce, western white pine, and mountain hemlock may appear. Understory shrubs include huckleberry, baldhip rose, and prickly currant; herbs and flowers here are bigleaf sandwort, wild ginger, anemone, arnica, trillium, brome, queencup beadlily, wood violet, and dwarf blackberry.

Above 4,800 feet the trees shade to subalpine fir, Englemann spruce, whitebark pine, and lodgepole pine. Ground cover includes huckleberry, beargrass, and, on damper north slopes, Cascades azalea, rustyleaf, and Labrador tea.

Wildlife common to the area includes mule deer, mountain goat, cougar, and black bear. Part of the Methow Valley mule deer herd, the largest in the state, spends summers in the wilderness and migrates in fall; fawns are born in the vicinity of Gilbert. Bald and golden eagles are often seen during the winter along the Methow River, and peregrine falcons are occasionally spotted during their spring and fall migrations.

Geology

The wilderness lies adjacent to the point of collision, some 60 million years ago, between the North Cascades micro-continent and the west coast of North America. Most of the rock in the area is metamorphic, formed from sedimentary and volcanic strata on the flanks of the two continents about 100 million to 140 million years ago. Their meeting resulted in tight folding and uplifting of this metamorphic base, forming the precursor to the Sawtooth Range of today.

Continued northerly movement of the micro-continent resulted in the Gardner Fault, which runs roughly along the ridgeline northeast of the Twisp River. This fault marks the west edge of the Methow graben, a wide strip of rock between this fault line and the parallel Pasayten Fault to the east that dropped relative to surrounding rock and was later overlaid with sedimentary deposits. A large granitic intrusion in the vicinity of Gilbert, at the head of the Twisp Valley, created the extensive mineral deposits along its margins that later brought prospectors to the region.

The U-shaped valley of the Twisp is characteristic of the sculpting of glaciers over the last 2 million years. Although most glaciers have disappeared from the area, small hanging ice fields on the north faces of a few peaks have extensive moraines below, testifying to their once-larger expanse. Creeks have more recently eroded narrow, deep V-shaped drainages that carve through many of the lateral ridges.

History

Alexander Ross, of the British North West Company, and three Indian guides explored the north end of the Twisp River in 1814. They probed northwest from South Creek, possibly through Rainy Pass, to the headwaters of the Skagit River. In 1853, Army survey crews under the command of Captain George B. McClellan, looking for possible railroad routes across the Cascades, tested the headwaters of the Twisp and found no practical route to breach the range. In 1882, another Army party, under Lieutenant Henry Pierce, searching for a military route across the Cascades, left the middle Twisp, crossed War Creek Pass, and continued on to Lake Chelan and beyond to the Skagit River.

The first mineral discoveries were made in 1884, and these brought hordes of prospectors to the area over the next six to ten years. The mining camp of Gilbert grew near the head of the Twisp River, and claims were soon plastered over most of Gilbert Mountain, Twisp Pass, Crescent Mountain, and Abernathy Peak. The ores were mostly silver-bearing, with some occur-

The Methow Valley boasts the largest herd of mule deer in the state.

rences of copper and placer gold. Although the surface ores had a high assay value, few mines had significant production, and by 1921 Gilbert lay deserted. Limited mining activity is still carried on at a few of the old claims.

ACTIVITIES

Hiking

LAKE CHELAN TRAILS

All trailheads on Lake Chelan must be reached via either private boat or passenger ferry from Chelan. Passengers can board or disembark at Prince Creek, Moore Point, and Stehekin; stops must be prearranged with the Lake Chelan Boat Company.

Trail #1247, Lakeshore Trail. 18 miles (14 miles in the wilderness)/e (H,S). This path runs through the north half of the wilderness bordering Lake Chelan; there are no trails along the precipitous south half of the shoreline. The trail runs from Prince Creek Campground, on the south, to Flick Creek Campground, just inside the Lake Chelan NRA on the north, then continues to Stehekin. As the way leaves Prince Creek (1,128 ft) it passes the lower end of Trail #1255, then gradually works up to 400 feet above the lake. It stays at this level, with minor ups and downs, as it crosses cascades of several creeks and periodically breaks into viewpoints of the lake and surrounding peaks.

The way wanders up to 1,720 feet, then drops in a few lazy switchbacks to Fish Creek. Here a spur leads west to Moore Point, one of the ferry stops. En route it passes the site of an old hotel, built in 1889–92 to accommodate the rush of prospectors, visitors, and settlers into the upper lake region. Trail #1248 heads east up the Fish Creek drainage, and Trail #1247 continues north near the 1,600-foot level to the NRA boundary.

Trail #1255, Prince Creek. 14 miles/m (H,S; B,M outside the wilderness boundary). From Trail #1247 (1,128 ft) switchbacks climb above the northwest side of the narrow, deep, lower

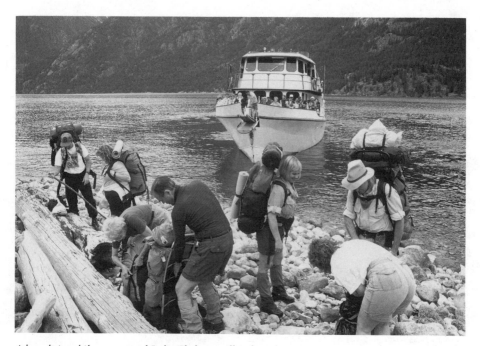

A boat brings hikers to several Lake Chelan trailheads.

Prince Creek drainage. The path then ascends gradually through a ponderosa forest, crosses the creek (2,715 ft), and continues up its east side to the confluence of the Middle and North forks (4,200 ft). Here, at a junction with Trail #1254, it swings east and leaves the wilderness.

Trail #1254, North Fork of Prince Creek. 2 miles/m (H,S). A short path follows the wooded southeast bank of the North Fork of Prince Creek, linking Trail #1255 (4,200 ft) to Trail #1259 (5,560 ft). In conjunction with Trails #1255, #1259, and #1249, it offers the shortest route to Surprise Lake.

Trail #1248, Fish Creek. 10 miles/m (H,S). From Trail #1247 (1,320 ft) this route ascends the steep sidehill above the north bank of Fish Creek to 2,400 feet, where Trail #1250A (#1245 on some maps) leaves to the southeast. The path continues its ascent above the creek, finally closing to it at the confluence of the North and East forks, the junction (3,560 ft) with Trail #1248A.

Trail #1248 follows the East Fork another 3 miles, staying within a few hundred feet of its bank, then crosses the creek to the lower end of Trail #1250. The ascending track crosses the creek three more times before it reaches an alpine meadow and meets Trail #1259 (6,750 ft). The two trails share the tread for 0.2 mile, then Trail #1248 heads uphill, crosses the outlet from Star Lake (7,173 ft), and climbs to Fish Creek Pass (7,500 ft), where it becomes Trail #411.

Trail #1248A, North Fork of Fish Creek. 3 miles/m (H,S). A link to Trail #1259 leaves Trail #1248 at the confluence of the North and Middle forks of Fish Creek. The grade through dense forest is steep, but eventually it levels at a meadow with the first of two crossings of the creek (both hazardous at high water). A more gradual ascent with a final steep scamper leads to Trail #1259 (5,640 ft).

Trail #1250, Indianhead Basin. 4 miles/m (H,S). From Trail #1248 (5,030 ft), switchbacks out of the East Fork of Fish Creek lead up the west bank of a tributary. The route rounds a nose into the Indian Creek drainage, crosses the creek, and follows gentle slopes below cliffs to the rocky head of the basin. The way climbs talus to a deep narrow col (7350 ft). Here are great views south to Finney Peak and the steep north face of the ridge between it and Surprise Lake. The route traverses east from the pass below a cliff band to join Trail #1249 (6,880 ft).

Trail #1249, Surprise Lake. 2.5 miles/m-d (H,S). Leaving Trail #1259 (6,530 ft) east of Baldy Mountain, this path climbs through forest and across rocky slopes to a broad saddle on the ridge to the south (7,050 ft). It descends the rocky sidehill west of the saddle, meets the upper end of Trail #1250, then swings east and switchbacks down a rough path to the west shore of Surprise Lake (6,150 ft). The long lake is wedged in a deep basin at the base of the 800-foot-high cliffs of Finney Ridge.

SOUTH NAVARRE CAMPGROUND TRAILS

Trail #1259, Summit Trail. 27 miles/m (H,S; B,M outside the wilderness). From South Navarre Campground (6,410 ft) the trail heads north for 10 miles to the Middle Fork of Prince Creek. Here it turns west and enters the wilderness at Chipmunk Pass (7,040 ft), on the divide between the Middle and North forks of Prince Creek.

The route drops steeply to a tributary of the North Fork and follows it down to the head of Trail #1254. A diagonal ascent through the forested basin east of Baldy Mountain leads to Trail #1249. The way climbs north from the basin to reach ridgetop meadows at a divide (7,640 ft) above the East Fork of Fish Creek.

The route switchbacks down a wooded cliff to the basin at the head of the East Fork of Fish Creek, then makes a long traverse through timberline parkland to pass Trail #1248. The path swings around the southwest flank of Gray Peak, where Trail #1259E heads uphill for Horseshoe Basin. After crossing a narrow saddle (7,390 ft), a short traverse to yet another pass (7,050 ft) leads to the headwaters of the North Fork of Fish Creek.

The route descends into forest as it heads north past Trail #1259B, then continues down to meet the upper end of Trail #1248A (5,640 ft). It swings west to follow the North Fork of Fish Creek to its headwaters, then climbs above them to a 7,240-foot pass where it enters the Lake Chelan NRA.

Trail #1259B, Eagle Pass. 1 mile/d (H,S). As Trail #1259 drops into the basin at the head of

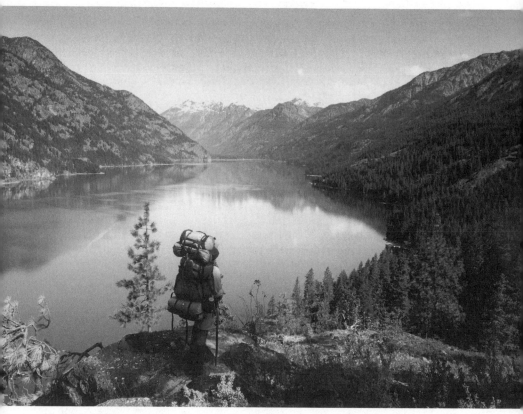

Trail #1247 follows the edge of Lake Chelan for eight miles, offering views up the long lake.

the North Fork of Fish Creek, a short, fading track climbs to Eagle Pass (7,450 ft), where it becomes Trail #410 from Eagle Creek.

BUTTERMILK–MISSION CREEK TRAILS

Trail #420, East Fork of Buttermilk Creek. 6.5 miles/m (H,S). The first 2 miles beyond FR 4300400 (4,750 ft) are on an abandoned road along the East Fork of Buttermilk Creek. At the road's end the track crosses the creek and continues a gentle ascent of the wooded creek bottom. The way crosses the creek twice near the head of the basin, where it becomes steep and rocky as it breaks into the talus and boulder slope on the north side of Hoodo Pass. The pass (7,630 ft) marks the wilderness boundary, where this trail becomes #1259C and drops down the south side of the pass to Trail #1259.

Trail #411, West Fork of Buttermilk Creek. 9.5 miles/m (H,S). At the end of FR 4300500 (3,800 ft), the way gradually ascends the wooded bottom of the West Fork of Buttermilk Creek drainage. After a potentially dangerous creek crossing at 0.1 mile, the path continues up the deep wedge-shaped valley, through boggy sections where the path closes with the creek. Near the head of the drainage, the route crosses to the southeast side of the creek; switchbacks gain a tree-covered bench. After another creek crossing, a steep ascent breaks into rocky scrub with a glimpse of talus marking the terminal moraine of a onetime pocket glacier on the north side of Star Peak. At Fish Creek Pass (7,530 ft) this route becomes Trail #1248 as it descends the west side of the range.

Trail #436, Buttermilk Meadows. 6.5 miles/m (H,S). This old stock drive high above the

West Fork of Buttermilk Creek may be difficult to follow in places. From the end of FR 4300560 (5,000 ft), the track heads southeast up a broad timbered ridge, then traverses the rim of Buttermilk Meadows, on the south slopes of Scaffold Ridge. The route contours a wooded bluff about 1,000 feet above the valley floor, then reaches a small unnamed lake (6,936 ft). After a lateral descent of steep slopes, the path joins Trail #411 (6,850 ft) at the last series of switchbacks climbing to Fish Creek Pass.

TWISP RIVER TRAILS

Trail #410, Eagle Creek. *7.3 miles/e (H,S).* At the end of FR 4420080 (3,010 ft) the path heads into the narrow Eagle Creek drainage to where the beak of Duckbill Mountain splits Eagle Creek from Oval Creek, its tributary to the south. This route continues up the densely forested bottom along Eagle Creek. At 5,700 feet the drainage widens to a wooded basin with a sprinkling of meadows. The track follows the creek west toward Battle Mountain, swings around the head of the basin, and with a few switchbacks reaches the parkland bench of Eagle Pass (7,280 ft). To the west the route becomes Trail #1259B.

Trail #410A, Oval Creek. *6.5 miles/m (H,S).* At the 2-mile point on Trail #410 (3,800 ft), this route crosses Eagle Creek and zigzags up a rib to get above a deep narrow cleft at the mouth of Oval Creek. The path then traverses to meet the rising creek as it heads up the narrow valley floor. The creek and trail continue in tandem as they ascend southwest for 5 miles. At the drainage-head basin, the trail climbs to the rock-rimmed cirque containing West Oval Lake (6,860 ft); it continues from here as Trail #410B.

Trail #410B, Oval Lakes. *2 miles/d (H,S).* From West Oval Lake, the way rounds a sharp rib to the south, then contours a small grass and talus basin to a saddle (7,650 ft) on the shoulder of Gray Peak. From the saddle, the track descends a gully and a forested rib to reach Middle Oval Lake (6,695 ft), hunkered beneath the sheer north face of Buttermilk Ridge. A short stroll east leads to East Oval Lake (6,656 ft).

Trail #408, War Creek. *9.3 miles/m (H,S).* From the end of FR 4430100 the route enters the mouth of the War Creek drainage (3,140 ft). Steep, forested valley walls sweep up 2,000 feet to enclosing ridgetops. The way follows the north side of the creek, climbing for 9 miles to War Creek Pass (6,780 ft). The ascent passes through the Douglas-fir, silver fir, and subalpine fir zones, presenting a botany lesson in the trees, shrubs, and grasses of each. At the pass the route enters the Lake Chelan NRA to meet the Boulder Creek, Purple Creek, and Summit trails.

Trail #414, Slate Creek. *5 miles/m-d (H,S).* From FR 44 on the west side of Little Slate Creek (2,860 ft), the route heads uphill in dense forest, picking its way up narrow benches in the steep side-slope. When these wide spots run out, switchbacks attack the slope directly, gaining the nose of a ridge at the wilderness boundary (4,800 ft). The uphill slog continues to the ridge crest (6,200 ft), where the climb slackens a bit and alpine meadows offer views of Midnight Mountain, Abernathy Ridge, and the vertical north face of Reynolds Peak. The way swings across a poorly marked parkland bench high above Little Slate Creek, crosses between bands of cliffs, and turns into the cirque enclosing Slate Lake (6,400 ft).

Trail #402, Reynolds Creek. *6.6 miles/m (H,S).* From the end of FR 4435015 (3,160 ft), the route heads into the narrow maw of lower Reynolds Creek to traverse a steep side-slope above the creek. The basin slowly widens, and meadows give glimpses of the 2,400-foot-high north face of Reynolds Peak. At a wooded bench below these cliffs, the path zigzags up to a tiny meadow flat, then struggles on, picking its way up a final rock cliff to Reynolds Pass (6,874 ft), the boundary with the Lake Chelan NRA. Although no trail continues south of the pass, a moderate cross-country scramble downhill can reach the Boulder Creek Trail.

Trail #401, South Creek. *7.8 miles/m (H,S).* From South Creek Campground (3,180 ft) the route heads into forest at the bottom of the deep V-shaped slopes of the South Creek valley. The track follows the creek west through avalanche-cut meadows in the ever-widening valley floor. These openings provide peeks at Crescent Mountain to the north and the long, imposing face of Rennie Peak to the south. The gentle grade continues up to the headwater basin, where a climb through flowered parkland reaches South Pass (6,300 ft), the Lake Chelan NRA border. Here an expansive view takes in nearby McAlester Mountain and the more distant icy summits of North Cascades National Park. Beyond, the path becomes the South Creek Pass Trail.

Trail #413, North Creek. 4.8 miles/m (H,S). The route starts amid prospect pockmarks alongside FR 4440 (3,662 ft), makes a couple of long swings uphill to pass a mine, then snakes along North Creek. Timber and meadows alternate as the valley bends from north to west and rounds the flank of Gilbert Mountain. At 3.6 miles the way passes the south end of Trail #476 (5,460 ft), a path that climbs steeply to a narrow notch (6,420 ft) through a long stretch of sawtooth pinnacles along the wilderness boundary, then enters the Liberty Bell Roadless Area. Trail #413 ascends to meadows; beyond a tiny tarn (5,700 ft) it splits, the south fork continuing to North Lake (5,780 ft), and the southwest fork climbing to mining operations in the cliffs above (6,600 ft).

Trail #432, Twisp Pass. 4.8 miles/m (H,S). The route leaves FR 4440 at Roads End Campground (3,690 ft) and heads up the glacier-cut Twisp River valley. In 1.5 miles the east rib of Lincoln Butte splits the Twisp into the North and South forks; this trail follows the South Fork, while Trail #426 heads up the North Fork. The track climbs the nose of Lincoln Butte to a clearing with great views of the sheer north faces of Crescent Mountain and companion peaks to the west. A traverse reaches cliffs, where the tread has been chiseled from a rock wall, then the way enters flower meadows as it continues to Twisp Pass (6,064 ft). Here it enters North Cascades National Park as the Twisp Pass (Fireweed) Trail.

Trail #426, Copper Pass. 4.8 miles/m (H,S). At 1.5 miles up Trail #432 (4,500 ft), the route heads up the North Fork of the Twisp River. This old prospector track between Gilbert and Stehekin was once abandoned, but was partially restored in the early 1980s by the volunteer efforts of outdoor groups. The lower portion of the route follows the wooded bottom of the North Fork to a small basin where the river splits into two major tributaries. The trail continues along the northwest branch and heads straight uphill with scarcely a breath-catching pause. The forest breaks into meadows, which yield to heather by the time the trail reaches Copper Pass (6,700 ft). The panorama of rugged peaks includes nearby Kangaroo Ridge, Early Winter Spires, and Stiletto Peak; beyond are Corteo Peak and the glaciated face of Goode Mountain. The trail continuing west down Copper Creek to Bridge Creek is brushy, but can be followed.

WOLF CREEK TRAILS

Trail #527, Wolf Creek. 10.3 miles/m (H,S). At the end of FR 5005 (2,700 ft), a long valley-bottom path heads west along the bank of Wolf Creek. Most of the lower valley is heavily wooded, though occasional meadows have early-season splashes of wildflower color. The route continues its gradual ascent along Wolf Creek to reach the broad expanse of Gardner Meadows (5,780 ft), with views up the vertical north face of Abernathy Ridge. The trail ends at the meadows, but skilled cross-country hikers can continue another mile up either fork of the creek to small alpine lakes.

Climbing

Although several peaks in the wilderness are in the 7,500- to 8,800-foot range, and many have massive near-vertical north faces, all of the summits can be reached by relatively simple scramble routes. The higher and more impressive peaks are listed here. Gilbert Mountain (8,023 ft) has a 600-foot north wall that encircles a small pocket of glacial ice. It can be climbed via the west ridge or south slope via mine trails to the upper slopes. Crescent Mountain (7,816 ft) has an abrupt north wall that continues west for almost 3 miles. Abernathy Peak (8,321 ft) is a rugged-looking pyramid at the west end of Abernathy Ridge.

Gardner Mountain (8,897 ft), the highest point in the Lake Chelan–Sawtooth Wilderness, has a massive 1,800-foot northeast face. A cross-country hike up the south slopes to the southeast ridge offers an easy summit route. Oval Peak (8,795 ft) is a large rounded dome, easily accessible from any side except via northeast cliffs. Courtney Peak (8,392 ft) is a triangular summit with a sheer 1,000-foot north face that rises above Oval Lakes; it is an easy ridge walk from Fish Creek Pass. Star Peak (8,690 ft), one of the highest summits on the Sawtooth crest, also is an easy ascent from Fish Creek Pass.

47

SAWTOOTH RIDGE

LOCATION: In Chelan and Okanogan counties, along the southeast side of the Lake Chelan–Sawtooth Wilderness

SIZE: 64,700 acres

STATUS: Semiprimitive Motorized

TERRAIN: Sawtooth Ridge, a sharp, high alpine divide, runs through the heart of the area. Creeks have cut deep lateral drainages that are separated by long ridges, narrow near the backbone crest and broader at lower elevations.

ELEVATION: 1,098 to 8,580 feet

MANAGEMENT: USFS, Wenatchee National Forest, Chelan Ranger District; and Okanogan National Forest, Twisp Ranger District

TOPOGRAPHIC MAPS: Billy Goat Mtn., Hungry Mtn., Martin Peak, Oss Peak, Prince Creek, South Navarre Peak

This area is a contiguous extension of the Lake Chelan–Sawtooth Wilderness, and should have been included within its boundaries. Unfortunately, acceding to multiple-use concepts, the Forest Service accepted existing motorized use of this portion of Sawtooth Ridge, and has

Crater Lake in the Sawtooth Ridge Roadless Area

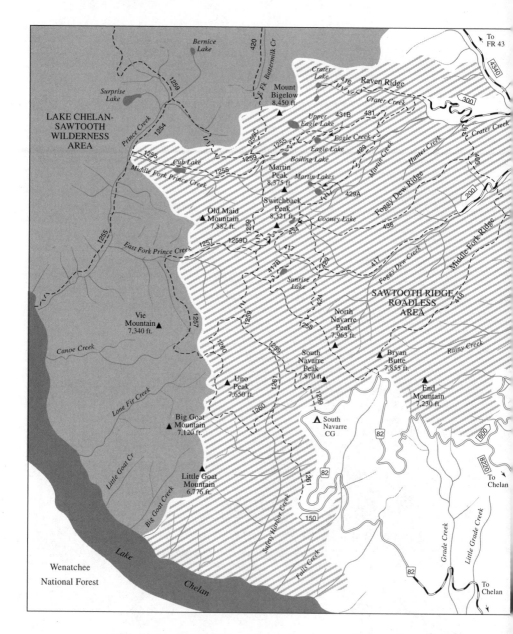

reconstructed 22 miles of trails, converting them to motorcycle highways. This use would have been precluded had the area been a part of the wilderness. Thankfully, a few trails (mostly old sheep drives) are too delicate, steep, or rough for motorized travel. These tend to follow the tops of the area's highest ridges, and therefore offer outstanding scenery. Short spur trails to six of the region's eight named lakes are also closed to motorized traffic, and another 15 or so smaller lakes can only be reached by cross-country scrambles.

Climate

Precipitation is relatively light, ranging from 18 to 23 inches, falling mainly as snow. Most of the snow is gone by the end of June, except at the highest elevations. Midwinter temperatures average in the 20s, with lows dipping to minus 30 degrees. Summers are warm, with average temperatures in the 70s and highs often near 100.

Plants and Wildlife

Lodgepole pine covers a large portion of the southern part of the area, but the mid-range elevations west of the crest have forests of Douglas-fir, silver fir, ponderosa pine, and western larch. Northeast of the divide the forest is composed mostly of lodgepole pine and western larch. Ridgetops have large meadows with a more open cover of white-bark pine, Englemann spruce, and subalpine fir.

The usual forest inhabitants include mule deer, cougar, and black bear.

Geology

All of the area is underlaid with Mesozoic and early Tertiary granitic rock, often exposed on south-facing slopes. Soils are granitic glacial till covered with volcanic ash of varying thickness, laid down in the last eruptions of Glacier Peak.

History

The meadows along ridgetops and in high basins have been used since the 1920s for grazing sheep; short sections of a long sheep drive from Chelan to the Pasayten still exist on the eastern slopes, and are still used for this purpose. A number of the area's trails were put in and maintained by shepherds.

ACTIVITIES

Hiking

EAST SLOPE TRAILS

Trail #405, Pasayten. 8.6 miles/m (H,S,B,M). This is one of the few remaining sections of an 80-mile-long sheep drive from the Chelan area north to the Pasayten highlands. Most of the route has been decimated by roads and logging, but this short piece is still used to access ridgecrest grazing trails. The north end of this trail segment starts at Crater Creek on FR 4340300 (3,201 ft) and switchbacks south to the top of Foggy Dew Ridge (4,550 ft), where it meets the east end of Trail #438. From here it drops steeply southeast to Foggy Dew Creek and FR 4340200 (2,922 ft). Switchbacks regain lost elevation, and the way joins Trail #418 atop Middle Fork Ridge (4,685 ft). After sharing a tread for 1.3 miles, this path leaves Trail #418 and traverses south to the Middle Fork of Gold Creek (3,270 ft). A short climb reaches a saddle in South Fork Ridge (4,005 ft), then the route descends to FR 4330100 (3,380 ft) in the South Fork of Gold Creek drainage.

Trail #431, Eagle Lake. 7 miles/m (H,S,B,M). From the end of FR 4340300 (4,750 ft) the route follows Crater Creek upstream to a fork in 1 mile, then swings south as it climbs around the nose of the ridge between Crater and Martin creeks. Long diagonal ascents linked by tailored-for-motorcycle switchbacks gradually work up the forested side-slope past the junction with Trail #429. The ascent becomes steeper as it passes Trail #431A to Upper Eagle Lake

Boiling Lake and the drainage of the Middle Fork of Prince Creek in the Sawtooth Ridge Roadless Area

(7,110 ft). Trail #431B descends from the first of the switchbacks below Horsehead Pass to Lower Eagle Lake (6,490 ft). The way climbs to Horsehead Pass (7,580 ft), where it continues west as Trail #1255.

Trail #429, Martin Creek. *8.9 miles/e (H,S,B,M).* From the 2.5-mile point on Trail #431 (5,720 ft), this route weaves down to cross Eagle Creek (5,235 ft), then gradually ascends side-slopes northwest of Martin Creek through old-growth forest. At 6.5 miles a side path reaches the twin Martin Lakes (6,729 ft and 6,820 ft) lying in larch-rimmed meadows. The route wanders gradually uphill around the headwaters of Martin Creek to meet Trail #434 (7,240 ft). A short descent southeast passes the west end of Trail #438, then the way drops down slopes above a fork of Foggy Dew Creek to end on Trail #417 (6,645 ft).

Trail #434, Cooney Lake. *1.5 miles/m-d (H,S).* In a meadow just 0.2 mile from Trail #429 lies Cooney Lake (7,241 ft), with more than a half-dozen small ponds above its west shore. A primitive path continues southwest from the lake, where tight switchbacks up a steep talus slope reach a notch (7,970 ft) on the east rib of Switchback Peak and the junction with Trail #417 from Merchants Basin.

Trail #438, Foggy Dew Ridge. *5.2 miles/d (H,S,B,M).* This sheep driveway runs along the crest of Foggy Dew Ridge. It leaves Trail #405 (4,550 ft) at a ridgetop saddle and climbs abruptly up a steep forested nose to a long gentle ascent atop the rounded crest. Breaks in the timber give views down into the Martin and Foggy Dew drainages, and occasional glimpses of the Sawtooth crest. The trail, unmaintained and indistinct in places, stays on the ridgetop for 3 miles to where the crest swings north around upper Hunter Creek. The way contours the hillside, maintaining a constant elevation until it joins Trail #429 (6,800 ft) a short distance below Cooney Lake.

Trail #417, Foggy Dew. 7.6 miles/m-d (H,S,B; M to Trail #429). From the end of FR 4340200 (3,440 ft) the track follows the north bank of Foggy Dew Creek, passing the flashing cascade of Foggy Dew Falls in 1.6 miles. The path continues upstream for 3.4 more miles to meet Trail #429, beyond which it is closed to motorbikes. Switchbacks leave forest for the meadows of Merchants Basin. Shortly Trail #417B heads south; Trail #417 continues up to Merchants Basin. An indistinct tread leads to switchbacks up talus slopes to a notch (7,970 ft) on the east rib of Switchback Peak, where Trail #434 is joined. The path now contours the south face of the peak to the Sawtooth crest (8,040 ft), where it continues west as Trail #1259D.

Trail #417B, Sunrise Lake. 0.75 mile/e (H,S). A short ascent from Trail #417 (7,160 ft) enters the pincers of two rock cliffs to reach the cirque holding Sunrise Lake (7,228 ft). The lake is rimmed by a small meadow with scattered larch and subalpine fir; above the trail climbs rock walls to the Sawtooth crest and Trail #1258.

Trail #418, Middle Fork Ridge (Bryan Butte). 10 miles/m (H,S,B,M). This unmaintained sheep drive starts from the end of a spur up the Middle Fork of Gold Creek off FR 4340 (2,200 ft). It continues up the creek to join Trail #405 and shares its tread to the top of Middle Fork Ridge (4,685 ft). The route heads southwest, keeping atop the broad ridge as it climbs through open forest and meadows with excellent views of the south end of the Sawtooth crest. At 7 miles the ridgetop narrows, with steep drop-offs on both sides; the trail stays steadfastly along its top. The path swings sharply south on a ridge north from Bryan Butte and ascends arrow-straight to the top of the butte (7,855 ft).

WEST SLOPE TRAILS

Trail #1258, Summer Blossom. 6 miles/m-d (H). Another old sheep driveway, improved in the 1930s by the CCC, leaves FR 82 (6,430 ft) in the Summer Blossom Basin and heads northwest along Sawtooth Ridge. Much of the way is in meadows and rocky flower gardens along the crest, where the tread is faint. Views of the peaks of the Glacier Peak Wilderness and the Methow Valley are priceless. The path strays off the ridge to avoid North Navarre Peak, but sightseers can scramble to its top (7,963 ft) for expanded scenic views. After meeting the upper end of Trail #424, the route slips from the crest to its upper west slope and bends around a rocky rib into Horsethief Basin. It continues to a saddle at the head of the basin (7,390 ft), where it merges with Trail #1259.

Trail #1259, Summit. 27 miles (11.5 miles to the wilderness boundary)/m (H; S,B,M to the boundary). Starting at the South Navarre Campground (6,630 ft), this trail runs north along the Sawtooth crest for 27 miles to the Lake Chelan NRA. The portion in the Lake Chelan–Sawtooth Wilderness is described in that section. From the campground the path descends through forest and meadow to Safety Harbor Creek, where it meets the north end of Trail #1261. It follows the creek northwest into Miners Basin to meet Trail #1260, then climbs steeply to reach the west slopes of Horsethief Basin. At the pass at the head of this basin (7,390 ft), the path meets Trail #1258. Switchbacks descend to the headwaters of the East Fork of Prince Creek, where a traverse of the basin meadows leads to Trail #1259D. The route continues north to the headwaters of the Middle Fork of Prince Creek. At the creek the route crosses Trail #1255, turns sharply west, and ascends steep side-slopes to Chipmunk Pass (7,040 ft), the wilderness boundary. En route it passes the lower end of Trail #1259C to Hoodo Pass.

Trail #1259D, Angel Staircase. 1.5 miles/d (H,S). The highest trail across Sawtooth Ridge ties Trail #1259 (6,990 ft) to Trail #417 at the Sawtooth crest (8,020 ft). The route is quite steep, with a faint tread through many switchbacks marked by cairns.

Trail #1255, Prince Creek. 14 miles/m (H,S; B,M to the wilderness boundary). From the wilderness boundary (4,200 ft) the trail follows the Middle Fork of Prince Creek east past Cub Lake (5,235 ft), crosses Trail #1259, then climbs to Boiling Lake (6,950 ft). From this pretty, meadow-rimmed lake, gentle switchbacks climb to Horsehead Pass (7,580 ft), and the path becomes Trail #431.

Trail #1259C, Hoodo Pass. 1.3 miles/e (H,S). The route leaves Trail #1259 (6,650 ft) and climbs gradually through a broad open timber-and-meadow basin to Hoodo Pass (7,430 ft), where it crosses into the wilderness and becomes Trail #420.

Trail #1261, Safety Harbor. 4.5 miles/m (H,S,B,M). Starting at the end of FR 8200150 (4,325 ft), the trail follows an old roadbed beside an abandoned aqueduct northwest for 2 miles, to where it meets Safety Harbor Creek and Trail #1260. Here the trail twists uphill alongside the creek to meet Trail #1259 (5,520 ft).

Trail #1260, Uno Peak. 6.5 miles/m (H,S,B,M). From Trail #1261 at Safety Harbor Creek (4,500 ft), the route heads up across the broad, steep, timbered southeast face of Uno Peak. Switchbacks lead to a ridge-crest notch where the way swings onto the south face of the peak and makes a diagonal ascent to another saddle on the west edge of that face. The route climbs along the west side of the peak, then drops to a bench above Miners Basin. It follows this bench around the head of the basin to meet Trail #1259 (6,260 ft).

Winter Sports

The main winter recreation in the area is snowmobiling on roads on the east side of the area. Check with local ranger districts regarding specific trails that are open to snowmobiling.

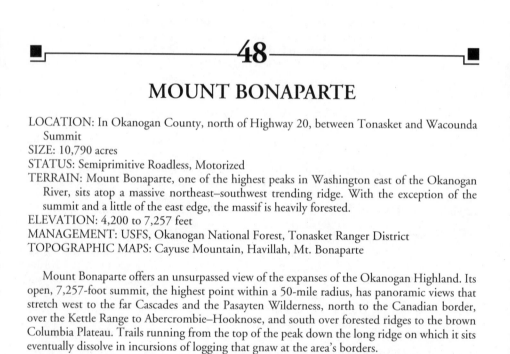

48

MOUNT BONAPARTE

LOCATION: In Okanogan County, north of Highway 20, between Tonasket and Wacounda Summit
SIZE: 10,790 acres
STATUS: Semiprimitive Roadless, Motorized
TERRAIN: Mount Bonaparte, one of the highest peaks in Washington east of the Okanogan River, sits atop a massive northeast–southwest trending ridge. With the exception of the summit and a little of the east edge, the massif is heavily forested.
ELEVATION: 4,200 to 7,257 feet
MANAGEMENT: USFS, Okanogan National Forest, Tonasket Ranger District
TOPOGRAPHIC MAPS: Cayuse Mountain, Havillah, Mt. Bonaparte

Mount Bonaparte offers an unsurpassed view of the expanses of the Okanogan Highland. Its open, 7,257-foot summit, the highest point within a 50-mile radius, has panoramic views that stretch west to the far Cascades and the Pasayten Wilderness, north to the Canadian border, over the Kettle Range to Abercrombie–Hooknose, and south over forested ridges to the brown Columbia Plateau. Trails running from the top of the peak down the long ridge on which it sits eventually dissolve in incursions of logging that gnaw at the area's borders.

Climate

The mean annual precipitation is between 13 and 14 inches. About a third of this falls between October and January, starting as rain and changing to snow by late November. Midwinter mean minimum temperatures run 14 to 16 degrees, and midsummer mean highs are in the high 80s to low 90s.

Plants and Wildlife

Lodgepole pine is dominant on the heavily forested slopes of Mount Bonaparte. Other species include Douglas-fir, western larch, and Englemann spruce, along with scatterings of ponderosa pine and subalpine fir. The south side of the mountain holds some good-sized stands of old-growth trees. Small meadows with subalpine vegetation coat the barren summit and a portion of the ridgetop on which it sits.

The lower portions of the mountain are a winter range for mule and white-tailed deer, and lower ridges are winter habitat for blue grouse. Occasionally coyotes, martens, and raptors such as golden eagles, hawks, and the rare great gray owl may be seen. The preponderance of lodgepole pine means few snags for typical cavity dwellers such as woodpeckers or porcupines, which are seldom found here.

Geology

Mount Bonaparte is at the northern edge of a massive granite dome that was intruded about 60 million years ago. As this dome rose, it dragged with it a fringe of older gneiss that surrounds this granite core. Surface soils are mostly glacial till left after the melting of continental ice sheets, plus more recent alluvium.

History

Mount Bonaparte is the primary fire lookout site for the Tonasket Ranger District; two generations of lookout structures are perched atop its summit. One, a hand-hewn log cabin built in 1914, is on the National Register of Historic Places. The more recent one is a conventional tower.

The old and new fire lookouts on the summit of Mount Bonaparte

ACTIVITIES

Hiking

Trail #304, Antoine Trail. 6 miles/m (H). The lower trailhead on FR 3230150 (4,400 ft) has been obscured by several clearcuts on the west side of Antoine Creek, so it may be difficult to find. If in doubt, follow the southeast rim of the cuts to pick it up as it parallels the creek, about 350 yards above its west bank. A gentle grade continues upstream, rounds the upper drainage, and heads north in a gradual ascent to the nose of the ridge to the east. It turns southeast up this broad ridge, climbing first through older fir and larch, then lodgepole pine. About 0.5 mile from the top of Mount Bonaparte it joins Trail #306 from Myers Creek (6,920 ft).

Trail #307, Fourth of July. 6.8 miles/m (H). From FR 3230 at the divide between Mill Creek and the North Fork of Siwash Creek (5,078 ft), the route heads east, then south along a bench, crosses the North Fork of Siwash Creek, then begins a long, gradual ascent of the wooded southeast side of the ridge running southwest from Mount Bonaparte. The way twists around minor ridges and basins at the head of Lightning and Pettijohn creeks. After traversing the steeper south flank of Mount Bonaparte, it weaves north to meet Trail #308 on the east side of the mountain (5,820 ft).

Trail #306, Myers Creek. 4.5 miles/m (H). The most direct route to the top of the mountain starts from FR 3300300 (4,640 ft). After negotiating a path through clearcuts, the way enters virgin forest and climbs south to meet Trail #308 (5,680 ft). More uphill grind reaches the top of Trail #304 (6,120 ft). The route breaks into subalpine trees and meadows at the summit (7,527 ft).

Trail #308, South Side Trail. 5.5 miles/m (H). FR 3300100 provides a new trailhead for this path, which once started 1,000 feet lower at Bonaparte Lake Campground (the lower trail section is still followable). The trail leaves the road (4,550 ft) and climbs southwest up the steep sidehill past Duff Spring to a cliffy area, switchbacks north, rounds a broad ridge nose, then meets Trail #307. The route traverses northwest through timber to merge with Trail #306 (5,680 ft).

—49—

PROFANITY

LOCATION: In Ferry County, along the Kettle Range, extending north from Highway 20 at Sherman Pass to Highway 602 at Deer Creek Summit

SIZE: 30,380 acres

STATUS: Semiprimitive Nonmotorized

TERRAIN: The north portion of the Kettle Range is a long north–south crest capped by a series of broad rounded summits. Lateral streams from this hydrological divide flow west to the Sanpoil and Curlew valleys, and east to the Columbia River.

ELEVATION: 4,250 to 7,135 feet

MANAGEMENT: USFS, Colville National Forest, Republic and Kettle Falls ranger districts

TOPOGRAPHIC MAPS: Big Goat, Cooke Mountain, Copper Butte, Edds Mountain, Malo, Mt. Leona, Sherman Peak

The long backbone of the Kettle Range is a distance hiker's nirvana, because its 30-mile-length is closed to motorbikes—a rarity for trails east of the Cascades. The entire distance is at ridgetop level, passing over a series of local high spots or near enough to them for view-seeking side trips. These summits have fascinating names—Jungle Hill, Wapaloosie Mountain, Scar Mountain, Midnight Mountain, Stickpin Hill, and Profanity Peak. For hikers who wish to

This fire lookout on the summit of Columbia Mountain was built in 1914. Only faint ruins remain today.

break the long crest trail into more digestible sections, several lateral access trails, 3 miles or less, intersect it from both sides of the ridge.

Early summer travelers are rewarded by a profusion of wildflowers in open alpine meadows, and in fall bird-watchers can spot raptors migrating through the region. Views from high spots are expansive but—as real estate agents put it, "territorial." Most open spots overlook a sea of rolling wooded hills on either side of the range that drop to unseen valley drainages and rise on the opposite side to distant ranges on the horizon.

Climate

Because the Kettle Range is a major obstacle to eastward-flowing weather systems, it tends to get more precipitation than areas of the Okanogan Highlands that border it on either side. Annual precipitation ranges between 28 and 35 inches, with more than half falling between October and March, a substantial portion of this in the form of snow. Periods of heavy rain also occur in May and June. Midwinter temperatures average in the 20s, with lows in the mid-teens. Summer temperatures average in the mid- to high 60s, with highs in the lower 90s.

Plants and Wildlife

Where the climax forest has not been touched by fire, the dominant species of trees are Douglas-fir, western red cedar, and subalpine fir, with Englemann spruce, quaking aspen, birch, and cottonwood in damper stream drainages. Understory vegetation for this segment of forest includes pinegrass, sedges, arnica, Oregon boxwood, huckleberry, trail plant, queencup beadlily, wood violet, and anemone. Dense stands of pole-sized western larch, lodgepole pine, and ponderosa pine have replaced large portions of the original forest consumed by large fires in 1929. Open slopes on drier southern exposures have a cover of fescues and sagebrush.

Wildlife includes mule and white-tailed deer, with the population shifting toward the latter

in recent years. Other forest inhabitants are black bear, cougar, bobcat, marten, lynx, ruffed and blue grouse, and snowshoe hare. The range is on the migration route for raptors such as golden eagles and peregrine falcons.

Geology

The northern portion of the range is composed mainly of older pre-Jurassic metamorphic gneiss, schist, and quartzite. About 60 million years ago this base was intruded in the south, near Sherman Pass, by younger granite. Soils are composed of volcanic ash, loess, and glacial till, with the ash component more heavily eroded on steeper south and west slopes. The northern portion of Profanity, in the vicinity of Mount Leona, has significant deposits of uranium, tungsten, silver, gold, and copper ores.

History

In 1872, a large area that includes the Kettle Range was designated as the Colville Indian Reservation. Its reservation status was short-lived, as the north portion of the reservation was opened to homesteading and mining in 1892. An Army group under the command of Lieutenant Henry H. Pierce was one of the first to explore the area; it crossed Sherman Pass in 1882. A second Army contingent traversed the region a year later, and the pass was named for its leader, General William Tecumseh Sherman, later of Civil War fame. An old stage road later crossed the range some 7 miles north of Sherman Pass, and its route is followed today by Trails #1 and #75.

The Colville National Forest was created in 1907, and the Forest Service built fire lookouts on two of Profanity's summits, Columbia Mountain and Copper Butte. Only faint remains of either exist today, but hikes to those summits still reward visitors with outstanding views.

ACTIVITIES

Hiking

The Profanity area is a narrow 30-mile-long strip of the Kettle Range between Sherman Pass on Highway 20, to the south, and Deer Creek Summit on Highway 602, to the north. Trail #13 runs the length of this backbone ridge, and all other trails in the area are primarily access routes to Trail #13.

Trail #13, Kettle Crest North. 29 miles/m (H,S,B). A long route atop the Kettle crest switchbacks north out of Sherman Pass (5,513 ft) to a bench, then contours the west flank of Columbia Mountain. As the forest breaks to meadows, a spur climbs southeast across an open hillside to a former lookout site atop the mountain (6,782 ft). Here are excellent views north and south along the crest, west to the Sanpoil River valley and Republic, and east across the Columbia River drainage. The crest trail swings west around a ridge finger, then returns east to a saddle (6,186 ft). It traverses the west and north sides of Jungle Hill, then zigzags down to meet the upper end of Trail #12. Switchbacks regain lost altitude as the way heads northeast into alpine meadows to the junction with Trail #15, just south of Wapaloosie Mountain. After rounding the west side of the mountain, a drop north down a rocky face leads to the east end of Trail #17 (6,570 ft) from Bracken Creek.

The path contours the west side of Scar Mountain, drops to a col (6,430 ft) to meet Trail #8 from the west, then climbs the ridge to the top of Copper Butte, the highest summit in the North Kettle Range (7,140 ft). Here are the remains of a lookout cabin, and views west to Republic, east to Colville, and southeast to Mount Spokane. A few gentle switchbacks down through lodgepole pine reach a saddle (6,050 ft) once crossed by a stage road over the Kettle Range. Trails #1, to the west and #75, to the east, follow its route.

The track continues through meadows with wide westward views as it gradually ascends to the south slopes of Lambert Mountain. The trail swings west across open slopes to meet Trail #47, then drops north across a steep, thickly forested sidehill. At a narrow saddle (5,648 ft) south of Mount Lenora, the way bends sharply east.

The trail contours a creek-head basin, then climbs to a narrow saddle (5,520 ft) on the west ridge of Ryan Hill. Switchbacks drop down the steep north shoulder of the hill to the head of a tributary of the South Fork of Boulder Creek, and the junction with Trail #30.

The route climbs a wooded knob to the north, descends to a pair of saddles west of Profanity Peak, and follows the west side of the ridge through a meadow, then Douglas-fir and lodgepole pine forest, to the east end of Trail #32. The way now swings east, drops to cross Indian Creek, then ascends to an old logging road atop Taylor Ridge (6,082 ft). After following the road a short distance, the trail shifts back to the crest, heads up and down over humps to the northeast, skirts the top of Sentinel Butte, and drops to the Deer Creek Summit Campground on FR 61 (4,630 ft).

WEST-SIDE TRAILS

Trail #12, Sherman. *1.1 miles/m (H,S,B).* This short hike leaves FR 20400065 just before it crosses the South Fork of the Sanpoil River (5,040 ft) and heads east into the forest. A gradual ascent passes through two small meadows, then a few switchbacks reach Trail #13 at a narrow saddle (5,840 ft) north of Jungle Hill.

Trail #17, Timber Ridge. *1.7 miles/m (H,S,B).* From a logging clearcut (5,520 ft) on FR 2040200, the path swings uphill northwest to gain a ridgetop meadow. It follows the broad forested crest of Timber Ridge east to a steeper, narrower rib, and ascends it to join Trail #13 atop a small knob (6,570 ft) between Wapaloosie and Scar mountains.

Trail #8, Marcus. *3.5 miles/m (H,S,B).* The route leaves the north side of FR 2040250 (4,750 ft) to wander up and cross the heads of three streams feeding the North Fork of the Sanpoil. An ascent, first in forest, then in dry side-slope meadows, reaches Trail #13 at a saddle (6,430 ft) on the ridge south of Copper Butte.

Trail #1, Old Stage Road. *5.8 miles/m (H,S,B, and Wagon).* Follow a piece of history, the old stage road across the Kettle Range, as it leaves FR 2165 (3,914 ft), crosses a bridge over Lambert Creek, and takes a few easy-grade switchbacks to gain a broad forested ridge crest. After following the ridge east a short way, the path makes a diagonal ascent across the north-facing slope of upper Lambert Creek basin. The trail swings northeast as it cuts up across the basin headwall to a saddle (6,050 ft) between Copper Butte and Midnight Mountain, where it meets with Trails #13 and #75.

Trail #47, Old Lambert. *1.6 miles/m (H,S,B).* The route leaves FR 2165300 (5,150 ft), passes a spring, and continues east through sidehill forest and meadow with broad views west to Curlew Lake. A steeper rib triggers a few switchbacks before Trail #13 is met (6,110 ft) northwest of Lambert Mountain.

Trail #32, Profanity. *1.5 miles/e (H,S,B).* Probably the easiest of all the west-side feeder routes to Trail #13, Trail #32 leaves the northeast side of FR 2160 (5,240 ft), waltzes a few hundred yards up to a broad wooded saddle, then turns southeast and wanders up an easy grade to Trail #13 at a 5,630-foot-high notch.

EAST-SIDE TRAILS

Trail #82, Sherman Pass. *4 miles/d (H,S,B).* Take Trail #96 northwest out of the Sherman Pass Campground (5,230 ft), and in 0.5 mile head north on Trail #82. The path crosses beneath a power line, climbs into the woods to the north, and swings around the head of a small stream to a narrow wooded divide (5,410 ft) between Sherman and Pass creeks. The track follows the rounded ridge to the northeast, descends to its steeper lower nose, then makes a lazy switchback down the east slope to cross Sherman Creek and join Trail #16 (4,280 ft) just east of FR 2030.

Trail #15, Wapaloosie. *3.5 miles/e-m (H,S,B).* Just after leaving FR 2030 (4,980 ft), this trail crosses the North Fork of Sherman Creek and heads up the lodgepole pine–covered slope in long gentle switchbacks. At 6,000 feet the path turns to a diagonal ascent south, across broad meadows on the east flank of Wapaloosie Mountain. Two more swings up through the meadows open views east of Graves and Mack mountains. The way then works around the south side of the mountain to join Trail #13 (6,860 ft).

Trail #75, Old Stage Road. *1.7 miles/m (H,S,B, and Wagon).* This is the eastern continuation of the old wagon road (reconstructed in 1992) that Trail #1 follows from the west. The gentle grade departs the west side of FR 2030 (5,478 ft), makes a pair of easy swings across the forested east slope, and gradually ascends to a saddle to meet Trails #1 and #13 (6,050 ft).

Trail #30, Ryan Cabin. 1.4 miles/e (H,S,B). From a common trailhead with Trail #71 (4,280 ft), this path turns northwest along a stream feeding the South Fork of Boulder Creek. A steady sidehill climb soon reaches Trail #13 (4,890 ft) as it descends the north flank of Ryan Hill.

Winter Sports

It only takes a couple of feet of snow to blanket the low ground cover of Kettle Ridge and open summer trails to cross-country skiing. Experienced skiers often head north from Sherman Pass, following the route of Trail #13 as far as skill and endurance can take them. The tour to the top of Columbia Mountain rewards the hardy with around-the-compass views of the Kettle Range and the drainages on either side, made even more beautiful by the crystal cover of snow.

At the north end of the Profanity area, at Deer Creek Summit, a Curlew conservation group has constructed and maintains a group of five nordic trails. Two follow old logging and jeep roads north from the pass for loops of 5 and 8 kilometers. South from the summit, one track traces the summer route of Trail #13 to the head of West Deer Creek, then returns north via abandoned FR 6110430. This loop is 10 kilometers, but a spur closer to the summit cuts the loop by a third. For the adventuresome, another old abandoned forest road at the south end of the longer loop continues west down Long Alec Creek, eventually coming out on County Road 582 east of Curlew. The length of this trip will vary, depending on how far the county has plowed the road, but it averages 16 kilometers (about 10 miles) and requires prearranged transportation at either end.

50

BALD SNOW–THIRTEENMILE– COUGAR MOUNTAIN

LOCATION: In Ferry County, in the Kettle Range, south of Highway 20 and east of Highway 21
SIZE: 41,920 acres
STATUS: Semiprimitive Nonmotorized
TERRAIN: Rolling to moderately steep ridges with a few deep, cliff-rimmed drainages. Mostly wooded except for the core area, which was burned by a major forest fire in 1988
ELEVATION: 3,100 to 7,103 feet
MANAGEMENT: USFS, Colville National Forest, Republic and Kettle Falls Ranger districts
TOPOGRAPHIC MAPS: Bear Mountain, Edds Mountain, Seventeenmile Mountain, Sherman Peak, Sitdown Mountain, Thirteenmile Creek

This area provides visitors with an opportunity to witness the rebirth of a forest. In the summer of 1988, lightning strikes in the White Mountain and Bald Mountain areas set six small spot fires. The extremely dry weather preceding the lightning storm, and the winds of up to 35 miles per hour that followed it, caused these small fires to merge and overwhelm fire-suppression efforts. The resulting inferno raged for nearly three weeks, consuming 20,126 acres before it was finally controlled. Nearly all of the Bald Snow Roadless Area was turned into charred snags, with only small, isolated patches of trees surviving. Salvage logging removed dead but marketable timber, and reforestation began, attempting to match planted seedling species with those that had previously existed in each section of the forest. As of this writing, six years later, vegetation is beginning to transform the blackened rocky landscape to a new, green, regenerated ecosystem.

Climate

The Kettle Range is a major obstacle to the west–east storm systems that cross this section of the state, and as a result it receives more precipitation than the drier highland valleys on either side. The mountains in the southwest Thirteenmile area are lower, and therefore drier, than those on the crest of the range. The Bald Snow area, abreast of the range, has an average annual precipitation of 35 inches, while Thirteenmile averages only 20 inches. About 50 percent of this occurs between October and March, much as snow. After a relatively dry spring, May and June often see extended rainy periods. Midwinter temperatures range between 10 and 20 degrees; summer highs are in the lower 90s, and sometimes warmer in the southwest part of the area.

Plants and Wildlife

In sections outside of the 1988 burn, the climax forest consists of Douglas-fir, ponderosa pine, western red cedar, and subalpine fir. In areas that had been burned over in the past, these species were replaced by dense stands of western larch and lodgepole pine. Forest composition varies with the moisture content of the soil; streams and damper areas also support Englemann spruce, quaking aspen, cottonwood, and birch. Drier south-facing slopes have larger open patches of grasses and forbs. The understory, depending on specific location, includes sedges, arnica, spirea, huckleberries, sweetscented bedstraw, hawkweed, Oregon boxwood, various species of rose, wood violet, and ninebark. Rarer sensitive species found in the

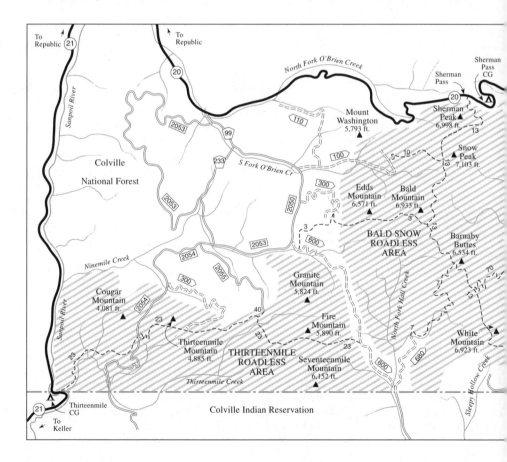

area are phacelia, twinflower, Umatilla gooseberry, Idaho gooseberry, Okanogan flameflower, and Robinson's onion.

Wildlife is plentiful in the forest; among the creatures that may be spotted on hikes here are mule deer, black bear, cougar, lynx, bobcat, coyote, wolverine, pine marten, snowshoe hare, blue grouse, and pika, and a variety of songbirds.

Geology

The Bald Snow–Thirteenmile area east of the line of summits between Mount Washington and Seventeenmile Mountain is underlaid with an intrusive granite dome that rose through the existing mantle about 50 million to 70 million years ago. Outcrops of this base granite are evident in many places along the Kettle crest. A north–south fault just west of this chain of summits marks an abrupt change from granitic rock to younger (50 million years old) andesite and rhyolite of volcanic origin. The soil cover of the area is composed of thick layers of glacial till left after several retreats of continental ice sheets, plus later additions of volcanic ash. Moderate amounts of tungsten and uranium ores are found in the western half of the region, and some zinc and silver composites occur south of Sherman Pass.

History

The entire area was once part of the Colville Indian Reservation, set aside in 1872. In 1892 reservation boundaries were adjusted, and the northern half of this region, which includes Bald Snow–Thirteenmile, reverted to public domain. The southern half remained, as it is today, the Colville Reservation. Four years later the north portion was opened to homesteading, but few

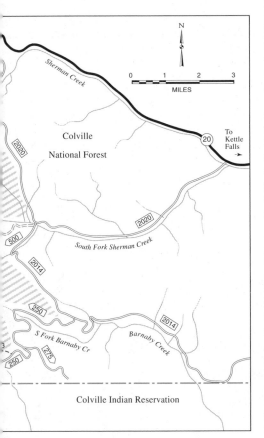

settlers arrived until the early 1900s. Despite having lost reservation status, the mountains just north of the boundary were of great significance to the Colville Indians. As a portion of the rite of transition into adulthood, tribe members sought out the summits as a place to seek contact with guardian spirits.

The first forest reserves in the state were created in 1897, and in 1907 the Colville National Forest was established. Over the next 25 years the Forest Service built fire lookouts atop Barnaby Buttes and White and Thirteenmile mountains, and trails were put in to supply the lookouts and accommodate fire-crew access to the area. None of these lookouts remains today.

ACTIVITIES

Hiking

There are two long trails in the area, Trail #13, running north–south along the Kettle Crest, and Trail #23, running east–west along the southwest border of the region. All other trails are feeders for these two.

Trail #13, Kettle Ridge South. *13.3 miles/ m (H,S,B).* This high ridgetop route offers wide burn-cleared views east to Lake Roosevelt (the Columbia River), west to the Okanogan Highlands, and north and south to the Kettle Crest summits. At the southeast side of Sherman Pass (5,587 ft), switchbacks

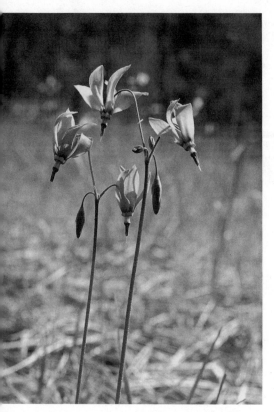

Shootingstars grow in dry, sunny areas of the old burn.

climb to the head of a fork of Pass Creek, then the route twists around flanking ridges northeast and east from Sherman Peak. At a saddle south of the peak (6,390 ft) the path switches to the west side of the crest and traverses the west slope of Snow Peak, passing the head of Trail #10 en route. The trail snakes over a ridgetop knob, returns to the east side of the crest, and traverses the east side of Bald Mountain. On the south flank of the mountain, it meets Trail #3 and returns to the ridgetop that trends southeast to Barnaby Buttes. The path crosses a broad low saddle between the two buttes, then continues south to meet Trail #70. A climb south through talus and boulders reaches a short spur to the summit of White Mountain (6,923 ft). From here the way is all downhill, first in tight switchbacks, then long ones, and finally a straight gradual descent to FR 2014250 (5,200 ft).

EAST SIDE OF KETTLE CREST TRAIL

Trail #70, Barnaby Buttes. 2.8 miles/e (H,S). This trail was once a supply road to the lookout atop Barnaby Buttes; although it reverted to trail status when the lookout was abandoned, it retains the wide tread and gentle grade of the old road. The last 2 miles of FR 2014500 to the trailhead (4,520 ft) are very rough, and impassable by low-clearance vehicles. The way starts in forest, passes through one steep stretch, then ascends gradually to meet Trail #13 at a saddle on the ridge south of Barnaby Buttes (6,050 ft).

WEST SIDE OF KETTLE CREST TRAILS

Trail #10, Snow Peak. 2.7 miles/m (H,S,B). After leaving FR 2050100 (5,120 ft) the route climbs diagonally up south-facing slopes to a broad ridgetop (6,100 ft), then follows the crest east to meet Trail #13 (6,300 ft) on the west side of Snow Peak. The entire way passes through the White Mountain burn; though new trees are not yet large enough to offer shade, grasses and wildflowers have recovered and add color to the hike.

Trail #3, Edds Mountain. 4.2 miles/d (H,S). The track starts at the end of FR 2050300 (4,884 ft) and heads steeply up slabs and boulder fields on the prominent ridge west from Edds Mountain. After crossing the south flank of the mountain (6,472 ft), the route drops to a broad saddle between Edds and Bald mountains (6,076 ft). The path then ascends the open ridge toward Bald, with views to the south down the broad Hall Creek drainage to the Colville Reservation. About 1,400 feet below the summit of Bald, the route starts a gradual descent east to join Trail #13 (5,920 ft). The tread may be hard to find in rocky or grassy areas, but cairns mark the way.

Trail #7, Barnaby Buttes. 7 miles/e (H,S). The route leaves FR 2050600 (3,420 ft) and follows gated FR 2050680 northeast up a creek basin for 3 miles before it degenerates to trail. The way continues to the head of the drainage, then climbs along the side of a gentle ridge in broken forest and meadows. Switchbacks climb to reach Trail #13 (6,180 ft) just west of the top of Barnaby Buttes.

The view from the summit of Thirteenmile Mountain, reached by Trail #23

Trail #23, Thirteenmile. *16.5 miles/m (H,S,B).* This path is west of the White Mountain burn, so it is blessed by a variety of forest cover, including magnificent old-growth stands of ponderosa pine. The east end of the trail starts from FR 2050600 at the head of a small Hall Creek tributary (4,327 ft). It climbs west through forest to a saddle on the ridge between Fire and Seventeenmile mountains (5,130 ft). Side trips can be made to the top of either for panoramic views of the area.

The track gradually winds down to the upper end of Thirteenmile Creek, where a spur leads north to a marsh at the end of FR 2055 (4,200 ft). The route climbs above the steep-walled banks of the creek and meanders west toward Thirteenmile Mountain. Just east of the mountain it touches the end of FR 2054300, then continues around the south side of the mountain through alternating patches of forest and meadow. A convoluted ridge is followed west to the canyon that contains FR 2054; the track drops and crosses the road (3,550 ft). The trail climbs out of the canyon, crosses a broad rib, and starts a twisting descent into the headwaters of the Sanpoil River; it meets the river at its confluence with Thirteenmile Creek. The remainder of the route follows the west bank of the Sanpoil as it winds south down a deep, narrow canyon with soaring rock cliffs on either side. The trail ends at the Thirteenmile Campground (2,020 ft) on Highway 21.

Winter Sports

On the plus side for the White Mountain burn, in winter the bare slopes offer limitless acres of deep, untracked powder snow for the enjoyment of skilled cross-country skiers. Summer Trails #10 and #13 are frequently used as access routes to reach the snow-clad ridges and bowls for fantastic runs unencumbered by timber.

51

JUNIPER DUNES WILDERNESS

LOCATION: In Franklin County, 16 miles northeast of Pasco, northwest of Pasco–Kahlotus Road
SIZE: 7,100 acres
STATUS: Designated Wilderness Area (1984)
TERRAIN: A low rolling landscape covered by sand dunes and groves of western juniper
ELEVATION: 750 to 1,130 feet
MANAGEMENT: US Bureau of Land Management, Spokane District
TOPOGRAPHIC MAPS: Levey NE, Levey SE, Levey SW, Rye Grass Coulee

Juniper Dunes is the last remaining vestige of the ecosystem that once covered nearly 250,000 acres between the Columbia and Snake rivers. It encompasses the largest sand dunes and the largest remaining natural groves of western juniper in the state. Strong, persistent southwesterly winds build dunes up to 130 feet high and more than 1,000 feet wide. This is the northernmost limit for western juniper—the groves in the wilderness are between 80 and 150 years old. This distinctive ecosystem is habitat for a unique group of mammal, bird, and plant species that have adapted to its demanding features. A number of other species of birds also migrate through the area seasonally.

Climate

The climate is that of a northern-latitude desert, with an average annual rainfall of only 7 to 8 inches, more than 80 percent of which occurs between the months of September and May. Since the area is cold during the winter, much of that season's precipitation occurs in the form of snow, about 13 inches annually. Minimum midwinter temperatures average in the low 20s, and the midsummer maximums are in the 90s, with many days above 100. Obviously the best times to visit are in the spring and fall.

Plants and Wildlife

The western juniper is the only significant tree species in the wilderness, however, there are more than 60 species of plants present. Among these are hoary aster, balsamroot, rabbitbrush, cryptantha, Russian thistle, milk vetch, psoralea, phacelia, yellow bells, blue flax, verbena, wheatgrass, wild rye, cordgrass, phlox, knotweed, larkspur, bitterbrush, prairie star, and blue-eyed Mary.

Larger mammals found in the area are mule deer, coyote, bobcat, badger, skunk, weasel, and porcupine. Smaller creatures include pocket gophers, kangaroo rats, pocket mice, harvest mice, deer mice, and grasshopper mice. (Those coyotes and bobcats have to eat something!)

The resident bird species include raptors such as red-tailed hawks, ferruginous hawks, Swainson's hawks, sparrow hawks, merlins, great horned owls, long-eared owls, and short-eared owls (more trouble for the mice). Other residents are quail, partridge, pheasant, magpies, ravens, and horned larks. Among summer-only visitors are mourning doves, kingbirds, Say's phoebes, violet-green swallows, shrikes, Macgillivray's warblers, orioles, blackbirds, cowbirds, and a variety of sparrows. Migrant bird populations include bluebirds, kinglets, pipits, vireos, Townsend's warblers, buntings, song sparrows, Canada geese, pintails, goshawks, sharp-shinned hawks, hummingbirds, night hawks, Lewis woodpeckers, sapsuckers, flycatchers, and pewees.

Reptiles here are not to be slighted; among these are skinks, four species of lizards, and six species of snakes (including rattlesnakes!).

Geology

The base rock below the wilderness is Columbia Plateau basalt. In Miocene times, about 15 million years ago, stretching of the earth's crust in southeastern Washington opened fissures from which enormous lava flows emerged and spread across the plateaus to the west. A succes-

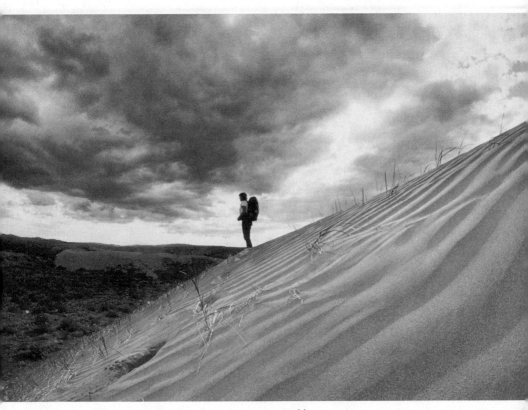

Windswept sand near a trailhead in the Juniper Dunes Wilderness

sion—maybe hundreds—of such basalt floods occurred over the following 4 million years, building up a thick crust of layered basalt.

About 10,000 to 12,000 years ago, the continental ice sheets that had covered most of the northern part of the present-day United States began to retreat. The melting glaciers formed huge lakes behind ice dams in northern Idaho and western Montana. When these dams gave way, immense floods swept across eastern Washington. The magnitude of the larger floods is almost unimaginable—in one, more than 500 cubic miles of water was released and flowed across the Columbia Plateau in a 2,000-foot-high surge. The floods carried away surface soils and carved deep channels in the basalt plateau, then fanned out and temporarily formed large lakes in central Washington before draining through gaps on the southwest side of the plateau into the Columbia River. These slack-water lakes, one of which formed above Juniper Dunes, deposited their finer sediments in the basins beneath them, providing the sand that is shaped by winds into today's dunes.

History

The area has been used since the 1960s for recreational activities, some benign such as picnicking, sightseeing, and nature studies, others more ecologically damaging such as camping, Air Force survival training, horseback riding, and motorcycle and offroad-vehicle (ORV) travel. Studies by the BLM in 1971 established the uniqueness of this ecosystem, and the bureau acquired and consolidated parcels of land from private owners. By 1975, 5,300 acres had been gathered and were designated an Outstanding Natural Area, which closed the area to grazing and ORV use. In 1984 an additional 1,800 acres were added, and the entire 7,100 acres were designated as the Juniper Dunes Wilderness.

ACTIVITIES

Hiking

There are no established trails within the wilderness, and only a half-dozen jeep roads make short probes into the perimeter of the area. All of the peripheral land is privately held, so at present there is no legal access to it without permission from surrounding landholders. The Juniper Dunes Ranch, on the north edge of the wilderness, permits access across their property at the end of Joy Road from February 1 to June 1, and from September 1 to October 15. No vehicles, camping, or hiking after dark are permitted.

Opposite: A bull elk in the Wenaha-Tucannon Wilderness Area

EASTERN WASHINGTON

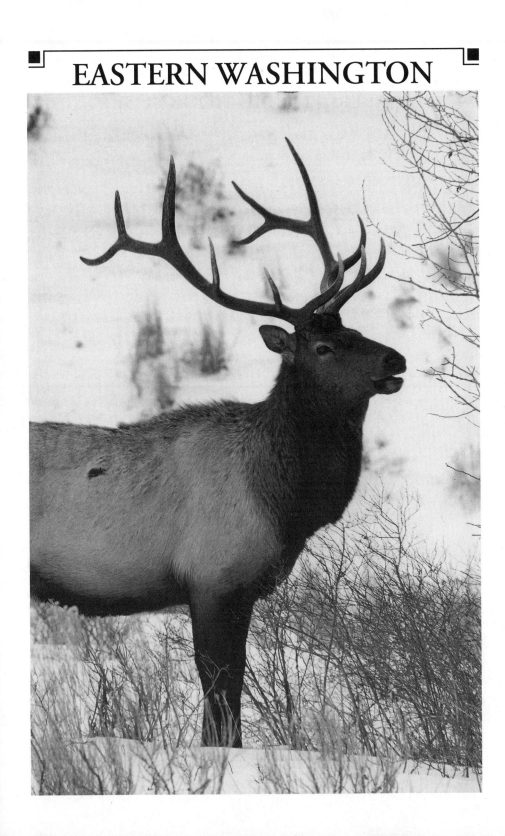

52

ABERCROMBIE–HOOKNOSE

LOCATION: In Stevens and Pend Oreille counties, on the west side of Highway 31, just south of the Canadian border
SIZE: 37,500 acres
STATUS: Semiprimitive Nonmotorized
TERRAIN: The area spans a long, rounded, north–south ridge that is the hydrologic divide between the Columbia and Pend Oreille rivers. The highest points have steep-walled, wooded cirques on their north or east sides. Creeks carve deep drainages east and west from the crest, defining lateral ridges that slope gradually to steep drop-offs into the valleys flanking either side of the area.
ELEVATION: 2,800 to 7,308 feet
MANAGEMENT: USFS, Colville National Forest, Colville and Sullivan Lake ranger districts; 1.5 sections under Washington State Department of Natural Resources management; some private inholdings
TOPOGRAPHIC MAPS: Abercrombie Mountain, Boundary Dam, Deep Lake, Leadpoint, Metaline

If you crave cross-country travel but don't warm to the possibility of bushwhacking or getting lost, then Abercrombie–Hooknose is the spot for you. Short (albeit steep) lateral trails, none exceeding 4 miles in length, reach broad, open meadows and lightly forested saddles along the 7-mile-long north–south backbone of the region. In early summer alpine meadows are ablaze with wildflowers, and in fall lower slopes provide ample patches of huckleberries on approach hikes.

Climate

The area is damper than most other portions of eastern Washington. It receives nearly 28 inches of precipitation annually, about half of which falls as snow, beginning in November and continuing until March. May and June also have periods of heavy rain. Temperatures are typical of the eastern part of the state, with midwinter minimums averaging in the teens, and summer maximums in the mid-80s, with some periods in the 90s.

Plants and Wildlife

A large portion of the area was burned in 1926, thus most of the forest cover is second-growth western larch and lodgepole pine, with occasional Douglas-fir and ponderosa pine that survived the blaze. Some of the wetter draws and west-side slopes have stands of old-growth Douglas-fir, western hemlock, and western red cedar. The understory here includes ninebark, snowberry, oceanspray, spirea, Oregon boxwood, and huckleberry.

A female white-headed woodpecker forages for insects on a dead branch.

At higher elevations Englemann spruce and subalpine fir stands are found, and damper locations on northern slopes and in ravines host vegetation such as Labrador tea and Cascades azalea. Drier south slopes have huckleberry, western juniper, arnica, serviceberry, huckleberry, and spirea. Meadow cover atop alpine ridges consists of bunchgrass, heather, moss, and lichen.

Found in the forest are mule deer, black bear, coyote, moose, elk, bobcat, cougar, grouse, pine marten, wolverine, goshawk, barred owl, and pileated woodpecker. Grizzly bears and gray wolves have been sighted occasionally. A small herd of mountain goats is located near Linton Peak, west of Metaline.

Geology

The high crest running through the Abercrombie–Hooknose region belies its origins, for it was once a broad coastal plain on the western flank of the North American continent. The plain built up over ancient continental crust, beginning over 600 million years ago. Throughout the ensuing Paleozoic era, deposition continued on the plain; layers of limestones alternating with black muds were transformed into slates and argillites.

About 200 million years ago, the North American plate was pushed westward by a flow of new crust in the mid-Atlantic trench, and its western margins were forced against, and then over, the continental crust of the Pacific Ocean. This collision folded and tilted the coastal plain upward in a series of fractured blocks. Pressures metamorphosed portions of these ancient sedimentary rocks, and granitic magma, heated by the subducting Pacific crust, intruded into the fault zones of the older rock. Erosion and continental glaciation smoothed this newly formed range, forming today's broad rounded ridges. Only Abercrombie and Hooknose mountains stood above the continental ice sheets. Alpine glaciers that formed on these two peaks carved the steep cirques that are now evident on their sides.

The oldest limestones and dolomites harbored solutions of lead, silver, and zinc ores that were trapped beneath the subsequent impervious layer of slate. Extensive mining that occurred

Underbrush of the Abercrombie-Hooknose Roadless Area provides habitat for ruffed grouse.

along the western flank of the region exploited these rich deposits. Later limestone deposits, concentrated closer to the top of the formation, were tapped for many years by a cement factory at Metaline.

History

The history of the Abercrombie–Hooknose area focuses on the development of its mineral wealth. The arrival of the Idaho and Washington Northern Railroad in 1910 created Metaline, a company town with one purpose in mind—the production of cement. Starting in the early 1900s, extensive mining for lead and zinc caused shafts to be sunk all over the tops of Gladstone and Red Top mountains. The demand for these ores peaked during World War I; today only a few mines remain active. In the Metaline vicinity, mining started in the 1930s. Small amounts of lead, zinc, and tungsten ores, and some placer gold, have been taken from that area.

The eastern boundary of the Abercrombie–Hooknose area is partially defined by large power transmission lines from Boundary Dam on the Pend Oreille River, just south of the Canadian border. The 340-foot-high dam is a Seattle City Light project that was completed in 1967.

ACTIVITIES

Hiking

Trail #502, Flume Creek. 4 miles/m (H,S). From the end of FR 350 (5,120 ft) the route heads west up a broad ridge, then across a steep sidehill to a scree slope where four long switchbacks gain the crest northeast of Abercrombie Mountain. The strenuous rocky route climbs southwest to the barren summit (7,308 ft), once the site of a fire lookout, with great views over northeast Washington. From Abercrombie, cross-country hikers can follow the open alpine crest northeast to Hooknose Mountain (7,210 ft), or chase cairns south along the open ridge to the upper end of Trail #117 and trek beyond, over several intermediate knobs, to Sherlock Peak (6,365 ft), nearly 5 miles to the south.

WEST-SIDE TRAILS

Trail #139, Sherlock Peak. 3.6 miles/m (H,S). From the end of FR 7078075 (4,620 ft), at the top of Gladstone Mountain, the track winds around a small knob, then climbs southeast across a steep wooded hillside, heavy with huckleberries in the fall. A few slow zigzags up the final slope reach a ridgetop meadow south of Sherlock Peak. An easy scramble to the north up the open crest reaches the summit (6,365 ft), with around-the-compass views of nearby Abercrombie and Linton mountains, the Columbia River, the Salmo-Priest Wilderness, and, in the distance, rugged North Cascades and Canadian peaks. The scenic cross-country ridgetop route north to Abercrombie is an easy hike.

Trail #123, South Fork Silver Creek. 3.6 miles/d (H,S). From the Y-intersection on FR 7078070, above the confluence of the forks of Silver Creek, take the branch to the southeast (3,160 ft) along an old jeep path into the woods. The gentle grade follows the huckleberry-rich creek bottom for about 2 miles before it takes on trail attributes and heads sharply uphill. Switchbacks climb the ever-steepening slope to gain a narrow saddle (5,450 ft) on the crest between Sherlock Peak and Abercrombie Mountain. From here hike cross-country to either of these two destinations via the north–south backbone ridge.

Trail #119, Silver Creek. 3.5 miles/d (H,S). From the intersection described above, take the northeast fork (3,160 ft) up the North Fork of Silver Creek. After a very brief stroll along the creek, it's uphill time, and seemingly endless switchbacks plow up the steep, timbered slope. A traverse from the last corner finds Trail #117 at a saddle (5,800 ft) on the west side of Abercrombie Mountain.

Trail #117, Abercrombie. 3.2 miles/m (H,S). From the end of FR 7078300 (5,000 ft), the way heads into second-growth timber where switchbacks climb to a ridgetop saddle and the junction with Trail #119. More zigs and zags up through an old burn break out into meadows and reach the crest south of Abercrombie Mountain; a large cairn marks the end of the formal trail (6,840 ft). The way north to the top of the mountain (7,308 ft) is obvious, marked by a sequence of small cairns.

53

SALMO–PRIEST WILDERNESS

LOCATION: In Pend Oreille County, south of the Canadian border, between the Pend Oreille River and the Idaho border
SIZE: Wilderness: 39,937 acres; adjoining roadless areas: 13,737 acres; 17,600 acres in northern Idaho have been proposed for addition to the wilderness
STATUS: Designated Wilderness (1984); adjoining areas are Semiprimitive Nonmotorized
TERRAIN: Two long northeast-to-southwest ridges are connected at their north ends by an east–west divide, capped by Salmo Peak. The westernmost ridge has very steep side-slopes below a narrow, rocky crest fringed with several glacial cirques. The easternmost ridgetop is lower, more rounded, and wooded. Both ridges are cut by several deep lateral drainages.
ELEVATION: 2,600 to 7,309 feet
MANAGEMENT: USFS, Colville National Forest, Sullivan Lake Ranger District; and Idaho Panhandle National Forest, Priest River Ranger District
TOPOGRAPHIC MAPS: Boundary Dam, Gypsy Peak, Helmer Mtn., Metaline Falls, Pass Creek, Salmo Mtn.

The Salmo–Priest Wilderness is the largest section of virgin forest in eastern Washington. However, even now its peripheral roadless areas are being chewed at by logging, and beautiful ridgetop vistas often include a substantial number of foreground clearcuts that degrade their aesthetic appeal. Trails that run the length of Crowell Ridge, on the west, and Shedroof Divide, on the east, offer extensive hiking and backwoods camping opportunities and broad scenic views of the Sullivan Creek drainage and Selkirk and Purcell mountains.

Climate

The north portion of the wilderness is one of the wettest sections of eastern Washington, averaging about 50 inches of precipitation annually, compared to 28.4 inches at Metaline Falls, at its southwest corner. Snow, which accounts for most of this precipitation, can reach depths of more than 9 feet and persist well into midsummer. Although average midwinter temperatures range from zero to the low teens, extremes of minus 40 degrees have been recorded. Summers are relatively mild, with highs in the 80s and occasional 90-degree days.

Plants and Wildlife

Most of the lower-elevation forest in the Salmo–Priest Wilderness consists of western red cedar, western hemlock, Douglas-fir, grand fir, and larch. At higher elevations, Englemann spruce and subalpine fir are introduced into this mix, and the highest crests are mostly meadows with a cover of fescue and beargrass.

One RNA has been designated in the wilderness, and two more are proposed in it and surrounding roadless areas. The Salmo RNA, established in 1973, consists of 1,390 acres between Salmo Divide and the South Salmo River. It typifies a timbered stream drainage, with old-growth stands of western red cedar, western hemlock, Douglas-fir, and Englemann spruce, and some areas of second-growth in spots burned by 1920s fires.

Round Top Mountain, at the southeast corner of the wilderness, has been proposed as another RNA. It is a gently rounded mountain covered with meadows and a few trees near the summit. Beargrass dominates portions of the meadows, which gradually taper to subalpine fir and isolated stands of whitebark pine. The other proposed RNA, Halliday Fens, lies in a roadless area on the west flank of the wilderness. This marsh, filled by wetland grasses, sedges, and forbs, is a habitat for seven state-listed sensitive plant species: yellow sedge, crested shield fern, green keeled cotton-grass, marsh muhly, hoary willow, McCall's willow, treelike clubmoss, and black snakeroot.

Among the wilderness wildlife are black bear, mule and white-tailed deer, elk, bighorn

South Salmo-Priest River, in the Salmo-Priest Wilderness

sheep, and a plethora of small rodents. Also found in the region are wolverine, badger, cougar, bobcat, pine marten, lynx, moose, goshawk, and pileated woodpecker. This is the only part of the state where woodland caribou are found, and one of the few areas where grizzly bear and gray wolf are known to exist.

Geology

This area is underlaid by some of the oldest rock in the state of Washington. This is the western fringe of the original North American continent; the base of Shedroof Divide, on the east side of the wilderness, is metamorphosed Precambrian sedimentary rock—phyllites and quartzites, more than 600 million years old. On the west side of the wilderness, the Crowell and Gypsy ridge area was once part of the younger western coastal plain of the North American continent. Westward drift of this continental plate caused it to ride over the Pacific Ocean crust, and the coastal lowlands were lifted and folded during early Paleozoic times to form this segment of the range. Continental ice sheets flowed across the area, grinding and rounding the mountains beneath them. Some of the higher portions of Crowell and Gypsy ridges stood above the ice sheets and were later sculpted by local alpine glaciers that left a chain of cirques in vertical sides of these two ridges. Soil in the valleys is primarily glacial till and alluvium, with a thin layer of volcanic ash from the last-gasp eruptions of the North Cascades volcanoes.

History

Aside from local Indian tribes, the first visitors were prospectors arriving in the late 1800s. Little is known of their efforts, and no productive mines are known to have existed in the wilderness.

Most of the trails throughout the area were cut in the early 1900s to support fire suppression and supply a chain of lookouts located along the higher summits. None of these lookouts is active today. As is obvious from the snarl of old logging roads and the clearcuts on the perimeter of the wilderness, logging has been the dominant industry in the region for the past 50 years.

ACTIVITIES

Hiking

HIGHWAY 31 TRAILS

Trail #522, Halliday. 7.8 miles/m (H,S,B).
From FR 180 (2,580 ft), the path heads northeast along a low wooded bench, rounds a steep ridge nose, then starts up a deep, wooded drainage. After a brief ascent, the way arrives at the west end of Halliday Fens, a treasure of biological diversity that hopefully will be set aside as a Research Natural Area. In ponds and marshes created by industrious beavers, this wetland boasts seven sensitive plant species. It is also a good spot for bird-watching. After a bench-top swing to the north, the track wanders along the northern perimeter of the fens, then makes a steady ascent to a broad wooded pass (4,080 ft) on the southwest side of Crowell Mountain. It then drops into the North Fork of Sullivan Creek drainage to meet Trail #507 (3,600 ft).

Trail #525, Slate Creek Cutoff. 5 miles/m (H,S). From FR 3155 (3,780 ft) the trail descends to cross the South Fork of Slate Creek, heads south across another creek, then climbs a forested ridge to a broad saddle. It drops off the saddle, wanders past a shallow pond, then resumes a gradual ascent around the basin at the head of Uncas Gulch. The route swings into the North Fork of Sullivan Creek drainage, where it joins Trail #507 (4,550 ft).

SULLIVAN CREEK TRAILS

Trail #507, North Fork of Sullivan Creek. 5 miles/m (H,S). From Trail #522 (3,620 ft), the route proceeds northeast above the North Fork of Sullivan Creek. It gradually ascends to a broad forested basin, then follows the creek as it twists uphill and southeast. After passing Trail

#525, the track switchbacks up the basin headwall and breaks into meadows on Crowell Ridge, where it meets Trail #515 (6,530 ft).

Trail #553, Red Bluff. *5.2 miles/m (H,S,B).* From the north side of County Road 9345 (2,580 ft), the trail climbs gradually northwest to the forested nose of a broad ridge, passing a few open spots that look south over Sullivan Lake. The route continues an easy ascent north, roller-coastering over intermediate knobs (3,700 to 4,100 ft). It switchbacks down a steep bank to the North Fork of Sullivan Creek, then climbs the opposite side to meet Trails #507 and #522 (3,720 ft).

Trail #515, Crowell Ridge. *7.8 miles/m (H,S).* The premier scenic route on the west side of the wilderness starts on the sharp ridge (6,260 ft) east of the Sullivan Mountain lookout. The track runs first through open timber, then into beargrass-studded meadows. It stays atop the narrow rib except when skirting minor ridgetop knobs. Steep walls drop northwest to a chain of cirques. After meeting Trail #507 at a saddle above Smart Creek, the path continues northeast atop the bare crest to a col (6,540 ft) between two talus-laden humps, where it drops down the southeast side of the ridge to the Leola Creek drainage to meet FR 2200 (5,650 ft) just above Bear Pasture.

From the ridgetop, the adventuresome can continue north cross-country along the bare rocky crest of Gypsy Ridge for about 4 miles. En route, hikers can cross the highest summit in the wilderness, Gypsy Peak (7,309 ft), or drop east off of the crest to either of two cliff-rimmed lakes, Watch Lake (6,471 ft) or Gypsy Lake (6,426 ft).

Trail #526, Thunder Creek. *5.3 miles/m (H,S).* From Gypsy Meadows (4,170 ft), walk gated FR 2220345 for 2.4 miles to the trail, which continues the gradual ascent south through huge old-growth timber. Sate yourself with trailside huckleberries in season as you head up the northeast side of Thunder Creek to meet Trail #512 (5,600 ft) between Thunder and Helmer mountains.

Badgers are among the varied wildlife found in the Salmo-Priest Wilderness.

Trail #511, Shedroof Cutoff. *1.7 miles/m (H,S).* The shortest east-side route to Shedroof Divide leaves the north end of Gypsy Meadows (4,340 ft), follows gated FR 2220280 north for a mile, then turns uphill to the east and climbs steadily up a small soggy gulch to Trail #512 (5,480 ft).

Trail #506, Salmo Basin. *8.8 miles/m (H,S).* This is the first leg of a popular and scenic 2- to 3-day loop that includes Trail #535 and a section of Trail #512. Just beyond the junction with the road to the Salmo Peak lookout, continue east on gated FR 2220 for 0.5 mile, where this trail heads north into the forest (5,920 ft). A pair of long lazy switchbacks work down into a drainage, passing through old-growth cedar and hemlock and a carpet of ferns and mosses reminiscent of the damp western Cascade forests. A long diagonal descent leads to more sweeping switchbacks that reach the South Salmo River (4,070 ft). Cross the river and turn east, making a gradual ascent to Crutch Creek. The path climbs away from the riverbank, enters Idaho, then bends north, staying high on the steep side-slope above the river. The river and trail once again twist east 0.5 mile south of the

Canadian border, then turn southeast, where the track climbs the drainage headwall to meadows at Snowy Top Pass (6,300 ft). Trail #506 becomes Trail #512 at this point. A strenuous cross-country scramble to the top of Snowy Top (7,572 ft) rewards the effort with a panorama of some of the wildest mountain country in northern Idaho, southern British Columbia, and northeastern Washington.

Trail #535, Salmo Divide. 3 miles/m (H,S). From the start of Trail #506 (5,290 ft), the route follows a closed road for a mile before becoming a true trail. It wanders along the forested top of Salmo Divide, between Salmo Mountain and Shedroof Divide, to link with Trail #512 (6,280 ft) at a saddle north of Shedroof Mountain.

PRIEST RIVER TRAILS

Trail #512, Shedroof Divide. 21.8 miles/e-d (H,S). The longest trail in the wilderness runs atop its eastern backbone ridge from the southeast tip of the area to just a mile short of the Canadian border. The entire distance is in semi-open to open timber, broken on occasion by alpine meadows. It offers wide views of the western portion of the wilderness, the Sullivan Creek drainage, and the upper Priest River country of Idaho. Starting on FR 22 just east of Pass Creek Pass (5,440 ft), the route heads north up the shoulder of Round Top Mountain. It skirts the east flank of the mountain, passes the upper end of Trail #320, and continues east of Mankato Mountain to reach a notch (6,491 ft) on the south ridge of Helmer Mountain.

The way drops to a divide (5,600 ft) between Thunder and Jackson creeks, passing Trail #526 from the west and Trail #311 from the east. The route climbs north, passes the upper end of Trail #313, then climbs over the top of Thunder Mountain (6,560 ft). The way follows the undulations of the divide as it continues north and passes the heads of Trails #312 and #511. A switchback ascent climbs toward Shedroof Mountain to 6,600 feet, where the route skirts the west flank of Shedroof and descends to a saddle to pass Trail #535.

Shedroof–Salmo Divide now bends northeast, rounds the head of Hughes Creek, and meets Trail #315. The crest is pursued north, to a spur to the lookout site atop Little Snowy Top (6,829 ft) with views encompassing the wilds of northern Idaho, northeastern Washington, and Canada. The way continues north past Trail #349, then joins Trail #506 at Snowy Top Pass.

EAST SIDE OF SHEDROOF DIVIDE TRAILS

Trail #320, North Gold. 3.3 miles/m (H,S). From Trail #512 (6,010 ft) north of Round Top Mountain, switchbacks and a poor tread drop swiftly into the upper Gold Creek basin; the grade then eases, meeting and following an old logging road for an easy descent to the end of FR 656A (4,350 ft).

Trail #311, Jackson Creek. 4.6 miles/m (H,S). From Trail #512 (5,600 ft), 1.7 miles south of Thunder Mountain, the trail drops through brush to a gradual side-slope descent above upper Jackson Creek. In 1.5 miles switchbacks descend the steep sidehill to close with Jackson Creek. The stream bottom is followed west from there to a broad, widening slope and Hughes Meadows (2,920 ft).

Trail #312, Hughes Fork. 7.5 miles/m (H,S). This seldom-maintained route departs Trail #512 (5,370 ft) 0.5 mile south of the junction with Trail #511. It drops quickly east down a brushy ridge crest, swings north into the Hughes Fork of the Priest River drainage, crosses the creek, and continues downstream above its north bank. It follows the stream as it bends south to end in Hughes Meadows on FR 662 (2,700 ft).

Trail #315, Upper Hughes. 5.3 miles/m (H,S). A brushy obscure tread leaves Trail #512 (5,930 ft) as it drops off the ridge 2 miles south of Little Snowy Top. The path continues south along the crest for a mile, then switchbacks down to a saddle where it meets an abandoned alder-choked logging road. This road is followed south for a little over 4 miles to a gate on FR 1343 (4,240 ft) near Cabinet Pass.

Trail #349, Little Snowy Top. 4.7 miles/d (H). From its intersection with Trail #512 (6,280 ft), this track makes a brutal teeth-jarring descent, losing nearly 4,000 feet of elevation in 1.5 miles via 72 switchbacks. After a no-bridge crossing of the Upper Priest River, the route ends on FR 308 near the river's east bank (2,960 ft).

54

GRASSY TOP

LOCATION: In Pend Oreille County, between Sullivan Lake and the Idaho border
SIZE: 25,216 acres
STATUS: Semiprimitive Nonmotorized
TERRAIN: An interconnected series of steep-walled forested ridges frame the headwaters and
drainages of Noisy Creek, Tillicum Creek, Sema Creek, and the South Fork of Granite Creek.
ELEVATION: 2,600 to 6,323 feet
MANAGEMENT: USFS Colville National Forest, Sullivan Lake Ranger District; Idaho Pan-
handle National Forests, Priest Lake Ranger District; three sections are owned by a private
timber company
TOPOGRAPHIC MAPS: Helmer Mtn., Metaline Falls, Monumental Mtn., Orwig Hump,
Pass Creek

On the west side of the area, slopes rise abruptly from Sullivan Lake to Hall Mountain,
where a high ridge runs southeast for more than 6 miles to Grassy Top Mountain. East of
Grassy Top, a rounded horseshoe-shaped chain of ridges joins High Rock Mountain, Tillicum
Peak, and Orwig Hump in enclosing the Tillicum Creek drainage. On the east these ridges drop
sharply to the North Fork of Granite Creek, pausing briefly in a midlevel bench 200 to 400 feet
above the creek. Although slopes on the north and south sides of the area have been heavily
logged, a fringe of untouched timber left along ridgetops mercifully hides clearcuts from most of
the trails. There is a fair chance of seeing Rocky Mountain bighorn sheep, which were introduced into the area, in the vicinity of Hall Mountain.

Climate

The average annual precipitation in the area is about 24 inches, most falling as snow, which
can reach depths from 3 to 6 feet, depending on elevation. Midwinter temperatures average in
the low- to mid-teens, with some below-zero stretches. Summer highs average in the mid-80s,
with occasional periods over 90.

Plants and Wildlife

The forest is a mixture of virgin old-growth and second-growth timber, the latter regenerating in areas burned by major fires in the 1920s. South-slope trees are mostly Douglas-fir and
ponderosa pine, with an understory that includes ninebark, snowberry, spirea, woods rose, and
oceanspray. Damper draws and north-slope forest stands hold western hemlock and cedar, with
ground cover of Oregon boxwood, queencup beadlily, oak fern, and huckleberry. The higher
elevations have a mix of subalpine fir and Englemann spruce, with whitebark pine included near
the top of Hall and Grassy Top mountains. On the ground here are beargrass, rustyleaf, Labrador tea, and huckleberry, with mosses and lichen coating open rock outcrops. Hooker's bluegrass, on the state sensitive species list, is found in the area.

Typical forest inhabitants include black bear, white-tailed deer, elk, cougar, bobcat, and a
variety of small animals. The area is also habitat for rarer creatures: moose, grizzly bear, gray
wolf, pine marten, and wolverine. Bighorn sheep are sometimes seen in the vicinity of Hall
Mountain, especially in early morning or late afternoon at salt blocks placed near the top of the
mountain. The State Department of Wildlife, in cooperation with the Sullivan Lake Ranger
District, maintains a winter feeding station for the sheep near the mouth of Noisy Creek. The
South Fork of Granite Creek is a spawning and rearing stream for Priest Lake cutthroat.

Geology

The base under the area is ancient metamorphosed Precambrian sedimentary rock that
formed on the original west coast of the North American continent. The south side of the area

has been intruded by a granitic batholith that has forced the original crust north along an east–west thrust fault at Pass Creek. Sullivan Lake and the region to the west of it are underlaid by the lateral moraine of continental ice sheets that pushed down the Pend Oreille Valley some 15,000 years ago. The same glacial advance is responsible for the rounded ridgetops, occasionally broken by rock outcrops, on the east side of the area. Surface soil is primarily glacial till, colluvium, and alluvium covered by a thin layer of ash from Cascade volcano eruptions.

History

Although the area is in territory traditionally used for hunting and gathering by the Kalispell Indians, no firm evidence of such activities has been found. Most of the trails were built in the 1930s to support fire lookouts that once existed on the six highest summits, and to provide backcountry access to fire crews. Some of this construction was carried out by the CCC, and vestiges of their camps may be found in the vicinity. During the same period there was also some prospecting, and about 200 claims were filed in the area. Recent mineral exploration in the eastern half of the region has focused on gold, silver, tungsten, lead, zinc, molybdenum, and uranium. Since the 1950s the major industry in the area has been logging, attested to by miles of side-slope clearcuts on the periphery of the Grassy Top area.

ACTIVITIES

Hiking

NORTH SIDE TRAILS

Trail #504, Sullivan Lake. 4.1 miles/e (H). This level path (2,600 ft) follows the east shore-line of Sullivan Lake between the Sullivan Lake Campground, on the north, and Noisy Creek Campground, on the south. Most of the way is in dense forest broken by open scree slopes with views up to Hall Mountain. The southern portion of the trail has easy access to the lakeshore, and the entire route is especially beautiful when the rich yellows and golds of fall are reflected in the deep blue surface of the lake.

Trail #540, Hall Mountain. 2.5 miles/e (H,S,B). FR 2200500 is closed to motorized traffic in spring and fall; check with the local ranger district for specific dates. From the end of FR 2200500 (5,300 ft), the track follows a short stretch of abandoned road up to a saddle (5,580 ft), the west end of Trail #533, and the north end of Trail #588. The route heads west along the south side of the grassy crest to the top of Hall Mountain (6,323 ft). The tread is rocky in places, but easy to follow. The mountaintop offers around-the-compass views of Sullivan Lake, the Salmo–Priest Wilderness, the remainder of the Grassy Top area, and the Pend Oreille Valley, as well as the possibility of close-up views of bighorn sheep.

Trail #533, Hall Mountain–Grassy Top. 5.1 miles/m (H,S,B). From the junction of Trails #540 and #588 (5,560 ft) east of Hall Mountain, the route heads east, then southeast along the contorted crest, sometimes on top, sometimes weaving from one side to the other. It reaches a saddle (6,160 ft) northwest of Grassy Top Mountain where it meets Trail #503. Most of the way is heavily wooded (thankfully) with few views of nearby clearcuts until it breaks into a sidehill meadow near its east end.

Trail #503, Pass Creek–Grassy Top. 7.7 miles/m (H,S,B). From FR 22 on the west side of Pass Creek Pass (5,360 ft), the trail drops to cross Pass Creek, switchbacks a few times up through dense forest, then swings south. A few more zigzags gain a ridgetop saddle (6,000 ft), where a wooded rib is followed southwest to join Trail #533. The path wanders across west-slope beargrass meadows before making the final ascent to the top of Grassy Top Mountain (6,253 ft) and broad views of the Salmo–Priest Wilderness and the Priest Lake area. The trail wanders through meadows southwest from Grassy Top for nearly a mile before it twists down a wooded nose to an abandoned logging road. The road is hiked west for about 3 miles to FR 1935030 on the North Fork of Harvey Creek (4,120 ft).

Trail #380 Willow Creek Cutoff. 0.5 mile/m (H,S). From a road-end clearcut on FR 1122 (5,350 ft), this short path saunters uphill to join Trail #379 atop the broad flat ridge (5,570 ft).

EAST-SIDE TRAILS

Trail #379, North Fork-Grassy Top. 7.7 miles/m (H,S). The route leaves the west side of FR 302 (3,250 ft), crosses the North Fork of Granite Creek, then attacks the steep face of a bluff in a series of switchbacks. A brief pause atop a midslope plateau gives way to an even steeper talus face, where more switchbacks gain the gentler, wooded east flank of High Rock. Here the path takes a straight shot west to the broad summit (5,570 ft).

The trail follows the flat, forested crest southwest for more than a mile, passing the upper ends of Trails #264 and #380 en route. At a junction with Trail #261, it bends northwest following a ridge toward Grassy Top. After wandering across two ridgetop knobs, the path gradually climbs to a rib running southwest. It turns up this narrow hogback, and breaks out into meadows studded with beargrass as it reaches the summit of Grassy Top and a junction with Trail #503 (6,253 ft).

Trail #261, Tillicum Creek. 4 miles/m (H,S). The first stretch of trail is on an abandoned section of FR 1103 (3,521 ft). In 0.4 mile, Trail #373 leaves to the southwest, and in another 0.5 mile the road becomes a trail and follows Tillicum Creek into a narrow, forested draw. The way bends north up a tributary stream and climbs the tightening sidehill slope toward a broad saddle on a spur from the east–west backbone ridge. A twist to the west and a diagonal ascent of

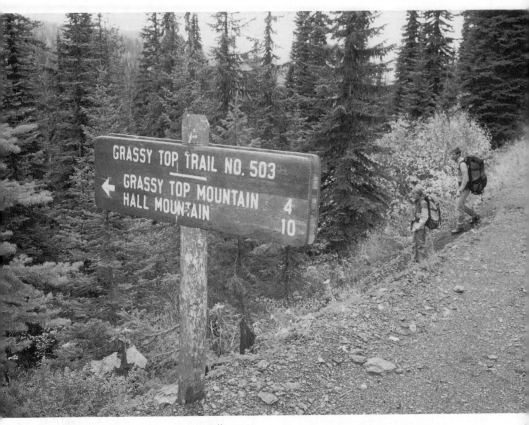

A trailhead sign in the Grassy Top Roadless Area

a broad, wooded slope leads to the crest. Here the track swings northeast and meets Trail #379 (5,620 ft).

Trail #373, Orwig Hump. *2.8 miles/m (H,S).* After leaving Trail #261 (3,555 ft), the route continues west on a jeep trail for nearly a mile before starting lazy switchbacks up the timbered slope to the south. It reaches the end of a finger ridge, then follows it southwest over an intervening bump, maintaining a steady ascent to the west shoulder of Orwig Hump just below its summit (5,210 ft). Here it meets Trail #284, descending from this old lookout site.

Trail #284, Tillicum Peak. *4 miles/m (H,S).* This route was once used to supply lookouts atop Orwig Hump and Tillicum Peak. It leaves FR 319 (3,520 ft) and works steadily uphill to the ridge running southeast from Orwig Hump. Once atop the ridge, a gentle grade goes arrow-straight to the old lookout site (5,330 ft). The path descends to the west, passes Trail #373, then follows the undulating crest west to the round, wooded summit of Tillicum Peak (5,740 ft). Here are views east down the wide Tillicum Creek drainage and south down the deep canyon of the South Fork of Granite Creek.

WEST-SIDE TRAILS

Trail #588, Noisy Creek. *5.3 miles/m (H,S,B).* From the end of an old mine road (3,280 ft) at the southeast end of Sullivan Lake, this path takes long switchbacks up the ridge, then drops into the deep, narrow, wooded Noisy Creek drainage. It follows the creek bank upstream for about 2 miles, then turns uphill to the north, where the tread continues up a hogback to the backbone ridgetop (5,580 ft) to meet Trails #540 and #533.

55

WENAHA–TUCANNON WILDERNESS

LOCATION: In Columbia, Asotin, and Garfield counties, in Washington, and in Wallowa
   County, Oregon. Spans the Washington–Oregon border southeast of Dayton, Washington
SIZE: Total: 177,465 acres; Washington: 111,048 acres; Oregon: 66,417 acres
STATUS: Designated Wilderness Area (1978)
TERRAIN: A high basalt plateau, incised with deep canyons cut by numerous creeks and rivers
ELEVATION: 1,700 to 6,387 feet
MANAGEMENT: USFS, Umatilla National Forest, Pomeroy Ranger District
TOPOGRAPHIC MAPS: (Washington) Deadman Peak, Diamond Peak, Godman Spring,
   Panjab Creek, Saddle Butte, Stentz Spring; (Oregon) Bone Spring, Eden, Elbow Creek,
   Wenaha Forks

The Wenaha–Tucannon area was once a huge basalt plateau, formed by millions of years of passive eruptions and volcanic flows through underlying dikes. Over the past 10 million years, streams have cut through this volcanic layer cake, creating a labyrinth of deep, steep-walled canyons. The original tableland surface has been reduced to long, narrow ridgetops and broad, forested mesas dividing the various drainages. Trails through the area generally stick to these crests, which often have clear, wide views of the surrounding ridges and the deep chasms between them. In most cases these ridges come to abrupt ends where creeks merge, and the gentle grades plunge precipitously down canyon walls for 2,000 feet or more to bordering streams. Some of the longer trails following streams and rivers through these narrow canyons offer a quick course in the region's geology, showcased in the multiple layers of basalt stacked in the walls above.

Climate

The mean annual precipitation varies with elevation, ranging from 24 inches in lower elevations to 32 inches at the highest points. Most of this falls between November and April as snow, which accumulates at depths up to 2 feet in the valley bottoms, and to 8 to 12 feet on ridge crests. Average midwinter lows are about 20 degrees; however, storms can easily drop temperatures to minus 20, and effectively much lower when the wind-chill factor is considered. Summer days are hot; highs average near 90, and days over 100 degrees are not uncommon, although evenings cool to the pleasant lower 70s.

Plants and Wildlife

The biosystems in the wilderness vary with elevation and climate. Lower valleys and creek bottoms are wooded, mainly with ponderosa pine and some occurrences of western juniper. Ground cover is mostly bluebunch wheatgrass, Idaho fescue, and Sandberg's bluegrass, with lesser occurrences of such shrubs, forbs, and annuals as western yarrow, sagebrush buttercup, cheatgrass brome, littleflower collinsia, and smallflower forget-me-not.

Above 4,500 feet the forest changes to lodgepole pine, with occurrences of western larch, grand fir, white fir, Englemann spruce, western white pine, and Douglas-fir. Interspersed among the trees are bitterbrush, penstemon, lupine, heartleaf arnica, and white hawkweed.

At the highest elevations within the wilderness, the dominant tree species is subalpine fir, with associated growths of Oregon boxwood and queencup beadlily. Ridges and south-facing slopes are frequently bare of trees, with a cover ranging from sagebrush and Sandberg's bluegrass at lower elevations to Idaho fescue, scarlet paintbrush, and rosy pussytoes higher up the slopes.

The 576-acre Rainbow Creek Research Natural Area, northwest of the confluence of Preacher and Rainbow creeks, was established in 1968. The RNA encloses a community of grand fir–white pine, grand fir–thinleaf huckleberry, and mixed conifers dominated by larch. Another proposed 1,665-acre RNA on the south side of the wilderness at Elk Flats–Wenaha Breaks holds grand fir–Pacific yew, grand fir–twinflower, and lodgepole pine–thinleaf huckleberry communities, and a low-elevation permanent pond.

The Wenaha-Tucannon Wilderness Area boasts one of the largest elk populations in the region.

Large herds of Rocky Mountain elk are found here, as are mule deer, white-tailed deer, black bear, cougar, bobcat, coyote, whistling marmot, and snowshoe hare. Avian inhabitants include bald and golden eagles, several species of hawks and owls, goshawks, quail, chukar, blue and ruffed grouse, and pileated, three-toed, and downy woodpeckers, as well as bluebirds and a variety of other songbirds. The warm, dry climate makes this ideal habitat for rattlesnakes.

Geology

When a volcanic island chain atop the Pacific Ocean plate impinged upon the westward-drifting North American continent in Miocene times, the oceanic crust was subducted below the continental rim. The magma melting from the diving ocean floor forced its way up through cracks in a north–south dike system near the Washington–Oregon–Idaho border, in a succession of massive basalt flows over a period of 20 million years. Individual flows (50 to 150 feet thick) are interleaved with significant biological growth, indicating multiple eruptive events over an extended period; in places the total of the flows is nearly 5,000 feet thick.

A long northeast–southwest fault along the west side of the wilderness marks the boundary between the Columbia Basin, which was depressed beneath the weight of the volcanic flows, and a bulging anticline that forms the Blue Mountain region, which includes the wilderness along the Washington–Oregon border. After this high volcanic plateau was formed, creeks and rivers cut deep canyons through the layered basalt to expose the geological structures that created the original tableland.

History

The Wenaha–Tucannon Wilderness was once the province of several Nez Perce Indian tribes, and many of today's trails throughout its expanse follow paths beaten by these natives. Trappers who entered the area in the 1880s used these paths, as did the sheepherders and cattlemen who followed them. In the 1930s this trail system was improved by the Forest Service to support grazing allotments and to assist in its fire-control mission.

During the late 1800s, the first settlers in the Blue Mountain region led a tenuous and hungry existence due to the scarcity of wild game in the area. In 1913, the Wenaha Game Protective Association was formed to introduce Rocky Mountain elk from Montana. The small new herds were protected by strict game laws and the creation of several game preserves; when hunting was first opened in 1927, the elk population had grown to one of the largest in the region, and it remains so today. In fact, hunters outnumber hikers as users of the wilderness.

ACTIVITIES

Hiking

WEST-SIDE TRAILS

Trail #3256, Sawtooth. 3.4 miles/d (H,S). The way leaves Burnt Flat Corral (5,600 ft), heads along the broad ridge to the south, and after a few ups and downs arrives at Burnt Flat (5,900 ft), a 150-acre bench covered with a mixture of lodgepole pine and subalpine fir. The trail becomes more challenging as it picks its way along the rough, rocky crest of Sawtooth Ridge to cross the border into Oregon. It follows the ever-narrowing divide between the North Fork of the Wenaha River and Beaver Creek, then descends a rib to the Wenaha River and Trail #3106 (3,000 ft).

Trail #3104, Slick Ear. 5.2 miles/m (H,S). From the end of FR 4600301 (5,100 ft), the route traces the semi-open crest south to the Oregon border, where it switchbacks steeply down into the Slick Ear drainage, then follows the creek bank south to join Trail #3106 (2,800 ft), just above the Wenaha River.

Trail #3103, Grizzly Bear. 7.5 miles/m (H,S). At the end of FR 4600300 (5,380 ft), this route heads southeast across a plateau lightly covered with subalpine forest. Meadow openings permit glimpses east into the rugged, steep-walled canyons of Butte Creek and its tributaries. The way descends the broad, flat, top of Grizzly Bear Ridge for more than 2 miles before starting a series of switchbacks down a steep canyon wall into Rock Creek. It follows the creek downstream to the Wenaha River and Trail #3106 (2,520 ft).

Trail #3112, East Butte. 6 miles/d (H,S). From the end of FR 4600300 (5,380 ft), the route heads northeast along the woods-and-meadow ridge that connects the tops of Twin Buttes. After reaching the north Twin, the way continues northeast, then starts a twisting descent of a steep, rocky canyon wall to the bank of Butte Creek. The stream is followed north 0.4 mile to the confluence of the East and West Forks of Butte Creek and Dickenson Creek, where the path meets Trail #3138 from the west (3,110 ft). The way now squeezes into the deep, steep-walled defile of the East Fork, and follows that stream in a steady climb to its headwaters. Zigzags reach Teepee Campground at the end of FR 4608 (5,500 ft).

Trail #3138, West Butte Creek. 8 miles/m (H,S). At Godman Campground (5,700 ft), the route leaves south from FR 46 and drops quickly down the ridgetop to Happy Valley (4,100 ft). It climbs to a notch, then descends

across the north end of the Rainbow Creek RNA to the banks of Rainbow Creek. The route parallels the creek as it bends east to the West Fork of Butte Creek. This fork is followed through ever-steepening canyon walls to the junction with Trail #3112 (3,110 ft).

Trail #3136, Turkey Creek. *4 miles/m (H,S).* Teepee Campground (5,500 ft) lies at the midpoint of Trail #3136. The route north is a wooded, valley-bottom trek that drops steeply to Turkey Creek, then follows the more gradual drainage floor north to join Panjab Creek and Trail #3127. The more popular segment winds through old-growth timber along the ridge east of the campground. After crossing West Butte Ridge, it descends to Oregon Butte Spring to meet Trails #3105 and #3113 (6,200 ft) on the north slopes of Oregon Butte. A short spur leads to the old lookout cabin atop the butte (6,387 ft), the highest point in the wilderness. Here are excellent views of the dozens of canyons that drop south to the Wenaha River and the forested ridges flowing north to the Tucannon River valley.

Trail #3105, Smooth Ridge. *15.8 miles/m (H,S).* From the junction with Trails #3136 and #3113, the route contours the east side of Oregon Butte to pick up the open ridge headed south. It follows a near-flat bench south for more than 3 miles to Lodgepole Spring. The way bends southeast across a divide, then makes a steep, wooded climb to top Weller Butte (5,540 ft). It then snakes east on the broad rim above the 2,000-foot-deep Crooked Creek drainage. After passing Trail #3126, the route begins a long, gentle descent of Smooth Ridge. This ends in a sudden switchback drop to the confluence of Fairview Creek and the Wenaha River (2,070 ft), where it ends on Trail #3106.

Trail #3126, Packer. *7.5 miles/m (H,S).* From Trail #3105 (4,780 ft), the route follows the south rim of the Crooked Creek drainage east, then gradually descends the broad ridge to the west rim of Crooked Creek canyon. It then weaves gradually down the west side of the canyon to join Trail #3100 near the mouth of First Creek (2,250 ft).

A rocky ridgecrest near Diamond Peak in the Wenaha-Tucannon Wilderness

NORTH-SIDE TRAILS

Trail #3129, Rattlesnake. 5 miles/m (H,S). At the mouth of Panjab Creek (2,970 ft), the route leaves FR 4713 and heads for the sky. Switchbacks work up to a just plain steep climb of the forested ridge leading south to Alnus Spring (5,200 ft). As a reward for the agony of the first 2.5 miles of trail, the remainder is near flat as it weaves through woods and grassland to end on Trails #3127 and #3113 (5,720 ft).

Trail #3100, Crooked Creek. 17.4 miles/m (H,S). Not for the claustrophobic, this long, rugged, creek-bottom route plumbs the deepest canyons in the wilderness. Starting on the north from Trail #3113 at Indian Corral (5,700 ft), the way drops immediately to the headwaters of Trout Creek, which it traces down through ever-deepening canyon walls to its confluence with Third Creek (3,250 ft). The snake-like path of this stream is followed down to its confluence with Crooked Creek (2,700 ft). To the south the canyon rim looms 2,000 feet above; to the north a mere 1,000 feet is needed to gain the ridgetop. At this point Crooked Creek flows east, but 2.5 miles downstream, at the junction with Trail #3124, the stream bends sharply south and the valley floor widens briefly to meadows at the lower end of Trail #3133 (2,350 ft). The route continues south along the creek, passes the east end of Trail #3126 (2,150 ft), then crosses the Oregon border. The creek is followed to its confluence with the Wenaha River and Trail #3106 (1,916 ft).

Trail #3135, Tucannon. 4.1 miles/e (H,S). From the end of FR 4712, along the Tucannon River (3,520 ft), this easy-grade path continues along the wooded riverbank to Bear Creek (4,130 ft) and the junction with Trail #3110.

Trail #3110, Bear Creek. 5.6 miles/m (H,S). From Trail #3135 (4,130 ft), on the Tucannon River, the route switchbacks uphill with a vengeance to Jelly Spring (5,440 ft). The worst is now over, as the way meanders south along a broad ridgetop bench with periodic meadow breaks and views of the north half of the wilderness. The route ends as it meets Trail #3113 (6,250 ft) just north of the summit of Diamond Peak (6,379 ft).

EAST-SIDE TRAILS

Trail #3113, Mount Misery. 16 miles/m (H,S). This is a scenic route with good views of the wilderness, short side trips to regional high spots, and very few ups and downs to make life miserable. From the end of the Diamond Peak Road, FR 4030 (5,900 ft), a half-mile stroll west leads to the junction with Trail #3110 and the spur to the top of Diamond Peak (6,379 ft). Just east, at Diamond Spring, the route meets the upper end of Trail #3124, then continues west along the crest past Sheephead, Squaw, Bear Wallow, Clover, and Bullfrog springs to meet Trail #3100 at Indian Corral (5,700 ft). Soon after, the way passes Trails #3127 and #3129, bends south, then wiggles along an easy semi-open ridgetop to meet Trails #3105 and #3136 on the north slope of Oregon Butte (6,170 ft).

Trail #3124, Melton Creek. 9.7 miles/m (H,S). The north end of the route departs Trail #3113 at Diamond Spring (6,185 ft) and soon starts the first of several series of knee-jarring switchbacks in its rapid descent to Melton Creek at Chaparral Basin (3,470 ft). The wooded creek bottom is followed south across at least two dozen steep sidehill gullies to join Trail #3100 where Melton Creek meets Crooked Creek (2,420 ft).

OREGON TRAILS

Trail #3106, Wenaha River. 22.3 miles/m (H,S). This long river-bottom trail runs east–west along the Wenaha River for the full width of the wilderness. The east end starts outside of the wilderness near Troy, Oregon, and in 9 miles reaches the wilderness at the junction with Trail #3100 at the mouth of Crooked Creek (1,916 ft). The way traces the twisting river course west, sometimes along the bank, and other times skirting a short distance up the canyon wall to avoid short riverside cliffs. After leaving Trail #3100, the way meets, in succession, east to west, Trails #3244, #3105, #3142, #3242, #3103, #3104, #3101, #3256, #3235, #3241, and #3237. At the confluence of the South Fork of the Wenaha and Milk Creek, the route swings south with the South Fork and climbs to join FR 6415 at Timothy Spring Campground (4,680 ft).

APPENDICES

APPENDIX A.
NATIONAL PARK AND FOREST SERVICE
RANGER DISTRICT OFFICES

Mount Rainier National Park, Tahoma Woods, Star Route, Ashford, WA 98304; (360) 569-2211

North Cascades National Park and Park Complex, 2105 Highway 20, Sedro Wooley, WA 98284; (360) 856-5700

Lake Chelan National Recreation Area and Stehekin District, PO Box 7, Stehekin, WA 98852; (509) 682-5675

Ross Lake National Recreation Area, Skagit and Wilderness Districts, 728 Ranger Station Road, Marblemount, WA 98267; (360) 873-4500

Olympic National Park, 600 East Park Avenue, Port Angeles, WA 98362; (360) 452-0330

National Fish and Wildlife Service, Nisqually National Wildlife Refuge, 100 Brown Farm Road, Olympia, WA 98506; (360) 753-9467

Bureau of Land Management, Spokane District Office, East 4217 Main Avenue, Spokane, WA 99202; (509) 536-1200

COLVILLE NATIONAL FOREST

Colville Ranger District, 755 South Main Street, Colville, WA 99114; (509) 684-4557

Kettle Falls Ranger District, 255 West 11th, Kettle Falls, WA 99141; (509) 738-6111

Republic Ranger District, PO Box 468, Republic, WA 99166; (509) 775-3305

Sullivan Lake Ranger District, 12461 Sullivan Lake Road, Metaline, WA 99153; (509) 775-3305

GIFFORD PINCHOT NATIONAL FOREST

Mount Adams Ranger District, 2455 Highway 141, Trout Lake, WA 98650; (509) 395-2501

Mount St. Helens National Volcanic Monument, Route 1, Box 369, Amboy, WA 98601; (360) 247-6644

Packwood Ranger District, Highway 12, Packwood, WA 98361; (360) 494-5515

Randle Ranger District, 10024 Highway 12, Randle, WA 98377; (360) 497-7565

Wind River Ranger District, MP 0.23, Hemlock Road, Carson, WA 98610; (509) 427-5645

KANIKSU NATIONAL FOREST

Priest River Ranger District, Route 5, Box 207, Priest River, ID 83856; (208) 443-2512

MOUNT BAKER–SNOQUALMIE NATIONAL FOREST

Darrington Ranger District, Darrington, WA 98241; (360) 436-1155

Mount Baker Ranger District, 2105 Highway 20, Sedro Wooley, WA 98284; (360) 856-5700

North Bend Ranger District, 42404 North Bend Way, North Bend, WA 98045; (206) 888-1421

Skykomish Ranger District, 74920 Northeast Stevens Pass Highway, PO Box 305, Skykomish, WA 98288; (360) 677-2414

White River Ranger District, 857 Roosevelt Avenue East, Enumclaw, WA 98022; (360) 825-6585

OKANOGAN NATIONAL FOREST

Tonasket Ranger District, 1 West Winesap, PO Box 466, Tonasket, WA 98855; (509) 486-2186

Methow Valley Ranger District, 502 Glover, PO Box 188, Twisp, WA 98856; (509) 997-2131

Methow Valley Ranger District, West Chewuch Road, PO Box 579, Winthrop, WA 98862; (509) 996-2266

OLYMPIC NATIONAL FOREST

Hood Canal Ranger District, PO Box 68, Hoodsport, WA 98548; (360) 877-5254

Quilcene Ranger District, PO Box 280, Highway 101, Quilcene, WA 98376; (360) 765-3368

Quinault Ranger District, South Shore Road, PO Box 9, Quinault, WA 98575; (360) 288-2525

WENATCHEE NATIONAL FOREST

Chelan Ranger District, 428 Woodin Avenue, PO Box 189, Chelan, WA 98816; (509) 682-2576

Cle Elum Ranger District, 803 West Second Street, Cle Elum, WA 98922; (509) 674-4411

Entiat Ranger District, 2108 Entiat Way, PO Box 476, Entiat, WA 98822; (509) 784-1511

Lake Wenatchee Ranger District, 22976 Highway 207, Star Route, Box 109, Leavenworth, WA 98826; (509) 763-3103

Leavenworth Ranger District, 600 Sherbourne Street, Leavenworth, WA 98826; (509) 782-1413

Naches Ranger District, 10061 Highway 12, Naches, WA 98937; (509) 653-2205

UMATILLA NATIONAL FOREST

Pomeroy Ranger District, Route 1, Box 53-F, Pomeroy, WA 99347; (509) 843-1891

State Parks Winter Recreation Office, PO Box 42662, Olympia, WA 98504-2662; (360) 753-5755

APPENDIX B.
RECREATIONAL GUIDEBOOKS

Arender, Barney. *Barney's Book on the Olympic Peninsula.* Olympia, Wash.: Nosado Press, 1990.

Beckey, Fred. *Cascade Alpine Guide, 1: Columbia River to Stevens Pass*, 2nd edition. Seattle: The Mountaineers, 1987.

———. *Cascade Alpine Guide, 2: Stevens Pass to Rainy Pass*, 2nd edition. Seattle: The Mountaineers, 1989.

———. *Cascade Alpine Guide, 3: Rainy Pass to the Fraser River.* Seattle: The Mountaineers, 1981.

Hansen, Mel. *Indian Heaven Back Country.* Beaverton, Ore.: The Touchstone Press, 1977.

Hooper, David. *Exploring Washington's Wild Olympic Coast.* Seattle: The Mountaineers, 1993.

Kirkendall, Tom, and Vicky Spring. *Cross Country Ski Tours 1, Washington's North Cascades.* Seattle: The Mountaineers, 1988.

———. *Cross Country Ski Tours 2, Washington's South Cascades and Olympics.* Seattle: The Mountaineers, 1988.

Landers, Rich, Ida Rowe Dolphin, and the Spokane Mountaineers. *100 Hikes in the Inland Northwest.* Seattle: The Mountaineers, 1987.

Mueller, Marge, and Ted Mueller. *The San Juan Islands, Afoot and Afloat*, 2nd edition. Seattle: The Mountaineers, 1988.

North, Douglas. *Washington Whitewater.* Seattle: The Mountaineers, 1992.

Olympic Mountain Rescue Group. *Climber's Guide to the Olympic Mountains*, 3rd edition. Seattle: The Mountaineers, 1988.

Portman, Sally. *Ski Touring Methow Style.* Lynnwood, Wash.: Washington Trails Association, 1985.

Prater, Gene. *Snow Trails: Ski and Snowshoe Routes in the Cascades.* Seattle: The Mountaineers, 1975.

Seeholtz, David. *Mount St. Helens, Pathways to Discovery.* Vancouver, Wash.: A Plus Images, 1993.

Shane, Scott. *Discovering Mount St. Helens.* Seattle: University of Washington Press, 1985.

Spring, Ira, and Harvey Manning. *100 Hikes in Washington's South Cascades and Olympics*, 2nd edition. Seattle: The Mountaineers, 1992.

———. *50 Hikes in Mount Rainier National Park*, 3rd edition. Seattle: The Mountaineers, 1988.

———. *100 Hikes in the Glacier Peak Region.* Seattle: The Mountaineers, 1988.

———. *100 Hikes in the North Cascades.* Seattle: The Mountaineers, 1988.

Spring, Vicky, Ira Spring, and Harvey Manning. *100 Hikes in Washington's Alpine Lakes*, 2nd edition. Seattle: The Mountaineers, 1993.

Strickland, Ron. *Pacific Northwest Trail Guide.* Seattle: The Writing Works, 1984.

Sutliff, Mary. *Entiat Country.* Lynnwood, Wash.: Washington Trails Association, 1985.

———. *Teanaway Country.* Edmonds, Wash.: Signpost Books, 1980.

Vielbig, Klindt. *Cross Country Ski Routes of Oregon's Cascades.* Seattle: The Mountaineers, 1984.

Wood, Robert L. *Olympic Mountains Trail Guide*, 2nd edition. Seattle: The Mountaineers, 1991.

INDEX

ABOUT THE AUTHORS

MARGE and TED MUELLER are outdoor enthusiasts and environmentalists who have explored Washington State's mountains, forests, deserts, and waterways for nearly forty years. They both have instructed mountain climbing through the University of Washington, and Ted has taught classes on cruising in Northwest waters. They are members of The Mountaineers and The Nature Conservancy, and Ted is a board member of the Washington Water Trails Association.

In addition to field work, research for *Exploring Washington's Wild Areas* included contacting every land management agency and representatives of each ranger district to ensure the completeness and accuracy of the text. Authors of the popular *Afoot and Afloat* series (The Mountaineers), this is the Muellers' ninth book.

ABOUT THE PHOTOGRAPHERS

TOM KIRKENDALL and VICKY SPRING, residents of Washington, are both experienced outdoor people. Both Tom and Vicky studied at the Brooks Institute of Photography in Santa Barbara, California, and are now building their careers together as outdoor photographers and guidebook authors.

Vicky and Tom are the authors of numerous hiking, cycling, and skiing books, as well as the recently published *Glacier National Park and Waterton Lakes National Park: A Complete Guide* (The Mountaineers).

THE MOUNTAINEERS, founded in 1906, is a nonprofit outdoor activity and conservation club, whose mission is "to explore, study, preserve, and enjoy the natural beauty of the outdoors. . . ." Based in Seattle, Washington, the club is now the third-largest such organization in the United States, with 15,000 members and five branches throughout Washington State.

The Mountaineers sponsors both classes and year-round outdoor activities in the Pacific Northwest, which include hiking, mountain climbing, ski-touring, snowshoeing, bicycling, camping, kayaking and canoeing, nature study, sailing, and adventure travel. The club's conservation division supports environmental causes through educational activities, sponsoring legislation, and presenting informational programs. All club activities are led by skilled, experienced volunteers, who are dedicated to promoting safe and responsible enjoyment and preservation of the outdoors.

If you would like to participate in these organized outdoor activities or the club's programs, consider a membership in The Mountaineers. For information and an application, write or call The Mountaineers, Club Headquarters, 300 Third Avenue West, Seattle, Washington 98119; (206) 284-6310.

The Mountaineers Books, an active, nonprofit publishing program of the club, produces guidebooks, instructional texts, historical works, natural history guides, and works on environmental conservation. All books produced by The Mountaineers are aimed at fulfilling the club's mission.

Send or call for our catalog of more than 300 outdoor titles:

The Mountaineers Books
1001 SW Klickitat Way, Suite 201
Seattle, WA 98134
1(800)553-4453